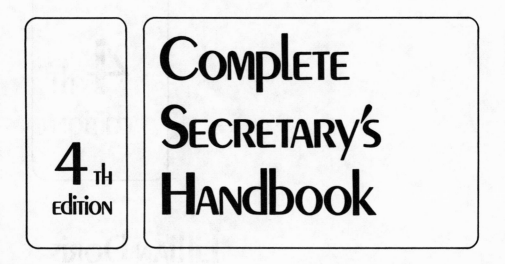

Complete Secretary's Handbook

4th **edition**

4 TH
EDITION

Lillian Doris
AND
Besse May Miller

PRENTICE-HALL, INC.

Complete Secretary's Handbook

revised by
Mary A. De Vries

ENGLEWOOD CLIFFS, N.J.

Complete Secretary's Handbook, 4th Edition
by Lillian Doris and Besse May Miller
revised by Mary A. De Vries

Prentice-Hall International, Inc., *London*
Prentice-Hall of Australia, Pty, Ltd., *Sydney*
Prentice-Hall of Canada, Ltd., *Toronto*
Prentice-Hall of India Private, Ltd., *New Delhi*
Prentice-Hall of Japan, Inc., *Tokyo*
Prentice-Hall of Southeast Asia Pte. Ltd., *Singapore*
Whitehall Books, Ltd., Wellington, *New Zealand*

Seventh Printing . . . . . November, 1981

Library of Congress Cataloging in Publication Data

Doris, Lillian.
  Complete secretary's handbook.

  Includes index.
    1. Office practice--Handbooks, manuals, etc.
  2. Secretaries--Handbooks, manuals, etc. I. Miller,
  Besse May, joint author. II. De Vries, Mary Ann.
  III. Title.
  HF5547.5.D6 1977   651'.4   76-40184
  ISBN 0-13-163402-X

Printed in the United States of America

A Word from the Reviser . . . . .
On the Increased Value This Edition Offers You—The Secretary

When I started to revise this book, I was pleasantly surprised and somewhat awed. It became clear, in going over every page carefully, that many of the principles and techniques described by Mss. Doris and Miller are still sound, and I knew it was important to preserve these excellent and enduring techniques. However, just as business methods change so do secretarial techniques, and it is in this area that the value of this handbook has been substantially increased.

Every chapter has been updated and now includes the latest techniques that secretaries in every type of business will find invaluable. Along with all the time-tested and proven techniques are many new and improved procedures that will help you achieve greater success as a skilled secretary. Organized in five parts, this new, revised edition presents up-to-the-minute information on everything you could possibly need to know about your work: how to improve your typing and stenographic skills, aids to quick filing and finding, the latest mail, phone, and telegraph regulations, how to handle employee problems, tips on good letter writing, keeping personal records for the manager—to name just a few.

The first section provides a broad range of practical "Techniques for General Secretarial Duties." Nine chapters with an all-new look reveal the secrets of effective reminder and follow-up systems, better filing and finding techniques, developing good typing and stenographic skills, how to handle in-and-out mail efficiently, postal guide and information, how expert secretaries use the telephone, telegraph and cable information, how to make travel arrangements, and business etiquette for the successful secretary. The vast amount of new and updated information in these chapters includes:

- an automated approach to reminder and follow-up problems (page 43)

- new systems and procedures for faster filing and finding (page 71)
- easy steps for taking and transcribing dictation (page 100)
- the latest mail, phone, and telegraph information (pages 114, 133, 146)
- how to make car rental arrangements (page 167)
- interviewing, training, and working with a new employee (page 197)
- tips on purchasing and storing supplies (page 70)
- current rules of basic office etiquette (page 182)

Handling correspondence involves much more than opening letters for most secretaries; it means writing letters—planning and composing them. Because this is so important, Part 2, "How to Write Good Letters," and Part 3, "How to Write Correctly," show you the fastest and easiest route to good grammar and good letter writing, including: the mechanics of business letters, forms of address for official or honorary positions, valuable aids for good letter writing, model business letters, correct word usage, spelling and word division, punctuation, and capitalization. Not surprisingly, there have been a number of style changes in recent years, and these chapters bring you up to date in this area, as well as offer some completely new and expanded sections. Here are just a few:

- examples of letters to process information and place orders (page 286)
- current definitions and examples of parts of speech and rules of grammar (page 309)
- a new list of 500 commonly misspelled words (page 370)
- an expanded list of abbreviations, with over a hundred additional entries (page 413)
- the modern way of capitalizing titles and terms (page 392)
- how to address a letter to a person holding several academic degrees (page 218)
- when to use Miss, Mrs., or Ms. (page 235)

Helping the manager with his personal records need not be a dreary or formidable task, as the fourth section of this book shows. "How to Handle Records and Correspondence for the Manager's Personal Matters" gives you the latest techniques and forms to use in keeping track of personal funds, investments, insurance, and taxes. But here, too, there have been changes in rules and regulations, and the four chapters have been completely updated, introducing items such as:

- a new, simplified form for recording investments (page 452)
- tips on how to examine insurance policies (page 457)
- new information on checking accounts (page 433)
- the latest regulations on income tax deductions for travel and medical expenses (pages 480, 484)
- how to record interest paid on personal debts (page 487)
- easy, new instructions for computing and recording the cost of securities (page 447)

Information processing is something that almost every secretary gets involved with to a considerable degree. Sometimes, though, the secretary seems to be constantly occupied with the search for information—for herself or himself, for the manager, for others. Therefore, Part 5, "The Secretary's Handy Information Guide," presents sources of information for the manager, and a quick reference guide to miscellaneous facts and figures. Both chapters have been heavily revised and updated, with a substantial amount of new information. For example:

- additional sources of general reference works, atlases, dictionaries, quotations, biographical information, periodicals, financial information, reference works on a specific subject, and securities services (page 499)
- how to find professional information (page 503)
- desk references for the secretary—general and secretarial books (page 531)
- a new exact interest table, 5% to 12% (page 526)
- a handy map of time zones and area codes (page 528)
- the metric system—a new, enlarged table (page 521)
- a twelve-year calendar: 1976-1987 (page 529)

Just as in previous editions, this essential information is presented in an easy-to-read, step-by-step manner, with a generous number of quick-reference charts and tables for instant fact-finding. It clearly illustrates how to handle every aspect of the secretary's job expertly and easily, and how to do it with the least possible amount of time and effort. The many new techniques are applicable to any type of office, which means you can use this new edition each day with complete confidence that you are developing and applying the latest and best in efficient secretarial procedures.

Mary A. De Vries

Acknowledgments

This fourth edition of the *Complete Secretary's Handbook* is the result of dedicated efforts by many people, as well as the valuable assistance of numerous business firms, educational institutions, and associations that supplied useful literature and other practical information. Their cooperative spirit and generous contributions have been most helpful. I want to thank those who gave substantial time and attention to this project, with suggestions, criticisms, and information, especially Sister Amy Hoey, president and professor of English, Mount Saint Mary College; Virginia D. Scott, public relations consultant; and Robert K. Scott, accountant and business consultant. In particular, I am grateful to Dr. Jacqueline F. Mara, associate dean and director of graduate studies, New Hampshire College, who provided expert guidance and consultation from beginning to end.

CONTENTS

How to Make and Use Calendars

Calendars that you should keep 31.   When to make up the calendars 32.
Checklist of recurring items 32.   How to use the tickler card file with
calendars 33.   Indefinite date reminders 35.   How to remind the manager
of appointments and things to do 35.   Reminders showing appointments
for a month 36.   Special reminders 38.   How to prepare a "contact
reminder" file 39.

The Facts of Follow-Up

Material that ordinarily calls for follow-up 40.   Follow-up methods 40.
Equipment for follow-up system 40.   Arrangement of folders for follow-up
41.   Operation of the follow-up system 41.   How to handle material in
the daily follow-up file 43.   Follow-ups on a small scale 43.   Use of
tickler card file for follow-up 43.   Information retrieval in follow-up
systems 43.

Developing Good Typing and Stenographic Skills (*Cont'd*)

Telegraph and Cable Information (*Cont'd*)

Chapter 8

How to Make Travel Arrangements 160

How to Make Travel Arrangements (*Cont'd*)

Chapter 9

PART 2

HOW TO WRITE GOOD LETTERS

Chapter 10

Mechanics of Business Letters *(Cont'd)*

Chapter 11

Forms of Address for Official or Honorary Positions

Model Business Letters *(Cont'd)*

Model Business Letters *(Cont'd)*

PART 3

HOW TO WRITE CORRECTLY

Chapter 14

Chapter 15

Chapter 16

Capitalization (*Cont'd*)

PART 4

**HOW TO HANDLE RECORDS AND CORRESPONDENCE
FOR THE MANAGER'S PERSONAL MATTERS**

PART 5

THE SECRETARY'S HANDY INFORMATION GUIDE

Chapter 23

Selected Sources of Information for the Manager *(Cont'd)*

Chapter 24

Quick Reference Guide to Miscellaneous Facts and Figures 510

Techniques for General Secretarial Duties

PART 1

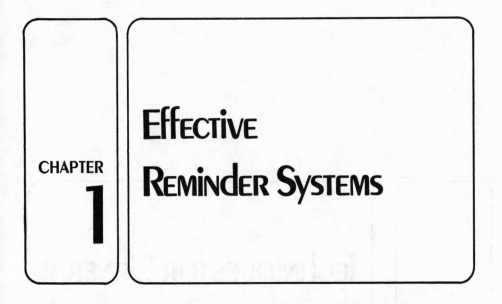

Effective Reminder Systems

Every secretary has the responsibility of seeing that certain things are done at certain times. Therefore, the need for an orderly and infallible system of "reminders" is obvious. Reminders are known by various names: calendars, tickler systems, "bring-up" files, future files, follow-up files. The details of a reminder system naturally differ slightly with the need of your office, but you can easily adapt the systems described here to your own needs. For any reminder system to function properly, the secretary *must* refer to it each day—no system is more perfect than the person handling it.

The practices described in this chapter fall into two parts: (1) how to make and use calendars and (2) follow-up files. Neither is a substitute for the other, although in many instances there is a choice as to which to use. For example, if a quarterly report must be considered on a certain day, you can put a notation on the calendar or a memorandum in the follow-up files.

Calendars that you should keep. Calendars are found in three basic styles: wall, desk, and pocket. Wall calendars are usually designed to show one day or one month at a glance, and occasionally a full year or several years (see calendar, page 529). Desk calendars, sometimes called diaries or journals, are available in a wide choice of sizes and types, including pads, book styles, combination memo-appointment, ring binders, spiral bound, and plastic or leather bound. They may be day-at-a-glance, week-at-a-glance, or month-at-a-glance versions. Most allow space for each day to write in appointments and memos. However, only certain styles have appointment spaces broken down into 15- or 30-minute intervals. There is such a wide selection that it would be wise to examine the supply at a local office supply or stationery store, and match size, type, writing space available, and practicality of each one with your own needs and those of the manager.

You will probably decide on three general categories for your office:

1. *Your own calendar.* Either a standard desk calendar pad or a yearbook, with 15-minute or 30-minute time divisions, would be a good choice in most situations. Many secretaries prefer desk calendars because the day's activities are then before their eyes constantly.

Enter notations of your own activities and business appointments as well as the manager's appointments and the things that you will have to remind him about. Enter any time-consuming task that must be done by a certain date sufficiently in advance to permit it to be done on time.

2. *The manager's calendar.* Again, a standard desk calendar pad or a yearbook would serve most purposes. Many managers prefer a yearbook because its contents are not visible to callers. The calendar or yearbook must be large enough to enable you to note the caller's affiliation and purpose of the call.

Enter all of the manager's appointments and the important days, such as his or her spouse's birthday, that he or she should remember. If the important days are not noted on the calendar, he or she may inadvertently make conflicting engagements. Do not enter in the manager's calendar items that are merely reminders to you, such as the date certain checks should be written. Although you enter reminders before the actual date on your own calendar, it usually is not necessary to do this on the manager's calendar. Watch his or her calendar closely for appointments he or she makes without telling you.

3. *Pocket memo calendar.* Note in a small pocket memo book the engagements that might conflict with future appointments that the manager makes. This memo book is for the manager to take with him or her to meetings, luncheons, on trips, and the like, where questions of future appointments might arise.

When to make up the calendars.   Keep a list of events that go on the calendars year after year (see checklist below). Early in October, enter all of the recurring items, events, and engagements for the forthcoming year in the calendar for the next year. If the manager makes important engagements far in advance, you may have to make up the yearly calendars even earlier. In preparing calendars, work from the list and not from the current year's calendar, because the dates for the events change. For example, if board meetings are held on the first Monday of every month, the actual dates vary from year to year. In making an entry, be certain that the date is not a Sunday or a holiday.

Enter notations of additional appointments or things to do as soon as you learn about them.

Checklist of recurring items.   Following is a list of recurring items that a secretary usually enters on the appropriate calendars for each year. You may not be concerned with some of them and will probably add many others that apply specifically to your position. If dates usually call for presents or cards, enter reminders about ten days before the date as well as on the date.

Family Dates
   Anniversaries
   Birthdays of all members of the manager's family and any other birthdays
      that he or she likes to remember
   Father's Day
   Mother's Day
Holidays
   Christmas. Since the purpose of this item is to bring up the gift and card
      lists, the entry date depends on the shopping conditions in your locality.

and on the number of presents. Six weeks is the average time required. (See also Holiday Presents on page 200.) Also enter the dates on which presents and cards should be mailed.

Easter

Election Day

Religious holidays

Thanksgiving

Valentine's Day

Meetings

Board meetings (company and outside directorates)

Business association meetings

Club meetings

Committee meetings (company and outside activities)

Luncheon meetings

Stockholders' annual meeting

Payment Dates

Contributions, under pledges or otherwise, to religious and charitable organizations. If weekly, enter each Friday as the date on which to draw the check.

Insurance premium due dates. See chapter 21 for special insurance records.

Interest on notes payable and maturity dates of notes. Enter notation about a week before due date. The manager's funds might be low or he might want to negotiate a renewal.

Interest on notes receivable and maturity dates of notes. If it is necessary to send a reminder to the debtor, enter ten days before the due date.

Periodic payments, such as salaries to servants, allowances to children, tuition payments, and the like. If the date the check should be prepared falls on a day that the office is closed, enter the reminder on the preceding day.

Renewal Dates

Driver's license and automobile registration

Hunting and fishing license

Subscriptions to periodicals

Tax Dates

Federal taxes. Enter tax items in your calendar in advance of the due dates to allow ample time for preparation of returns. State and local taxes. (See page 473, chapter 22.)

How to use the tickler card file with calendars. The use of a 3″ by 5″ card tickler file will reduce the necessary work in preparing a calendar. A card tickler file has a tabbed guide for each month of the year and 31 tabbed guides, one for each day of the month. The daily guides are placed behind the current month guide. Memoranda are made on cards, and the cards are filed behind the daily guide according to the date on which the matter is to be brought up.

Recurring items can be put on one card, and the card can be moved from week to week, month to month, or year to year. Thus, if a certain check is made out each Friday, you can make one card and move it each week, instead of making 52 entries in the calendar. Furthermore, you can put all necessary information on the card so that you, or anyone else, can make out the check and mail it without referring to any other material. For example, if an insurance policy is payable semiannually, the card would show (1) due dates, (2) amount of premium, (3) type of coverage, renewal dates and expiration date, (4) identification by company and policy number, (5) agent's name, (6) insured, and (7) property covered. See page 463 for an example of a tickler card for the expiration of an automobile policy. If interest on a mortgage is payable quarterly, the card would show (1) due dates, (2) amount of interest, (3) to whom payable, (4) where to send check, (5) brief description of property covered by mortgage, (6) amount of mortgage. See Figure 1.

```
Int. due quarterly--15th of Jan., Apr., July, & Oct.

Amt. $200.  Make check to:  Estate of Harvey Adams
            Send check to:  Mr. Ralph Jones
                            Attorney for Estate of
                            Harvey Adams
                            75 Fifth Avenue
                            New York, N.Y.  10003

Mortgage for $20,000 on 71st Street Dwelling
```

FIGURE 1   INTEREST PAYMENT REMINDER

A recurring problem in many offices is the loss of material through lending practices. Files and other material are removed and the borrower forgets to return them, or the secretary who suddenly is asked to produce a certain file cannot locate it. A charge-out tickler file is the ideal solution in these situations. A tickler card is prepared for each withdrawal. A supply of preprinted cards can even be placed in a conspicuous place for borrowers to select one to fill out at times when they remove material in the absence of the secretary. Information should contain (1) the file caption, (2) name of borrower and his or her department, (3) dates of correspondence involved, (4) date of removal, and (5) date for follow-up. The completed card is filed behind the day of the month designated for follow-up, and another charge-out slip is placed in the regular files.

A card tickler file *does not* take the place of a calendar for noting appointments. All engagements and appointments, even regularly recurring ones, should be entered on the calendar; otherwise, whenever you want to make an appointment for the manager, you will have to look not only at the calendar but also at the tickler cards. Refer to both the calendar and the tickler file each morning.

Indefinite date reminders. A manager might want to be reminded from time to time of a particular matter until it has been acted upon. For example, he or she might want to be reminded to go over a certain file of material. This kind of item should be included from time to time in the typed schedule of appointments and things to do that you place daily on the manager's desk. There are two ways of reminding yourself of the item:

1. Make a notation on *your* calendar at short intervals.
2. If you keep a card tickler file, note the item on a card and move the card from time to time.

Matters to come to the manager's attention in connection with any unscheduled but definite event are best handled by placing a reminder memo in an appropriately labeled folder for the event. For example, if the manager wants to be reminded to call upon a certain customer the next time he goes to Chicago and the date of his trip has not been scheduled, make a folder marked "Chicago Trip" and put in it the necessary reminder memo. When the date of the trip is settled, give your employer the entire folder or include the item in a typewritten schedule of matters pertaining to the trip. If the event is of such rare occurrence that you would need a reminder that there is such a folder, do not use a folder but make the notation on your calendar or in the card tickler file as described above.

How to remind the manager of appointments and things to do. Each morning place on the manager's desk a "Today's List" of appointments and special things to be done. It is advisable to prepare this list at the end of the previous day's work. Make a carbon copy for your own use.

Figure 2 illustrates a daily appointment list.

```
┌──────────────────────────────────────────────────────────┐
│                                                          │
│       APPOINTMENTS FOR MONDAY, APRIL 5, 19__             │
│                                                          │
│   10:00 A.M.   Special Dictation-Speech for Ad Club     │
│                                                          │
│   10:30        Conference-proposed personnel booklet    │
│                                                          │
│   11:00        Mr. Simmons--new labor course            │
│                                                          │
│   12:00        Employees' meeting--annual report on     │
│                profit-sharing plan                       │
│                                                          │
│    1:00 P.M.   Luncheon at Ad Club with Y & R           │
│                representatives                           │
│                                                          │
│    3:30        Mr. Dressler                             │
│                                                          │
│    4:00        Executive Committee meeting              │
│                                                          │
│    5:00        Sales Staff meeting, through dinner      │
│                                                          │
│                                                          │
└─────────⌇────────────────────⌇──────────────⌇───────────┘
```

FIGURE 2   DAILY APPOINTMENT LIST

Memorandum paper, about 6″ by 9″, is desirable for this purpose. At the time of each appointment give your employer any material he or she will need for it. For example, before the 12:00 appointment shown in Figure 2, hand the manager the material that has been prepared for making the report.

To remind the manager of a task that he should do, place the file on his desk. If he has said that he wanted to do a certain thing in connection with the matter, attach a reminder to the file. For example, suppose he told you, "I want to wire Robertson on Friday if we don't hear from him." On Friday you type a memo, "You wanted to wire Robertson," and attach it to the Robertson file before placing it on your employer's desk. If possible, draft the wire and give that to him with the file folder.

Some executives make a practice of calling their secretaries into their office daily to discuss pending matters and things to be done. This is the ideal arrangement. For this discussion, take with you a list of things to do and any material pertaining to them. Your employer will give you instructions on one matter after another.

Reminders showing appointments for a month.   Many managers like to see the month's engagements at a glance. There are calendars designed for this purpose, usually on cardboard about 9″ by 11″. Figure 3 is an illustration of such a calendar. Note that under the arrangement of dates on this calendar, every Sunday in the month is on the top row, every Monday on the next row, and so on.

NOVEMBER

	Sunday, 7th	Sunday, 14th	Sunday, 21st	Sunday, 28th
Monday, 1st	Monday, 8th	Monday, 15th	Monday, 22nd	Monday, 29th
Tuesday, 2nd	Tuesday, 9th	Tuesday, 16th	Tuesday, 23rd	Tuesday, 30th
Wednesday, 3rd	Wednesday, 10th	Wednesday, 17th	Wednesday, 24th	
Thursday, 4th	Thursday, 11th	Thursday, 18th	Thursday, 25th Thanksgiving Day	CALENDAR
Friday, 5th	Friday, 12th	Friday, 19th	Friday, 26th	
Saturday, 6th	Saturday, 13th	Saturday, 20th	Saturday, 27th	

FIGURE 3   APPOINTMENT CALENDAR FOR A MONTH

Figure 4 is an example of a four-week schedule, which is typed each week. Note that it lists holidays, evening social functions, and things to be done, as well as appointments. The question marks indicate uncertainty. (WL stands for Weekly Letter.) If the schedule is to remain on your employer's desk, he or she might like to have it mounted on cardboard to facilitate handling. Either staple or paste the corners to the cardboard. When your employer is planning to be away from the office for a week or so, he usually likes to know what is on his calendar for that period before he completes his plans. Use the setup shown in Figure 4 for this purpose.

<u>APPOINTMENTS</u>

Nov.	15 Mon. -		- WL-269
		- 12:00 Noon	- Preliminary Meetg. - Cleve. Engrg. Soc.
		- 3:00 P.M.	- Apex Bd. Meetg.
''	16 Tues.-	1:30 P.M.	- Engineering
''	17 Wed. -	5:30 P.M.	- Cath. Char. - Parlor B - Cleve. Athletic Club
		- 6:00 P.M.	- ? Union Club-Ohio Pub. Expenditure Coun.-WTH
''	18 Thur.-	6:30 P.M.	- Foremen's Dinner - Lake Shore Ctry. Club
''	19 Fri. -	12:15 P.M.	- ?Amer. Trade Assn. Executives - Public Libr.
		- 6:? P.M.	- Cleve. Engrg. Soc. Panel

Nov.	22 Mon. -		- WL-270
''	23 Tues.-	1:30 P.M.	- Engineering
''	24 Wed.		- Sandusky
''	25 Thur.-		- Thanksgiving
''	26 Fri. -	Evening	- Apex Dance - Lake Shore Ctry. Club

Nov.	29 Mon. -		- WL-271
		-	- Check to W. Shaw
''	30 Tues.-	1:30 P.M.	- Engineering
Dec.	1 Wed. -		- Sandusky
''	2 Thur.-		- Talk at Cincinnati - Wm. Campbell
''	3 Fri. -		-

Dec.	6 Mon. -		- WL-272
''	7 Tues.-	1:30 P.M.	- Engineering
		- 6:00 P.M.	- Loyal Service CIub - Carter Hotel
''	8 Wed. -		- Sandusky
''	9 Thur.-		-
''	10 Fri. -	10:00 A.M.	- VCMA Meeting - Hotel Cleveland

FIGURE 4   FOUR-WEEK SCHEDULE

Special reminders.   A manager may find it useful to have the secretary give him or her a 3″ by 5″ or 4″ by 6″ reminder card each evening when leaving the office. This contains not only a list of

activities for the following day, but also reminders of certain things
that he or she should do at home. Figure 5 is a typical reminder card
for a manager who lives in the suburbs.

```
Reminder for WEDNESDAY, May 19 19--
Tell Mrs. Adams that her draperies will be delivered Mon.
Get exact dimensions of kitchen cabinet
8:30--Parent-Teacher gathering at Westchester High
Pack bag for Dinner at Waldorf (White Tie)

10:30----Mr. John Brown
11:30----Portfolio Committee meeting
12:30----Luncheon for Mr. Robert St. John, Pres. Reynolds
            Inv. Assn., at Advertising Club
 2:30----Mr. Smith's office: 250 Broadway, Room 1200
            re: Texas bonds

Evening
 7:30----Reception, Grand Ballroom Waldorf-Astoria
 8:30----Dinner in honor of Dr. Thompson
            Chauffeur will return at 11:00, Park Ave. entrance
```

FIGURE 5   SPECIAL REMINDER CARD

How to prepare a "contact reminder" file.   If your employer makes
numerous contacts throughout the year, it is difficult for him or her
to remember everyone and the circumstances of the meeting. Yet it
may be necessary for him or her to be able to recall names and
connections. A "contact reminder" file is useful for this purpose. A
loose-leaf, leather notebook, 5" by 7¾", or 4" by 6", makes a handy
contact reminder file for recording the name of the person your
employer meets, his or her affiliations, and the circumstances of the
meeting. It is advisable to put on the record any personal items that
might be helpful to your employer in recalling the individual. Thus,
if the person sent cigars or flowers at Christmas, or a booklet
published by his or her company, or your employer sent him or
someone related to him something special, make a notation on the
record.

The secretary to the chairman of a large bank follows the practice
of making three copies of each entry. She files them alphabetically,
one under the name of the individual, another under the name of the
company, and the third under the name of the city where the
company is located. Thus, if the manager is to meet the officials of
the Bates Company, she turns to the B's and makes a list of all the
officers of the Bates Company whom the manager has met and the

circumstances of the meetings. Or, if he is going to Chicago, she turns to the C's and makes a list of the names, titles, and connections of people in Chicago whom he has met.

It takes time to keep a record of this type up to date, and your employer's cooperation is necessary to keep it properly. It is, however, invaluable if he or she travels or has many business contacts. The personal notations are especially valuable to persons who are candidates for public office.

Periodically, it is necessary to review all record-keeping methods and ask yourself: (1) is the procedure still required, or have changes in operations made it obsolete? and (2) are any new records requiring still more new records to keep track of the old ones? (See page 70) The need to employ cost-cutting practices in many offices makes an analysis of current systems a necessity. With this in mind, it may be wise to ask the manager, if you are in doubt, about any system that appears to have diminished in usefulness or any records that are rarely used any more.

THE FACTS OF FOLLOW-UP

Material that ordinarily calls for follow-up.   The following items ordinarily call for follow-up.

1. Matters that are referred to other executives or departments for information or comment.
2. Correspondence or memoranda awaiting answer.
3. Orders for future delivery, both those that you receive and those that you place.
4. Items that come up for periodic consideration, such as company reports of various kinds, tax matters, contract renewals, and the like.
5. Promises to be carried out in the future.

Follow-up methods.   In any tickler or follow-up system, one of two methods must be used: (1) the material to come up for action at a certain date must be placed in the tickler or (2) a notation or reminder of that material must be placed in the tickler while the *material itself remains* in its proper place *in the regular files*. The latter method is preferable for the secretary and is the only one described here.

Equipment for follow-up system.   Numerous styles of equipment for follow-up purposes are on the market, but many secretaries for busy executives have found the follow-up file system described here, or a variation of it, practical, efficient, and time saving.

The only equipment necessary is a file drawer and file folders. Make a set of file folders consisting of (a) 12 folders labeled from January through December, (b) 31 folders labeled from 1 through 31, and (c) 1 folder marked "Future Years." If you have a heavy volume of follow-up material, it is advisable to have two sets of folders labeled by days—one for the current month and one for the succeeding month.

Tabbed guides marked 1 through 31 and removable separators tabbed with the month will make it easier to locate a particular folder, but these are not necessary to the efficient functioning of the system.

Arrangement of folders for follow-up.   Arrange the folders labeled by days in numerical order in the front of the file. Place in these the follow-up material for the current month. The folder labeled for the current month is at the back of the other monthly folders ready to receive any material to be followed up in the same month next year. Immediately following the numerical daily folders is the folder for the forthcoming month, followed by the folder for the succeeding month, and so on. Figure 6 is a diagram of the folders when Friday, April 16, is the current day.

A variation of this plan is to arrange the files labeled by months in calendar sequence. Thus, January is always the first month-by-month folder. Some secretaries prefer this arrangement because the folders remain in the same position. In this case, as the folder for each day is emptied, it is placed in position for the next month.

Operation of the follow-up system.   1. Make an extra copy of correspondence or memoranda that requires a follow-up, preferably on paper of a different color. Mark on the extra carbon the date on which it is to be followed up. When there is no carbon copy of material for follow-up, write a brief memo for the tickler file. For example, if your employer gives you a newspaper clipping and tells you to bring it to his attention on the 30th of the month, prepare a tickler memo for follow-up on the 30th, but file the clipping so that you can put your hands on it if your employer wants it before the 30th. The memo should indicate where the material is filed. File any pertinent papers in the regular files.

2. Place material that is to be followed up in the current month in the proper date folders. Each day transfer the empty daily folder

back of the folder for the forthcoming month. Thus, you always have 31 daily folders for follow-ups, part of them for the remaining days in the current month and part of them for the first part of the forthcoming month. Place material that is to be followed up more than 30 or 31 days in the future in the proper month folder, regardless of the day of follow-up. See Figure 6, which is a diagram of the arrangement of folders on April 16. On that day, current material to be followed up from April 16 through May 14 is placed in daily folders; material to be followed up after May 14 is placed in the proper month folder. Material that had already been placed in the May folder will not be refiled in the daily folders until May 1st. (See next step.)

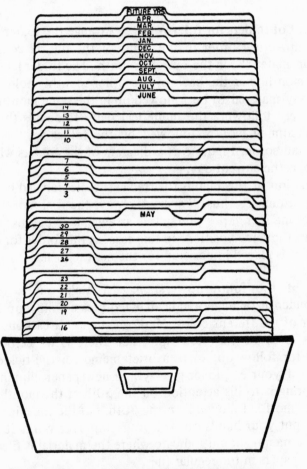

FIGURE 6   DIAGRAM OF FOLLOW-UP FILES

3. On the first of each month, transfer the material from the folder for that month into the folders labeled by days. To avoid filing material for follow-up on Saturdays (if the office closes), Sundays, or holidays, reverse the folders for those days so that the blank side of the label faces the front of the file. Notice in Figure 6 that the folders for April 17, 18, 24, 25, and 31 (since April has only 30 days), and May 1, 2, 8, 9, and 15 are blank. The empty folder for the current month is then transferred to the rear of the other month-by-month folders—or to its proper calendar sequence if that arrangement is used.

How to handle material in the daily follow-up file.   Each day when you examine your follow-up file you will find that a large part of the correspondence has been answered without a follow-up. Destroy these carbons or memoranda. If a heavy schedule keeps you from giving attention to all the material in the daily folder, mark the less-important items for follow-up at a later date.

Move indefinite follow-ups forward from week to week until a definite date is established or until the matter is completed. This procedure is often referred to as "combing-back."

Follow-ups on a small scale.   When you have only a small amount of correspondence or other matters to follow up, a set of follow-up file folders is not necessary. Mark the carbons with the follow-up date and file them chronologically in one folder, with those marked for the earliest follow-up on top.

Use of tickler card file for follow-up.   A tickler card file is as useful as follow-up file folders for any type of material except correspondence. You can type a notation for yourself on a card and place it in a tickler card file as easily as you can type a memorandum and put it in a file folder. But it is a waste of time to make a card notation of correspondence when you can make an extra carbon at the time of transcription. Therefore, unless you have only a small amount of correspondence to follow up, and handle it as described in the preceding paragraph, use follow-up file folders instead of a card tickler.

Information retrieval in follow-up systems.   There are times when the process of following up also requires the collection of massive amounts of information—too much for a secretary to begin searching for manually in the regular files. Follow-up systems that often require a fast method of data collection may involve business records, such as accounts payable and receivable. Follow-up systems, in fact, are used with almost all items that require renewals or sequences of notices, such as invoices, purchase and job orders, leases and mortgages, various types of applications, tax and check records, bids, and insurance files, to name just a few. Often it is not enough for a secretary to be reminded to follow up on something, such as past-due accounts. Quite probably, in instances like that, the facts related to some accounts must be reviewed, and many companies have turned to high-speed equipment to locate such information instantly. Some data-retrieval machines are electronically coded to locate and convey regular files in a matter of minutes or seconds.

The process gaining in popularity, however, is that of micro-filming. This involves photographing documents at reduced sizes and developing the noncombustible film. Depending upon company policy, the secretary then may be instructed to destroy the original. When review is required, the film may be retrieved instantly and viewed in magnified size on a screen. Some film readers will also make a photocopy of the document being displayed at the same time. The need to control or reduce storage space is a prime consideration in the purchase of these systems. Also, the need to retrieve massive amounts of data rapidly may be a key factor.

The cost of information-retrieval systems used in follow-up activity varies, depending upon the system's size and complexity (e.g., whether a film reader must have photocopy capability, or whether such a feature is of little value). An evaluation of desired features and capabilities must, of course, be conducted as part of a larger justification analysis. It must be determined carefully, for example, whether actual savings and/or increased income through increased output will exceed the cost of acquiring and maintaining the new system. Numerous factors must be considered, such as volume of work, processing time requirements, cost of alternative systems, and labor and storage space costs under each system. A study of these and other cost items, along with specific advantages and disadvantages of the proposed system, will tell if the new equipment is truly justified. The secretary can often contribute to justification considerations by writing for literature on new systems and equipment, and by making a study of the steps involved and her own time in performing certain tasks manually.

CHAPTER
2

BETTER Filing
aNd FiNdiNg TechNiques

Although a company may have a central filing department, a
fully centralized filing department is seldom found in actual
practice. There are always papers, such as executives' files,
confidential files, corporation and financial papers, and so on,
that are and should be kept in private or departmental offices
rather than in a centralized filing department. The secretary
is frequently in charge of these private and departmental files.
She or he also keeps the employer's personal correspondence
and papers in private files. This chapter explains what the
secretary must know about filing to carry out filing responsibilities efficiently and in accordance with modern practices.

SYSTEMS OF FILING

Basic filing systems. The basic filing systems are alphabetical, geographical, numerical, and decimal. The following paragraphs explain briefly how to use each of these. As requirements differ from office to office, and as others may have to use your system in emergency situations, you may wish to prepare a file manual for your office explaining the system and the steps involved in (a) preparing material for filing, (b) filing it, and (c) retrieving it from the files.

Alphabetical filing. Ninety percent of all filing is alphabetical. The use of an alphabetical system in name and subject files is described on pages 47-52.

Numerical filing system. The numerical filing system requires numbers on the file folders, which are arranged numerically. This is an indirect method of filing since it must be used in connection with a cross-index that shows what the number stands for; an index card is made for each folder and the cards are arranged alphabetically.

The advantages of the system are the rapidity and accuracy of refiling and the opportunity for indefinite expansion. However, these advantages are more than offset by the disadvantage of having to maintain the auxiliary card index and to make two searches, one of the index and the second of the files, every time papers are withdrawn or filed.

The numerical system is used mainly in files where each of the jobs, clients, or subjects has a number that acts as an identification mark (e.g., requisitions, orders, bills, invoices); for the filing of confidential records; for handling a rapidly growing file; and in files where extensive permanent cross-reference is necessary.

Geographical filing system. Under the geographical filing system, material to be filed is classified; first, according to the name of the state; then, according to cities or towns; and last, according to the names of correspondents in each city or town. Equipment houses supply standard sets of guides, which consist of a set of state guides subdivided by auxiliary sets of county or city guides. This type of file also requires a cross-index. A name card is prepared showing the geographical location. The cards are filed alphabetically. If the location is not known, reference is made to the name in the cross-index to determine the location. This system is used principally by sales organizations where a review of the activity in any given territory is of more importance than the name of a company or individual.

Decimal system of filing.   The decimal system of filing is based on the Dewey decimal system used in some public libraries and in some highly specialized businesses. All the records in an office are classified under ten or fewer principal headings, which are numbered 000 to 900. Each heading is divided into ten or fewer subheadings, which are numbered from 10 to 90, preceded by the applicable hundreds digit. Each subheading may be subdivided into ten or fewer headings, which are numbered from 1 to 9, preceded by the appropriate hundreds and tens digits. If necessary, these headings may be further subdivided and numbered from .1 to .10, and so on, under the appropriate full number. The following example illustrates a breakdown of books on Useful Arts under the Dewey classification used in libraries.

Useful arts	600
Engineering	620
Canal engineering	629

The secretary is seldom called upon to install a decimal system of filing. Should it become necessary, consult books describing the Melvil Dewey system, which can be obtained at most public libraries.

NAME AND SUBJECT FILES

Adaptation of files to needs.   A secretary ordinarily files papers according to *name* or *subject,* using one of the basic systems of filing or an adaptation of it. For some records, a name file under an alphabetical system should be used; for others, a subject file arranged under a numerical system is more appropriate. Thus, the secretary in a lawyer's office will use the numerical system for litigated cases, with cross-reference index cards under the names of all the parties to the litigation. She or he will also have an alphabetical file with a folder under the name of each client for correspondence that does not relate to litigated matters. The secretary to a sales manager will probably have an administrative file classified according to subject and another file classified according to name for correspondence with district managers and salespersons.

Name file.   The easiest and quickest method of filing is to classify material according to name and to file it alphabetically. This system should be used whenever possible because no cross-index or list of files is necessary. Rules for indexing and alphabetizing names are given on pages 52-58.

Folders. Make a folder for each correspondent or name, if there is sufficient material to justify a separate folder. From three to ten papers justify starting a folder. Arrange the papers within the folder by date with the latest date on top.

Miscellaneous folder. Make a miscellaneous folder for each letter of the alphabet and place it behind the last name folder under the particular letter. File any material for which there is no separate name folder in the miscellaneous folder, alphabetically rather than by date. This keeps all papers relating to a particular name together. When they reach the required number, three to ten, make a separate folder.

Voluminous correspondence with the same person. If correspondence with the same person or firm is voluminous, separate it into date periods. You may obtain folders with printed date headings (Figure 7), or you may type the dates on your labels.

Correspondents with the same name. On folders for correspondents with the same name, use a different-colored label. The distinctive color is a signal to use extra precaution in filing or in looking for filed material. Thus, if you use blue labels and you have a folder for *Abernathy, Edgar, Sr.* with a salmon label, you know immediately that you also have a folder for *Abernathy, Edgar, Jr.,* with a blue label.

Subject files.   Some material does not lend itself to classification by name and must be classified by subject. The installation of a subject file requires great care. You should not attempt to choose the subject headings until you are thoroughly familiar with the material that is to be filed in your office. The list should be comprehensive and yet simple enough to avoid confusion. Subject headings must be specific, significant, and technically correct. Select nouns whenever possible, for they are more specific than other words.

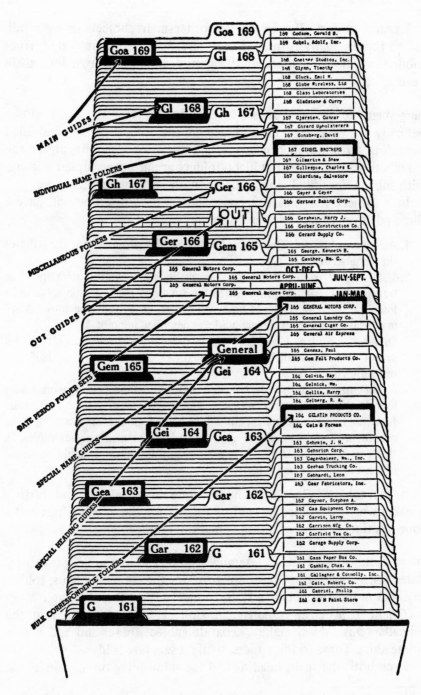

FIGURE 7   ALPHABETICAL NAME FILE ARRANGED IN FOUR POSITIONS

Expand subject files by adding other main subjects or by subdividing those already in use. If necessary, subheadings may be further subdivided; but for a secretary's purpose, a breakdown into main headings and subheadings is generally adequate.

Arrangement of subject files.   Subject files may be filed alphabetically or they may be arranged in any logical order[1] and filed according to a numbering system. Secretaries generally prefer the alphabetical system. All subject folders are arranged alphabetically, with subheadings filed alphabetically under each main heading.

In a subject file that has main and subheadings, you will have a three-position arrangement as follows:

1. *Alphabetical guides.* These may be cardboard separators with the letter of the alphabet at the left.
2. *Main subject guides.* These may be cardboard separators with metal or transparent plastic tabs into which the names of the main subjects can be inserted. These tabs should be in the center. Or a "miscellaneous folder" may be used as a main subject guide, as described in point 4.
3. *Subheading folders.* Use right-position tabs for these folders. Folders with precut tabs are available with tabs of varying widths (e.g., half cut, one-third cut, etc.).
4. *Miscellaneous folder for each main heading.* Label the miscellaneous folder like the guide and use a label different in color from that on the regular folders. Place the miscellaneous folder behind all the other folders. The miscellaneous folder may be used instead of the main subject guides. In that case the folder should have a center-position tab and should be placed in front of the subhead folders.

If the subject file has main headings, subheadings, and further breakdowns, use guides instead of folders for the subheadings and a four-position, instead of a three-position, arrangement.

Folders in the subject file.   Arrange the papers in a subject folder by date, with the latest date on top. In the miscellaneous folder, material is filed alphabetically by subject rather than by date. When sufficient papers on a particular subject are accumulated in the miscellaneous folder, make a separate subject folder and add it as a subheading. Three to ten papers justify a separate folder.

Type both the main heading and the subheading on the file labels.

---

[1] In a standard classification adopted by the American Institute of Architects, the subjects are arranged according to the order of procedure in building. Thus, *excavation* comes ahead of *acoustics.*

For convenience in filing and finding, type the subheading on the first line and the main heading on the second line, indented two spaces or in parentheses. If you have a red and black ribbon on your typewriter, type the main heading in red to distinguish it more readily from the subheading.

Index to subject file. For subject files, it is generally advisable to keep either an alphabetical list or a card index of the subjects: (1) to prevent filing material under a new heading when you already have a folder for the subject; (2) to enable a substitute, an assistant, or your employer to locate things in the file.

Alphabetical list. Type in one alphabetical list the main headings and subheadings, the main headings in full caps and the subheadings in initial caps. After each subheading, type in parentheses the main heading under which the subheading is classified. Leave sufficient space between the items to permit additions of new subjects. *Keep the list up to date.* An alphabetical list will usually be adequate where the files are not extensive and additions are infrequent. Here is the arrangement of an alphabetical list of subject files:

Applications (Personnel)
CONTRACTS
EXPENSES AND EXPENSE ACCOUNTS
FORM LETTERS
Holidays (Personnel)
Hotels, Reservations (Travel)
INSURANCE
INVESTMENTS
Itineraries (Travel)
Leases (Contracts)
MEETINGS
Minutes (Meetings)
PERSONNEL
TRAVEL

Card Index. Make an index card for each subject heading and subheading. Show for each subheading the main heading under which it is classified. When a subject heading is not self-explanatory, describe on the card the material covered by it. Also, make cross-reference cards for subjects on which there is insufficient material to justify a separate folder and for subjects under which material might logically have been classified but for which you chose another heading. Thus, as the secretary to a department head you might have a main heading "PERSONNEL." As you have only a few papers relating to "Lunch Hour," you decide to file this material in the miscellaneous "PERSONNEL" folder. Make an index card for the subject "Lunch Hour" and indicate on the card that material relating to it is filed in the miscellaneous "PERSONNEL" folder. File all the cards alphabetically.

The card index is usually preferable for extensive, growing files because it is easily kept up to date.

Combined name and subject file.   If you have only a name file and occasionally have material that should be filed by subject, or if you have a subject file and occasionally have material that should be filed by the name of the individual, you can combine the occasional folders with your main file. For example, in a name file you might include a folder labeled "Applications" to receive the few applications that you keep in your files. Put a cross-reference sheet under the name of the applicant in the miscellaneous folder for the letter with which the surname begins. Or in a subject file you might include a folder labeled with a person's name, which would actually be a subject.

Chronological filing.   Many secretaries find still another type of file, the chronological file, to be useful in addition to, not instead of, other filing systems. This auxiliary file contains carbon copies, in chronological order, of all outgoing letters, memorandums, notices, and reports. A chronological file is useful when trying to locate material the content of which has been forgotten. When, for example, the manager says to you, "What was it we asked the city for about eight months ago?" You can simply look at the correspondence in the chronological file for the period in question. A chronological file is also a convenient way of recalling what went on during a given period. For example, when the manager has been out of town for a week or so, a quick look at the chronological file will help to bring him or her up to date on what has transpired during his or her absence.

A chronological file is also known as a *reading* file.

HOW TO INDEX
AND ALPHABETIZE

Indexing.   Indexing, as applied to filing, is the arrangement of the names on the folder tabs or on cards for filing purposes. The folders or cards are then arranged in alphabetical order. You must know how names are indexed before you can consider them for alphabetizing.

Individual names. Individual names are indexed by the surname first, then the given name or initial, and then additional names or initials.

Name	Index as
L. Vosburgh Lyons	Lyons, L. Vosburgh
James G. Mellon	Mellon, James G.
R. S. Andrews	Andrews, R. S.

Business concerns, organizations, and institutions. When organization names are composed of names of individuals, follow the order that applies to individual names; otherwise, each word comprising the name is considered in the order in which it appears.

Name	Index as
James G. Mellon & Son	Mellon, James G., & Son
J. P. Goode, Inc.	Goode, J. P., Inc.
Myron, Bache & Adams Co.	Myron, Bache & Adams Co.
National City Bank	National City Bank
National Development Co.	National Development Co.

When an institutional name contains the name of the type of institution, such as *Bank* of America or *University* of Illinois, the distinctive word is used first for filing purposes.

Name	File as
Bank of America	America, Bank (of)
University of Illinois	Illinois, University (of)

Basic rules of alphabetizing. Alphabetize by words, according to the first word in the name *as indexed.* When the first word of two or more names is the same, alphabetize according to the second word, then according to the third.

Index and File as
Brown, Albert A.
Brown, George
Brownell, Edward

Names of unequal length. The basic rule of alphabetizing by words results in the following simple rule: When two or more names are of unequal length but contain the same word or words and are spelled the same up to and including the last word of the shorter name, index and file the shorter name first.

Order

Brown, G.
Brown, George
Brown, George A.
State Bank
State Bank and Trust Company

Precedence of letters. 1. *Letters used as words.* One or more single letters used as words are treated as words. The group beginning with letter names is arranged alphabetically and precedes word names.

Order

A A Club
A C E Letter Co.
AWVS
Abbey Coat Co.
Admiration Cigar Co.

2. *Ampersand symbol.* The ampersand symbol (&) is not considered a letter and is disregarded in determining alphabetical sequence.

Index and File as

A & B Co.
Abernathy Stores, Inc.
Adams Hardware, Inc.
Adams & Rawlins, Inc.

Hyphenated names. Treat names composed of letters, words, or syllables joined by one or more hyphens as one word. When the hyphen is used instead of a comma in a firm name, the individual parts of the name are treated as separate words. You know that the hyphen replaces the comma when the names of two individuals make up the firm name.

Index and File as

Evers-Harper & Co.
   (hyphen used instead of comma)
Evers, Warren D.
Ever-Sharp Products Corp.
Up-Stairs Dress Co.
Upton-Smith, Edward L.

Abbreviations.   Abbreviations, such as Chas., Co., Geo., Jas., St., Wm., and the like, are alphabetized in the same sequence as if spelled in full. Spell out on file labels for ease in filing.

Names	File as
St. John's Church	Saint John's Church
Jas. Sanders	Sanders, James
Jane Sanders	Sanders, Jane
Wm. Smith	Smith, William
Willis Smith	Smith, Willis

Sometimes an abbreviated name is the actual legal name of the person or company. In this case, use the abbreviated spelling in filing.

Compound firm names.   1. When a firm name consists of a compound word that is sometimes spelled as one word, sometimes as two or more words, index as written but treat as one word in alphabetizing.

Index and File as
Lockport Engine Co.
Lock Port Fisheries
Lockport Mansions, Inc.
New Amsterdam Bakery, Inc.
New York City Bank
Newark Rubber Co.
North, R. S.
North East Commodities, Inc.
Northeastern Burlap Co.

2. Opinion differs as to whether compound geographic names, such as New York, should be treated as one or two words in alphabetizing. Adopt a rule and follow it uniformly. In the example above, compound geographic names are treated as two words.

Sr., Jr., 2nd.   Retain designations that follow names, such as Jr., III (Third), in indexing and filing, and alphabetize according to the designation. The order is as follows: 2nd (Second), III (Third), Jr., Sr.

Index and File as
White, John, 2nd
White, John, III
White, John, Jr.
White, John, Sr.

Surnames with prefixes.   When individual surnames are compounded with prefixes, such as D', De, Del, De La, Di, Fitz, L', La, Las, Los, M', Mc, Mac, O', San, Santa, Ten, Van, van Der, von, von Der, and other similar prefixes, index as written, and treat as one word in alphabetizing, disregarding the apostrophe, the space, or the capitalization, if any.

> *Index and File as*
> Damata, J.
> D'Amato, P.
> D'Arcy, A. C.
> De Lamara, A. D.
> De La Mare, A. D.
> Madison, R. L.
> McIntyre, A. C.
> Mead, Robert A.
> Tenants' Committee, Inc.
> Ten Eyck, E. M.

Articles, prepositions, and conjunctions.   Disregard articles, prepositions, and conjunctions in determining alphabetical sequence. The words in parentheses in the following examples are disregarded.

Names	*Index and File as*
F. A. Madison	Madison, F. A.
(The) Marine Bank	Marine Bank, The
Geo. Mathews	Mathews, Geo.
Society (of) Arts (and) Sciences	Society of Arts and Sciences
Society (for the) Prevention of Cruelty	Society for the Prevention of Cruelty

Articles, prepositions, and conjunctions in foreign languages.
Consider an article in a name in a foreign language as part of the word that immediately follows it; treat prepositions and conjunctions as separate words in determining alphabetical sequence.

Names	*Index and File as*
C. H. Deramer	Deramer, C. H.
Der Amerikaner	Der Amerikaner
Société des Auteurs et Peintres	Société des Auteurs et Peintres
Société des Auteurs, Musiciens et Compositeurs	Société des Auteurs, Musiciens et Compositeurs

Words ending in "s."   When a word ends in "s," index and file as spelled regardless of what the "s" denotes (whether possession, with or without the apostrophe, or a singular or plural ending).

Index and File as
Girl Scout Council
Girls' Service League
Girly Shoe Store
Smith, John
Smith's Delicatessen
Thompson, R. S.

Names containing numbers.   When a name contains a number, alphabetize as if the number were spelled in full. Spelling out the names on the file labels facilitates the filing.

Names	*File as*
28 Sutton Place, Inc.	Twenty-Eight Sutton Place, Inc.
2059 Third Ave. Corp.	Twenty Fifty-Nine Third Ave. Corp.
The 21 Club	Twenty-One Club, The

Exception: Numbered streets and branches of organizations numbered consecutively should be arranged in numerical sequence. Thus, Branch Number 4 precedes Branch Number 5, although if the numbers were spelled out and alphabetized, Branch Number Five would precede Branch Number Four.

Government offices.   Index and file names of government offices under the names of the governing body, with the names of the departments, bureaus, or institutions as subtitles.

Federal	*State*
United States Government	Mississippi (State of)
Treasury (Dept. of)	Education (Dept. of)
Accounts (Bur. of)	Rural Education (Div. of)

County	*City*
Suffolk (County of)	Memphis, Tennessee
County Clerk	City Planning Commission

Titles.   1. Titles are disregarded in indexing and filing but are usually written in parentheses at the end of the name.

Exceptions: If the name of an individual contains a title and a given name, without a surname, consider the title as the first word.

Names	Index and File as
Dr. J. C. Adams	Adams, J. C. (Dr.)
Sister Mary Brown	Brown, Mary (Sr.)
Madame Celeste	Madame Celeste
Miss Helen Marsh	Marsh, Helen (Miss)
Count Carlos Sforza	Sforza, Carlos (Count)

2. If a *firm name* contains a title, consider the title as the first word.

Index and File as
King Edward Hospital
Sir Walter Raleigh Tobacco Co.
Uncle Sam Produce Co.

Married women. Index and file names of married women according to their married surnames, followed by their first names. Show the husband's initial or name in parentheses on the file label when it is convenient or important to have this additional information.

Name	Index and File as
Mrs. Robert E. (Ada R.) Brown	Brown, Ada R. (Mrs. Robert E. Brown)
Mrs. Albert S. (Mary L.) Brown	Brown, Mary L. (Mrs. Albert S. Brown)

AIDS TO FAST FILING AND FINDING

Time-saving techniques in filing and finding. An efficient secretary will quickly learn how to apply a few simple, time-saving techniques to filing duties. Most of the following will not only save precious minutes each day, but will make your job much easier.

1. Visit showrooms and write to suppliers to request free sales literature to get ideas on new and effective filing materials and equipment, filing systems, and efficient office layouts.
2. Learn the pros and cons of different systems thoroughly, including advanced techniques such as microfilming and automated storage and retrieval, before you set up a new system or revise the present system in your office.
3. Avoid fatigue, which cuts work speed and performance, by using filing

techniques and aids such as (a) stools with rollers, so you may sit down during extended periods of filing; and (b) tables with rollers or trays that attach to file drawers, to keep material for filing at arm's reach. Keep heavy documents where it isn't necessary to lift or carry them far; store seldom-used materials in the higher and lower drawers or on top and bottom shelves; and always work from the side, not the front, of a file drawer.

4. File daily. Large stacks of accumulated filing can complicate the task and make it tiresome.

5. Simplify the step of sorting and organizing the material to be filed by using sorting trays, racks, or carts, whichever suits the type and volume of work you have. Use rubber fingers if you must leaf through large stacks of correspondence. Different-colored carbons, according to subject, will also speed the sorting process.

6. Use supplies and equipment that encourage rapid visual location. Examples are (a) visible files, including trays, holders, stands, loose-leaf books, and desk-top organizers, along with transparent guides, binder and shelf clips, and pockets—all for quick visual identification of contents; and (b) color-coded files, both file folders and storage containers, for instant recognition of files and contents and easy-to-spot misfiles. Circular, rotating files and open-shelf filing also permit fast and easy location and retrieval, especially in combination with color-coding.

7. Avoid mishaps, such as (a) toppling a file cabinet by pulling out more than one drawer at a time; (b) spilling the contents of a folder by not resting it properly upon removal or by not using both hands while filing material in it or retrieving material from it; or (c) ruining a folder while pulling it out by grasping only the tab.

8. Keep the size of folders manageable—open new ones if necessary. Leave several inches for such expansion in each file drawer and on each shelf.

9. Use a guide for every six to eight folders and place folders *behind* the guides. Investigate the use of file and desk drawer dividers to aid further in compartmentalizing and organizing contents.

10. Speed the labeling process with such products as pressure-sensitive labels, preprinted tabs, and continuous-feed labels for typing. Some tabs are removable; and some have transparent windows for reuse, which means it's a simple matter to salvage and use old folders again merely by a quick tab change or by inserting a newly typed label.

11. Always position records in their folders face up with the top toward the left; the document with the most recent date goes in front. Fold oversized papers with the data on the outside.

How to type index tabs and labels. For best results in typing tabs, guides, and folder labels, observe the following rules:

Use the briefest possible designations. Abbreviate, omitting punctuation whenever possible. Index tabs need to be legible only at normal reading distance. Guide labels should be legible at two or three feet. File drawer labels should be legible at six to ten feet.

Use initial caps whenever needed. Full caps, especially in elite and pica type, do *not* increase the legibility of label designations; they decrease the amount of light background in the vicinity of the letters and make reading more difficult. Do not underline.

Folder labels. The most important part of a folder label is the eighth of an inch immediately below the scoring (the place at which the label is folded when it is pasted on the folder tab). Frequently this space is the only part visible in the file. Therefore, write in the first typing space below the scoring. Typing should begin in the first or second typing space from the left edge of the label, except for one or two character designations. If this is done, all folder labels in the file drawer will present an even left margin.

Use initial caps and indent the second and third lines so that the first word of the first line will stand out.

In typing labels for a numbered subject file, leave space between the number and the first word; type the subject in block form. Avoid exceptionally long file numbers if possible. For proper arrangement of various label designations, see Figure 8.

Guide labels. For file guide labels, use the largest type available. Begin the typing as high on the label as the guide tabs will permit. Center one- and two-character designations. Start all other designations in the second typing space from the left edge. Use abbreviations or shortened forms and omit punctuation, except for large numbers such as 10,000, 175,000.

File drawer labels. In preparing labels for file drawers, use the largest type available. Center the typing on the label and leave a double space above and below detailed reference information. It is better to print file drawer labels because type is not legible at a distance.

Cross-reference. Frequently, material may be filed logically under one or more names or subjects. In those cases, file the paper under one name or subject and cross-reference under the other. For example, a letter from Mr. Remsen might relate to Mr. Abernathy. The most reasonable place to file the letter is under *Abernathy,* but a cross-reference should be made under *Remsen.* Write the cross-reference on colored cross-reference sheets, about 8½″ by 11″. They

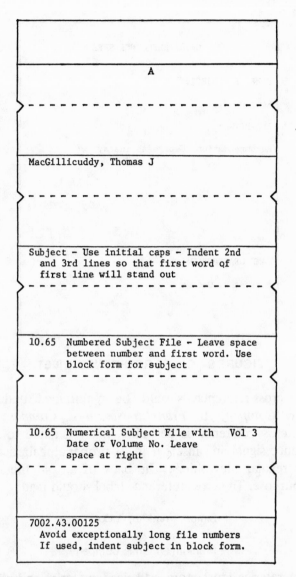

A

MacGillicuddy, Thomas J

Subject - Use initial caps - Indent 2nd
and 3rd lines so that first word of
first line will stand out

10.65   Numbered Subject File - Leave space
        between number and first word. Use
        block form for subject

10.65   Numerical Subject File with   Vol 3
        Date or Volume No. Leave
        space at right

7002.43.00125
        Avoid exceptionally long file numbers
        If used, indent subject in block form.

FIGURE 8   PROPER ARRANGEMENT FOR LABEL DESIGNATIONS

may be purchased in pads at any stationery store. The cross-reference sheet should contain the information shown in Figure 9. If Mr. Remsen has a regular folder, put the cross-reference sheet in it; if not, put it in the miscellaneous folder under R.

A permanent cross-reference is usually maintained when a name or subject can be filed under more than one designation. For example, a

```
┌─────────────────────────────────────────────────┐
│              CROSS-REFERENCE SHEET              │
│                                                 │
│   NAME OR SUBJECT:                              │
│                                                 │
│   Remsen, S.J.                                 │
│                                                 │
│   REGARDING:                                   │
│                                                 │
│   Recommendation, George Abernathy             │
│                                                 │
│                                                 │
│                               DATE:            │
│                                                 │
│                               May 11, 19--     │
│                                                 │
│                                                 │
│                                                 │
│   (see)                                        │
│                                                 │
│   NAME OR SUBJECT:                             │
│                                                 │
│   Abernathy, George                            │
│                                                 │
│                                                 │
└─────────────────────────────────────────────────┘
```

FIGURE 9 CROSS-REFERENCE SHEET

permanent cross-reference should be maintained under *Simon, Franklin, & Company* to *Franklin Simon & Company*. When a permanent cross-reference is desirable, make a guide to serve as a cross-reference signal and insert it in its proper alphabetical position among the regular file folders. The back of an old file folder will serve this purpose. The cross-reference label should read:

> Simon, Franklin, & Co.
> see
> Franklin Simon & Company

Many secretaries must store odd-sized material or bulky objects (blueprints, film, etc.) in a special place. A cross-reference sheet in the regular files may be desirable in such cases.

Cross-reference labels should be in a color different from the color of the labels on the regular folders. *Use cross-reference sheets freely.*

There are instances when frequent reference or the need for full information immediately may preclude the use of a standard cross-reference procedure. A photocopy of the document in question placed in the regular files would be preferable for such situations.

How to prepare material for filing.   To prepare material for filing, do the following:

1. Check to be certain the material has been released for filing. (This may be indicated simply by a brief notation on the document or by a rubber-stamped FILE notice.)
2. If you have more than one category of files, segregate papers into the different categories: personal correspondence, business correspondence, documents, and the like. Use one of the sorting aids described on page 59.
3. Check through all papers that are stapled to see whether they should be filed together.
4. Remove all paper clips.
5. Mend torn papers with cellophane tape.
6. Note on the paper where it is to be filed. For a *name file,* underline the name in colored pencil; for a *subject file,* write the main heading and subheading in the upper right-hand corner. Place guide or file number, if used, in the upper right-hand corner.
7. Circle an important word or words in colored pencil to facilitate location of a particular paper when it is wanted.
8. Make necessary cross-reference sheets as each letter or paper is handled.

Control of material taken from the files.   To control material taken from your files, use guides the same height as the file folders but of different-colored stock, with the word OUT printed on the tab. The OUT guide provides space on which to make an entry of the date, the material taken, who has it, and the date it should be returned. See Figure 10. Place the guide in the files where the removed material was located.

DATE	MATERIAL	DATE REMOVED	TO BE RETURNED	CHARGE TO WHOM	REMARKS

FIGURE 10   OUT CARD

A secretary in a private office does not put an OUT guide in the file every time she or he withdraws material for the manager. The guide is used under these circumstances: (1) Someone outside the immediate office wants the material. (2) The employer expects to take the material out of the office, say, when he or she goes on a trip. (3) The secretary expects the employer to keep the material a week or so, say, to prepare a report.

Guides for the files. Frequent guides make filing and finding easy. Therefore, it is usually advisable to put guides between at least every six or eight folders.

Alphabetical index guides come in divisions of from 25 to 2,000. The 25 division has a guide for each letter from A to Z, with Mc added and XYZ combined in the last guide. Although in alphabetizing, names beginning with Mc are treated in regular alphabetical sequence (see page 56), Mc is included as a letter in a 25-division index for the convenience of those who have more than three or four names beginning with Mc. The Mc guide precedes the M guide. In an index with more divisions, the Mc guide is in its proper alphabetical position, between the M and the N guides.

To determine which division you need, count the number of drawers of filing material. The following table shows the division required for a given number of drawers.

For	1 drawer	25 division
For	2 drawers	40 division
For	4 drawers	80 division
For	6 drawers	120 division
For	8 drawers	160 division
For	12 drawers	240 division
For	16 drawers	320 division

For geographical index guides, see page 46.

How to find a lost paper. When you, or someone else, has misfiled a paper, and you have to find it, you can shorten your search by looking in the most likely places for misfiling it:

1. Look in the folders that precede and follow the folder the paper should be in.
2. Look under consonants that look alike either handwritten or typed—for example, *N, M, W, U,* and *V.*
3. Check under other vowels than the correct one. For a name beginning with *Ca,* look under *Ce, Ci, Co,* or *Cu.*

4. Abbreviations are easily misfiled. For example an abbreviation of James Sanders may have been incorrectly labeled and filed under Sanders, *Jas.,* instead of Sanders, *James;* or an abbreviation of *Saint* may have been incorrectly labeled and filed under *St.* instead of *Sa.*
5. If more than one name is in the subject of the lost paper, look under each name, even though the paper should have been filed under the first name in the subject.
6. Look for a possible "charge-out" or "transferred" withdrawal that may not have been recorded.
7. As a last resort, check your sorter, behind the file cabinet or your desk, or even in the wastebasket.

HOW TO MODERNIZE AND STREAMLINE YOUR FILES

Eliminate follow blocks.   If you are jamming records into a 26-inch file drawer that also contains a follow block about ¾-inch thick, you are losing between 1 and 1½ inches of drawer space in each drawer. With four or five drawers in each cabinet, you are losing up to 7½ inches of drawer space in each cabinet. Substitute hanging folders and pockets and portable drawer dividing units for the bulky follow blocks.

Use hanging folders and hanging pockets.   Hanging folders and hanging pockets solve space problems for many secretaries. If your files did not come equipped with this feature, you can purchase metal frames in either letter or legal size, depending on the size of the cabinet drawer and the type of papers to be filed. The metal frame fits into the file drawer (from which the follow block has already been removed) and hanging folders and hanging pockets are ready to be dropped into place. The hanging folder serves as a guide card, folder, and separator all in one.

Although hanging *folders* have numerous advantages, you will not save space if you use too many in one drawer. Since two hanging folders take up ½ inch of space, a dozen of these folders would take up 3 inches of space, robbing you of more drawer space than you save by removing the follow block.

Hanging *pockets* seem to be the most space-saving of all divider devices. Pockets hold individual folders neatly in place and unlike hanging folders, expand freely. If the material in your drawer is filed by subject, and your subjects are divided into four main categories, use four roomy hanging pockets in which to insert individual folders. Material that is numerically arranged can easily group itself in pockets by the 10s, or 100s, depending on the amount of material in each numbered section. Even alphabetically arranged material can be divided by means of a hanging pocket. Label one pocket "A to F," the second pocket "G to M," and so on. Material is never lost by slipping under other folders onto the floor of the drawer. Folders are held firmly in place and never slip or slide under one another.

How to use portable drawer dividing units.   A portable drawer divider is another device to eliminate bulky follow blocks. The divider is a lightweight metal "skeleton" that separates and supports file folders and is easily inserted into a drawer. Its strong bottom stand holds folders upright and prevents loss through slipping.

This dividing unit serves other purposes, too. It can be inserted into a desk drawer to hold miscellaneous papers, brochures, stationery, and other supplies. It can be used on the desk top, in lieu of a more elaborate desk-top organizer, to hold letters or magazines. It is adjustable, so that sections can be expanded or narrowed, as needed.

Eliminate magazines, bulky brochures.   File cabinets should not be piled high with old copies of magazines, brochures, and other printed material. Late issues of important periodicals should be on display for easy accessibility, not tucked away in file drawers where they are of no use to anyone. After periodicals have been read by those who are interested, they have served their purpose and current issues should be substituted for them.

If it is necessary to keep dated printed matter for *infrequent* reference purposes, it should be stored in a less-accessible place. Material that must be kept filed and ready for *quick* reference should be stored as compactly as possible. Here are two ways of saving space through compact placement:

1. Narrow pamphlets and brochures, only a fraction of the size of the folder that holds them, should be stacked in double or triple rows, lengthwise, within the folder.
2. Printed matter that is clipped or bound on one edge should be equalized by alternating the papers within the folder: half of the bulky edges to the right side of the folder and half to the left.

Eliminate duplications.   Bulky files are greatly reduced when duplicate papers are deleted from active files. Duplications often occur in the following areas:

1. Carbon copies of memos and letters
2. Galleys, page proofs, and paste-ups
3. Reprints of published letters and reports
4. Identical copies of published brochures

If you are in the habit of making two or three carbons for each letter or report you type, consider reducing the number of copies you make. Unless the manager has need of extra copies for some special purpose, you may be cluttering your files with unnecessary copies of memos and routine letters. Condense and centralize your files wherever possible, to avoid overlapping. If you keep a "carbon copy file," and also a "follow-up file" in addition to the manager's complete file, you may be doubling the amount of work necessary to complete your tasks.

Unless you plan to distribute additional copies of brochures or reports, the filing of identical copies of printed matter is unnecessary. Many secretaries retain three copies of this type of material and send the remaining copies to storage spaces located in a remote part of the building.

Remove thick backings of clippings and photos.   Photographs and clippings that must be filed need support and protection against loss or tearing. Although cardboard backing is often used, it is unnecessarily thick for filing. Manila tag is a better choice because it is sturdy and yet takes up much less space. Celluloid envelope sheets are probably the best protection for photographs and clippings, and they are less bulky than manila tag sheets, but they are the most expensive method of preservation.

Transfer little-used or odd-sized material.   Odd-sized and bulky materials such as blueprints or tape reels should not occupy valuable space in the regular files. Instead, they should be moved to suitable containers and merely cross-referenced in the regular files. Correspondence, papers, and records that cannot be destroyed but are referred to only occasionally should be transferred to storage to save floor space. Transfer files save time in filing and finding; they also release expensive equipment for active files. Some correspondence should not even be retained, such as standard inquiries and form-letter replies. If the inquiry represents a prospective customer or sale, the name and address can be transferred to a card file or a mailing list.

Here is a list of ideas to facilitate the transfer of files that must be retained.

1. Plan the new file well in advance of the transfer date.
2. If the entire file is to be transferred, leaving only guides in the file drawers, prepare new folders for the new file beforehand. Prepare only those folders that will be definitely needed. Use a new color for folder labels and indicate the year as well as the title.
3. If the folders and the guides are to be retained in the file, prepare a new set of cheap folders to hold the material in the transfer drawers. Put titles on these folders identical with those in the current file and have them ready in advance of the transfer date.
4. If the space is available, keep the old files in the office for a few weeks until sufficient material for reference purposes accumulates in the new files.
5. Make sure ample storage space is available for the old files and that the transfer files or boxes fit the conditions in the storage location.
6. To avoid interference with general office procedures, plan to have the transfer operation done after hours. Plan for enough help to complete the entire job in one evening. For most efficient results, have two persons work on each drawer—one pulling out the folders and the other packing them in the transfer files. If folders and labels have not been prepared in advance, have a typist do this work during the transfer operation.
7. Label all transfer files or boxes. Indicate contents of file, dates, and so on clearly on labels and affix them to the containers so that they can be easily read.
8. Pack transfer files or boxes tightly—two drawer-length transfer units will hold the contents of three filing cabinet drawers.

Develop a file retention program.   Although it is necessary for a secretary to have a retention and disposal program for filing materials, it is not her or his responsibility to decide what should be kept and what should be destroyed.

Business matters. If your company has established a procedure for the destruction of papers, you should be guided by this method. If no such policy exists, the manager should determine the period of retention for all types of documents and letters. How long a paper will be retained depends on legal considerations such as the statute of limitations or other requirements, and the manager's desires.

The preparation of any destruction schedule must take into account (1) the statute of limitations, (2) other laws that may apply to particular items,[2] and (3) studies that have been made of how long business firms usually retain various types of papers. If space is at a premium and it is absolutely necessary to keep some types of correspondence for many years, some companies make microfilm copies, which take up little space.

Personal matters. Two factors will determine how long to keep personal papers and records: the statute of limitations and the manager's desires. The secretary is advised to compile for her or his own use a retention schedule that meets the employer's desires. To make the schedule the secretary should do the following:

1. List alphabetically all types of personal papers and records in the files.
2. Rule three columns to the right of the listed items.
3. In the first column, insert the statute of limitations requirements in your state, or other legal requirements.
4. In the second column, show what you suggest as the period of retention. There are no established practices that can be used as guides for retention of personal papers, as there are for business records.
5. Have your employer indicate in the third column his or her wish as to the period of retention for each item.
6. Retype the schedule with just one indication of years—the time approved by your employer.

Safeguard your files and important documents.   So much attention is given to filing systems that basic precautions for safety are often ignored in an office. As a separate record or as part of the retention records mentioned above, you should ask the manager to indicate which business and personal papers are confidential. All such items should be stored in cabinets with security locks.

Other considerations in filing and storing materials are fire, loss, humidity, and cleanliness. Each of these must be considered when selecting appropriate filing and storage equipment.

Use of color-coding to enhance your filing system.   Color-coding, as used in both folders/tabs and containers, can be applied to any filing system, and it can be as simple or as intricate as you like. Quick storage and retrieval and ease in spotting misfiles are the more obvious benefits of this technique.

---

[2]For example, the provisions of the Fair Labor Standards Act (Wage-Hour Act) and of the Federal Insurance Contribution Act (old-age, survivor and disability benefits) must be taken into account in scheduling the destruction of payroll and other employee information records called for by these acts.

Color can be applied numerically (e.g., black = 10; red = 20; green = 30, etc.) or by subject (e.g., black = Insurance; red = Real Estate; green = Investments). Some offices are using color to make evaluations as well (e.g., black = a good, prospective customer; red = a potential, but difficult customer; green = an unlikely prospect). The uses of color are almost limitless. Manufacturers of supplies and cabinets have complete systems already designed, and sales literature describing them is available free for the asking.

How to determine if a file is really necessary. Files are intended to organize information in such a way that it can be retrieved with a minimum of time and effort. Therefore, the temptation to over-organize is strong, and the secretary should view each new file critically:

1. Will the proposed new file make it possible to locate information faster and easier than in present files?
2. How often will the file be used—often, occasionally, seldom?
3. Will the file require an increase in the number of carbon copies and photocopies (and thus in typing and copying time and costs) of certain correspondence?
4. Will the file increase the number of hours devoted to filing and related duties?
5. Will the file affect file container and storage space requirements?
6. Will the file require other new files (e.g., check-out, cross-reference, etc.) in order to maintain it properly?
7. Very simply, do the pros outweigh the cons?

How to order and store supplies. It is often a secretary's job to purchase and store supplies for herself or himself and the manager. This involves a knowledge of what is needed and when, where to go to get it, and where to store it until time for use.

A larger company will have a special department that orders and stocks supplies for use in offices within the company. In such cases a secretary must complete a company order form and present it at the stockroom. Supplies may not always be available and requests should be made far enough in advance to allow for ordering if necessary. In a small office, a secretary may simply be asked to go to a local office supply store and purchase (probably by charge account) the necessary supplies. At the time the supplies are ordered, you should keep a copy of the purchase order and check off items as they are received.

Some form of regular inventory control is needed, regardless of the size of the office. A typed list of supplies on hand, and average quantity used during certain periods (e.g., monthly), would be the simplest method. Such an inventory control sheet would have several columns, recording the quantities left on hand at certain dates (e.g., the end of each month). When the sheet indicated that a certain supply would be exhausted in another month, it would be time to reorder. As an example, the following entry would indicate on April 30 that it is time to reorder memo pads:

Item	Av. Qty. Used/Mo.	On Hand				
		Jan. 31	Feb. 28	Mar. 31	Apr. 30	etc.
memo pads	12	48	36	24	12	etc.

Storage is frequently more of a problem than purchasing. Lack of organization will complicate the task of taking inventory periodically. Many of the same rules applied to the filing of regular correspondence can be used here. Seldom-used supplies, for example, should go on the top and bottom shelves or toward the back in a storage closet. Materials should be grouped for ease in locating and in estimating quantities. Mark packages for quantity as they arrive—don't trust your memory to hold until the end of the month. As supplies are removed during the month, cross out that quantity and jot the new balance on the front package. At the end of the month record the last balance on your inventory control sheet.

If you have doubts about quantities needed or length of time required on items that must be ordered, play it safe—order far in advance, several months if necessary, and order more than you believe necessary.

Automated procedures in handling information. The storage of information and its retrieval are processes that have been automated in many offices. Although there will always be certain materials that require manual filing and retrieval, vast quantities of information can only be processed, stored, and located by sophisticated equipment. Along with data-processing machines and the small-to-large computer installations, the larger company may well house sophisticated storage and retrieval devices. Automated equipment in this category is often large and capable, at the push of a button, of locating sizable containers in storage modules and transporting them to a predetermined location. After use, the push of another button will return the container of files to its storage module.

Other equipment and processes store material in reduced form or size, such as microfilm, punched cards, magnetic tape, magnetic cards, edge-punched cards, and printouts (machine forms). Microform encompasses microfilm, microcard, microfiche, and ultrafiche. Of these, microfilming is the best-known method of transferring documents onto a roll of film (the other three processes simply refer to cards or sheets of film rather than rolls). After microfilmed documents are reduced and stored on film, they can be viewed on a screen when desired and, with certain equipment, they can be photocopied at the same time. Original, full-size files can then be destroyed, and only the film retained, with a savings in storage space of up to 98 percent. Moreover, the film is noncombustible, reducing the danger of loss through fire. Microfilm has special benefits in the storage and retrieval of extensive or continuous records, such as mailing lists, accounts receivable, personnel forms, and stock certificates, or bulky items such as engineering drawings.

Automated procedures for handling information basically are intended to lower or control costs by reducing such factors as space and labor requirements, and by increasing such factors as efficiency and output. Justification of sophisticated storage and retrieval equipment, however, is quite complex. A detailed analysis is necessary not only to compare all pertinent cost and production factors, but also to project growth and consider the effect of all related factors in the future. The secretary should be alert to signs that suggest a need for expansion: delays in processing, an increasing volume of work, and so on. It is none too soon at that time for her or him to begin collecting information on new systems, and to prepare a written report of the processing problems and requirements encountered. All of this will be helpful to the manager when the question of a new system arises and a justification analysis must be undertaken.

CHAPTER 3

Developing Good Typing and Stenographic Skills

There are two basic instructions for increasing speed and accuracy in typing:

1. Keep your eyes on the text you are reading, not on the typed material.

2. Use your fingers only, thereby eliminating useless motion. This chapter gives suggestions for handling special typing problems and for doing everyday typing with extra skill.

Know your typewriter. Take a few moments to become familiar with your machine. Learn the things it can do—how it can make your work go faster and more smoothly. All typewriter companies supply booklets describing the mechanics and special uses of their machines; these booklets are well worth studying. If the former user of your typewriter did not leave the booklet in the desk, ask the typewriter company to send you one.

In addition, keep abreast of new developments in both machines and accessories, such as ribbons. You can do this easily by reading sales literature and by observing displays when you visit office equipment and supply stores and manufacturers' showrooms. Each year typewriter manufacturers introduce equipment with new features that can make your job easier and improve the quality of your work.

How to keep your typewriter in good repair. Keep your typewriter in good condition by observing these instructions.

1. Keep your machine covered when not in use.
2. Move the carriage to the extreme right or left when erasing to prevent eraser dust from clogging the machine.
3. Oil sparingly—just an occasional drop on the carriage rails is sufficient. (*Note:* Some new machines no longer require this and it may, in fact, be harmful.)
4. Use only light oil—preferably a 3-1 quality that will not gum; never use Dictaphone oil or motor oil.
5. Never oil any other part of the typewriter—wait for the repairperson to oil your machine generally.
6. Clean the type with a good quality brush and type cleaning fluid or, preferably, a plastic type cleaner. Liquid cleaner is not recommended for electric typewriters.
7. Wipe off the entire machine occasionally with a soft cloth slightly dampened with cleaning fluid; never use alcohol, which would destroy the finish on your typewriter.
8. Use properly inked ribbons for the style of the typeface.
9. Change typewriter ribbons when necessary.
10. If your machine receives heavy use, consider a maintenance contract whereby it will be cleaned and serviced regularly.

Standard rules for spacing. Usage has established the following standard rules for spacing:

One space:
　　After a comma
　　After a semicolon
　　After a period following an abbreviation or an initial
　　After an exclamation mark used in the body of a sentence
　　Before and after "x" meaning "by," for example, 3" x 5" card
Two spaces:
　　After a colon
　　After every sentence
　　After a period following a figure or letter at the beginning of a line in a list
　　　of items
No spacing:
　　Before or after a dash, which is two hyphens
　　Before or after a hyphen
　　Between quotation marks and the matter enclosed
　　Between parentheses and the matter enclosed
　　Between any word and the punctuation following it
　　Between the initials that make up a single abbreviation, for example,
　　　C.O.D.
　　Before or after an apostrophe, unless it begins or ends a word

Never separate punctuation from the word it follows. For example, do not put a dash at the beginning of a line.

How to type on printed forms.　　When preparing to type on printed forms, check their alignment by holding several copies up to the light or against a window, before typing them.

Insert all the forms, without carbon paper, in the machine and then insert the carbon paper as described on pages 80-81.

If your "window test" proved that the printed material on the sheets was not correctly aligned, try sticking a pin through the forms at several points along the extreme margins (do this after inserting the carbon paper), lining up the forms accurately as you do so. Then you can make frequent "pin checks" and adjust the forms as you type.

Use your variable line spacer to align the type so that the tails of the longer letters (y, p, g, and the like) rest on the lines printed on the form.

How to get the same number of lines on each page.　　In typing jobs that run four or more pages, it is desirable, and sometimes necessary, to have the same number of typewritten lines on each page except the first and last.

Some typewriters come equipped with a numbered strip at the left edge of the platen. With this kind of machine, try the following:

1. Feed each page into the machine in alignment with the number one.
2. Note the number on which you begin typing the first line of your model page. Start all pages on the same number.
3. Note the number on which you type the last line of your page. Finish all pages on the same number.

When your typewriter is not equipped with a numbered strip.　Here is a simple way of getting the same number of lines on a sheet.

1. Type the first sheet.
2. Lightly mark the next sheet with pencil.
3. Indicate the first line by having your pencil mark in line with the bottom edge of the first line of type, so you can align your machine on the mark.
4. Make the second pencil mark about four lines before the final line of type so that you can see the pencil mark as it comes out of the carriage. You will then know you have four more lines to type to complete the page.

How to draw lines on work in the typewriter.　To draw *vertical lines,* release the platen as for variable spacing. Roll the platen up while holding a pencil point firmly at the desired spot, not through the ribbon.

To draw *horizontal lines,* lock the shift key and release the ribbon as for making stencils. Insert the pencil (or even a pen may be used) in the fork of the ribbon guide. Then move the carriage across the paper until the line is completed.

On an electric typewriter with an automatic (repeat) underscore key, horizontal lines may easily be drawn with the underscore. Using an underscore key that is not automatic requires too much time, especially when many lines must be drawn.

Some typewriters have a special place to insert a pencil when drawing lines, but inserting the pencil in the fork of the ribbon guide does the trick if your machine does not have this extra convenience. Remember to hold the pencil firmly. Brace it against the machine, if you like.

What to do about rush telegrams and memos.　It is not necessary to remove your work from the typewriter when you have to type a rush telegram or memo. Just do the following:

1. Backfeed the paper and carbons that are in the machine until the paper shows a top margin of about two inches.

2. Insert the first sheet of the rush work behind the material you are typing, against the paper table, just as if nothing were in the typewriter.

3. To make carbons of the telegram, insert the second sheet of the telegram against the coated side of the carbon paper that is already in the machine. Thus, the second sheet of the telegram is between the carbon and the second sheet of your letter. Do the same for each carbon that you have in the typewriter. (You must insert a sheet for each carbon in your machine to prevent the typing from showing on the carbon copies of your work.) For additional copies add carbon sheets in the usual manner.

4. Turn the platen knob until the telegram blanks are in position for typing.

5. After typing the message, backfeed until you can remove the telegram from the machine.

6. Forwardfeed to the point at which you stopped writing your letter or other work and continue with your typing.

Typing drafts of letters or other material.   Write the word "Draft" in capitals across the top of every draft to avoid mistaking it for the finished copy.

In retyping a rough draft, study the corrected page, noting:

1. Portions marked for omission
2. Additional material to be inserted
3. Transpositions
4. Corrections in spelling, punctuation, and the like

Note carefully the changes in each sentence before typing.

How to type above and below the line of type—use of line retainer lever.   When you must type above or below the line—for a chemical formula, to express degrees of temperature, to refer to footnotes, or to mention a few instances—use the line retainer lever, sometimes called the "line position reset." It is surprising how many secretaries do not know this helpful gadget exists. It can be found on almost all makes of typewriter, although the position varies with each machine, of course. When this lever is used, the platen can be revolved to any point to write the subscripts or other characters. When the lever is engaged again you will be able to return the platen to the same spacing position at which you were originally typing.

The line retainer lever is not the same as the variable line spacer. Although the variable line spacer will permit you to revolve the platen freely, it will not permit you to return the platen automatically to the same relative spacing position.

Always use this automatic line finder when feeding typed material back and forth in preference to rolling the material into position without using it. The use of the line finder not only permits much quicker positioning, but also helps to prevent carbon smudges and wrinkling.

How to type small cards.   It is easier to type a series of small cards if you chain feed them from the front of the platen. After typing the first card, feed backwards until the card has a top margin of about three-quarters of an inch. Insert the next card so that the bottom of it will be held in place by the card just completed. Each succeeding card will be held in place by the card preceding it. The cards automatically pile up against the paper table in the order in which they are inserted in the machine.

How to type narrow labels.   By using this simple system, you will be able to type narrow labels with both hands, thus avoiding typing with one hand while holding the label with the other:

1. Make a horizontal pleat about an inch deep in a sheet of paper.
2. Feed the sheet of paper into the machine in the regular way, maintaining the pleat so the folded edge will be up when the material is in writing position. This pleat will form a shallow pocket.
3. When the pocket appears at the front of your platen, insert the label, or several of them, in the pocket.
4. Feed all the material back so that you can type on the label.

Shortcuts for typing envelopes.   1. Fold a piece of heavy paper through the center. Insert the folded end into the roller of the typewriter and roll it through until it extends about an inch above the front scale. Now insert the envelope at the front of the roller, behind the folded paper. (The flap of the envelope should be at the top, turned away from you.) Turn the roller back as many spaces as you need to bring the envelope to the proper position for addressing. Type the address and then turn the roller up enough spaces for you to lift out the envelope. The folded paper is then in place for the next insertion.

2. *Chain-feeding* is a quick method of addressing numerous envelopes. Use the same system as described above for small cards. The envelopes will pile up on the paper table in the same order in which they are typed. This saves the trouble of re-sorting them.

When the flaps on the envelopes you are typing are thick or wide, your typing may be ragged. It is then better to chain-feed from the back of the platen. To do this, open the flap of the next envelope to be typed and insert it between the first envelope and the paper table, before removing the first envelope. A twirl of the platen knob removes one envelope and automatically brings the next one into position to be typed.

Tabulator uses. The tabulator is used not only to type tables but for (1) placement of the date line, (2) paragraph indentations, (3) placement of the complimentary close and signature line.

Typing numbers in columns. When typing columns of Arabic or Roman numerals, plan the spacing so that the right-hand edge is even. Use the tabulator.

VIII	3,078
XI	99
M	204
XIX	12
II	5

Typing numbers in letters or manuscript. Numbers ten and under should be spelled out. "Some firms spell out all numbers under one hundred.)"

Fractions. Fractions are hyphenated when the numerator and denominator are both one-word forms, such as *one-third, one-hundredth,* but omit the hyphen between the numerator and the denominator when either one or the other, or both, contain hyphens, such as *one twenty-fifth* and *twenty-five thirty-sevenths.*

How to type on ruled lines. In typing on ruled lines, make certain that the typing is adjusted so that the bases of letters that extend below the line of the type (y, g, and p) just touch the ruled line.

How to center headings. Electronic typewriters automatically perform functions such as centering. To center manually, count the letters, spaces, and punctuation marks in the heading. Subtract one-half the number from the point on the typewriter scale that coincides with the center of the paper. (For example, if the paper extends from 0 to 102 on the scale, the center of the paper will be at 51 on the scale; if the paper extends from 0 to 90, the center will be at 45 on the scale.) The remainder will show the point on the typewriter scale at which the heading must begin. Thus, if your heading contains 26 characters, and your center point is 51, your starting point will be 38 (51 − ½ of 26).

from 0 to 90, the center will be at 45 on the scale.) The remainder will show the point on the typewriter scale at which the heading must begin. Thus, if your heading contains 26 characters, and your center point is 51, your starting point will be 38 (51 - ½ of 26).

Or the starting point may be determined by beginning at the center point and backspacing once for each two characters in the heading while spelling out the heading. In spelling the heading, include spaces and punctuation marks as though they were letters. This will place the machine at the proper starting point.

If part of the left margin is to be used for binding, the starting point will be moved toward the right one-half the number of spaces cut off for binding. For example, if 35 is the starting point gauged by the entire width of the paper, and 10 spaces are to be allowed for binding purposes, the starting point will be 40.

How to make special characters not included on your typewriter. You can overtype one standard character with another to form special characters that may not be on your typewriter:

¶	Paragraph mark	P and 1
÷	Division sign	Colon and hyphen
£	Pound Sterling sign	f and t, or L and f
ç	Cedilla beneath "c"	c and comma
!	Exclamation sign	Apostrophe and period
=	Equation sign	Hyphen—use ratchet detent lever and turn platen slightly
[ ]	Brackets	Underscore and diagonal

You can type one character over another without backspacing by holding down the space bar as you type, except when using an electric machine with an automatic space bar.

Tips on how to feed numerous sheets of paper to the typewriter. Every typist experiences difficulty in inserting numerous sheets of paper or bulky carbon packs in the typewriter. Try these methods:

1. To insert a bulky pack, release the paper feed and insert the paper sheets and carbon into the feed roll, then return release lever.
2. Feed the paper sheets in without carbons, rolling the platen knob enough for the paper feed rollers to get a grip. Then insert carbon sheets one by one, making sure the shiny, or carbon, side faces you. Then twirl the pack into typing position.

3. Several sheets of paper and carbon may be inserted in the typewriter easily by placing them beneath the flap of an envelope. The platen, however, does not grasp a large pack as readily, and the alignment is not as perfect as when the device described below is used.

4. When you have a very large carbon pack to insert, try making this device:

(a) Fold a 5″ by 8½″ strip of flimsy manila tag (an inexpensive file folder will do) across the center, lengthwise.

(b) Cut three U-shaped slots across the upper half of the folded strip, about one-half inch from the crease.

(c) Lift up and bend backward the tongues formed by the slot.

(d) Insert the assembled sheets of paper in the folded strip.

(e) Feed the tongues from the U-slots into the typewriter. The platen grasps them more readily than it does a thick pack of paper.

(f) Remove the folded strip before beginning to type.

(See Figures 11 and 12.)

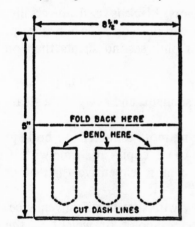

FIGURE 11   DEVICE FOR FEEDING
PAPER TO TYPEWRITER
—PROCESS OF MAKING DEVICE

FIGURE 12   DEVICE FOR FEEDING PAPER TO TYPEWRITER,
WITH PAPERS INSERTED

HOW TO SOLVE
SOME CARBON PROBLEMS

Selecting the best carbon paper for the job.   Select the heaviest carbon paper that will yield a sharp impression. Thin paper is required for making a large number of copies at once, whereas heavy paper, because of its durability, should be used if only one or two copies are needed. Carbon paper is offered on the market today in three general weights and in a single-weight film or plastic:

Type	Yield
Lightweight	1 to 10 copies
Medium weight	1 to 5 copies
Heavy weight	1 to 2 copies
Film (plastic)	1 to 10 copies

Carbon paper is made in several colors. Black is used universally; blue is the prevailing color for pencil carbon work. Carbon imprint shows up better on white, yellow, or pink second sheets than on blue, green, russet or cherry.

To avoid curling and wrinkling, keep carbons carefully in the desk, with the coated side down, out of the sunlight, and away from steam pipes.

The new film (or plastic) paper, being more durable, can be kept and used longer and one can make up to ten copies at a time with it. Two disadvantages are that it is much more expensive than other paper and it is available only in black.

Some offices are concerned primarily with speed and convenience, and not with any particular selection of color or weight in the preparation of carbon copies. Two popular products meeting those requirements are the treated carbonless paper (multiple sets not requiring any carbon paper between sheets) and the single sheet of tissue with a single sheet of lightweight carbon paper attached at one end. The best way to make a choice is to ask your local office supply store to give you samples and prices of each that you can use to compare results.

Carbon shortcuts.   1. Cut a small triangle off the upper left corner of the carbon paper so that when you take hold of the upper left corner you are grasping the writing paper but not the carbon. Let the carbons extend slightly beyond the bottom edge of the copy sheets. This makes separating the copy sheets from the carbon easier. (Carbon paper can be bought with the corner already cut.)

2. To insert red figures or letters in the carbon copy of a report without removing the report from the typewriter, simply insert a small piece of red carbon behind the black carbon in the desired position, type the red copy, remove the red carbon, and proceed with the work.

A sheet of heavier paper placed at the back of a carbon pack will prevent manifold paper from creasing and "treeing" with carbon lines.

Keep your carbon paper stored away from sunlight and heat.

What to do when you must type on carbon copies only.   Occasionally you may want to indicate some information on the carbons of a letter that you do not want to show on the original, or perhaps you want it to show on just one or two of several copies. If this is a matter of just a few words, insert a small scrap of paper over the original letter and an additional scrap over each of the carbons on which you do not want the notation to appear. Type the notation and then remove the scraps of paper. The notation will appear only on those copies before which you did not insert a scrap of paper.

However, you may get a slight indentation on the original page. To avoid even that, try the following when you wish to indicate something on the carbon copies but not the original:

If the information is to appear at the top of the carbon copies:

1. Insert your paper in the usual way.
2. Use your paper release lever to free the paper.
3. Move the carbon pack an inch or so above the original.
4. Return your paper release lever to the "tight" position.
5. Feed the material back and type in the information.
6. Feed the material forward again.
7. Use the paper release lever and align the original with the carbon pack. Return the paper release lever to the "tight" position and you are then ready to type your letter.

If the information is to be shown on the bottom of the carbon copies:

1. Position the machine exactly where you want the material to appear.
2. Use your paper release lever.
3. Slip the original out of the machine without disturbing the carbon pack, engage the paper release lever, and begin typing.

Caution: It is necessary to position the machine before removing the original because after the original is removed the first piece of carbon covers up the carbon copy of the letter you have typed. Do *not* try to remove the first carbon sheet. Its removal will smudge the carbon copies and drag them out of alignment.

HOW TO CORRECT
TYPING ERRORS

A good secretary seldom makes a typing error—she or he could not have succeeded in her or his chosen career if she or he had been careless about the basic skill of typing. However, if you make errors, there are two steps you can take to correct them: (1) overcome your poor typing habits and (2) acquire the art of making neat erasures.

Suggestion for overcoming poor typing habits. For a week or two make a notation of every typing error you make. Then study and analyze them. You will find repetition of the same type of errors—transposing certain letters; omitting letters; striking one letter in lieu of another one near it, and so on. Then, *get out your typing books*—or buy a new one. Select the drills that apply to your poor typing habit and practice, practice, practice. If you cannot find a drill that applies to your poor typing habit, practice typing the word in which you made the error, and words similar to it. Of course, you cannot practice during your work hours, but if you do not have a typewriter at home, you can stay at the office late, come in early, or use part of your lunch hour for practice, but *practice.* The improvement will soon be obvious not only to you but to the manager.

How to erase neatly. If you have time, use two erasers—a hard one and a soft one. They may be combined into one eraser. Move the carriage as far to the side as possible so that paper and eraser fragments will not fall into the typewriter mechanism. Start with the soft eraser to remove the excess surface ink. Then change to the hard eraser to remove the imbedded ink. Finally, use the soft eraser again to smooth off the surface. When erasing, rub with short, light strokes.

A sharp razor blade may be used on a good grade of paper to remove punctuation marks and the tails of letters.

If you accidentally move the roller or the paper, making it difficult to retype a letter on precisely the spot of the error, try using your stencil lever and make a test. The letter will strike the paper and leave a faint indentation but no black ink that must be erased again if your alignment is off.

Caution: Insert a steel eraser guard (on many typewriters, your typewriter scale often serves as a guard) between the carbon paper and the copy. The eraser guard is heavy enough to protect the other copies under it and is easy to handle. Or you may use a celluloid eraser shield, but *do not use little pieces of paper* in back of each carbon sheet. You might accidentally leave one of them in your work.

New methods of erasing.   New methods of erasing are being developed all the time. Ask your purchasing department or stationery supplier to investigate some of the following for you, or investigate them yourself. The cost may be worth the time saved in neat erasures in letters that can be sent out without retyping. (But don't fool yourself by thinking that the manager will not know the erasures are there!)

1. An eraser made of glass fibers is on the market. It will permit you to erase on the original without the impression of your erasure going through to the carbon. Be sure to move your carriage to the right or left when using the eraser, and do not handle the glass part of it.
2. Electric erasers, some battery operated, are available.
3. Special correction paper (or tape) is available for erasing typing errors. All you have to do is backspace to the point of the mistake, whether it is a single letter or a complete word, place the correction paper over the error, and retype *the error.* This results in a blank space in which you now type the correct word or letter. There is also a companion product for erasing errors on carbon copies. These correction papers are available in different colors to match the color of the typing paper.
4. At least one major manufacturer now offers an electric typewriter with a built-in correcting key. A device feeds a roll of correction paper and the erasure is made in a manner similar to that described in item 3 above.
5. Correction fluid is popular for work where it is unimportant if the correction is noticeable as it leaves a white blot on the paper (or a colored spot, if colored fluid is being used on colored paper). An obvious spot on the paper would not matter, for instance, in copy being prepared for printing, on notes the secretary writes to herself, or possibly on a first draft that will instantly be marked up without ever leaving the office.

How to make corrections on carbons.   Corrections on carbon copies are often much fainter than the rest of the typing. To avoid this, make the correction as follows: After the necessary erasure has been made, adjust the ribbon control indicator to stencil position. Put the carriage in the proper position and strike the proper key. This will leave the impression on the carbon copies, but the original will still be blank. Then switch the control indicator back to the ribbon, place the carriage in position, and again strike the proper key. This permits a perfect match of the typing on the original and will leave the typing on the carbon copies with an equal density of color.

How to erase near the bottom of a page. To erase on a line near the edge of the page, feed the sheet back until the bottom of the paper is free of the platen. Erase, and turn the page back into position for typing.

How to make corrections on bound pages. Corrections can be made on pages that are bound at the top. Insert a blank sheet of paper in the typewriter, as though for typing. When it protrudes about an inch above the platen, insert between it and the platen the unbound edge of the sheet to be corrected. Turn the platen toward you until the typewriter grips the sheet to be corrected. You can then adjust the bound sheet to the proper position for making the correction.

Corrections cannot be made on pages that are bound at the side without unstapling them.

How to make corrections near the bottom of a page. To erase on a line near the bottom of the page, do not remove the paper from the typewriter. Simply feed the sheet backward until the bottom edge is free of the platen. Make the erasure and turn the page back into position for typing. (Remember to use your automatic line finder when feeding sheets back and forth.)

HOW TO TYPE A TABLE

Measurements for typing tables. The following information will be helpful in planning the arrangement of a table.

> 6 line spaces equal 1 inch, measured vertically.
> 10 spaces of pica type equal 1 inch, measured horizontally.
> 12 spaces of elite type equal 1 inch, measured horizontally.
> A sheet of paper 8½″ by 11″ has 85 spaces of pica type on a horizontal line.
> A sheet of paper 8½″ by 11″ has 102 spaces of elite type on a horizontal line.
> A sheet of paper 8½″ by 11″ has 66 vertical line spaces.

Planning the arrangement. Before beginning to type a table, carefully plan the arrangement. Keep these thoughts in mind:

1. Tables usually have three parts: a title, columnar headings, and a stub (the headings down the left side), which is equivalent to a column in planning the arrangement.
2. Align figures on the right, words on the left (see Figure 13).
3. Center columnar headings, gauging the center by the longest item in the column. Notice how, in Figure 13, "Shares" is centered in relation to the number with the most digits, and "Held" is centered under "Shares."

CLASSIFICATION OF STOCKHOLDERS

December 6, 19--

	Stock- holders	Percent	Shares Held	Percent
Women	31,402	41.60	2,254,582	24.07
Men	23,285	30.84	2,161,751	23.08
Fiduciaries	14,658	19.42	1,488,444	15.89
Joint Accounts	3,024	4.00	96,898	1.03
Institutions	1,164	1.54	230,773	2.46
Corporations and Partnerships	829	1.10	237,124	2.53
Nominees	511	0.68	2,319,731	24.77
Brokers	266	0.35	295,987	3.16
Insurance Companies	233	0.31	204,729	2.19
Investment Trusts	118	0.16	76,459	0.82
	75,490	100.00	9,366,478	100.00

FIGURE 13 TABLE SHOWING PROPER ALIGNMENT OF WORDS AND FIGURES

Vertical spacing. Allow three line spaces between the title and the subheading, if any, or between the title and columnar headings. Allow two line spaces between the subheading and the columnar headings, and two line spaces between the columnar headings and the items in the column. Therefore, a table with a subheading has ten line spaces in addition to the items in the table (assuming that the title, subheading, and columnar headings take a line each). If the table is short, double space between the items to give the typed page a more balanced appearance.

In Figure 13, the date is in the position of the subheading.

Headings of tables. Center the headings and subheadings of tables in the same manner that you center any other headings. Remember to make an allowance if part of the left margin is to be used for binding.

How to make top and bottom margins even. Here is what you do to make the top and bottom margins even:

1. Figure the number of line spaces on the paper that you are using.
2. Count the lines in the table and add the number of lines and spaces to be covered by the title and subheadings.
3. Subtract the total from the number of line spaces on your paper.
4. Divide the difference by two. The result is the number of line spaces in the top and bottom margins.

How to make the side margins even. To make side margins of a table even, follow these directions:

1. Figure the number of spaces across the paper that you are using. If part of the left margin is to be used for binding, subtract those spaces from your count.
2. Count the number of characters in the longest line in each column, including the stub as a column, and total them.
3. Subtract the total found in Step 2 from the number of spaces found in Step 1. This gives the number of spaces that are available for left and right margins *and* to separate the columns.
4. Decide how many spaces you want between each column. This varies with the amount of available space.
5. Multiply the number of spaces to be put between each column by the number of columns, *not* including the first column.
6. Subtract the result found in Step 5 from the result found in Step 3, and divide by 2. This gives the number of spaces to be allowed for each side margin.

Where to set the tabulators. Before beginning to type a table, set your tabulators as follows:

1. Set the left-hand margin at the point found in Step 6 above. This is the point where the stub or left-hand column begins.

2. Space once for each character in the longest line of the stub, space once for each space that separates the columns (see Step 4), and then set the first tabulator key.
3. Beginning at the point where the first tabulator key was set, space once for each character in the longest line of the second column, space once for each space that separates the columns, and then set the second tabulator key.
4. Follow the same procedure until the tabulator key is set for the starting point of the last column.

HOW TO PREPARE REPORTS

The reports referred to here are those written by someone other than the secretary and given to her or him in draft form to be prepared for presentation. The reports may be informal, set up in letter form, or formal. Each of these types will be described in this section, but first the techniques of report preparation will be explained.

Preliminary study of draft.   Before typing a report in final form, read over the entire handwritten or rough draft with these purposes in mind:

1. To see that each sentence makes sense. If you cannot understand something in the report, do not hesitate to ask the meaning of the sentence or paragraph and have it clarified.
2. To correct mistakes in English.
3. To identify or supply the headings and subheadings so that you can visualize the report in final typewritten form. Headings help to bring out the organization of the report and to disclose weaknesses in the arrangement of the material.

The suggestions given below, if followed, will yield a report that will command attention for its professional appearance.

Headings.   The body of a report is usually divided into topics and subtopics with headings. In setting up the headings, keep this thought in mind: *Topics of equal importance should be given equal emphasis.*

How to show emphasis. Emphasis is shown in typed material by centering and by the use of caps, spacing, underlining, or a combination of these techniques. Underlining important topics in red adds emphasis and improves the appearance of the report. Headings of the same relative importance should be identical in form.

Patterns of headings. In typing a long report, make a pattern of the style of headings that you intend to use throughout the report. The following pattern is adequate for the average report:

<u>FIRST</u> <u>TOPIC</u> <u>HEADING</u>
SUBDIVISION HEADING
<u>Minor</u> <u>subdivision</u> <u>heading</u>

If the report requires more breakdowns, the following pattern may be followed:

<u>FIRST</u> <u>TOPIC</u> HEADING

SUBDIVISION HEADING

<u>Subordinate</u> <u>Heading</u>

Minor Heading

<u>Least</u> important subdivision heading

If the report requires only topic headings and subdivision headings, follow the style illustrated under *wording of headings,* below.

Note that when the letters are spaced, there is a double space between words. Use triple space between a center heading and the text that precedes it; use double space between the heading and the text that follows.

If upper and lower case is used, capitalize only the important words. Only the first word in a minor subdivision heading is capitalized.

Wording of headings. 1. Headings should be short, striking, and descriptive of the topic being discussed. If it is impossible for a heading to be lively and descriptive at the same time, select the descriptive heading.

2. Headings should be uniform in grammatical construction, if possible. Thus, if a subheading is introduced with a participle, other subheadings under that topic should be introduced with a participle.

Note the effective use of short, imperative sentences in the following headings and subheadings from a report outlining a plan for strengthening a company's marketing program.

IMPROVE THE PRODUCT LINE
Pretest New Products
Shorten the Length of the Line

Reduce Percentage of Low-Volume Items
Improve Colors in Lower Price Lines
STRENGTHEN FIELD SELLING EFFORTS
Clarify Territorial Boundaries
Relieve the Overburdened Sales Force
Improve the Sales Compensation Plan
Develop More Appealing Displays
Improve Field Supervision

Paper used in typing reports.   Reports are usually written on plain white paper, 8½" by 11". Occasionally long reports are written on legal-size paper (8½" by 13"), but letter-size paper is preferable.

Use a good quality paper for the original. Lightweight paper may be used for duplicate originals when several copies are made. If the report is in letter form, the first page may be written on letterhead paper.

Proper spacing.   Formal reports are usually double spaced. However, if the report is to be duplicated or numerous copies are to be mailed, single spacing will save labor, paper, and postage. Use a double space between paragraphs of both single-spaced and double-spaced material.

Indent and single-space quoted or extracted material. If the report has much quoted material, double-space the report to make the quoted material stand out.

Reports in letter form are usually single spaced.

Margins for an attractive appearance.   Use ample and uniform margins at top, bottom, and sides. A one-inch margin is appropriate, *exclusive* of the part of the page that is used for binding. Thus, if ¾ of an inch is used for binding, the bound edge (left side or top) has a margin of 1¾ inches instead of 1 inch.

The first page of the report and the first page of each chapter should have a two-inch margin at the top.

The left margin of indented material is even with the paragraph indentation of the main part of the report.

Numbering pages.   Number the pages of the table of contents and any other pages that precede the report proper with small Roman numerals, thus: i, ii, iii, iv.

Number all pages of the report proper, the appendix, and the index with Arabic numerals, starting with 1. Place the numbers in the center of the page, one-half inch from the bottom. The pages of a report that is bound on the left side may be numbered in the top right-hand corner.

Numbering appendices.   Letter the appendices in sequence: A, B, C. Capital letters are used instead of Roman numerals because chapters are usually numbered with Roman numerals. Each appendix also has a subject or title.

Numbering within the reports; indentation.   A report should make use of numbering and lettering schemes, in addition to headings, to simplify the reading. There are no fixed rules as to numbering schemes, but the following three patterns are among those commonly used. Notice that, whatever the scheme, topics of equal importance are given equal emphasis in the arrangement. Follow the scheme consistently throughout the report.

Pattern 1	Pattern 2	Pattern 3
I.	I.	I. . . . .
1.	1.	A. . . . .
(a)	A.	1. . . . .
(b)	B.	2. . . . .
(1)	(1)	(a) . . . . . .
(2)	(2)	(b) . . . . . .
2.	2.	B. . . . .
II.	II.	II. . . . .

Observe the following rules within the numbering and lettering scheme:

1. Follow Roman numerals and Arabic numerals with a period.
2. Do not use a period after a number or letter in parentheses.
3. Use a double space between paragraphs carrying a number or letter just as you would between other paragraphs.
4. Determine how far you will indent each of the groups in your numbering and lettering scheme, indenting each successive group at least five spaces more than the preceding group, and maintain the same indentation plan throughout the report. Thus, in Pattern 1 the left-hand margin of paragraphs lettered (a), (b), etc. would be indented at least five spaces more than paragraphs numbered 1, 2, and so on, and the left-hand margin of paragraphs numbered (1), (2), and so on would be indented at least ten spaces.

5. Indent the first line in a main paragraph ten spaces. Indent the first line in an indented paragraph five spaces more than its own left-hand margin, or use the block form.

Informal report. An informal report may be set up in letter form. The parts of an informal or letter report are the heading, date, address, salutation, body, complimentary close, and signature. Instead of the regular address and salutation, the salutation may begin with the word "To." The complimentary close is usually "respectfully submitted." The signature usually consists of the firm name written in longhand.

Formal report. A formal report includes the following parts, in the order listed:

1. Cover or title page.
2. Table of contents.
3. Body, consisting of introduction, development, conclusion or recommendation, and date.

A formal report may also include: (1) a letter of transmittal, which follows the title page; (2) a list of illustrations, which follows the table of contents; (3) an appendix, which follows the body; (4) a list of references and bibliography; and (5) an index, which follows the bibliography. These five parts are not included ordinarily in the average report, but only in unusually long, formal reports.

Title page. All formal reports have a title page. Informal or letter reports do not. Usually the title page is the front cover, but if a report is enclosed in a binder, the title page is the first page beneath the cover.

Items that go on the title page. The items of information on the title page are: (1) the title of the report, (2) to whom submitted, (3) by whom submitted, and (4) the date.

Dividing items into more than one line. When an item on a title page is written on more than one line, divide the material at a logical point. Adjectives and articles are not separated from the word they modify, a preposition is not separated from its object, and a line does not end in a conjunction. Thus, the title "The Participation of the White-Collar Worker in Modern Labor Unrest" should not be divided between "Collar" and "Worker," although this division makes a more even distribution of the letters in each line. That title should be written as follows:

Report on
THE PARTICIPATION OF THE WHITE-COLLAR WORKER
IN MODERN LABOR UNREST

Arrangement of items. The items on the title page are centered horizontally on the available space, exclusive of the part taken up by binding or fastening. With a left side fastening, allow ¾ of an inch for binding. The centering point on the typewriter scale is then moved seven spaces to the right of the actual center for *pica* type and nine spaces for *elite.*

Separate each item on the title page by at least four line spaces to give the page a balanced appearance, but use only two spaces between the lines of an item. Figure 14 is an example of a well-balanced title page.

Table of contents. The table of contents consists of the numbers (if any) and titles of the chapters or topics and the number of the page on which each begins. Prepare the table of contents after the final draft of the report has been completed and the pages numbered.

Arrangement. Center the table of contents horizontally and vertically. Double space a short table, single space a long table. List the chapter or topic numbers at the left, space three times, and follow with a list of the titles. List the page numbers on the right-hand margin.

Leaders. Use periods as leaders to guide the reader's eye across the space between the title and the page number. Space once between each period. To align the periods, always begin the first dot of the leaders at an even number on the typewriter scale.

Binding or fastening of the report. Staple short, informal reports in the upper left-hand corner.

Fasten formal reports along the left-hand margin or across the top, but preferably on the side. Use brads, paper fasteners, or staples for fastening. Formal reports are presented in special holders, binders, or folders; sometimes they are laced together on the left side with a cotton lace.

Footnotes in reports. If there are many footnotes in a report, number them consecutively, from 1 to 99. Start with 1 again after 99. In a report that is divided into chapters, begin with 1 in each chapter. Place the footnote figure (called a superior figure) after the

A PROPOSED DESIGN FOR THE ILLUMINATION

OF THE MUNICIPAL AIRPORT

DALEWILD, NEW YORK

Submitted to

Mr. O. T. Webster

Head, Design Department

City of New York

By

Randall H. Rice

Head, Illumination Division

Lumen Corporation

May 17, 19--

FIGURE 14   TITLE PAGE OF A FORMAL REPORT

word in the text to which the footnote applies. In a double-spaced paragraph it would appear thus:

Only one real solution is offered:[1] To . . . .

In a single-spaced paragraph it would be written as follows:

Only one real solution is offered /2/: To . . . .

If there are only a few footnotes in the report, you may use an asterisk, dagger, or other similar character instead of superior figures.

Place the footnote to the text at the bottom of the page on which the superior figure appears; place the footnote to a table, however, at the bottom of the table.

To separate the footnote from the text, allow two lines of space below the last line of text, make a line with the typewriter about two inches long, and then allow another line of space before typing the footnote. Precede the footnote with its corresponding superior number or symbol.

Examples of different types of footnotes are given below; they constitute a style for citing articles and books and for making acknowledgments. Underscore as shown.

Citation of a book:

Robert Semenow, Questions and Answers on Real Estate, 8th ed. (Engle-wood Cliffs, N.J.: Prentice-Hall, Inc., 1975), p. 111.

Citation of an article:

R. H. Lubar, "Plan for Tax Reform," Fortune, March 19——, pp. 92-96.

Acknowledgment of credit:

Acknowledgment is made to Charles Berg for the data on housing.

Bibliography to a report.   A report may contain at the close (1) a list of references and (2) a bibliography. The list of references shows all sources from which material in the report was drawn. The bibliography contains a list of publications on the subject of the report. Both lists are typed in the same style.

How to type a bibliography.   *Books.* The citation of a book in a bibliography contains the following:

1. Name of the author
2. Title of the book
3. City in which publisher is located

4. Name of the publisher

5. Year in which the book was published

Arrange the items alphabetically by authors' names, the last name first, in the following form:

Semenow, Robert. Questions and Answers on Real Estate. Englewood
Cliffs, N.J.: Prentice-Hall, Inc., 1975.

The form in which the author's name is cited in the bibliography should be the form in which it appears on the title page of the book. Thus, if the name on the title page is Robert Semenow, the form in the bibliography should be "Semenow, Robert." If, however, the name on the title page is R. Semenow, the form in the bibliography should be "Semenow, R." If an item has two or more authors, it is not necessary to reverse any names, except the one that appears first, which is reversed to aid alphabetical arrangement.

If a bibliography contains more than one item by the same author, arrange them alphabetically according to title.

Bibliographies may be further classified according to the types of printed material: books, book reviews, pamphlets, indexes, guides, reference works, and the like.

Magazine articles. The citation of magazine articles in the bibliography should be in the following form:

Lubar, R. H. "Plan for Tax Reform," Fortune, 19 March 19___, pp. 92-96.

Checklist for reports.

1. Has the report been read carefully, word for word?
2. Have all typographical errors been corrected on the original and on all copies?
3. Are the pages numbered correctly?
4. Has a consistent style of headings and numbering been followed throughout the report?
5. Have all statistics been checked against their sources?
6. Have all cross-references been checked?
7. Are footnotes in proper sequence with corresponding references in the text?
8. Are mathematical tables and computations accurate?
9. Are proper names spelled correctly?
10. Are all pages firmly stapled in the binding?
11. Are the pages arranged in proper sequence in the binding?

HOW TO PREPARE
MINUTES OF MEETINGS

Every manager spends a great deal of time in meetings, many of which are formal. Accurate minutes of meetings of stockholders, directors, and committees are essential. If you are a secretary in a small corporation, it might be your job to prepare minutes of meetings of stockholders and directors. If you are a secretary in a large corporation, you are frequently required to prepare the minutes of important committee meetings. Preparation of minutes, especially if you attend the meeting and take notes of it, can be a most interesting job.

The following suggestions apply to minutes of any meeting. The suggestions are especially helpful because preparation of minutes is not usually a daily routine job.

Preparation of draft of minutes. Write the minutes immediately after the meeting while events are still fresh in your mind.

If you do not attend the meeting, you might write the minutes by expanding the corporate secretary's notes. For example, the notes will show that a certain resolution was unanimously adopted. The minutes will be expanded to read:

On motion duly made and seconded, the following resolution was unanimously adopted:
RESOLVED, That . . . .

To write minutes from notes made by another, you must have before you all papers, documents, and reports that were discussed at the meeting.

More than likely, the corporate secretary will dictate the minutes to you if you are his or her secretary. Your immediate superior will dictate to you minutes of committee meetings that you do not attend.

Submit a draft of the minutes to the corporate secretary (or to your immediate superior) for review and correction. Never write minutes in the minute book without first writing a draft.

How to prepare minutes in final form. Standard paper for minute books is of a special quality—smooth, heavy, and durable. Manufacturers and stationers who specialize in corporate supplies can supply it. Both sides of the paper are written on. Of course, you can use any kind of loose-leaf book and any kind of durable paper for minutes of committee meetings. If the paper is not heavy, do not write on both sides of it. Pages of a minute book may be numbered for convenience. Some of the larger corporations have strict rules about the uniformity of arrangement of minutes. Independently of rules, a secretary should take particular pains with details about the typing, arrangement, spacing, and general appearance of the minute book. The following is a suggested list of rules relating to the form to be followed in typing the minutes in final form for the minute book:

1. Capitalize and center the heading designating the meeting.
2. Indent paragraphs ten spaces.
3. Indent names of those present or absent 15 spaces.
4. Double space the text.
5. Double space between each paragraph, and triple space between each item in the order of business.
6. Indent resolutions 15 spaces and single space them.
7. Capitalize the words "Board of Directors" and the word "Corporation" when reference is made to the corporation whose minutes are being written. References to specific officers of the corporation may be capitalized or in lower case, but the capitalization should be consistent.
8. Put captions, if used, in the margin in capitals or in red type.
9. Leave an inch and a half outside margin.
10. Capitalize all letters in the words "Whereas" and "Resolved," follow by a comma, and begin the word "That" with a capital.
11. When sums of money are mentioned in a resolution, write them first in words and then in figures in parentheses.
12. Number each page at the bottom, in the center of the page.

HANDLING MATERIAL FOR PRINTING

Regardless of the nature of the business in which you work, you will at times be called upon to help prepare material that is to be printed. You may or may not do some of the writing. It probably will be your responsibility to get the material ready to send to the printer and to follow through from manuscript to final printing. It will pay you to get in touch with the printer and discuss the project with him as early in your planning as possible.

Typing the manuscript.   The following rules should be observed in typing the manuscript for copy to be set in type:

1. Type on 8½" by 11" white bond, using one side of the paper. Make carbon copies, but always send the original to the printer.
2. Use a carbon ribbon (as opposed to fabric) for sharp, clean copy.
3. Keep the typewritten line to six inches.
4. Use double spacing.
5. Keep the right-hand margin as even as possible, to help you later in estimating the length of the copy.
6. Indent paragraphs at least five spaces.
7. Type headings and subheadings in the position they are to occupy on the final printed page.
8. Leave a margin of at least one inch on all four sides and keep each page as nearly uniform in length as possible.
9. Set off quoted material from the rest of the text (a) by single spacing the extracted material; or (b) by indenting it from the left margin or from both the left and right margins.
10. Type footnotes double spaced and full measure separate from the manuscript, unless there are very few, in which case they may be typed at the bottom of the text page.
11. Cross-references to material appearing in other parts of the manuscript should read "see page 000," but be sure to put in the correct reference numbers when you receive the final page proofs.
12. If you need to write instructions to the printer somewhere on the copy to be printed, use a light-blue pencil as this color will not reproduce.

See chapter 24, pages 512-513, for guides to proofreading and marking copy.

TAKING AND TRANSCRIBING DICTATION

Taking dictation.   Although some managers write out their letters in longhand, taking dictation is a daily or at least a frequent occurrence for many secretaries. Whether dictation is handled by machine or person-to-person, observing a few simple rules will simplify the entire process:

1. Make it a practice right away in the morning to sharpen pencils (preferably medium soft lead) and have one or more shorthand notebooks ready, with rubber bands to secure completed pages. Have paper clips handy to clip certain pages together if desired. Finally, have special files or other pertinent material ready to take with you when the manager calls.
2. Use a colored pencil to write or mark special instructions in your notebook.

3. Leave space between letters or somehow keep them separate in your notebook—do not run one into another. There may be changes or copy to insert later and space will be needed then.

4. If the manager does not specify, ask about the type of item—letter, memo, or other; the number of carbon copies and to whom; the addressee's name and address; any other special instructions, such as if there is a "subject" line or enclosures.

5. During dictation, place your notebook on the desk or rest it in a comfortable position for writing and flipping over filled pages without pausing. Date the first page at the bottom where it is easy to see when paging through the notebook later. Do not hesitate to speak up if the dictator is talking too fast or if you do not understand something. Most of the material you will record in shorthand, but an unfamiliar word is best written out in longhand. Remember that accuracy is of the utmost importance.

6. After taking the dictation, double-check spelling of names, addresses, and unusual words.

7. If you are having difficulty, it may be necessary to take a refresher course or at least work on troublesome words and symbols after hours.

Transcribing dictation. Transcribing the notes or tapes is just as important as taking the dictation. Most secretaries will want to begin as soon as possible, while everything is fresh in mind. If a transcription machine is used, it is necessary to be thoroughly familiar with it before beginning. Observing a few basic rules will simplify the entire process of transcribing the notes or tapes.

1. Clear your desk and organize the necessary materials for transcription—stationery, envelopes, erasers, and so on. A copyholder or some support should be set up for the shorthand notebook, and the typewriter should be checked for a fresh ribbon and clean keys.

2. Reread all dictation (or listen to the tapes or belts), organize it in order of importance, and solve such problems as paragraphing, missing punctuation, or errors in spelling before you begin typing. Most managers will expect their secretaries to polish and rephrase awkward passages.

3. Estimate the length of the letter so it is positioned attractively on the stationery—this will take practice before you know how much typed copy comes from one of your notebook pages or from a transcription belt or tape.

4. If you cannot find a time of day to transcribe without interruption, have a colored pencil ready to mark the spot on your notebook where you stop each time. A transcription machine will automatically remain at the point where you stop it. When you complete a letter, draw a diagonal line

through your notes or on the identification strip that accompanies a transcription belt or tape.

5. Place the addressed envelope over the typed letter, along with carbon copies and enclosures, and leave it face up on the manager's desk for his or her signature. After it is signed, proceed with filing and mailing, as described in chapters 2 and 4.

Word processing.   Taking and transcribing dictation are sometimes referred to as word processing. In a sophisticated word processing (WP) and administrative support (AS) system, usually found in larger companies, secretaries are categorized as administrative or correspondence. Administrative secretaries handle phones, do accounting, process mail, file, and do research. Correspondence secretaries, however, primarily transcribe dictation material at high word rates.

The correspondence secretary must have high-level typing and stenographic capabilities; the training of both secretaries, though, must equip them with language, editorial, and many other skills. Emphasizing the expanding duties and the increasing importance of the secretarial role, the National Secretaries Association has a Certified Professional Secretaries program in which they grant a certificate to qualified secretaries who pass an extensive exam on diverse subjects such as business and public policy, financial analysis, and decision making.

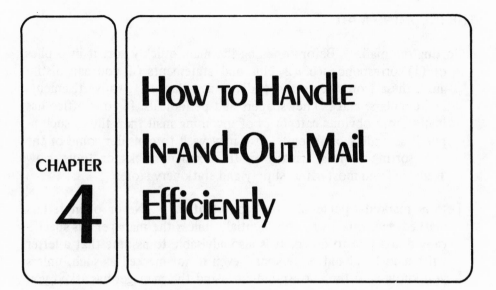

CHAPTER

4

How to Handle In-and-Out Mail Efficiently

Efficient handling of the mail by a secretary relieves the manager of attention to details that would otherwise consume much of his or her time. The mail in an office may be classified broadly as "incoming" and "outgoing." In this chapter, therefore, we describe efficient procedures for handling various types of incoming mail, and the preparation of outgoing mail. This chapter also recommends a procedure for handling the mail when the manager is away from the office. The next chapter covers domestic postal service and international mail.

THE INCOMING MAIL

Sorting the mail.   Before opening the mail, quickly sort it into piles of (1) correspondence, (2) bills and statements (if you can distinguish these from the correspondence at a glance), (3) advertisements and circulars, and (4) newspapers and periodicals. If your office has many more obvious categories of incoming mail than these, such as purchase orders or receipts, you may wish to consider some of the new sorting devices, usually in the form of racks or trays, now available from most office supply and stationery stores.

Letters marked "personal" or "confidential."   Never open letters marked "personal" or "confidential" unless the manager has specifically asked you to do so. It is also advisable to assume that a letter written in longhand is personal, even if not marked as such, unless you know who the correspondent is and the manager has asked you to open the letter.

Correspondence.   Give the correspondence your first attention. Before slitting the flaps of the envelopes, strike the lower edge of the stack of letters on the desk to lessen the possibility of cutting the contents with the letter opener. Do this also if you use one of the new electric letter openers, as they shave a fraction of an inch off the top of the envelope. When using a hand letter opener, have the flaps of the envelopes facing upward. First slit all the envelopes and then remove the contents, making certain that no enclosures are left inside. Attach the enclosures to the letters.

If the address of the sender is on the envelope but not on the letter, attach the envelope to the letter. Otherwise, put the envelopes aside until all the mail is completely processed and you know that you will not have to check the envelopes for overlooked contents or addresses. If the letter is undated, the postmark date should be recorded. Ask the manager if he or she would also like to have all mail rubber-stamped with the date received.

Sort the letters into three piles: (1) those that require the manager's attention, (2) those that require the attention of someone outside your office, and (3) those that require your attention. This applies also to interoffice memoranda. As you sort the letters, check the enclosures. If any are missing, look in the envelope that was put aside for this purpose. If the enclosure cannot be found, make a notation on the letter to that effect. When the nature of the enclosure is such that the letter cannot be answered without it, put the letter in the pile that requires your attention.

Mail that requires the manager's attention.   Strive to have the manager's mail on his or her desk before he or she gets to the office. At any rate, get it there as quickly as possible.

Since the file of previous correspondence relating to a current letter will facilitate action, attach the incoming letter to the file before giving it to the manager. Type copies of incoming letters that are written in longhand, if not easily read.

Arrange the manager's mail in the order of importance, with the most important on top. Some managers with many outside activities like to have the mail relating to personal matters segregated from that relating to company business. For handling the mail when the manager is out of the office, see page 109.

Ask the manager if he or she would like to have you annotate his or her mail—underline or otherwise point out the key points in lengthy letters and perhaps jot down useful facts on them. For instance, if a letter asks him or her to speak at a luncheon, you might underscore the time, place, etc., and in the margin of the letter remind him or her of any conflicting appointment. There are yellow marking pens available in office supply stores that can be used to underscore or circle words without leaving marks that will show if the letter is photocopied.

Mail that requires action or attention by others.   When sorting the mail, place in separate piles correspondence that your immediate office cannot dispose of without information or assistance from someone else in the organization and correspondence that should be routed to others.

For the purpose of getting the desired action, have forms, similar to the one shown in Figure 15, printed or reproduced by an inexpensive mechanical process. Check the action you want taken, staple the form to the incoming correspondence, and forward it to the individual to whose attention it is directed. If necessary, attach the pertinent file or previous correspondence.

If several people should see the correspondence, use mimeographed (or duplicated) routing slips similar to the one shown in

FROM THE PRESIDENT'S OFFICE:

☐   Please answer direct.

☐   Please prepare reply for president's signature.

☐   Please furnish information for president's reply.

☐   Please refer to the appropriate person to handle.

☐   Please discuss this with the president.

☐   Is it possible for the company to meet this request?

☐   Please note and return.

☐   _____

Thank You.

FIGURE 15   "ACTION REQUESTED" SLIP

Date: 3/5/--

(To be routed in the order numbered)

2 Mr. Edwards		*ARE*	3/7
1 Mr. Roberts		*LR*	3/6
4 Mr. Jones		*B.J.*	3/10
3 Ms. Nelson		*E.N.*	3/8
Mr. Ellis			
5 File			
Please initial, date, and forward.			

FIGURE 16   ROUTING SLIP

Figure 16. Place the numerals 1, 2, 3, etc. in front of the names on the slip in the order that each person should receive the mail. The names are already on the slip but the order of routing varies.

When you attend to part of a letter. If you attend to part of a letter before sending it to someone for further attention, mark the paragraph that has had attention. Write the date and "done" or "noted" in the margin and initial.

Daily mail record.   Keep a simple daily record of all mail sent *out* of your office for action by another person. This applies to telegrams and reports as well as letters. The purpose of the record is twofold: It serves as a check on the receipt and disposition of mail that gets misplaced and for follow-up, if necessary.

For the daily mail record, use loose-leaf sheets with vertical columns headed "Date," "Description," "To Whom Sent," "Action To Be Taken," and "Follow-up." See Figure 17. If you keep the record with pencil or pen instead of typing it, the sheets should have lines drawn between entries. Double space between each entry on the typewriter.

DAILY MAIL RECORD

Date	Description	To Whom Sent	Action To Be Taken	Follow-up
3/5	Spellman, Preface to Corp. Sec'y, 3/3	L. Rogers	Approval	3/8
3/5	Brown of U. of Wis. request for free copy of Credits & Collections 3/3	Andrews	Reply	

FIGURE 17   DAILY MAIL RECORD

In the "Date" column, show the date on which the material is sent out of your office. Under "Description," note the date of the communication, name of the sender, and the subject matter. "To Whom Sent" obviously refers to the person to whom you sent the material. In the "Action To Be Taken" column note the action that was checked on the slip that you attached to the communication before forwarding it. Write the deadline date for disposition in the follow-up column if it is necessary to follow up to see that proper action is taken. When the matter has had the necessary attention, draw a line through the entry.

In some organizations, certain department heads receive all of the mail of the department in order that they may assign the correspondence to the appropriate person for reply. In such cases the daily mail record is particularly important.

Mail that requires your attention.   When sorting the mail, include in a separate pile the letters that you will answer for the manager's signature, as well as those that you will write over your own signature. See chapter 13.

Newspapers and periodicals.   Select the ones that your employer likes to read. Unwrap, flatten out, and put in a folder labeled "Newspapers and Periodicals." Put the folder on his desk, or in his briefcase if he prefers to take material of this kind home.

Send the other newspapers and periodicals to the persons in the organization who need them or put them on the shelves for reference. If your employer is paying for a periodical that he or she does not want, that is not needed by someone in the organization, or that is not valuable as reference material, ask him or her about canceling the subscription.

Advertisements and circulars.   The educational value of advertisements and circulars is often overlooked. They are frequently a convenient and free source of information about such things as availability and trends in new products and procedures, or reminders of important meetings and other business-related events. Some of this material will doubtless interest your employer or another department in your company. For example, a lawyer is usually interested in the advertisement of law books that he does not have in his library; executives are always on the lookout for cost-cutting ideas. If an order blank is enclosed with an advertisement, clip it to the advertisement.

Frequently, in the advertisements you will find solicitations for contributions. Put these in a separate folder and handle in the manner described for charitable contributions on page 203.

The mail will include material about investments. Handle this as described on page 446.

Bills and statements.   These are filed until a designated time of the month. Therefore, do not open them until you have disposed of the other mail. In fact, if you are particularly rushed and there is a large stack of them, you might put them aside until you have time to attend to them. See pages 442-443 for how to handle bills and statements.

How to handle incoming mail when the manager is away.   The manner in which you should handle the mail when the manager is away from the office depends, of course, upon his personal preference. You can adapt the procedure recommended here to his or her wishes:

1. If the manager makes a practice of telephoning his office each day, sort the correspondence according to company matters and outside matters. Also jot down the gist of each letter so that you can report to him readily.
2. Telephone or wire him about anything urgent that requires his immediate personal attention if he does not call you.
3. Acknowledge all correspondence, whether personal or business (see page 282), if he is to be away more than a few days.
4. Dispose finally of as much of the mail as possible by covering the subject of the letter in your acknowledgment or by referring letters to other people in the organization for reply.
5. Copy all mail that requires the manager's personal attention and forward the copies to him.
6. Number consecutively the packets of mail that you send to your employer. In this way he can tell whether or not he receives all the mail that you send him. Numbering the packets is particularly important when the manager is traveling from place to place.
7. If the manager is on a vacation and does not want mail forwarded to him, hold the letters that require his personal attention and indicate in your acknowledgment when a reply might be expected.
8. Keep the accumulated mail in folders marked "Correspondence to be signed," "Correspondence requiring your attention," "Correspondence to read" (letters that have been answered but in which he will probably be interested), "Reports," and "General reading material" (miscellaneous items of advertising and publications that he might want to read).

OUTGOING MAIL

Getting signature to outgoing mail.   When you give letters to the manager for his or her signature, separate those that he or she dictated from those that you or someone else wrote for his or her signature.

The most usual method of giving letters to a dictator for signature is to remove the carbon copy and insert the flap of the envelope over the original letter and its enclosures. Many executives are interested only in the letters, however, and consider envelopes a nuisance. The practice of giving the manager letters without envelopes also has this advantage: You can get the letters to him for signature more quickly because you can address the envelopes from the carbon copies or after he returns the letters to you. Of course, you never file the carbon copies until after the letters are signed and you have made the necessary changes on the copies.

Assembling the mail.   When the mail has been signed, bring it back to your desk and assemble it for actual mailing. Check each letter for these three things:

1. Has the letter been signed?
2. Are all enclosures included?
3. Are the inside address and the envelope address the same?

How to fold and insert letters in envelopes.   Letters written on full-size letterheads for insertion in long envelopes should be folded as follows: one fold from the bottom, about one-third of the way up; a second fold from the bottom to within one-sixteenth of an inch of the top. Insert in the envelope, top up.

Letters written on full-sized letterheads for insertion in short envelopes should be folded as follows: one fold from the bottom to within one-quarter of an inch of the top; a second fold from right to left, about one-third of the way across; a third fold from left to right within one-quarter of an inch of the right edge. Insert with the right edge up.

Letters written on half-size letterheads should be folded as follows: one fold from right to left, about a third of the way across; a second fold from left to right, leaving about one-sixteenth of an inch between the edges at the right. Insert in a small envelope with the right edge up.

Letters should be inserted into envelopes in such a manner that when the letter is removed from the envelope and unfolded, the type side should be up.

Enclosures.   When it is necessary to fasten enclosures together or to a letter, use staples. The U.S. Postal Service objects to pins or metal clips because the pins injure the hands of postal employees and the clips tend to damage post office canceling machines.

1. *Enclosures the size of the letter.* These are easily folded and inserted, with their accompanying letters, into commercial envelopes of the ordinary size. If the enclosure consists of two or more sheets, staple them together but do not fasten the enclosed material to the letter. Fold the enclosure, then fold the letter, and slip the enclosure inside the last fold of the letter. Thus, when the letter is removed from the envelope, the enclosure comes out with it.

2. *Enclosures larger than the letter.* These include booklets, pamphlets, prospectuses, catalogs, and other printed material too large to fit into a commercial envelope of ordinary size. These are generally mailed in large manila envelopes. Enclosures of this kind may be handled in one of four ways.

(a) The letter is inserted with the enclosure in the large envelope, which is sealed. In this case first-class postage is charged for both the letter and the enclosure.

(b) A combination envelope is used. This is a large envelope with a flap that is fastened by a patent fastener of some kind, *but not sealed.* A smaller envelope of commercial size is affixed on the front of this envelope in the process of manufacture. The letter is inserted into the small envelope and the flap is sealed. Postage is affixed to the large envelope at third-class rate and to the small envelope at first-class rate.

(c) The enclosure may be sent, *unsealed,* in one envelope and the letter, *sealed,* in another.

(d) A letter may be enclosed with a parcel if postage is paid on the letter at the first-class rate. (See page 120.)

3. *Enclosures smaller than the letter.* When enclosures are considerably smaller than the letter, staple them to the letter in the upper left-hand corner, on top of the letter. If two or more such enclosures are sent, put the smaller one on top.

TIMELY SUGGESTIONS FOR BOOSTING YOUR EFFICIENCY IN THE MAILING DEPARTMENT

Have a well-equipped mail desk.   Your job of getting out the mail does not get simpler if you have a mailing department. You still have to decide the best method of sending out your mail. Although a knowledge of the basic postal rates, and ways to use them properly, is essential (see chapter 5), a well-equipped mail desk can prevent actual mail handling from being a wearisome task.

Devices and supplies that can end some of the drudgery are now on the market, including convenient desk-top postage scales, postage meters, rubber stamps, colorful press-apply mailing labels, and a variety of mailing envelopes and package sealing tapes.

1. *End the "lick and stick" office drudgery.* Postage meters are now available for even the smallest office. You get rid of stamps, prestamped envelopes, and lick-and-stick mailing. You "dial" and print your own postage as and when you need it, day or night, for any kind or class of mail. Postage meter equipment generally consists of two parts: an office mailing machine and a detachable postage meter. The United States Postal Service licenses the meter. Your employer can buy the mailing machines, but must lease the meter from an authorized manufacturer who is responsible to the post office for its proper operation, maintenance, and replacement, when necessary. To buy postage, you simply send your meter to the nearest post office to have it set. You pay postage in advance, just as when buying ordinary stamps. The postage meter not only eliminates stamp licking, but eliminates the need for keeping loose stamps, protects postage against loss, waste, and stamp borrowing. The equipment will also seal envelopes while applying postage.

Caution: Never guess at the amount of postage required—always use your scales.

2. *Use rubber stamps.* If you regularly send letters with special classifications, have a rubber stamp made with the necessary information, such as "Priority Mail" or "Special Delivery." These low-cost stamps save time for you in two ways: They save you the trouble of positioning and typing the instructions and they are more readily noticed by postal employees.

Five ways to speed post office processing.   You can speed your letters on their way faster if you take these steps:

1. Place the correct zip code in the address.
2. One of the preliminary steps in the post-office processing of mail is to sort the local mail from the out-of-town mail. Unless your daily mail is limited to just a few pieces, the way it leaves your office is important to fast handling. Stack and tie your mail in local or out-of-town bundles with addresses facing the same direction.

3. When you send a special class of mail, such as special delivery or priority mail, to the post office, place these letters in special bundles placed on top of the other mail. The postal employees can then spot them more easily.
4. You can save as much as a full day in delivery by getting your mail out in the morning, instead of late in the afternoon. Although this is not always practical for all mail, you should try to see that out-of-town mail is sent as early in the day as possible.
5. Keep in mind the pickup times at your local collection box for timing your mailings.

Cut rising mailroom costs.   The costs of communicating by mail increase each year, but there are ways you can combat rising mailroom expenses: (1) Double-check to be certain that everyone on your mailing list *must* receive a copy of your communication; (2) if you find that you often mail several letters every couple of days to the same person, look into the possibility of combining mailings into one letter; (3) try to eliminate unnecessary enclosures; (4) use routing slips instead of mailing numerous carbon copies; (5) consider microfilm if constant bulk mailings are a problem in your office; (6) where possible, use the telephone for local contacts—it's faster and cheaper; and (7) above all, keep your letters brief and to the point—long-windedness costs money in extra postage.

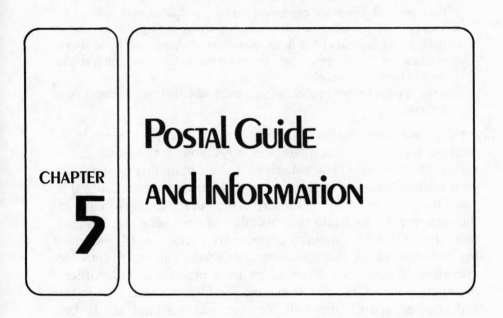

CHAPTER
5

Postal Guide
and Information

In this chapter the rules and regulations that affect all kinds
of mail that the secretary is likely to handle are given. The
fees and rates are subject to change. You can get the current
information by calling the local post office.

Sources of information. The U.S. Postal Service has printed chapters 1 to 6 of the *Postal Manual* for general public sale. Chapter 1 relates to domestic postal service; chapter 2 to organization and administration; chapters 3 to 6 cover postal procedures, personnel, transportation, and facilities.

These chapters contain regulations and procedures. They explain the services offered, prescribe rates and fees, and prescribe conditions under which postal services are available.

In order that purchasers of this material may keep up to date with current information and changes as they occur, a loose-leaf supplementary service is included. The manual and supplementary service are sold on a subscription basis only.

The Directory of Post Offices, sold on a subscription basis, lists all post offices arranged alphabetically by states. International mail regulations are described in the *Directory of International Mail,* publication 42.

These publications are available from the Superintendent of Documents, U.S. Government Printing Office, Washington, DC 20402.

DOMESTIC POSTAL SERVICE

Classes of mail and special services. There are four classes of mail: first, second, third, and fourth. First-class mail consists of sealed matter and also of certain items that the U.S. Postal Service considers first-class matter whether sealed or not (see the following list). If the distance between points merits air transport, first-class mail is sent by air. Second-class mail consists of newspapers and periodicals; third-class mail, of unsealed and marked sealed matter weighing less than 16 ounces; fourth-class mail, or parcel post, of packages weighing 16 ounces or more. Figure 18 presents specified delivery times applicable to each class.

The special services, or forms of handling, that the U.S. Postal Service provides are:

Special Delivery	Insured
Registry	Certified

Certificate of Mailing
Collect on Delivery
Special Handling
Business Reply Mail
Stamps by Mail

Self-service Postal Centers
Money Orders
Premium Services (Mailgram;
Express Mail;
Controlpak)

CLASS OF MAIL	POST OFFICE SERVICE STANDARD
First Class	Contact your local post office for areas receiving next-day delivery
First Class Transient	Not specified (applies to complete copies of a publication mailed by other than publisher only)
Third Class Single Piece	Not specified
Third Class Bulk	Not specified (Minimum 200 pieces of same size)
Fourth Class Parcel Post	Local: overnight Zone 2: second day Zone 3: third day Zone 4: fourth day Zone 5: fifth day Zone 6: sixth day Zone 7: seventh day Zone 8: eighth day

FIGURE 18   DELIVERY TIMES PER CLASS OF MAIL

Details of the various classes of mail and the special services are explained in subsequent paragraphs of this chapter.

Mailable items and how to dispatch them.   The following list shows the class of mail by which to send each item.

Item	*How to Send*
Birth Announcements	First class
Bonds: negotiable	Registered first class
Nonnegotiable	First class or certified first class
Books	Fourth class

(Special rates apply to books. The book may be autographed. Mark the package "Special Fourth-class Rate: Books.")

Catalogs . . . . Third, fourth class
 (Special rates apply to printed catalogs individually addressed, consisting
 of 24 pages or more and not weighing over 10 pounds. Each piece must be
 clearly marked "Catalog.")
Checks, Filled Out . . . . First class
 Canceled . . . . First class
 Certified . . . . Registered first class
 Endorsed in blank . . . . Registered first class
Circulars . . . . Third class
Currency . . . . Registered first class
Documents: No intrinsic value . . . . Certified mail
 With intrinsic value
 Signed originals . . . . Registered first class
 Copies . . . . First class
Drawings . . . . Third class
Form Letters . . . . Third class
 (Check with the post office for the category of third-class mail best suited
 to your needs.)
Greeting Cards . . . . First class
Jewelry . . . . Registered first class
 (Limit of liability is $10,000–$1,000 if commercial or other insurance is
 also carried.)
Letters
 Carbon copies . . . . First class
 Duplicate copies . . . . First class
 For delivery to addressee only . . . . Registered (or
              certified) first class
 Form (see Form Letters)
 Handwritten or typed . . . . First class
Magazines . . . . Second class
Manuscript . . . . Fourth class, insured
              (Mark the package
              "Special Fourth-class
              Rate.")
 Accompanied by proof sheets . . . . Third or fourth
              class, depending on
              weight
(Corrections on proof sheets may include insertion of new matter, as well
as marginal notes to the printer. The manuscript of one article may not be
enclosed with the proof of another unless the matter is mailed at the
first-class rate.)
Merchandise (see Packages)
Money Orders . . . . First class
Newspapers . . . . Second Class

Packages
　　Up to 16 ounces . . . . Third class
　　16 ounces and over . . . . Parcel post
　　(Packages may be sealed if they bear an inscription authorizing inspection by the postmaster. Packages containing articles valued at not more than $200 may be insured, but if they contain articles valued at more than $200, they should be sealed and registered. First-class postage will then apply, and the liability limit is $10,000.)
　　Containing personal messages (See *Combination Mail*, page 120)
Periodicals . . . . Second class
Photographs . . . . Third class
　　(Wrap with a cardboard protection and mark the envelope "Photograph—Do Not Bend." Photographs may be autographed.)
Postal Cards . . . . First class
Post Cards . . . . First class
　　(In order to be mailed at post-card rates, cards cannot be smaller than 4¼ by 3 inches or larger than 6 by 4¼ inches. Cards exceeding 6 by 4¼ inches require postage at the first-class rate for letters. If the card is enclosed in an envelope, it cannot be mailed at the post-card rate. Cards carrying a statement of a past-due account cannot be mailed at the card rate because they must be enclosed in an envelope.)
Plants, Seeds, Cuttings, Scions, Bulbs, Roots . . . . . . Third class or parcel
　　　　　　　　　　　　　　　　　　　　　　　　　　　　　　　　 post depending on
　　　　　　　　　　　　　　　　　　　　　　　　　　　　　　　　 weight
Printed Matter
　　Less than 16 ounces . . . . Third class
　　16 ounces and over . . . . Fourth class
Stock Certificates
　　Negotiable . . . . Registered first class
　　Nonnegotiable . . . . First class or
　　　　　　　　　　　　　　　　　　　　　　　　　　　　　　　 certified
Tapes and Cassettes
　　Nonpersonal . . . . Special fourth class,
　　　　　　　　　　　　　　　　　　　　　　　　　　　　　　　 marked "Sound
　　　　　　　　　　　　　　　　　　　　　　　　　　　　　　　 Recording"
　　Personal . . . . First class
Typewritten Material (see Manuscript) . . . . First class

First-class mail. *Rate basis.* The rate is based on the ounce, or fraction thereof, up to 13 ounces. First-class mail weighing over 13 ounces is based on pound and zone rates (priority mail).

　　Preparation for mailing. Seal. Mark or stamp oversized or odd-shaped envelopes "First Class" very plainly. (You can buy first-class mail stickers and also large envelopes with first-class mail borders.) If the flap is not gummed, seal with glue or mucilage.

Instructions and postal regulations. All sealed matter is first class unless it qualifies as third or fourth class and is properly marked.

When first-class matter is included with second, third, or fourth, postage at the first-class rate is required for the letter. The package should be marked "Letter Enclosed." ECOM (electronic-originated mail) is a new subclass of first-class mail being designed to provide two-day message service. As with mailgrams, Western Union will transmit messages and the Postal Service will deliver them.

Second-class mail (transient, copies mailed by public). *Rate basis.* The rate is based on a set fee for the first two ounces and an additional amount for each additional ounce or fraction thereof, or at the fourth-class rate, whichever is lower.

Weight limit. None.

Preparation for mailing. Do not seal. Address an envelope, slit the ends, and wrap the entire newspaper or periodical in it. Write "Second-Class Matter" above the address, "To" in front of the address, and "From" in front of the return address. To call attention to a special passage in the text, mark with symbols, *not words,* in colored pencil. Write "Marked Copy" on the wrapper.

Second-class mail (publishers). *Rate basis.* The rate basis varies with the weight, frequency of publication, percentage of advertising, and zone.

Instructions and postal regulations. Only newspapers and periodicals published at least four times a year bearing a printed notice of second-class entry are admissible for mailing to established lists of paid subscribers.

Publications produced by stencil or hectograph methods are not admissible as second-class matter. The entire newspaper or periodical must be mailed; otherwise, the *higher* third-class rate applies on material weighing up to 16 ounces.

Third-class mail. *Rate basis.* The rate is based on a minimum of two ounces with an increase for each two ounces or fraction thereof, without regard to zone.

Weight limit. Up to 16 ounces. The same material becomes fourth class or parcel post when mailed in packages weighing 16 ounces or over.

Preparation for mailing. Third-class mail is subject to postal inspection, but may be sealed if clearly marked "Third Class" on the outside. It is advisable to designate the contents on the wrapper, such as "Merchandise" or "Printed Matter."

Instructions and postal regulations. Writing, except something in the nature of an autograph or inscription, is not permitted on third-class matter. If you are concerned with *bulk rate mail,* go in person to the post office for information and instructions.

"Do not open until Christmas," or a similar legend, may be written on the wrapper; other directions or requests may not.

Corrections of typographical errors may be made.

Fourth-class mail (parcel post).   *Rate basis.* The rate is by the pound, according to distance or zone. A fraction of a pound is computed as a full pound. To find the zone of the place of destination, telephone the post office, Parcel Post Information, or refer to the *Directory of Post Offices* for the zone key for your city.

Weight limit. Sixteen ounces or more and not more than 40 pounds when going between post offices with greater than 950 revenue units within the 48 contiguous states. All other parcels may not exceed 70 pounds.

Size. For parcel post going to post offices with greater than 950 revenue units, the size limit is 84 inches in length and girth combined; to post offices up to 949 revenue units, the size limit is 100 inches. The length is the distance from one end of the package to the other, not around it; and the girth is the distance around the package at its thickest part. For example, a parcel 35 inches in length, 10 inches in width, and 5 inches in thickness is 65 inches in length and girth combined (35" plus 10" plus 10" plus 5" plus 5").

Preparation for mailing. Bear in mind that parcels sent through ordinary handling (see special handling of parcel post below) are likely to be handled roughly. Be sure that the contents are solid. If they are crushable, pack in an extra-heavy cardboard box.

Instructions and postal regulations. Do not seal the package unless it bears an inscription that it may be opened for postal inspection.

Combination mail. No communication may be enclosed with a parcel unless additional postage is paid. Invoices and customer's orders that relate entirely to the articles may be enclosed. When articles are being returned for repair, exchange, or credit, no communication, such as "Please credit my account," may be included unless additional postage is paid, but the sales slip may be enclosed. Seasonal greetings may be enclosed.

A letter may be enclosed with a parcel if postage is paid on the letter at the first-class rate and on the package at the parcel-post rate. The mail will be dispatched as fourth-class matter. Beneath the postage and above the address, write the words "First-Class Mail Enclosed."

Special-handling postage entitles fourth-class mail to the same handling as is given to first-class mail, but not to special delivery by the office of destination. Nor does special handling ensure the safe delivery of the mail.

Special fourth-class mail. The special fourth-class rate applies to books of 24 pages or more of which at least 22 are printed, films of 16 mm or narrower width, printed music in bound or sheet form, printed objective test materials, sound recordings, playscripts and manuscripts for books, and loose-leaf pages and binders containing medical information. Each parcel should be labeled "Special 4th Class Rate" and should include a description of the item, such as "Books" or "Printed Music."

Priority mail—airmail for heavy pieces. For mail over ten ounces to be sent by air, priority rates apply. Any mailable matter except that liable to damage by freezing or explosion by high altitude (e.g. aerosol products) may be sent by priority mail. If you must mail such products, be sure to use third class or parcel post, which are not automatically sent airmail to distant points.

Rate basis. The rate for matter weighing over ten ounces to four and a half pounds is based on the pound and half pound. The rate for parcels weighing five pounds to seventy pounds is based on the pound. All rates are calculated according to zones and miles.

Weight and size limits. Priority mail may not exceed 70 pounds or 100 inches in length and girth combined. Parcels weighing less than 15 pounds and measuring over 84 inches but not exceeding 100 inches in length and girth combined are chargeable with a minimum rate equal to that for a 15-pound parcel for the zone to which addressed.

Preparation for mailing. Seal all priority mail and request priority mail postage at the post office.

Instructions and postal regulations. Priority mail may be registered, insured, or sent C.O.D. or special delivery if the charges for these services are paid in addition to the regular priority mail rate.

Registered mail. This service offers additional safeguards for the transmission of valuable mail. Mail may be registered for any amount.

Indemnity. When registered mail is lost, rifled, or damaged in transit, the U.S. Postal Service will pay an indemnity up to $10,000 if no commercial or other insurance is carried; the limit is $1,000 if other insurance is carried. In the event of a loss, go immediately to the nearest post office and fill out the forms required by the postal authorities. Your employer will probably have to sign the claim form.

Fee basis. The fee for registering mail is based upon the declared actual value of the goods, not just the amount of indemnification desired. Thus, if the value of the package is $1,000,000, the fee on that basis is charged, but the U.S. Postal Service will pay only $10,000 in case of loss. A small additional fee is charged for a return receipt and a larger fee for delivery to the addressee only.

Preparation for mailing. All registered mail, except second- and third-class mail valued at not more than $100, must be sealed. Seal with glue or mucilage.

Write the value on the face of the matter being mailed, near the space for the stamps.

Print or stamp "Registered," "Registered, Return Receipt Requested," or "Registered, Deliver to Addressee Only"—as the case may be—in the space below the stamps, above the address. These instructions on the wrapper serve only as a reminder to the person mailing the letter or package. The postal employees will ignore them unless the proper fee is paid at the time of mailing.

Instructions and postal regulations. Mail without intrinsic value may be registered for the minimum fee or *certified* (see below). Registered mail closes earlier than ordinary mail at the post offices. Priority mail may be registered. Registered mail may be sent C.O.D. Write the name of the addressee on the back of the receipt given to you by the post office. This is to enable you to identify the receipt. Mail at the post office; *do not* deposit in a mailbox.

Certified mail.   First-class mail without intrinsic value may be *certified.* The sender gets a receipt, and a record of delivery is kept at the office of address. Return receipts are available for an extra fee as is special delivery service.

Certificate of mailing.   The sender may establish that he has mailed an item by purchasing a *certificate* showing that the item was mailed.

The certificate does not provide for insurance; it furnishes evidence of mailing *only*.

Insured mail.   Third- and fourth-class mail may be insured. First- and second-class mail cannot be insured; such matter should be registered.

Indemnity. The indemnity limit on insured mail is $200.

Fee basis. The insurance fee depends upon the declared value of the mailed matter.

Preparation for mailing. Do not seal, but wrap securely. Under the return address write "Return Postage Guaranteed."

Special regulations. All insured mail is sent with the understanding that forwarding or return postage is guaranteed.

The priority mail system handles insured mail if it is sent at the priority mail rate of postage plus insurance fees.

Return receipt may be had for an extra fee.

Mail at the post office; *do not* deposit in a mailbox.

Special delivery.   For the payment of a fee, any class of mail may be sent *special delivery*. Special delivery postage provides immediate delivery by the office of destination. See also *special handling* of fourth-class mail.

C.O.D. mail.   Domestic third- and fourth-class mail and sealed matter of any class bearing postage at the first-class rate may be sent C.O.D. (collect on delivery). The sender must pay the postage and the C.O.D. fee, but may include these in the price of the article that is to be collected upon delivery. The maximum amount that may be collected on any single C.O.D. is $300. The collections are sent to the sender by the post office in the form of a money order.

The sender of a C.O.D. parcel must guarantee return and forwarding postage. C.O.D. mail may be sent special delivery or special handling if fees applying to these services are paid in addition to postage and C.O.D. charges. The priority mail system handles C.O.D. mail if it is sent at the priority mail rate of postage plus C.O.D. charges.

Business reply mail.   The sender who wishes to encourage responses by paying the postage for those responses may use the business reply service. Application is made by filling out U.S. Postal Service Form 3614, for which there is no charge. The mailer pays a $30 fee and guarantees that he will pay the postage for all replies returned to him. Two options are available: (1) If an advance deposit is made at the post office, the mailer must pay an accounting charge of $75 plus 3.5 cents per piece returned. (2) If no deposit is made, there is no accounting charge; however, the mailer must pay 12 cents for each piece returned.

Business reply mail must be identified as such in large letters on the address side of the envelope. Also appearing on the same side must be the permit number, the name of the post office issuing the permit, and the words "No Postage Stamp Necessary if Mailed in the United States." The envelope must also carry the words "Postage Will be Paid by Addressee" or the inscription "Postage Will be Paid by" over the name and address of the person or business firm to which the mail is being returned.

Stamps by mail.   This service makes it possible to buy limited amounts of postage stamps through the mail. In locations where the service is offered, an order blank obtained at the post office provides for the customer to indicate the stamps he wants to buy. The order and the customer's check are mailed postage free to the post office and the stamps returned through the mail. A nominal fee is charged to cover handling costs.

Self-service postal centers.   Self-service postal centers provide round-the-clock, seven-day-a-week mailing service for letters and parcels. Automatic vending equipment enables the customer to purchase individual stamps, books of stamps, postal cards, stamped envelopes, and parcel insurance. Some of these units are located in post office lobbies; others are at shopping centers, college campuses, and other places of pedestrian access. Some are located for automobile drive-up.

Money orders.   Postal money orders provide for sending money through the mail safely. Fees depend upon the amount of the money order, which may be purchased and redeemed at any post office. The amount of a money order is limited to $300.

Premium services.   *Mailgram.* Mailgram is a combination letter and telegram designed to provide overnight service to addresses in the continental United States. The customer presents his message to a Western Union Office or toll-free to a Western Union centralized telephone operator. The message is sent electronically to a teleprinter at a post office near its destination. There it is placed in a distinctive envelope and delivered to the ultimate destination by a regular postal service letter carrier. Most mailgrams are delivered the next business day. Businesses can originate mailgrams directly from their Telex or TXW machines. Large volume users may also originate messages by computer. Call your local Western Union office for details. (See *First-class mail*, page 119, for information on a two-day message service.)

Express mail. Express mail is a high-speed intercity delivery system geared to the special needs of business and industry for fast, reliable transfer of time-sensitive documents and products. The service is customized to the mailer's specific needs using a network linking 58 major metropolitan areas of the United States plus several foreign countries. Call your post office for more specific information on express mail, including the five different system options available.

Controlpak. The U.S. Postal Service has developed controlpak to assure maximum safety to mailers of credit cards and other high-value items that previously presented a security problem. The controlpak mailer prepares individual pieces of his mail in the usual way, addressing each envelope and affixing postage at the first-class rate. He then sorts the pieces by five-digit zip codes, packages each *group* in a special controlpak plastic bag, and heat-seals the bag against theft. The bag is addressed to the post office, station, or branch represented by the five-digit zip code. It is transported within the registered mail system to that destination, where it is opened under controlled, accountable conditions, and the individual pieces are made available to the carrier for final delivery.

How to reduce postage costs.   Money can be saved by knowing how and when to use the various types of mail service. Here are a few suggestions to reduce postage costs.

1. Use business-reply envelopes instead of stamped self-addressed envelopes. Today business-reply envelopes are used mainly with sales letters to make it easier for a prospect to buy. With bills or statements a self-addressed envelope is enclosed, but usually without prepaid postage.
2. Mail early in the day to get the fastest service possible. This is especially important for first-class mail to distant points, which must meet plane schedules.
3. Eliminate special delivery if letters will reach their destination in time for the first mail delivery.
4. Economies are possible if you know how and when various classes of mail can be used.
5. If you have several letters for the same person, put them in one envelope.

6. Send all material to the same branch office in one envelope. Postage is paid on so much per ounce or fraction, and combining fractions saves ounces. Saving is also made on envelopes.
7. Write communications to branch offices on memo paper. This reduces the weight of the mail going to branch offices.
8. Pack priority mail and other parcels in the lightest weight materials possible without sacrificing sturdiness.
9. Give thought to the weight of paper and envelopes used for normal correspondence. Reduced weight need not mean sacrifice of quality.
10. Do not send paper clips through the mail.
11. When you send a letter with material that does not require first-class postage, use specially constructed envelopes that have one part for the first-class letter and another part for the lower class material.

Forwarding mail.   Make changes of address on mail to be forwarded in *ink*, not pencil.

First-class mail will be forwarded for a period of one year from one post office to another without additional charge.

Second- and *third-class* mail will be forwarded for a period of 90 days, without additional postage, to a known address in the local area.

Fourth- and *second-class* mail (after 90 days) can be forwarded from one post office to another on a "postage due" basis, with the addressee paying the additional charges when certain postal regulations regarding envelope endorsement are met. There are no extra charges for forwarding this mail within a district. Check with your post office for detailed instructions regarding provisions for forwarding second-, third-, and fourth-class mail, and for obtaining the new address for your records.

Special delivery mail may be forwarded under the same rules that apply to mail sent by regular delivery, but will not be delivered as special at the second address if an attempt was made to deliver it at the first address unless the sender has guaranteed the additional postage at time of mailing.

Return of mail.   Put a return address on the upper left-hand corner of every piece of mail that you send out.

First-class mail will be returned to the sender free of charge.

The rules governing the return of *second-class mail* are detailed and exacting; consult the postmaster if you have a problem.

Third- and fourth-class mail will be returned to the sender and the return postage collected on delivery when the sender's address is in the upper left-hand corner and when the pledge "Return Postage Guaranteed" appears immediately under the return card. Otherwise, the postmaster will notify the sender that the mail is not deliverable and that return postage is required but he will not return the matter until the sender pays the necessary amount.

Upon request, address corrections will be sent to the mailer for a fee.

INTERNATIONAL MAIL

Foreign or international mail is mail deposited for dispatch to points outside the continental United States and its territories and possessions. Foreign mail is classified as postal union mail and parcel post.

Postal union mail.   This category of international mail is divided into LC mail and AO mail. LC mail (letters and cards) consists of letters, letter packages, aerogrammes, and post cards. AO mail (other articles) includes printed matter, matter for the blind, and small packets.

Letters and letter packages.   *Rate basis.* The rate is based on the ounce or fraction thereof, varying according to the country of destination and for surface or air transport.

Instructions and postal regulations. Do not use envelopes of weak or unsubstantial paper.

Typewritten material must be sent under the classification of "letters" and cannot be sent at the cheaper rate applicable to printed matter.

Write the words "Letter (lettre)" on the address side of letters or letter packages that may be mistaken for other articles by reason of their volume or packing. Airmail should be clearly designated by "Par Avion" in writing or in label form.

Merchandise that is liable to customs duty may be forwarded in letters or letter packages to many countries, prepaid at the letter rate of postage, if the importation of the article is permitted by the country of destination. Check with the post office regarding the appropriate form to be filled out and label (s) to be affixed.

Some countries will not accept merchandise sent at the letter rate of postage. Refer to Publication 42, *International Mail,* or consult the post office for restrictions and requirements in the country of destination.

Aerogrammes.   Aerogrammes consist of sheets that can be folded in the form of an envelope and sealed. They can be sent to *all foreign countries* at a uniform rate. Messages are to be written on the inner side of the sheets, and no enclosures are permitted.

Aerogrammes with printed postage and airmail markings are sold at all post offices. Aerogrammes manufactured by private concerns, if approved by the U.S. Postal Service, are also accepted for mailing after the required postage has been affixed.

Post cards.   *Rate basis.* The rate varies according to country of destination, with surface or air rates applying.

Dimensions. Only single cards are acceptable in international mail. Maximum size, 6 by 4¼ inches; minimum, 5½ by 3½ inches.

Printed matter.   *Rate basis.* The rate is based on two ounces or fraction thereof, with surface and air rates applying.

Instructions and regulations. Printed matter may be sealed if postage is paid by permit imprint, postage meter stamps, precanceled stamps, second-class or controlled circulation indicias.

Write "Printed Matter" on the wrapper and specify the type of printed matter, such as "Books" or "Sheet Music," since special rates apply to these categories.

The following are considered printed matter: newspapers and periodicals, books, pamphlets, sheet music, visiting cards, address cards, greeting cards, printing proofs (with or without the relative manuscripts), unframed photographs, engravings, albums containing photographs, printed pictures, drawings, plans, maps, patterns to be cut out, calendars (except calendar pads with blank pages for memoranda), catalogs, prospectuses, advertisements, notices, matrices of material similar to paper or cardboard. Reproductions of handwriting or typewriting obtained by means of the printing press, mimeograph, multigraph, or similar mechanical process are accepted as printed matter.

Matter for the blind.   Consult the post office regarding matter admissible in international mail as matter for the blind.

Rate basis. Surface rate, free; air rate, by the ounce or fraction thereof according to AO rates.

Instructions and regulations. The weight limit is 15 pounds. Do not seal.

Small packets.   This is a class of postal union mail designed to permit the mailing of small items of merchandise and samples. The postage rates are lower than for letter packages or parcel post.

Rate basis. The rate is based on four ounces or fraction thereof, with surface and air rates applying.

Instructions and regulations. May be sealed. The weight limit is two pounds, except for some countries for which the limit is one pound.

Mark the address side of the packet "Small Packet" or its equivalent in a language known in the country of destination. Small packets, whether or not they are subject to customs inspection, must bear the green customs label, Form 2976.

You may enclose in small packets a simple invoice and a slip showing the names and addresses of the sender and addressee of the packet.

Small packets may not contain any letter, note, or document having the character of actual personal correspondence; coins, bank notes, paper money, postage stamps (canceled or uncanceled), or any values payable to the bearer; platinum, gold, or silver (manufactured or unmanufactured); precious stones, jewelry, or other precious articles.

Some countries will not accept small packets. Refer to the *Postal Manual,* chapter 2, or consult the post office for restrictions and requirements in the country of destination.

Special services for postal union mail.   Registration, return receipt, special delivery, special handling, and airmail are available to practically all countries. Insurance and certified mail are not available for postal union mail. Consult the post office for details on special services.

Parcel post.   Parcel post may be sent to almost every country in the world, either by direct or indirect service. The parcels are sent from the United States by surface vessel or by airplane to a port in the country of destination, or to a port in an intermediate country to be sent from there to the country of destination. In the latter case, the parcels are subject to transit charges in the intermediate country.

The customs and other restrictions and regulations vary with the country of destination. Before preparing a parcel to be sent to a foreign country, consult postal authorities or Appendix B, Publication 42, *International Mail.*

Preparation for mailing. Pack in canvas or similar material, double-faced corrugated cardboard boxes, solid fiber boxes or cases, thick cardboard boxes, or strong wooden boxes of material at least half an inch thick. Do not pack in ordinary pasteboard containers. It is permissible to use heavy wrapping paper or waterproof paper as the outside covering of a carton or box, but it may not be used as the only covering of the contents. Boxes with lids screwed or nailed on and bags sewed at the openings may be used, provided they conform to the special provisions of the country of destination.

Do not deposit packages in a mailbox, but take them to the post office for mailing.

Special services available for parcel post.   Registration, special delivery, insurance, and air service are available to some countries. Special handling entitles parcels to priority handling between the mailing point and the U.S. point of dispatch; fees vary. C.O.D. and certified mail are not available for parcel post.

SPECIAL ZIP CODE TIPS
THAT SPEED DELIVERY
OF YOUR MAIL

Traditional addressing of envelopes formerly preferred by the U.S. Postal Service and executives must give way to progress and the machine age. The following recommendations for addressing envelopes are in conflict with traditional styles. Address your *letter* in the traditional style if you wish (it takes more time), but speed delivery of your mail by using the following tips on the envelope address. Of course, follow the manager's wishes.

1. *Always* use the two-letter abbreviation of a state plus the zip code. Capitalize both letters of the abbreviation; do not put periods between the letters—thus, New Jersey—NJ. Do not use any punctuation between the state abbreviation and the zip code, *nor between the city designation and the state abbreviation.*

2. Use only two spaces between the state abbreviation and the zip code—do not arbitrarily place the zip code at any place on the envelope where you think it looks attractive. This position is important because of the use of electronic equipment in "reading" the address.

3. Major addressing systems have a maximum 23-position line for city-state-zip code designation. The U.S. Postal Service has therefore prepared abbreviations for long post-office names for use with the zip code. These city abbreviations are also useful for window envelopes. From the U.S. Postal Service, Washington, DC 20260 (or perhaps from your local post office) you can get a booklet showing the official abbreviations of all of these localities with long names. Shown here are the traditional abbreviations and the two-letter abbreviations used in connection with zip codes (Figure 19).

4. When nine-digit zip codes are available, use them to facilitate sorting and delivery of commercial mail.

A zip code directory is available for reference in every post office. Copies also may be purchased through the U.S. Government Printing Office in Washington, DC 20402.

Traditional and U.S. Postal Service Two-Letter Abbreviations

State	Traditional Abbrev.	Postal Abbrev.	State	Traditional Abbrev.	Postal Abbrev.
Alabama, State of	Ala.	AL	Nebraska, State of	Nebr.	NE
Alaska, State of	Alas.	AK	Nevada, State of	Nev.	NV
Arizona, State of	Ariz.	AZ	New Hampshire, State of	N.H.	NH
Arkansas, State of	Ark.	AR	New Jersey, State of	N.J.	NJ
California, State of	Calif.	CA	New Mexico, State of	N.M.	NM
Canal Zone	CZ	CZ	New York, State of	N.Y.	NY
Colorado, State of	Colo.	CO	North Carolina, State of	N.C.	NC
Connecticut, State of	Conn.	CT	North Dakota, State of	N.D.	ND
Delaware, State of	Del.	DE	Ohio, State of	Ohio	OH
District of Columbia	D.C.	DC	Oklahoma, State of	Okla.	OK
Florida, State of	Fla.	FL	Oregon, State of	Oreg.	OR
Georgia, State of	Ga.	GA	Pennsylvania, Commonwealth of	Pa.	PA
Hawaii, State of	Hawaii	HI	Puerto Rico	P.R.	PR
Idaho, State of	Ida.	ID	Rhode Island and Providence Plantations, State of	R.I.	RI
Illinois, State of	Ill.	IL	South Carolina, State of	S.C.	SC
Indiana, State of	Ind.	IN	South Dakota, State of	S.D.	SD
Iowa, State of	Iowa	IA	Tennessee, State of	Tenn.	TN
Kansas, State of	Kans.	KS	Texas, State of	Tex.	TX
Kentucky, Commonwealth of	Ky.	KY	Utah, State of	Utah	UT
Louisiana, State of	La.	LA	Vermont, State of	Vt.	VT
Maine, State of	Maine	ME	Virgin Islands	V.I.	VI
Maryland, State of	Md.	MD	Virginia, Commonwealth of	Va.	VA
Massachusetts, Commonwealth of	Mass.	MA	Washington, State of	Wash.	WA
Michigan, State of	Mich.	MI	West Virginia, State of	W.Va.	WV
Minnesota, State of	Minn.	MN	Wisconsin, State of	Wis.	WI
Mississippi, State of	Miss.	MS	Wyoming, State of	Wyo.	WY
Missouri, State of	Mo.	MO			
Montana, State of	Mont.	MT			

FIGURE 19 U.S. POSTAL SERVICE ABBREVIATIONS

CHAPTER 6

How Expert Secretaries Use the Telephone

Two factors control the value of the telephone in business contacts—the user's telephone personality and efficiency, and the services offered by the telephone company. This chapter is divided, therefore, into (1) your telephone personality and (2) telephone services.

YOUR TELEPHONE PERSONALITY

Rules of telephone courtesy. The following simple rules constitute the basis of courteous and efficient telephone usage:

1. Answer calls promptly.
2. When you leave your desk, arrange for someone to take your calls. Leave word where you can be located by telephone and when you will return.
3. Keep pad and pencil handy.
4. In asking a caller to wait, ask, "Will you please hold the line while I get the information?" and wait for the reply. When you return to the telephone, thank the caller for waiting. If it will take you some time to get the information, offer to call back.
5. If you have to put the receiver down for any reason, put it down gently.
6. Do not interrupt or be impatient. Listen attentively. Do not make the other party repeat because of inattention on your part.
7. Do not try to talk with a cigarette, pencil, or chewing gum in your mouth.
8. When you have finished talking, say, "Thank you, Mr. Smith," or "Goodbye," pleasantly and replace the receiver gently. Let the caller hang up first.

Placing calls for the manager. The correct practice to follow when you place calls for the manager has developed from expediency. When *you* place the call, it is your privilege to get the person called on the wire before connecting the manager. Assume that you are calling Ms. Nelson for the manager, Mr. Owens. When you get Ms. Nelson's secretary on the wire, you say, "Is Ms. Nelson there, for Mr. Owens of XYZ Company?" Then Ms. Nelson's secretary will put Ms. Nelson on and trust to your good judgment and care to see that Mr. Owens comes on the line promptly. (When a secretary calls your employer, you reciprocate the courtesy.) When Ms. Nelson comes on the line, say to her, "Here is Mr. Owens, Ms. Nelson," and establish the connection between the two at once.

You must be extremely careful not to keep the person called waiting for your manager to take the call. Don't make the call unless he or she is available. On the other hand, it is your job to see that the manager does not hold the phone needlessly. When you are calling a person whose secretary is cooperative and dependable, there is no difficulty because you and she or he can connect your parties simultaneously.

There is an exception to this procedure. If you call a close friend or a person to whom deference is due by the manager, connect the manager as soon as you talk to the secretary at the other end of the line. Tell the manager that the person he or she is calling will be on the line immediately and let him or her receive the call direct. Some secretaries follow this procedure at all times. However, the practice described above is preferred because the person making the call is alert to take it and, therefore, time for both the caller and the person called is saved in the long run.

Some secretaries refuse to put their executives on the line when called until the caller is on the line. If this is their attitude, don't act stubbornly—just connect your manager with the secretary. She or he is undoubtedly acting under orders.

Now that direct dialing makes it so simple to place a call, more and more executives are placing (and taking) their own calls.

When you answer and screen calls for the manager.   Many executives now take their calls directly without having them go through a secretary, unless they are in a conference or do not wish to be disturbed for some other reason. Then, of course, there are some junior executives who think it gives them prestige to have a secretary answer the phone. The junior executive might have his or her hand on the receiver just waiting for the secretary to answer the phone and give the go-ahead signal.

When you are answering the manager's phone and a secretary calls and tells you that "Ms. Nelson of ABC is calling Mr. Owens," ask her or him to wait a moment and announce the call to your manager. Say to the calling secretary, "One moment, please," and tell your manager that "Ms. Nelson of ABC is calling." Your manager will then pick up the phone and wait until Ms. Nelson is connected with him. Or perhaps the other secretary has learned that you are cooperative and she or he puts Ms. Nelson on the line at the same time that you connect the call with your manager.

Screening calls for the manager. Screening calls is far more complicated than just answering the phone for the manager. Many modern executives do not require that their calls be screened, but some are in vulnerable positions where their calls must be screened or they would spend their time answering unnecessary calls.

A polite way of asking who is calling is, "May I tell Mr. Owens who is calling?" Or, "May I ask who is calling?" A legitimate caller seldom objects to giving his or her name. Almost all callers not only volunteer their names but also briefly state their business.

If the party calling does not want to give his or her name, you have the right to insist, politely but firmly, that he or she do so. As a matter of fact, you have no right to put through calls without first screening them, when this is expected of you, and without knowing that the manager is willing to talk. If the caller insists upon withholding his or her name, you might say, very politely, "I'm very sorry but Mr. Owens has someone with him at the moment. If you cannot tell me who is calling, may I suggest that you write to him and mark your letter 'personal'? I'll be glad to see that he gets it at once."

Finding the purpose of a call is necessary when a person telephones for an appointment.

In a new position you are not familiar, of course, with the names of people who have legitimate business with the manager. It is then better for you to err by putting through a few unnecessary calls than by delaying or rejecting important ones. As you become familiar with the manager's business and his or her associates, use your judgment about putting through calls from persons whose names mean nothing to you. Or you can say that the manager is not available at the moment and ask for the caller's telephone number. Then investigate the call and, if necessary, check with the manager. If he or she wants to talk, call the party back in a few minutes. If you learn that the call is a nuisance call, handle it yourself.

Your telephone conversation.   Plan your telephone conversation before placing your call. Know your facts. Know the points you want to cover. If necessary, have an outline of them before you while you talk. Have all records and other material before you. This is particularly important for out-of-town calls.

Keep your telephone conversation brief but not to the point of curtness. Take time to address people by their names and title and to use expressions of consideration, like "Thank you," "I am sorry," and "I beg your pardon." Always say, "Yes, Mr. Adams," or "Yes, sir," not "I see." Avoid slang and expressions such as "Yeah," "Uh-huh," and "Uh-uh."

The importance of your telephone voice.   As you are not face-to-face with your listener, the only way you can show interest in a telephone conversation is by a warm and cordial tone. Today, when the major portion of business contacts are made by telephone, the importance of a gracious and friendly personality, as evidenced by your telephone voice, cannot be overestimated. Guard against the tendency to let your voice become mechanical and without expression. Hold the mouthpiece about one inch from your lips and talk in a pleasant, conversational tone. It is not necessary to shout—just speak distinctly and clearly.

Most important of all is your enunciation. Several numerals and consonants sound much alike over the telephone and, unless spoken with special distinction, cause confusion.

TELEPHONE SERVICE

How to place a local call.   1. Do not call information for a number except when you cannot find it in the telephone directory.

2. Give the person you are calling ample time to answer before you hang up.

3. When the person called answers, identify yourself immediately: "This is Miss Edwards of Prentice-Hall." Or, where appropriate, "Good morning, Mr. Brown [or simply "Mr. Brown"], this is Miss Edwards of Prentice-Hall."

4. If the person who answers the phone is not the one you want or does not identify himself, ask pleasantly for that person and announce your name. "May I speak to Mr. Brown, please? Miss Edwards (of Prentice-Hall) calling."

5. When you do not want any particular person, state your wishes in a nice way, preferably in the form of a request.

> *Examples:* "The rug department, please."
> "I should like some information about————."
> "Please take an order for————."

How to answer incoming calls.   1. Identify yourself.

When there is no switchboard: "Brown & Co., Miss Edwards."

When the operator has previously answered the call: "Advertising Department, Miss Edwards speaking." If several people have the same extension line that you do, it is sometimes confusing to identify yourself. If the caller has asked for another individual, he might think he has the wrong line. Just answer the phone by saying, "Advertising Department. May I help you?" If the caller has asked for someone else, he is actually not interested in your name at this point.

Your own phone: "Miss Edwards speaking."

Another person's phone: "Mr. Brown's office." Where desirable, also give your own name, for example, "Mr. Brown's office, Miss Edwards speaking."

2. When you answer someone else's telephone, and the person called is not available, offer to take a message. Make a record of the caller's name, his affiliation, his telephone number, and the time that he called. See that the person called gets the message immediately upon his return.

3. Do not transfer calls unless necessary.

4. If the person called is talking on another line or is not immediately available for some other reason, ask the caller if he or she prefers to hold the line, to call back, or to leave a message. Go back on the line at near intervals if he or she is holding to give the caller a chance to leave a message

How to transfer calls. Never transfer a call if you can handle it properly yourself or can have the appropriate person take care of it. If you cannot take care of the call yourself, handle it in one of the following ways.

1. Say that you will refer the matter to the appropriate person. In some cases you will want to indicate that the person calling will be called back, but in other cases this will not be necessary.

> *Examples:* "That is something Mr. Rogers looks after. If you wish, I'll tell him about it, and I'm sure he will give it prompt attention."
>
> "That is something Mr. Rogers handles. If you wish, I'll refer it to him and ask him to call you back."

2. Offer to transfer the person calling to someone who can take care of his or her call.

> *Example:* "That is handled by our Credit Department. If you wish, I'll have you connected with them."

3. If you do not know who should handle the matter, tell the person calling that it is not handled by your department but that you will refer it to someone who will take care of it.

> *Example:* "I'm sorry, but that is not handled in this department. If you wish, I'll refer the matter to the appropriate person and ask him to call you back."

When you transfer a call, make sure that the person calling knows what you are doing. Signal the switchboard attendant *slowly* to get her attention. Explain the situation to her so that she will not have to ask the person calling to repeat.

> *Example:* "Will you please connect Mr. Smith [or, "this call"] with Mr. Rogers in the Credit Department?"

Wait for the attendant's reply to be sure she understands correctly.

4. If you offer to transfer the caller and he is annoyed because he has already been transferred several times, apologize, ask him to give you his telephone number and name, and tell him that you will get the appropriate person to return his call within a few minutes.

Of course, you will see that anything you have promised the caller receives prompt attention.

Wrong number!   *You get a wrong number.* If you place a call and receive what appears to be a wrong number, immediately check the telephone number. But do not say, "What is your number?" or "Who is this?" Use, instead, a question that will be more likely to get the information you want, such as, "I beg your pardon, but is this 353-2000?" If it is evident that some error was made, express regret in some way, even if you were not responsible. For example, "I am sorry you were disturbed." If the call was placed through a long-distance operator, and it is obvious that she made an error in dialing, report it to her immediately and you will not be charged for the call.

Someone calls you by mistake. Nothing can be as annoying to a busy secretary trying to get out a rush job as answering the telephone and having the caller say "Wrong number," or simply bang down the receiver. Frequently the caller does not realize he has the wrong number and you receive calls that are not meant for you or anyone else in your office. You should be as tactful with the callers who dialed by mistake as you are with anyone calling on business. Inform the caller politely that he has reached a wrong number, and ask him to check if he has dialed the number he wanted. You might say, "This is the Novelty Publishing Company, and we have no Mr. Brown in this office, sir. Are you sure you dialed the right number?"

If your calls come through a switchboard operator and he connects a call to you through error, signal him and ask him to transfer the call to the appropriate person. Be careful to keep any trace of annoyance out of your voice; the caller can hear what you say to the operator.

You will also get (and place) some wrong interoffice calls. It is sometimes difficult to refrain from telling the caller to learn how to dial, but, as a good secretary, you will be polite—even when the same person repeatedly dials your number by mistake.

Caution: Never abruptly announce, "Wrong number," and hang up. The person who dialed the wrong number may be a customer of your company who read the wrong number from a desk telephone list. He or she may be a personal friend of the manager who confused your number with a similar number on the personal telephone list. You cannot afford to be impolite to people who get wrong numbers.

Station-to-station and person-to-person long-distance calls. A station-to-station call (see the reference to direct distance dialing under "How to place out-of-town calls" below) is made when the caller is willing to talk with anyone who answers the telephone. A person-to-person call is made when the caller must talk to some one person in particular and asks the operator to connect him with a particular person, department, or extension telephone. The three-minute initial period rates for these calls are substantially higher than those for station-to-station calls.

Although a station-to-station call is cheaper, in a few cases it is more economical in the long run to make a person-to-person call. If the person with whom you wish to speak at the called point is extremely difficult to locate, use the person-to-person call, for the time spent in locating the person may run up the cost of a station-to-station call higher than the cost of a person-to-person call.

Variation in rates. Reduced rates apply at certain times daily and all day on Saturday and Sunday to various points. Reduced rates are also in effect at night and on Sunday on calls to many foreign countries. The time at the dialing point governs the application of reduced rates. Consult the front pages of your telephone directory to find out when they are applicable.

Rates on operator-assisted out-of-town calls are based on so much for the first three minutes and for each minute thereafter. Dial-direct calls are based on so much for the first minute and for each minute thereafter. Telephone directories usually give the rates between the principal cities.

How to place out-of-town calls. Direct dialing of long-distance, station-to-station calls is possible throughout this country. You dial the area code number consisting of three numbers and then dial the desired number. You will find in the local telephone directory the code numbers for the various sections in the country. (See also the map of area codes in chapter 24, page 528.) In some sections, it is necessary to dial "1" (or possibly some other digit) before dialing your area code and number. Direct distance dialing is far less expensive than, and thus preferable to, operator-assisted calls. If you reach a wrong number by direct dialing, contact an operator immediately and explain what happened. She will make certain that there is no charge for the call.

When you must place a person-to-person call. Give the operator the name of the place you are calling, then the area code and telephone number you want, and if you wish to talk to a particular person, give his name next. For instance, "Washington, DC, 202-981-4884, Mr. Ames." As soon as you give the operator the name of the place you are calling, she or he begins to make the connection without waiting for the number and name of the person called.

Always supply an out-of-town number if possible.

Stay on the line until the call is completed. You can then supply additional information to the operator or immediately name an alternate to whom you will talk. When a call cannot be completed at once, the operator will follow it up at your request. At regular intervals she or he will try to make a connection with the number you want. Because the operator will do this, it is not necessary to ask her or him to "try it again" or to request another operator to put the call through.

If you do not know the out-of-town number you wish to call, dial the area code, then 555-1212. For example, if you want a telephone number in Westchester County, New York, dial 914-555-1212. An operator in Westchester County will answer and you ask for the telephone number of the party you want to call. The operator will give you the number. There is no charge for this service. Even when you are placing a person-to-person call through the operator, you should ask for the number you want before calling.

Charges on out-of-town calls.   Keep a record of all out-of-town calls so that you can verify the telephone bill and can allocate the charges to the proper account. Your company probably requires certain forms to be filled out on long-distance calls. Be careful to observe these requirements when you place a call through the company switchboard.

You can get the long-distance charge on a call at the time you make it if you ask the operator for it.

If a call must be placed from an outside telephone, there are three ways to handle the charges: have the operator charge the call to your office phone, use a credit card, or place the call collect. The operator may call your office to be certain the charges will be accepted if you ask to charge the call to your office phone. Credit cards are especially convenient when travelling. You simply give the long-distance operator the card number and the number you wish to call. The charges will appear on the next telephone statement. Calls may be placed collect by specifying this when you give the operator the number you wish to call. The person receiving the call, if he accepts it, will then pay the charges.

Messenger calls.   If it is necessary to reach someone who does not have a telephone, the operator at the called point may be authorized to send a messenger for the person desired. Whether or not the call is completed, the caller pays the cost of the messenger's service, which is in addition to the regular person-to-person charge for the call.

Appointment calls.   In placing a person-to-person call, you may specify a certain time that you will talk with a person. The telephone operator will try to put the call through at the exact time. The charge is the same as for a person-to-person call. The advantage of an appointment call is that it saves time.

Conference calls.   Conference service makes it possible for an executive to be connected simultaneously with a number of other stations. No special equipment is required. Suppose that your employer needs to discuss a contract provision with three other people (or any number up to ten) who are in different cities. By means of a conference call he and the other persons can talk back and forth over long-distance as though they were grouped around a conference table.

If your employer so desires, he can speak to a gathering of employees in different cities instead of to individuals. He can do this by having the telephone company install loudspeaker equipment appropriate for the number of listeners. A control dial permits volume adjustment.

In arranging a conference call, ask the long-distance operator to connect you with the conference operator and explain to her the setup you want.

IDDD (International direct-distance dialing).   This service is available from certain cities in the United States to certain countries overseas. To place a call to any of the 18 participating countries, you dial the international access code, country code, city code, and then the local telephone number, which could be a two- to seven-digit number. Check with your local business office for specific information.

Mobile calls—air-land-marine.   You can make local and long-distance calls to automobiles, trucks, aircraft, boats, and ships. Ask the operator for the mobile, marine, or high seas operator, and give her the number and party you wish to reach.

See chapter 7 for information regarding the sending of cables and telegrams by telephone.

Telephone convenience aids.   The telephone company has many devices that increase the usefulness of the telephone system for outside and interoffice calls. They add immeasurably to the convenience of executives and secretaries.

Discuss your telephone problems with the manager. If you are in a large company, the manager will take the matter up with the appropriate person or tell you to. If you are in a small company, the manager will probably give you authority to discuss the problem with the telephone company—if the manager agrees with you, of course. The telephone company can recommend a plan best suited to your needs.

It would be futile to describe here the numerous devices, such as hold buttons and audible and visible signals, that are available. Many even more useful types are being manufactured and placed on the market from time to time.

Companies other than the telephone company also manufacture useful devices that may be attached to the telephone system. The telephone company now permits the use of some of these devices; formerly it did not. Advertisements of these devices will cross your desk from time to time. Do not just throw the ads in the wastebasket without looking at them—they may describe just what you need.

YOUR TELEPHONE
REFERENCE BOOKS

The telephone directory.   The *telephone directory* lists all the business and personal phones in your community, except unlisted numbers and newly installed telephones. The listings include the names of the individuals or companies, their street addresses, and their telephone numbers. They are arranged alphabetically. See the sections on indexing and alphabetizing in chapter 2 for the alphabetical order in which (1) names consisting of letters, e.g., A & Z Pharmacy; (2) compound names, e.g., *North Western* Airlines and *Northwestern* Airlines; and prefixes, e.g., *de Quincy,* are listed.

The telephone directory also helps you by suggesting alternate spellings of a name. At the beginning of the list of telephone subscribers named *Swaringen,* for example, you will find a note reading, "See also Swearingen, Swearingin."

If you make frequent calls to cities other than those listed in your local telephone directory, you can obtain directories for those areas by calling your local telephone business office and requesting them.

Your desk telephone book.   There will be some telephone numbers that you call very often in your work. The handiest way to keep these numbers readily available is a small desk telephone book. Numerous sizes and styles are for sale in stationery stores.

In addition to numbers called frequently on company business, keep the following telephone numbers in your desk telephone list:

Airlines	Railroads
Building manager or superintendent	Residences of employees in your office
Emergency calls (Fire, Police,	Stationer (office supplies)
Ambulance, etc.)	Telegraph office
Express office	Travel agency
Messenger service	Typewriter repairs
Post office	Weather

Personal numbers for the manager. Also keep in your desk telephone list the following personal telephone numbers for your employer:

Bank	Florist
Dentist	Friends whom he or she calls
Doctors	frequently
Family (residence and business)	Garage

Organizations to which he or she belongs
Services (dry cleaner, tailor, etc.)

Stores that he or she trades with
Theater ticket agency

You will have to make a new book from time to time because additions, deletions, and changes will make your book list illegible.

SPECIAL SUGGESTIONS TO INCREASE YOUR SECRETARIAL EFFICIENCY ON THE TELEPHONE

Never ask a caller to wait while you get information and then stay away from the phone so long that he or she hangs up before you return.

When making a business call, identify yourself without waiting to be asked who is calling.

When you receive a call for someone who is not in the office, make a note of it and *do not* forget to give the person the note.

When making a number of calls on a line serving several people, try to space your calls so that others may have a chance to use their phones.

When you place or receive a call for the manager, *do not* get into an argument with another secretary about whose executive should be put on the line first.

When you are making a call for the manager, be sure he or she is ready to speak as soon as the person you are calling is on the line.

Don't chat with a friend who calls you during business hours as though you were at home; *do not* chat with someone who calls the manager.

Before you start a lengthy explanation or conversation with a busy person, ask if the time is convenient for him.

When you make a call, wait for six or seven rings before hanging up.

CHAPTER 7

Telegraph and Cable Information

Up-to-date knowledge of the various types of services that telegraph, cable, and radio companies offer and of their use prevents needless expense. Telegraph companies, both domestic and international, are constantly improving their services and adding new types of services to meet changing business needs. From time to time they issue advertising material and circulars that are well worth the time it takes to read them. These circulars and the personal advice of experienced telegraph people are obtainable at any local office of Western Union, ITT World Communications, and RCA Communications.

Territory covered by domestic telegraph service. Domestic telegraph service includes messages sent by wire to any point in the continental United States, Canada, Mexico, and Saint Pierre and Miquelon Islands. Messages sent to other points are classified as cablegrams.

Classes of domestic service. The classes of domestic telegraph service are (1) fast telegram, (2) mailgram, and (3) night letter.

Fast telegram. The fast telegram is quicker than any other class of service. The charge is based on a minimum of 15 words, with an additional charge for each word in excess of 15. Nothing is gained by condensing the message to less than 15 words. The address and signature are not counted as words. Code may be used. You can get a schedule of rates from Western Union.

Mailgram and ECOM. Mailgrams may be sent by toll-free telephone call, telex, TWX, computer, or tape. Each message is routed by wire to the post office nearest the addressee and printed out individually. Preferential treatment is given to mailgrams assuring their delivery in the next regular mail after being received at the post office—either the same day or the next morning. Similar to the mailgram, ECOM (electronic computer-originated mail) is a new subclass of first-class mail being designed to provide two-day message service.

Night letter. A night letter is the least expensive message service. Delivery is made on the morning of the next day, or the morning of the next business day in the case of a business message. A night letter may be filed with the telegraph company at any time up to 2:00 a.m. The charge is based on a minimum of 100 words, with an additional charge for each *group* of 5 words in excess of 100. The cost of a 100-word night letter is less than the cost of a 15-word fast telegram. If a full rate or fast telegram costs $4.75, the charge for a night letter going to the same city would be about $4.00. Nothing is gained by condensing the night letter to less than 100 words.

Telegraph rates between principal towns. The secretary who sends a number of telegrams should obtain a chart compiled by Western

Union that enables the user to find the rate for a 15-word telegram to the principal cities in every state.

How to type a telegram.   Most companies simply telephone their messages to Western Union. However, if yours is one that prepares typed copy for delivery to Western Union, the following guidelines are useful.

1. The number of copies depends upon the requirements of your company. Four is the usual number if the telegram is to be picked up by a messenger.
   a. The original for pickup by the telegraph messenger
   b. A carbon copy for confirmation by mail
   c. A carbon copy for your file
   d. A carbon copy for the accounting department (or for your telegraph account file if you pay your employer's telegraph bill)
2. Check the class of service in the form provided on the telegraph blank—domestic service in the upper left corner, international service in the upper right corner. Also type the class of service two spaces above the address.
3. Type the date and hour in the upper right corner, two spaces above the address.
4. Omit the salutation and complimentary close.
5. Double space the message.
6. Do not divide words at the ends of lines.
7. Type as you would any other material. Use caps only for code words.
8. In the lower left corner type:
   a. Reference initials
   b. How the message is to be sent—"Charge," "Paid," or "Collect"
   c. Address and telephone number of the sender, unless printed on the blank
9. If the telegram is to be charged, type the name of the charge account in the space provided on the blank.

How to send the same message to multiple addresses.   If you want to send the message to a number of people, type the telegram text only once. List the names and addresses on a special sheet obtainable from Western Union (or on a plain sheet). Above the list type "Please send the attached message to the following 12 (whatever the number is) addresses."

HOW CHARGES FOR TELEGRAMS ARE COUNTED

Addresses.   No charge is made for essential material in one complete address. A charge is made for alternate names or addresses. No charge is made for notations, such as "personal," "will call," and the like. The telegram may be addressed to the attention of a specific individual without charge.

Signature and address of sender.   No charge is made for the name of the sender. The city and state from which the message is sent are included in the dateline free of charge, but a charge is made for the sender's street address if it is to be transmitted. The signature may include the company name and the name of the individual sending the telegram without charge, but a charge is made for the name of a department added to such a signature.

States, countries, and cities.   In the message itself, names of states, countries, and cities are counted according to the number of words they contain. For example, "New York City" is three words, "United States" is two. Running the words together as "Newyork" does not affect the count. If the names are abbreviated, they count as one word. Thus, "NYC" is one word.

Abbreviations.   Abbreviations that do not contain more than five letters are counted as one word. They should be written without spaces or periods—COD, UN, FOB.

Initials.   If separated by a space, initials are counted as separate words, but if written without spaces, they are counted as one word for each five letters or fraction thereof. Thus, R L is counted as two words, but RL is one word.

Personal names.   Personal names are counted in accordance with the way they are usually written. Thus, Van der Gren is counted as three words; Van Dorn, as two words; and O'Connell, as one word.

Mixed groups of letters and figures.   Mixed groups of letters, figures, and the characters $, /, &, #, ' (indicating feet or minutes) and " (indicating inches or seconds) are counted at the rate of five characters, or fraction thereof, to the word in messages between points in the United States and between points in Mexico. Thus, "one hundred" is counted as two words, but 100 is counted as one word; $34.50, as one word (the decimal is not counted); 44B42, as one word, but 1000th (six characters) is counted as two words.

In messages sent to Canada and Saint Pierre and Miquelon Islands, each figure, affix, bar, dash, and sign in a group is counted as a word.

Punctuation marks.   Punctuation marks are not charged for, but the words "stop," "comma," and the like are counted.

Compound words.   Compound words that are hyphenated in the dictionary are counted as one word. Thus, "son-in-law" is one word. Combinations of two or more dictionary words are counted according to the number of words of which they are composed. Thus, "highschool" and "Newyears" are each counted as two words.

HOW TO ECONOMIZE ON TELEGRAMS AND CABLEGRAMS

Plans for economy.   In trying to make economies in the use of telegraphic service, consider three things.

1. The urgency of the message
2. Time differentials
3. The wording of the message

Urgency of message.   In some cases delivery on the same day may be essential; in others delivery on the morning of the following day would be satisfactory. The fastest service is, of course, the most expensive; it should therefore be used where speed is necessary. A description of the various types of domestic messages is given on page 147; of the various types of cable and radio messages, page 152.

Time differentials.   Consider the variations in standard time in different parts of the United States and in different countries in choosing the class of service by which to send a message. The following is an illustration of how money can be saved by giving considerations to time differentials.

At 3:30 in the afternoon a secretary in San Francisco is told to send a 19-word telegram to New York City. Since it is 6:30 in New York City and the people to whom the message is being sent have probably left the office for the day, the secretary suggests sending a night letter. The rate for a night letter is, let us say, $4.00. By considering the time differential, the secretary saves her company approximately 30 percent on one telegram without affecting the delivery time of the telegram.

The following list shows the standard time in different parts of the country when it is 12 o'clock noon Eastern Standard Time, and Figure 20 shows the location of time belts in the United States.

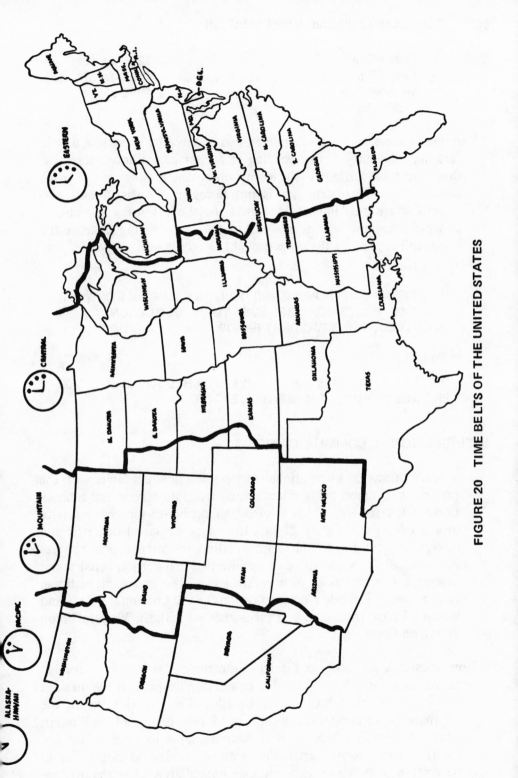

FIGURE 20   TIME BELTS OF THE UNITED STATES

```
Eastern Time  . . . . . . . . . . . . . . . . 12:00 noon
Central Time  . . . . . . . . . . . . . . . . 11:00 a.m.
Mountain Time  . . . . . . . . . . . . . . . 10:00 a.m.
Pacific Time  . . . . . . . . . . . . . . . .  9:00 a.m.
```

Wording of message.   Much money can be saved by exercising a little care and ingenuity in the wording of a message. Although terseness should not be carried to the point where the message is not clear, complete sentence structure is not necessary. Verbs, nouns, and adjectives are the important words. In the following example a 23-word telegram was nearly cut in half by deleting unnecessary words and expressing the same thought clearly in only 14 words.

23 words:

> WE ARE IN NEED OF PRICE AND DELIVERY SCHEDULE ON YOUR AEC-1400 PROCESSOR. BELIEVE YOUR QUOTATION OF 14 AUGUST CONTAINS TWO-DIGIT ERROR.

14 words:

> REQUEST NEW PRICE AND DELIVERY SCHEDULE ON AEC-1400 PROCESSOR. AUGUST 14 QUOTE IN ERROR.

INTERNATIONAL COMMUNICATIONS

Many forms of international services are now available, with the two most common being international telegram service and international telex service, which is direct subscriber-to-subscriber service over a teleprinter. Figure 21 lists the major classes of domestic and foreign service; for complete information on international services you can call the local office of an international carrier, listed under Telegraph Companies in your yellow pages. The major international carriers are ITT World Communications, RCA Communications and Western Union International (not associated with the Western Union Telegraph Company).

How messages are sent to foreign countries.   Messages to foreign countries are sent by cable, radio, or satellite facilities. If the message is to be sent by telex, it may be filed directly with any of the international carriers; if it is to be sent by cablegram, call the Western Union Telegraph office. If it is desired that a message go by any specific international carrier, the name of the desired carrier should be written or typed on each message immediately after the destina-

Domestic Service	
Class	*Nature of Service*
Fast telegram	Fastest (same-day or next-day) delivery
Mailgram	Fast (next regular delivery after receipt at P.O.) delivery
Night letter	Least expensive service.

Foreign Service	
Class	*Nature of Service*
Full-rate messages	Standard fast service
Letter telegram, or night letter	Overnight (least expensive) service
Shore-to-ship/ship-to-shore	Radio communication at sea
Radio photo service	Photo transmission by radio
Overseas Telex service	Direct, two-way communication by keyboard

FIGURE 21   MAJOR CLASSES OF DOMESTIC AND FOREIGN SERVICES

tion. (Example: Via ITT, Via RCA, Via WUI.) This routing of international messages will often save time in the transmission of the message, and involves no extra cost. The services and rates described below are available through all international carriers except where otherwise indicated.

Full-rate message (FR). This is the standard fast service for messages in plain or secret (coded or cyphered) language. The charge per word varies according to the destination and generally does not exceed 34 cents per word. There is a minimum charge of seven words. Both the address and the signature are counted in the charge. See page 158 for the method of determining charges.

Letter telegram (LT). Letter telegrams (sometimes known as night letters) provide an overnight service designed for messages of some length that need not arrive before the next day. Letter telegrams may be written in plain language only; however, registered code addresses may be used (see below). The charge for letter telegrams is half the full-rate charge per word with a minimum of 22 words. The address and signature are counted in the charge as well as the indicator "LT,"

Aleutian Islands Tutuila, Samoa	Alaska Hawaiian Islands	Tahiti	SanFrancisco & Pacific Coast	Chicago Central America (except Panama) Mexico, Winnipeg	Bogota, Havana Lima, Montreal Bermuda New York, Panama	Buenos Aires Santiago Puerto Rico Lapaz, Asuncion	Rio, Santos Sao Paulo	Iceland	Algiers, Lisbon London, Paris Madrid	G.M.T.
1:00pm	2:00pm	2:00pm	4:00pm	6:00pm	7:00pm	8:00pm	9:00pm	11:00pm	MIDNIGHT	0000
2:00pm	3:00pm	3:00pm	5:00pm	7:00pm	8:00pm	9:00pm	10:00pm	MINUIT	1:00am	0100
3:00pm	4:00pm	4:00pm	6:00pm	8:00pm	9:00pm	10:00pm	11:00pm	1:00am	2:00am	0200
4:00pm	5:00pm	5:00pm	7:00pm	9:00pm	10:00pm	11:00pm	Medianoche	2:00am	3:00am	0300
5:00pm	6:00pm	6:00pm	8:00pm	10:00pm	11:00pm	MIDNIGHT	1:00am	3:00am	4:00am	0400
6:00pm	7:00pm	7:00pm	9:00pm	11:00pm	MINUIT	1:00am	2:00am	4:00am	5:00am	0500
7:00pm	8:00pm	8:00pm	10:00pm	Medianoche	1:00am	2:00am	3:00am	5:00am	6:00am	0600
8:00pm	9:00pm	9:00pm	11:00pm	1:00am	2:00am	3:00am	4:00am	6:00am	7:00am	0700
9:00pm	10:00pm	10:00pm	MIDNIGHT	2:00am	3:00am	4:00am	5:00am	7:00am	8:00am	0800
10:00pm	11:00pm	11:00pm	1:00am	3:00am	4:00am	5:00am	6:00am	8:00am	9:00am	0900
11:00pm	Medianoche	MINUIT	2:00am	4:00am	5:00am	6:00am	7:00am	9:00am	10:00am	1000
MIDNIGHT	1:00am	1:00am	3:00am	5:00am	6:00am	7:00am	8:00am	10:00am	11:00am	1100
1:00am	2:00am	2:00am	4:00am	6:00am	7:00am	8:00am	9:00am	11:00am	NOON	1200
2:00am	3:00am	3:00am	5:00am	7:00am	8:00am	9:00am	10:00am	MIDI	1:00pm	1300
3:00am	4:00am	4:00am	6:00am	8:00am	9:00am	10:00am	11:00am	1:00pm	2:00pm	1400
4:00am	5:00am	5:00am	7:00am	9:00am	10:00am	11:00am	Mediodia	2:00pm	3:00pm	1500
5:00am	6:00am	6:00am	8:00am	10:00am	11:00am	NOON	1:00pm	3:00pm	4:00pm	1600
6:00am	7:00am	7:00am	9:00am	11:00am	MIDI	1:00pm	2:00pm	4:00pm	5:00pm	1700
7:00am	8:00am	8:00am	10:00am	Mediodia	1:00pm	2:00pm	3:00pm	5:00pm	6:00pm	1800
8:00am	9:00am	9:00am	11:00am	1:00pm	2:00pm	3:00pm	4:00pm	6:00pm	7:00pm	1900
9:00am	10:00am	10:00am	NOON	2:00pm	3:00pm	4:00pm	5:00pm	7:00pm	8:00pm	2000
10:00am	11:00am	11:00am	1:00pm	3:00pm	4:00pm	5:00pm	6:00pm	8:00pm	9:00pm	2100
11:00am	Mediodia	MIDI	2:00pm	4:00pm	5:00pm	6:00pm	7:00pm	9:00pm	10:00pm	2200
NOON	1:00pm	1:00pm	3:00pm	5:00pm	6:00pm	7:00pm	8:00pm	10:00pm	11:00pm	2300
1:00pm	2:00pm	2:00pm	4:00pm	6:00pm	7:00pm	8:00pm	9:00pm	11:00pm	MIDNIGHT	2400

FIGURE 22   INTERNATIONAL TIME CHART

which must be inserted before the address. Letter telegram messages are delivered generally after 8:00 a.m. local time the day after filing. Certain Pacific and European countries have special rules.

Shore-to-ship and ship-to-shore radio.   This service permits communication by radio with individuals aboard ships at sea. Give the name of the passenger (in full since there may be more than one with the same last name aboard), his or her stateroom (if known), the ship, and the radio station in the address.

> Walter Scott
> Stateroom 61B
> SS LIBERTE
> Newyorkradio (Via ITT or RCA)

Addresses and signatures are counted as in other international messages. Messages may be filed with ITT World Communications or

Bengasi, Berlin Oslo, Rome, Tunis Tripoli, Warsaw Stockholm	Cairo, Capetown Istanbul, Moscow	Ethiopia, Iraq Madagascar	Bombay, Ceylon New Delhi	Chungking Chengtu, Kunming	Celebes, Hong Kong Manila, Shanghai	Korea, Japan Adelaide	Brisbane, Guam Melbourne, New Guinea, Sydney	Solomon Islands New Caledonia	Wellington* Auckland*
1:00am	2:00am	3:00am	5:30am	7:00am	8:00am	9:00am	10:00am	11:00am	11:30am
2:00am	3:00am	4:00am	6:30am	8:00am	9:00am	10:00am	11:00am	MIDI	12:30pm
3:00am	4:00am	5:00am	7:30am	9:00am	10:00am	11:00am	Mediodia	1:00pm	1:30pm
4:00am	5:00am	6:00am	8:30am	10:00am	11:00am	NOON	1:00pm	2:00pm	2:30pm
5:00am	6:00am	7:00am	9:30am	11:00am	MIDI	1:00pm	2:00pm	3:00pm	3:30pm
6:00am	7:00am	8:00am	10:30am	Mediodia	1:00pm	2:00pm	3:00pm	4:00pm	4:30pm
7:00am	8:00am	9:00am	11:30am	1:00pm	2:00pm	3:00pm	4:00pm	5:00pm	5:30pm
8:00am	9:00am	10:00am	12:30pm	2:00pm	3:00pm	4:00pm	5:00pm	6:00pm	6:30pm
9:00am	10:00am	11:00am	1:30pm	3:00pm	4:00pm	5:00pm	6:00pm	7:00pm	7:30pm
10:00am	11:00am	NOON	2:30pm	4:00pm	5:00pm	6:00pm	7:00pm	8:00pm	8:30pm
11:00am	MIDI	1:00pm	3:30pm	5:00pm	6:00pm	7:00pm	8:00pm	9:00pm	9:30pm
Mediodia	1:00pm	2:00pm	4:30pm	6:00pm	7:00pm	8:00pm	9:00pm	10:00pm	10:30pm
1:00pm	2:00pm	3:00pm	5:30pm	7:00pm	8:00pm	9:00pm	10:00pm	11:00pm	11:30pm
2:00pm	3:00pm	4:00pm	6:30pm	8:00pm	9:00pm	10:00pm	11:00pm	MINUIT	12:30am
3:00pm	4:00pm	5:00pm	7:30pm	9:00pm	10:00pm	11:00pm	Medianoche	1:00am	1:30am
4:00pm	5:00pm	6:00pm	8:30pm	10:00pm	11:00pm	MIDNIGHT	1:00am	2:00am	2:30am
5:00pm	6:00pm	7:00pm	9:30pm	11:00pm	MINUIT	1:00am	2:00am	3:00am	3:30am
6:00pm	7:00pm	8:00pm	10:30pm	Medianoche	1:00am	2:00am	3:00am	4:00am	4:30am
7:00pm	8:00pm	9:00pm	11:30pm	1:00am	2:00am	3:00am	4:00am	5:00am	5:30am
8:00pm	9:00pm	10:00pm	12:30am	2:00am	3:00am	4:00am	5:00am	6:00am	6:30am
9:00pm	10:00pm	11:00pm	1:30am	3:00am	4:00am	5:00am	6:00am	7:00am	7:30am
10:00pm	11:00pm	MIDNIGHT	2:30am	4:00am	5:00am	6:00am	7:00am	8:00am	8:30am
11:00pm	MINUIT	1:00am	3:30am	5:00am	6:00am	7:00am	8:00am	9:00am	9:30am
Medianoche	1:00am	2:00am	4:30am	6:00am	7:00am	8:00am	9:00am	10:00am	10:30am
1:00am	2:00am	3:00am	5:30am	7:00am	8:00am	9:00am	10:00am	11:00am	11:30am

RCA Communications directly, or with the Western Union Telegraph Company who will transfer them to the international carrier indicated by the routing indicator marked on the message.

Radio photo service. This service covers the transmission of photographs by radio. Among the types of material suitable for transmission are financial statements, machine drawings, production curves, fashion designs, architectural designs, typewritten matter, printed matter, affidavits, contracts, signatures, and business and legal papers of all kinds. Photo service is available to the public through Mackay Radio and RCA Communications, Inc.

Registered code addresses. A charge is made for both the address and the signature in all messages sent to foreign countries. However, a registered code address and signature may be used. They obviate the expense incurred in using full addresses and signatures. Registered code addresses must be arranged locally. They may be registered with the Central Bureau of Registered Addresses, 67 Broad Street, New York, NY 10004; with international carriers maintaining offices in Washington, DC and San Francisco (ITT World Communications and RCA Communications); or with any Western Union Telegraph Company office. The addresses need only be registered with one carrier in each city, which will supply the local office of other carriers with each new registration.

Direct international services.   Recent technical advances in overseas communications are making it possible to obtain direct and private connections for one- or two-way keyboard operation across the oceans. Western Union Cables has inaugurated a service of this type, known as International Metered Communications, providing a direct teleprinter connection between the New York and London offices of the subscriber, over which keyboard conversations are carried on as desired. This service is paid for on the basis of electrical pulses.

Similar in operation, but charged for on a time basis, International Telex Service provided by Mackay Radio and TEX service provided by RCA Communications offer teletypewriter-to-teletypewriter service with a large number of countries. Charges vary from $2.00 to $3.00 per minute, with a three-minute minimum. All TWX subscribers may use this service to place calls or to send cablegrams and radiograms as the TWX system is now owned by Western Union and has been integrated with the telex system by computer.

Another service that comes in this category is Leased Channel Service, which offers an economical means of direct wire communication to large-volume users. This service permits the user to rent a channel, operated at a desired speed, on a daily basis.

International time charts.   The ITT World Communications Time Chart is shown in Figure 22. When passing a line to the left, subtract one day. When passing a line to the right, add one day. The simplified chart illustrated in Figure 23 was also compiled by the ITT World Communications System. It shows how to calculate time in foreign countries when you know Eastern Standard Time.

Overseas telex service.   Many firms now have teleprinters in their offices. These are machines similar to typewriters that communicate directly with another similar machine in other parts of the world to

To determine STANDARD TIME overseas
add (+) to or subtract (-) from
EASTERN STANDARD TIME as indicated:

	E.S.T.		E.S.T.		E.S.T.
Afghanistan	+9½	Finland	+7	Norway	+6
Albania	+6	Formosa	+13	Pakistan	+10 (5)*
Algeria	+6	France	+6	Panama	0
Argentina	+2	Germany	+6	Paraguay	+1
Aruba	+½	Ghana	+5	Peru	0
Australia	+15 (1)*	Great Britain	+5	Philippines	+13
Austria	+6	Greece	+7	Poland	+6 (6)*
Azores	+3	Guatemala	-1	Portugal	+5
Belgian Congo	+6 (2)*	Haiti	0	Puerto Rico	+1
Belgium	+6	Hawaii	-5	Rhodesia	+7
Bermuda	+1	Hungary	+6	Roumania	+7
Bolivia	+1	Iceland	+4	Salvador (El)	-1
Borneo (Br)	+13	India	+10½	Saudi Arabia	+8 (7)*
Brazil	+2 (3)*	Iran	+8½	Singapore	+12½
Bulgaria	+7	Iraq	+8	Spain	+6
Burma	+11½	Irish Republic	+5	Surinam	+1½
Canal Zone	0	Israel	+7	Sweden	+6
Ceylon	+10½	Italy	+6	Switzerland	+6
Chile	+1	Japan	+14	Syria	+7
China	+13 (4)*	Korea	+13½	Thailand	+12
Colombia	0	Lebanon	+7	Tunisia	+6
Costa Rica	-1	Luxembourg	+6	Turkey	+7
Cuba	0	Madagascar	+8	Union of South Africa	+7
Curacao	+½	Malaya	+12½	USSR	+8 (8)*
Czechoslovakia	+6	Morocco	+5	Uruguay	+2
Denmark	+6	Netherlands	+6	Venezuela	+½
Dominican Republic	0	Netherlands Antilles	+½	Vietnam	+12
Ecuador	0	Newfoundland	+1½	Virgin Islands	+1
Egypt	+7	New Zealand	+17	Yugoslavia	+6
Ethiopia	+8	Nicaragua	-1		

Note: (1)* Brisbane, Canberra, Melbourne,
New South Wales, Sydney, Queensland.
(2)* Leopoldville.
(3)* Rio de Janeiro, Sao Paulo, Santos.
(4)* Hong Kong, Peiping, Shanghai, Tientsin.
(5)* Karachi   (6)* Warsaw   (7)* Djeddah   (8)* Moscow

FIGURE 23   INTERNATIONAL TIME DIFFERENTIALS

give a "conversation in writing." All of the international carriers provide their own teleprinters in the cities in which they operate. In other places, Western Union Telegraph Company telex machines or Western Union TWX machines connect with the international carriers.

If you have a machine furnished by one of the international carriers, you will have with it an instruction booklet showing how to make international calls. If the machine is a Western Union Telegraph Company telex machine or a Western Union TWX machine, you must call the international carrier first and then select the number overseas. It is best to obtain the instruction book for your particular machine from one of the carriers. This will give you all the details.

In telex, charges are based on time used, as with a telephone, rather than the number of words sent. The speed of operation on international circuits is about 66 words per minute, set by an international standard. Some telex machines have tape perforators that allow the message to be prepared beforehand and then transmitted automatically at the full speed of the machine. Minimum charge to most parts of the world is three minutes, but some countries with fully automatic service have a one-minute minimum.

International leased channel service. This service provides a private telegraph channel available to a company between two points on a daily basis. It is rented from the international carriers on a fixed charge regardless of usage. This permits greater speed and economy for high volumes. A much larger quantity of information can be sent at a much lower cost than by either message or telex. It is a channel rented on a daily basis for any one of a number of different speeds.

The Pocket Guide. ITT World Communications, 67 Broad Street, New York, NY 10004, issues a kit called the Pocket Guide to International Communications that serves as a reference guide and information kit for different types of international communications. It answers questions on all types of problems encountered when sending messages or telex calls overseas. It includes factual information on holidays in various countries, a slide computer for finding the time in various parts of the world, and an introductory booklet on how to get the most efficient and economical service when communicating abroad.

HOW CHARGES FOR CABLES ARE COUNTED

Addresses. In the address, the name of the place of destination, including the name of the country when it is necessary, is counted as one word regardless of the number of letters it contains. The names of persons or streets may be run together and counted as 15 letters, or fraction thereof, to the word. For example: STJAMESSTREET is one word, but St. James Street is counted as three words. Registered code addresses may be used.

Signature and address of sender.   A charge is made for each word, but the cable need not be signed or it may be signed with a code signature.

Plain language messages.   In plain language messages, each word containing 15 letters or less is counted as one word; each word containing more than 15 letters is counted at the rate of 15 letters to the word.

Code messages.   Secret language words (code or cypher) are counted at the rate of five characters, or fraction thereof, to the word. These messages may only be sent full rate.

Mixed groups of letters and figures.   A group of figures, or figures and letters, is counted at the rate of five characters, or fraction thereof, to the word. These may be sent in LT telegrams. Dollar signs or pounds sterling signs cannot be sent, and if written in the message will be translated into DLRS or POUNDS and charged at the rate of one word. Fractions bars, commas, and decimals are counted with figure groups as a character each.

Abbreviations.   Commercial marks and abbreviations, such as FOB (free on board), CIF (cost, insurance, and freight) and the like are permitted and are counted as one word for every five characters. Abbreviations contrary to common usage will be sent as code words and as such must be sent full rate.

Punctuation.   Punctuation marks, hyphens, and apostrophes are not transmitted except where expressly requested, and then they are charged as a separate word each.

How to Make
CHAPTER
8
Travel Arrangements

In this space age of travel, it is not unusual for a manager to make weekly trips across the continent, or overnight trips to a nearby city—or he or she may commute regularly to Europe. The trips may be for business, pleasure, or a combination of business and pleasure. The manager may schedule trips in advance or make them unexpectedly, but you have to be prepared to handle your secretarial responsibilities in either case. This chapter not only gives you basic travel information, but suggests how you can carry out your secretarial responsibilities by speeding the manager on a successful mission.

Use of travel agents. A travel service is indispensable in making plans for foreign business; many business concerns also have an agency make all travel reservations for domestic business trips as well. A company may open an account with an agency and be billed once a month, thus avoiding the nuisance of paying for numerous tickets throughout the month.

A travel agent will procure all the necessary tickets, map out an itinerary, arrange hotel accommodations, arrange to have a rented car awaiting the manager at his or her destination, and perform many other services that will save you time and worry. You can make one phone call and be sure of getting the best schedule and best routing, even though more than one airline is involved. The travel agent represents all companies and is partial to none. (For use of travel agents for extensive trips, see pages 175-177.)

Even if your company has an account with a travel agency, you act as liaison between the agency and the manager. It is your responsibility to see that the desired arrangements are provided without any inconvenience to the manager.

Your responsibilities in arranging the manager's business trips. In arranging a business trip for the manager, here is what you do:

1. Get transportation information and submit a time-and-route schedule to the manager.
2. Make transportation and hotel reservations. (If it is necessary to write for reservations, follow the sample letters on pages 287-288.)
3. Pick up the tickets.
4. Prepare the travel itinerary and appointment schedule.
5. Assemble business data and supplies to be taken on the trip.
6. Prepare baggage identification labels and furnish baggage information.
7. Make financial arrangements for the trip.
8. Give the hotel confirmations and tickets to the manager.
9. If there are to be any formal occasions, such as dinners and conventions, try to find out what type of formal attire your employer will need to take.

How to get information about transportation. The manager will usually tell you which mode of transportation he or she intends to use. Sometimes certain information is needed to make a choice, such as:

1. What airline or railway may be used
2. Time schedules
3. Plane and train (dining and sleeping facilities, etc.) accommodations
4. Car rental arrangements at destination
5. Cost
6. Baggage facilities

MAKING TRAVEL AND HOTEL RESERVATIONS

Checklist of information needed from the manager.   Today's business executive usually travels by plane, but circumstances may prompt him to choose an overnight sleeper. Therefore, before making reservations for the trip, you will have to know not only where the manager plans to go, but also the method of transportation he or she prefers. You need the following information to make travel and hotel reservations:

1. Destination
2. Desired departure time (morning, afternoon, evening, or night)
3. Desired arrival and departure times for stopovers
4. Preferred transportation (plane, train, or automobile)
5. Travel accommodations desired
6. Whether or not a rental car is desired
7. Hotel preference and accommodations desired at destination

For an automobile trip, the manager will want to know the routes, day-to-day mileage, and the cities or towns at which to stop overnight.

How to submit preliminary time and route information to the manager.   If there is more than one airline servicing the city that the manager is planning to visit, list each airline together with departure and arrival times and submit the schedule to your employer so that he or she may determine which one is the most convenient.

In some cases railway transportation may be more convenient or desirable. If traveling by train is more convenient, give the manager a schedule showing information about departure and arrival times, railway lines to be used, and ticket information.

If the contemplated trip has several laps, submit the information for each lap on a separate sheet. This information is also helpful when making reservations.

List the major car rental facilities available in each city on the itinerary.

Planes and trains are usually scheduled on Standard Time at the place named in the timetable—Eastern Standard, Central Standard, and so on. (See page 151 for a time zone map.) Call the change in time to the manager's attention so that he will not think the trip consumes more or less time than it does.

What to do about delay in getting reservations. Frequently you cannot get space when you try to reserve it. The airline or railroad will then enter your request and notify you if the space later becomes available. In this case also put in your request with another airline or railroad. *As soon as you are given space on one line, cancel your requests to the others.* You keep the good will of transportation companies by promptly canceling any space that you are not going to use.

Payment for, and delivery of, tickets. Airlines and railroads, especially airlines, make it easy to obtain and pay for tickets. Most companies whose personnel travel extensively open charge accounts with some airlines and railroads. Individuals who make many trips can open similar accounts on the basis of their personal credit and receive credit cards. Each airline has its own method of making travel easy for the manager and of saving the secretary time otherwise used in picking up tickets and paying for them. Even if the manager does not have a charge account with the airline, if time is available you can telephone the airlines (some of them), make your reservation, and request that the ticket be mailed. Immediately upon receipt of the ticket in your office, send a check to the airline. Of course, the ticket is not valid until the airline receives the manager's check. When you make an arrangement of this kind, you must be sure that there is ample time for receipt of the ticket by you, and, in turn, receipt of the check by the airline. Should the manager change plans before you mail the check, simply return the unused ticket to the airline.

Careful check of the tickets. Always be sure to check any tickets carefully against the information you gathered in making the reservation.

Plane tickets. Check plane tickets for these points:
- Are the flight numbers correct?
- What about time of departure?

- Is the plane leaving from the airport you assumed it was leaving from?
- Is the city of destination the city to which your employer wants to travel?
- And last but not least, is the reservation on the airline you assumed it was on? The *name* of the airline is not on the ticket; only the *airline letter code* appears on the ticket. If the trip has several laps the ticket will show the code of the airline being used for each lap. Letter codes for the major airlines follow.

AIRLINE LETTER CODES FOR MAJOR AIRLINES

AC	Air Canada	KL	KLM
AF	Air France	LH	Lufthansa German Airlines
JM	Air Jamaica	MI	Mackey International Airlines
NE	Air New England	NA	National Airlines
FJ	Air Pacific	NY	New York Airways
AS	Alaska Airlines	NC	North Central Airlines
AZ	Alitalia	NW	Northwest Airlines
AL	Allegheny Airlines	OA	Olympic Airways
TS	Aloha Airlines	OZ	Ozark Airlines
AA	American Airlines	PW	Pacific Western
BN	Braniff International Airways	PA	Pan American World Airways
BA	British Airways	PI	Piedmont Airlines
CO	Continental Airlines	QF	Qantas Airways, Ltd.
DL	Delta Air Lines	SN	Sabena World Airlines
EA	Eastern Airlines	SK	Scandinavian Airlines
AY	Finnair	SO	Southern Airways
FL	Frontier Airlines	SR	Swissair
HA	Hawaiian Air	TP	TAP
RW	Hughes Air West	TI	Texas International Airlines
IB	Iberia Airlines	TW	Trans World Airlines
LL	Icelandic Airlines	UA	United Airlines
IN	Irish International Airlines	RG	Varig Airlines
JL	Japan Air Lines	WA	Western Airlines

Train tickets. Before giving train tickets to the manager, check them carefully for information similar to that for the plane tickets. Check these points: time, date, destination, train number, accommodations, and railway station.

How to make hotel reservations. If you are using a travel agent, the agent will take care of hotel reservations according to your specifications or will make suggestions regarding hotel accommodations. If your employer has no hotel preference, is not familiar with the hotels in a city where he or she expects to stop, and is not using a travel agent, you can get detailed information by consulting the latest editions of *Hotel Guide and Travel Index,* published by Ziff-Davis Publishing Company, Inc., 1 Park Avenue, New York, New York 10016, and the *Official Hotel Red Book and Directory,* published by the American Hotel Association Directory Corporation, New York. The number of rooms and the price enable you to judge the class of hotel. Or you can call a local hotel association or write to the Chamber of Commerce in the city of destination.

Some credit card organizations, associations, and larger hotel and motel chains provide a nationwide reservation service. Information in the folders offered to members of the American Automobile Association and in *Lodging for a Night,* a book published by Duncan Hines, Inc., New York, guides the traveler to good hotels, inns, overnight guest houses, and motels in the United States, Canada, and Mexico.

When making a hotel reservation, give the name of the person for whom the reservation is to be made, the time of arrival and probable time of departure, and the type of accommodation desired. Also inquire about the checking-out time and include this information in the memorandum that you give your employer when he starts on his trip. The reservation can be made by telephone, telegraph, or letter. Examples of letters making hotel reservations are given on page 288.

Always get confirmations of hotel reservations in writing or by wire and attach them to the copy of the itinerary that your employer takes with him (see Figure 24). This applies whether you make the reservation for your employer or whether it is made for him by someone in the place to which he is going.

If you must reserve rooms for a large meeting, such as a conference, it is best to speak directly with the sales manager at one of the larger hotels in the city where the meeting is scheduled. Hotels provide valuable assistance in arranging for group reservations, in selecting appropriate meeting rooms and other facilities, and in handling the many other details that are involved.

SECRETARIAL PREPARATIONS FOR THE MANAGER'S BUSINESS TRIP

When you make travel and hotel reservations for the manager, you

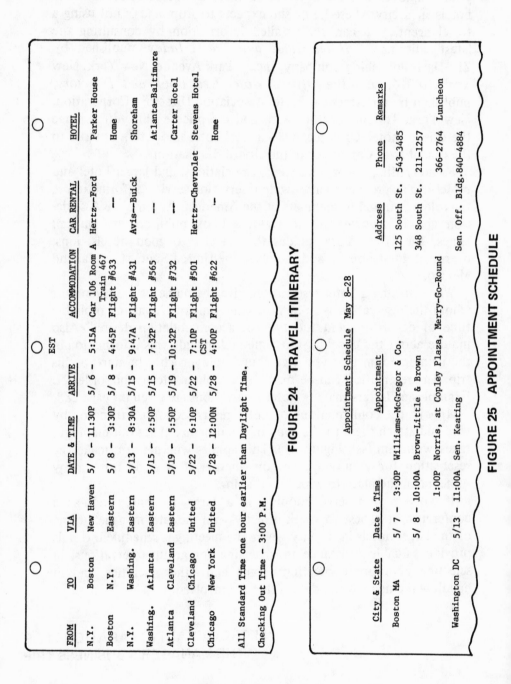

FIGURE 24 TRAVEL ITINERARY

| | | | | EST | | | |
FROM	TO	VIA	DATE & TIME	ARRIVE	ACCOMMODATION	CAR RENTAL	HOTEL
N.Y.	Boston	New Haven	5/ 6 – 11:30P	5/ 6 – 5:15A	Car 106 Room A Train #467	Hertz—Ford	Parker House
Boston	N.Y.	Eastern	5/ 8 – 3:30P	5/ 8 – 4:45P	Flight #633	—	Home
N.Y.	Washing.	Eastern	5/13 – 8:30A	5/15 – 9:47A	Flight #431	Avis—Buick	Shoreham
Washing.	Atlanta	Eastern	5/15 – 2:50P	5/15 – 7:32P	Flight #565	—	Atlanta-Baltimore
Atlanta	Cleveland	Eastern	5/19 – 5:50P	5/19 – 10:32P	Flight #732	—	Carter Hotel
Cleveland	Chicago	United	5/22 – 6:10P	5/22 – 7:10P CST	Flight #501	Hertz—Chevrolet	Stevens Hotel
Chicago	New York	United	5/28 – 12:00N	5/28 – 4:00P	Flight #622	—	Home

All Standard Time one hour earlier than Daylight Time.

Checking Out Time – 3:00 P.M.

Appointment Schedule   May 8–28

City & State	Date & Time	Appointment	Address	Phone	Remarks
Boston MA	5/ 7 – 3:30P	Williams-McGregor & Co.	125 South St.	543-3485	
	5/ 8 – 10:00A	Brown-Little & Brown	348 South St.	211-1257	
	1:00P	Norris, at Copley Plaza, Merry-Go-Round		366-2764	Luncheon
Washington DC	5/13 – 11:00A	Sen. Keating	Sen. Off. Bldg.	840-4884	

FIGURE 25 APPOINTMENT SCHEDULE

are acting as his or her travel agent. There are also many secretarial jobs relating to necessary preparations for the manager's trip.

How to make car rental arrangements. On a trip involving several stops, the manager may prefer to travel from city to city by car or may prefer to have a car available for appointments within a particular city. The major car rental facilities at each stop should be listed on the itinerary you prepare. If he indicates that a car will be needed, you can phone in advance for reservations and have a car waiting for him at the airport or train station. Upon arrival he need only show his driver's license; payment is most frequently arranged by use of one of the major credit cards.

How to prepare the itinerary and hotel information. Type an itinerary for the manager showing points of departure and arrival; airline or railroad; dates and time of departure and arrival; accommodation; available car rental facilities; hotel. Figure 24 is an illustration of an itinerary.

Type the itinerary on strong, durable paper in triplicate—a copy for the manager, a copy for his or her family, and a copy for your file. Also make a copy for anyone in the organization who needs it and is entitled to it. If you are working with a travel agent, he will prepare the itinerary.

How to compile the manager's appointment schedule. Prepare a schedule of all the appointments the manager has on the trip. Include in the schedule the following: city and state; date and time; name, firm and address of the individual with whom the manager has an appointment; phone number; any remarks or special reminders about the visit. Figure 25 is an illustration of a schedule.

If the manager has previously met any of the individuals with whom he or she is to do business, make a notation of the circumstances of the meeting. You will have this information available if you keep the "contact reminder" file described on page 39.

Assembling data for the manager's business appointments. Place together the papers relating to each matter the manager is to attend to on his trip. He will want letters or memos concerning the problem he wants to discuss and also any other pertinent information that is in his file. Use a rubber band or large paper clip to bind together the papers pertaining to each matter, and clearly label each packet.

☐ Stationery of all kinds   ☐ Pens and pencils

☐ Envelopes, plain   ☐ Erasers

☐ Envelopes addressed to the company   ☐ Clips

☐ Large manila envelopes   ☐ Scissors

☐ Memo paper   ☐ Rubber bands

☐ Stenographer's pad   ☐ Blotters

☐ Legal pads   ☐ Cellophane tape

☐ Carbon paper   ☐ Calendar

☐ Address book   ☐ Mail schedules

☐ Legal folders   ☐ Pins

☐ Business cards   ☐ Bottle opener

☐ Dictation equipment   ☐ Ruler

☐ Mailing folders or boxes for dictation belts or tapes   ☐ Band-Aids.

☐ Cash   ☐ Aviation guide

☐ Personal checkbook   ☐ Timetable

☐ Office account checks   ☐ Stamp pad & rubber stamps

☐ Expense forms   ☐ Postage stamps

☐ Other office forms

FIGURE 26   CHECKLIST OF SUPPLIES FOR TRIP

Packing supplies for the trip.   Make mimeographed or duplicate lists of the stationery and supplies that your employer needs when he goes on a business trip. Use the lists as checklists when you pack the supplies so that you will not forget anything. The list in Figure 26 suggests items that he might need.

Baggage.   Your employer may want to know the baggage allowance that will be checked without charge on his railroad or plane ticket and the limitations on the dimensions of baggage. You can usually find all of this information in the timetables.

Prepare identification labels for each piece of baggage. Labels are available at ticket offices and baggage counters. Keep a supply on hand.

For short trips some executives use a combination suitcase and briefcase, or an attaché case with a divider that snaps down on one side. With clothes under the divider, the manager can go from plane to appointment without having to stop at a hotel and unpack. Then, too, there is no time wasted waiting for luggage at the airport.

Travel funds.   A businessperson uses one of the following plans for keeping a supply of funds while traveling.

1. *Personal checks.* A person who travels extensively usually has credit cards from the hotels where he or she stops. It is then easy to cash checks at the hotels.

2. *Traveler's checks.* These are available in denominations of $10, $20, $50, and $100. Citibank of New York and Bank of America sell their own traveler's checks (Citibank's traveler's checks are called First National City Bank Traveler's Checks); other banks sell American Express Traveler's Checks. You can, of course, purchase them direct from the American Express Company. To purchase traveler's checks for your employer at his or her bank, fill out the bank's application form, which provides a space for the total amount of checks and the denominations desired. Your employer will have to sign the checks in the presence of the bank's representative. If the account is particularly valuable, the bank's representative will come to your office; otherwise, your employer must go to the bank.

3. *Letters of credit.* A person traveling to a foreign country usually buys a letter of credit from his bank if he wants to have funds of $1,000 or more. You can fill out the application for your employer, but, as in the case of traveler's checks, he must complete the

transaction in the presence of the bank's representative. A letter of credit testifies to the holder's credit standing, serves as a letter of introduction to leading banks, and can be drawn against at banks in every part of the world until the face amount of the letter of credit has been exhausted. Many travelers find it advisable to purchase both traveler's checks and a letter of credit when planning a trip to a foreign country.

To a great extent, the manager uses credit cards in lieu of cash. Each company has its own procedure for paying the traveling expenses of its employees. The above methods are for personal funds and for the businessperson who uses his or her own funds for travel.

Use your contacts to make hard-to-get reservations.   If the manager travels frequently, become acquainted with a *passenger representative* for each airline and railway in your community. They are usually cooperative and frequently send you their cards unsolicited because they want your business. It is always good policy to build up good will with the passenger representatives.

Airlines and railway companies usually keep space in reserve for emergencies. Corporations whose officers and employees travel extensively frequently have a contact among the higher officials of the travel lines. These contacts can usually secure a space for you in emergencies, but *do not* call on them except in an emergency.

Or call on your secretarial friends in the travel field when the emergency is acute. You can return the favor when she or he needs help in your field. Don't make a habit of imposing on your friends.

A compact method of preparing travel information.   Type the itinerary and schedule of appointments in a small, top-bound notebook. You can do this by backfeeding (see page 80) the pages of the notebook into the typewriter. You can also put other information and reminders in the notebook. If it is spiral-bound, the manager can also use it for writing memos to send to you and other executives of the company.

Build your own travel and hotel information library.   Keep a reference shelf of timetables for airlines and railroads and of roadmaps. Whenever you take a trip, go to an airport, railroad station, or hotel, pick up new timetables.

MAKING AIRPLANE
TRAVEL ARRANGEMENTS

Where to get information about airplane travel.   You can get information about airplane travel from the following sources:

1. *Official Airline Guide.* The best published source of airline information is the Official Airline Guide published by Reuben H. Donnelley, 2000 Clearwater Drive, Oak Brook, Illinois 60521. Cities in the United States, Canada, and United States possessions are listed alphabetically. Under each city the airlines servicing that city are listed, together with the page numbers for the respective airline schedules. The guide index also indicates the availability of a car rental service and/or air taxi service for each city. International flight information is also included. It may be obtained through yearly subscription or by purchase of single copies.

2. *Timetables of separate airlines.* Find out which lines may be used for the proposed trip and get the timetables of those lines.

3. *Telephone information.* By telephoning the local airlines' information or reservations number, you can get any desired information for a specific trip.

If your task involves arranging air travel for a large group—perhaps for a conference—contact several major airlines and inquire about their special services for conference travel. Some will offer a number of attractive packages, including reduced group rates and block reservations from selected cities, and some will even do a promotional mailing, free of charge, to everyone registered for the conference or to prospective attendees.

What plane accommodation does the manager want?   The majority of companies require their officials to travel economy class on planes, if expedient. Most flights have both first class and economy class. Exceptions are shuttle flights, such as those between Washington and New York. These flights have only one class of travel. Reservations are not available, but the airline guarantees passage even if a second plane has to be placed in service for the scheduled flight.

Always find out if meals or snacks are available on the flight you are inquiring about. On most flights during a meal hour, meals or so-called snacks are available. The traveler can usually get a cocktail without charge at meal time in first class, but must pay for it in economy class.

How to make plane reservations. When you telephone for reservations, get the name of the person to whom you are talking and give that person your name, so that if you must call again to clarify any part of the itinerary you will be able to speak with the same person.

Explain clearly what reservations you want. Give the reservations clerk the following information:

1. Points of departure and destination
2. Date and time of departure desired
3. Flight number
4. Class of accommodation desired

Your conversation might follow this pattern:

"This is Miss White of Wilson Motors Corporation. I would like to make a reservation for Mr. Joseph Lawrence of this company on Delta Airlines flight 210 from Jackson to New York, economy class, at 9:30 a.m. Central Standard Time, on April 14. Is space available?"

"Yes, Miss White. We have economy class space available on Flight 210 on April 14, but that flight leaves at 9:48 a.m."

"That will be satisfactory. At what time does the plane arrive in New York?"

"It arrives at New York Kennedy Airport at 1:56 p.m. New York (Eastern) Standard Time."

"What is the fare?"

"The fare is $100 each way."

(Note: The airline may also offer an excursion rate for the same accommodations. Inquire about this. If the required travel days are satisfactory for the manager's plans, book passage or him at the excursion rate.)

"Thank you very much. Please book Mr. Lawrence on that flight. And may I have your name in case any question arises?"

"Surely. Just ask for Robert McIntyre at the reservations desk. And now may I have complete information about the passenger?"

"The reservation is for Mr. Joseph Lawrence, Wilson Motors Corporation, 1070 North State Street, Jackson. The phone number of the company is 535-4800, and Mr. Lawrence's home phone number is 566-2453."

"Thank you, Miss White. I have Mr. Lawrence booked on that flight."

If the trip involves stopovers or plane and train reservations. When the manager plans to make several stopovers on his trip, give the reservation clerk the approximate times that he wants to depart from, and arrive at, various stops, and the accommodations desired. The reservations clerk will work out the best possible schedule for you. He will probably have to call you back because he will have to check with other airlines. It is most important that you get his name when making reservations for a trip with several laps.

If one lap of the trip is to be by train, the airline reservation clerk will also make that reservation for you.

MAKING TRAIN
TRAVEL ARRANGEMENTS

Where to get information about trains. You can get information about travel by train from the following sources:

1. *The Official Guide of the Railways.* This publication, issued monthly by the National Railway Publications Company, 424 West 33rd Street, New York, New York 10001, contains all the schedules or timetables of all the railroads in the United States, Canada, and Mexico, with a description of the accommodations on each train. It also shows mileage between stations and contains maps of individual roads. It can be subscribed for by the year or single copies can be purchased for a few dollars.

2. *Timetables.* Contact your local Amtrak or major railroad agent regarding timetables, and ask to be put on their respective mailing lists. In this way you will always have on hand their latest timetables.

3. *Travel agent.* A travel agent will handle reservations on railroads, look up all schedules, and provide you with a complete itinerary.

What train accommodations does the manager want? The manager might travel economy class on a plane, but he or she is not likely to travel by coach on a train. Each timetable gives the accommodations or "equipment" offered by the scheduled trains, or gives a reference to a page where that information can be obtained. You can tell from this whether the train carries a diner, club car, observation car, and the like, and the type of sleeping accommodations carried.

In addition to upper and lower berths, the usual sleeping accommodations are:

Compartment. A private room containing lower and upper berth, with toilet facilities in the same room.

Bedroom. A private room containing lower and upper berth, the lower berth serving as a sofa for daytime use; also toilet facilities in the same room.

Roomette. A private room, intended primarily for single occupancy, with a bed folding into the wall and containing a sofa seat for daytime use; also toilet facilities in the same room.

How to make train reservations. The procedure for making train reservations is similar to that for obtaining plane reservations. An intelligent idea of what you want before you phone Amtrak or a major railroad will help immeasurably.

Be sure to give the reservations clerk complete and clear information on the point of departure and destination, time, train number or name, and the accommodation desired. When the exact reservations that you want are not available, ask the reservations clerk to suggest something that is available.

Unlike the airlines, *a railway will not make reservations for the entire trip if the trip is broken by plane travel.*

MAKING AUTO TRAVEL ARRANGEMENTS

Where to get information for automobile trips. You can use the following sources in arranging business trips to be made by automobile.

American Automobile Association. If your employer travels by automobile a great deal, he or she will find it advantageous to be a member of the American Automobile Association, which has a travel service available to plan any trip a member wants to take. The AAA headquarters is located at 8111 Gatehouse Road, Falls Church, Virginia 22042. To secure travel service, telephone or mail your request to the nearest branch of the AAA, and routings will be forwarded to you, or get them in person by calling at the nearest AAA branch. The club's travel department assists its members in these ways:

1. Advises them how to go, where to stop, and what to see.
2. Prepares a special Triptik. This consists of detailed up-to-the-minute strip maps with mile-by-mile routing marks for the entire journey. The Triptik

also shows detours. The reverse side of the Triptik lists recommended hotels and official AAA service stations on the way. In addition, the AAA outlines in color, on a map covering the entire trip, the route to be taken.
3. Provides last-minute information on weather and highway conditions.
4. Assists in selecting and securing motel and hotel accommodations in advance of the trip.

Members also receive a number of AAA travel guides and directories covering outstanding points of interest.

Note: Other automobile travel associations also offer similar services.

FOREIGN TRAVEL AND PLEASURE TRIPS

Travel agencies. If your employer is planning a trip to a foreign country, for either business or pleasure, or a trip in this country, it is advisable to make arrangements through an accredited travel service. Travel agents offer complete service in all matters pertaining to travel throughout the world. Since it is their business to keep in touch constantly with air, rail, and steamship lines everywhere, as well as commercial and resort hotels, they are able to make advance arrangements for you. In addition, travel bureaus have circulars and booklets describing foreign countries and each part of this country. From these the traveler can decide where he wants to go and what he wants to see.

The traveler pays no additional fee for the services of a travel agency. However, if plans are canceled the agent may charge for the services rendered and to cover such out-of-pocket expenditures as long-distance phone calls or wires. In some cases the agent also charges for railway transportation arrangements, but not in the case of prearranged vacation package trips.

How to select a travel agent. If you have not had experience with a qualified travel agent, select one who is a member of a nationally known association. The American Society of Travel Agents, Inc., familiarly known as ASTA, has members in the principal cities of the United States and Canada. The members may be recognized by the ASTA emblem, which they are permitted to display if they are in good standing. You can get the name of an ASTA member situated near your office by writing to the executive offices of the association, located in New York City. There are, of course, many reliable agents that are not members of ASTA, but the code of ethics of this association is high and its members, therefore, are dependable and efficient.

What the secretary should tell the travel agent.   When you ask an agent to arrange a trip for your employer, tell him or her the number in the party, names, ages, sexes, and, if the trip includes a foreign country, citizenship. Also indicate where your party wants to go, dates of departure and return, mode and class of travel, and the approximate amount that can be spent. The travel agent will be able to tell you the classes of travel and rates on a particular airline or steamship and on the trains in the foreign countries and recommend hotels to conform to your budget.

What a good travel agent will do for you.   The following is some of the assistance that a travel agent is able to give you:

1. Prepare and submit a tentative itinerary, which the traveler can change or adjust.
2. Make all travel, hotel reservations, and sightseeing arrangements for the entire trip.
3. Tell you what documents the traveler must have, such as passport, health and police certificates, and the like, and how to get them. The service will get them for you unless a personal appearance is necessary. *The secretary has the responsibility, however, of seeing that her employer has all the necessary documents.*
4. Supply in exchange for dollars a small amount of currency of the country to be visited, for tips, taxi fares, and the like. The agent will also assist in getting a letter of credit or traveler's checks.
5. Advise as to all regulations, such as restrictions on currency and customs requirements.
6. Have a foreign correspondent meet the traveler on arrival, take care of baggage, and see him through customs.
7. Have a rental car waiting for the traveler at his destination, whether it be Toledo or Tokyo.
8. Arrange personal and baggage insurance and even provide rain insurance (a sum designed to console in the event rain mars the trip).
9. Help the traveler take advantage of money-saving travel rates, such as excursion or group rates.
10. Arrange for interesting side trips to points of interest or special events in the particular area in which the traveler will be.

When your employer is unable to decide upon a definite itinerary.   A traveler abroad who has all reservations made and confirmed in advance travels with the greatest ease and comfort. It sometimes happens, however, that it is impossible for your employer to know where he or she will be able to go, and when. If plans are uncertain, give the travel agent the names of the places in which your employer expects to need hotel reservations, approximate dates, and how much per day he or she will spend for hotel expenses. The agent will do the following things:

1. Send you the name of a desirable hotel in each place.
2. Write to each of the recommended hotels asking them to give your requests their best attention.
3. Advise the agent's foreign correspondent in each city of the approximate date of arrival.

Passports.   Application for a passport may be executed before a clerk of a federal court, a state court authorized to naturalize aliens, an agent of the State Department, or a post office authorized to grant passports. Passport agents of the State Department are located in New York City, San Francisco, Chicago, Los Angeles, Boston, and New Orleans. In Washington, DC applications are executed in the Passport Division of the Department of State.

The following is a brief summary of the essential requirements for making application for a passport when the applicant is a native American citizen or a naturalized citizen.

A native American citizen must submit a birth certificate with his application, to prove citizenship. Birth certificates must show that the birth was recorded within one year from date of birth. If this certificate is not obtainable, the applicant must submit an affidavit executed by a person who has personal knowledge of the place and date of birth. If an affidavit of a relative or attending physician cannot be obtained, an affidavit of some other reputable person, preferably a blood relation, with knowledge of the facts should be submitted. The person must have known the applicant for several years. The affidavit should state how knowledge of the place and date of birth was acquired.

The traveler must establish his identification to the satisfaction of the passport agent. This may be done by presentation of one of the following documents containing the signature of the applicant and either a photograph or a physical description of the applicant:

1. Prior United States passport
2. Certificate of naturalization
3. Driver's license
4. Federal, state, or municipal government identity card
5. Industrial or business identity card or pass

Two standard passport photographs must be submitted. The passport fee is $10.00 plus a $3.00 execution fee.

A passport is valid for five years after which it is necessary to apply for a new passport.

A naturalized citizen must present his naturalization papers and be identified in the same manner as a native-born citizen.

Applications of persons going abroad on business in pursuance of a contract or agreement with a federal government agency must be accompanied by a letter from the head of the firm, or, in his absence, from the person in charge. The letter must state the position of the applicant, his destination (or destinations), the purpose of the trip and the approximate length of stay.

Visas. After the traveler gets his passport, his next step is to get visas for the countries that require them. Your travel agent will tell you whether or not a visa is required. Generally, the passport must be presented and a visa form filled out. The various countries have a number of special requirements, such as additional photographs, police and health certificates, vaccinations, and inoculations. Usually there is a visa fee. The length of time required for processing a visa varies with the country.

Customs information. Anyone going to a foreign country should know in advance the United States customs laws and regulations covering purchases made in a foreign country and brought into the United States. A competent travel agent will usually supply you with this information, as well as with details about customs requirements in countries to be visited.

Whether or not you use a travel service, send for *United States Customs Information for Passengers from Overseas.* If your employer is going to visit western hemisphere nations, send for *Customs Hints for Returning Americans—Visitors from Canada, Mexico, and Other Western Hemisphere Nations.* These pamphlets, available from the United States Treasury Department, Bureau of Customs, Washington DC, furnish the traveler with the general information he needs about United States customs laws and regulations.

Special duties in connection with a foreign business trip.   When the manager travels abroad *on business,* you have certain duties that you do not have in planning a pleasure trip. In addition to the duties that you have when your employer makes a business trip in this country, you should do the following:

1. Ask your travel agent or the consulates about the special requirements imposed on *commercial* travelers but not on *pleasure* visitors. *This is most important.*

2. Compile a list of officers and executives of each firm with whom your employer does business in the foreign countries to be visited. A loose-leaf, leather notebook, about 6" by 4", is convenient for this purpose. (See also the contact reminder file on page 39.)

3. Compile pertinent data on all recent deals completed with each firm, together with data on pending deals. You should have a manila folder for each company or individual to be visited.

4. Write letters for the manager's signature requesting letters of introduction from banks, individuals, business houses, and the like to their foreign offices. Such introductions are very helpful to a commercial traveler. The following is a form that you can adapt to your own purpose:

Mr. Alexander N. Gentes
Second Vice-President
Guaranty Trust Company
140 Broadway
New York NY 10006

Dear Mr. Gentes:

On April 24 I am leaving for Europe on a business trip. I will call on publishers and booksellers in London, Paris, Zurich, Brussels, Amsterdam, Copenhagen, Oslo, Stockholm, and probably Barcelona. It has occurred to me that a letter to your correspondents in each of these cities might be helpful to me. I would appreciate it very much if you would supply me with such a letter.

I expect to gain a good deal of first-hand information on general conditions in all of these countries, as well as more specific data on books and publishing matters. Of course, I will be glad to make available to you upon my return any information that may interest you.

Sincerely yours,

Kenneth M. Winston
Manager, Foreign Division

5. Write letters to the firms on whom the manager expects to call to announce his travel plans, the dates of his proposed stay in the city concerned, his local address, and the like. These letters are written over the manager's signature, or in the name of the president of the firm he represents. Although you might not draft these letters, you must remind the manager to dictate them well in advance of his trip.

6. Write an announcement of the manager's visit to different trade or professional magazines published in the city or country to be visited. The announcement should give the address where the manager can be reached while there, as well as the dates of his proposed visit. If you use a good travel agent, he or she will prepare an itinerary of the entire trip and make extra copies for distribution.

7. Write a letter for the manager's signature six weeks or two months in advance of his or her trip, to:

Travel Officer, International Trade Service Divisions
Special Services and Intelligence Branch
Department of Commerce
Office of International Trade
Washington DC 20230

This letter should state the purpose of the manager's trip and should include his itinerary. The Department of Commerce sends airgrams, via its bulletins, to all Foreign Offices announcing the visit.

8. Get a letter of authority, addressed "To Whom It May Concern," from the chairman or president authorizing the manager to represent the firm. This is especially valuable in dealing with immigration or customs authorities.

9. Assemble data on the trade conditions, political aspects, geography, climate, customs, and the like of each country to be visited. If your employer makes frequent trips abroad, you should also accumulate such material throughout the year from trade journals. Mark with colored pencil the items of interest to the manager.

10. If your company subscribes to the Dun & Bradstreet credit service, get a card from them authorizing the manager to call on their foreign offices for credit information. This is a service that Dun & Bradstreet offers its subscribers.

Guide to travel information.   An intelligent traveler for pleasure is always interested in material about the places he or she is going to visit. An enormous number of travel books, guides, and other material have been published and can be obtained in libraries, bookstores, at travel bureaus, railroads, airlines, automobile associations, and hotels. Ask your employer the type of information that interests him. Then consult the Cumulative Book Index under "Voyages and Travel" and other classifications there noted, for titles. You can also get advice from your local bookstore, which will usually obtain for you any book it does not happen to have on hand.

Because many travel guides undergo frequent revision, always find out the date of the latest edition before acquiring a travel book.

The following classification of travel material will help you work out with your employer what he or she may want to take on the trip: (1) handbooks for foreign countries, (2) condensed guides for more than one country, (3) books on subjects of regional interest, (4) books on sports in various regions, (5) histories, (6) books about cities, (7) books that tell where to eat, and (8) books to read for entertainment.

CHAPTER 9

BUSINESS ETIQUETTE fOR THE SECRETARY

If you know "how to do" any secretarial task the way it should be done, then, subconsciously perhaps, you know the etiquette and manners involved in that task. Most of the chapters in *Complete Secretary's Handbook* tell you how to do a task the way it should be done. You therefore automatically use proper business etiquette and good manners in doing that task. For example, how could you possibly use the telephone expertly (chapter 6) without proper business etiquette and good manners?

There are many problems of etiquette and good personal relations not directly involved in a particular task. This chapter calls to your attention many of these little things that help make you a *successful secretary*.

One of the most important aspects of a secretary's work is the way in which she or he handles visitors. The secretary is a reflection not only of the company's public relations image—as is the receptionist—but of the manager's image. The secretary is a key figure in building good will both for the manager and for the company through her or his attitude, regardless of the relative importance of each caller. All of the qualities essential for success in the secretarial profession are brought into play: poise, tact, social adaptability, good judgment, and good manners.

In the secretary's contact with callers, she or he is always conscious of a double duty: first, to serve the manager and to give his or her wishes precedence and, second, to serve the visitor.

How to be of help to the manager in handling callers. An executive rarely tells you what he or she expects of you in your role as receptionist. Sometimes he or she will give you explicit instructions about a particular caller, but will expect you to do the following without instructions.

1. Find out the name of the caller, company affiliation, and the purpose of his or her visit. Remember names and faces so that you can greet frequent callers more cordially.
2. Maintain the good will of the person by making his or her contact with the firm pleasant and satisfactory. Make him or her comfortable while waiting to see the manager.
3. Judge which callers the manager will welcome, which he or she wants to avoid, which should be seen by someone else in the organization, and which you should take care of yourself.
4. Make explanations to those callers whom the manager will not see, without antagonizing the caller.

In addition, an executive expects the secretary to keep the appointment records, write letters pertaining to appointments (see page 284) and furnish him or her with reminders of appointments (see page 35).

Methods of receiving callers. Different organizations have different methods of receiving callers. In large companies all callers go to a reception desk where a trained receptionist takes care of the preliminaries and advises the secretary that the caller has arrived. The secretary then goes to the reception office and escorts the visitor to the manager's office, if he has an appointment. Simply say to the visitor, "Mr. Gray? I'm Mr. Roberts' secretary. Will you come with me, please?" You then usher the caller to the manager's office. Do not attempt to carry on a conversation with him, but do respond cordially to any remarks or questions of his.

In small companies, the telephone operator may double as receptionist, or a messenger or some other person who has been trained in the preliminaries greets the visitor.

Greeting a caller.   Formality is appropriate in greeting an office caller. You should say, "How do you do?" or "Good morning," or "Good afternoon"—not "Hello." Let the caller make the first gesture toward shaking hands.

If your desk is at the entrance of the office, or in a convenient or conspicuous location, you need not rise to speak to a caller unless he or she is a person of considerable importance or much older than you.

After your greeting, if the caller does not volunteer any information, your next move is to ask, "May I help you?"

Finding the purpose of a call.   A secretary is usually expected to ask why a caller wants to see the manager, not only when the caller comes to the office unexpectedly but when he or she telephones for an appointment. This is one of the most difficult jobs that confronts a secretary, especially in a new position. Of course, when a visitor presents a card you are usually able to tell the reason for the visit; also, in many cases you know the purpose of the visit from previous correspondence or visits. The "voice with a smile" is never more useful than when you are trying to get information from a caller or when you are refusing to let him see the manager. This duty requires discretion, tact, and patience. Fortunately, a visitor who makes a call in good faith rarely objects to telling the purpose of the visit.

Several approaches are suggested here for finding the purpose of a call. Keep in mind that these suggestions are for the secretary who has instructions not to admit a caller unless the purpose of the call is known.

The caller enters your office or you greet him in the reception room. You might say:

"Good morning, Mr. Jones. I'm Mr. Brown's secretary. He's busy at the moment, but is there anything I can do for you?"

Or: "Good morning. I'm Mr. Brown's secretary. He's not in the office at present, but is there anything I can do for you?"

Or: "Good morning, Mr. Jones. I'm Mr. Brown's secretary. What can I do for you?"

Or: "You're waiting to see Mr. Brown? I'm Miss Edwards, Mr. Brown's secretary. Can I be of any help to you?"

Caller states his business, which is of interest to your employer. You might say:

"I'm sorry, I can't arrange a definite engagement right now because I don't know what additional commitments Mr. Brown has made since I last saw him, but if you'll let me have your telephone number I'll call you either later today or surely tomorrow morning and arrange an appointment for you. I know Mr. Brown will be glad to see you."

Or you arrange a definite appointment at that time.

Or you take him in to see your employer, or arrange for him to see an assistant, or handle the matter yourself, as the occasion requires.

Caller refuses to state business, probably saying it's personal. You might say:

"I'm sorry, but I'm afraid I can't ask Mr. Brown to make an appointment without telling him what you want to discuss. Could you give me a general idea?"

Or: "I'm sorry, Mr. Jones, but Mr. Brown is only able to see people by appointment. As I make all his appointments, I'll have to ask you what you would like to discuss with him."

Or: "I'm sorry, Mr. Jones, but I'll have to know what you want to see Mr. Brown about, because that's the first thing he'll ask me. If I don't know I'll simply have to come back and ask you again—which I'm afraid would be a waste of your time."

Caller still refuses to tell you why he wants to see your employer. You might say:

"I'm really sorry, Mr. Jones, that I can't help you, but those are our office rules, and Mr. Brown expects me to observe them. Without some indication of the business that you want to discuss, I'm afraid there's no way I can help you. I'm very sorry."

Or: "In that case, Mr. Jones, perhaps you could write Mr. Brown a note. Just tell him briefly what you want to see him about and ask for an appointment. Then he can make his own decision."

Or: "That's unfortunate, Mr. Jones, because until I know what you want to discuss with Mr. Brown, I won't be able to make an appointment for you."

Making a caller comfortable. Show a caller who is to see your employer where to leave his or her hat, coat, briefcase, and any other articles that he or she will not need for the appointment. Offer to hang up the caller's coat.

When the caller has to wait, ask him to have a seat, indicating a chair. If he has to wait any length of time, offer him a newspaper or magazine. If the caller deserves special attention, ask him, "Is there anything I can do for you while you're waiting?" The caller will then frequently say that he would like to look up something in the telephone directory, or make a call, or see someone else in the organization. Offer to look up a number for him, but do not insist. If he wishes to phone, show him to a private phone if there is one available. He may wish to make a call on a confidential matter, so be sure not to show any unnecessary interest.

Do not begin a conversation with a waiting visitor; but if he shows an inclination to talk, respond. Talk on topics in which he is likely to be interested—a trip he has recently taken, or current topics—but avoid controversial issues. Do not tell the manager's friend a story you know the manager would enjoy telling himself or herself—a story about a hole-in-one at golf, or news about his or her family. If the visitor asks questions about the business, reply only in generalities.

How to announce a caller. When the manager is ready to receive a guest, you may do one or two things. If the caller is known to the manager and has visited the office before, you may nod to him and say something to the effect that, "Mr. Wilson is free. Won't you go right in?" However, if it is the caller's first visit, or he is an infrequent caller, accompany him to the door of the manager's office, open it if it is kept closed, step to one side and say, "Mr. Wilson, Mr. Smith." *Or* "Mr. Wilson, this is Mr. Smith."

When older people, dignitaries, or women are announced in a business office, it is considered proper to mention the guest's name first. For instance, should a church dignitary visit the manager, the polite announcement would be: "Bishop McLeish, Mr. Wilson." (Refer to the chart in chapter 11 for the proper titles by which to announce officials and dignitaries.)

A caller with an appointment. If you have a receptionist, give her a list of appointments each day. She will then be in position to handle your callers courteously and efficiently. Where a receptionist serves numerous executive offices, the company might not follow the practice of supplying her with a list of appointments for various managers, but the practice promotes efficiency.

When a caller with an appointment arrives, notify the manager immediately unless he is in a conference that cannot be interrupted. You may say to him over the interoffice communication system, "Mrs. Carter is here for her ten o'clock appointment. May I bring her in?" If the caller is already in your office, near your desk, it is better to go into the manager's office and tell him that the caller has arrived. When the manager is ready to receive the caller, say, "Will you come with me, Mrs. Carter?" and introduce her as described above.

If the manager has to keep a caller with an appointment waiting, explain the delay: "Mr. Grant has someone with him at the moment, but he'll be free in a few minutes. Will you have a seat?" If the delay will last for any length of time, tell the caller the approximate time she will have to wait. She can then judge whether she wants to wait or make a later appointment. (Of course, if you know that your employer is not going to be able to keep an appointment promptly, you will notify the appointee before she leaves her own office.)

When the manager is not in his office. On occasion an executive might have been called out of his office just before a visitor arrives. When this happens, apologize for the manager and explain the circumstances.

You can say, "Good morning, Mr. Hughes. Mr. Smith was called into the plant about ten minutes ago because of a production problem. He should be back any minute now. Do you mind waiting?"

If an unexpected emergency will keep the manager out of his office for more than a few moments, you might explain his absence this way:

"Good morning, Mr. Hughes. I'm so sorry, but Mr. Smith was called to the office of the chairman of the board a little while ago. I'm not sure when he will be back. I tried to reach you, but your secretary said you had already left. Can you wait?" The visitor can then decide whether to wait, come back later, make another appointment, or even see someone else—the manager's assistant, for instance.

A caller who has no appointment, but whom the manager will see. Usually when a person the manager will see calls at your office without an appointment, you know him well enough to greet him by name: "How are you, Mr. Douglas? It's so nice to see you again." You might inquire about his family or ask him about his vacation. Then ask him the nature of the unexpected visit. After you learn the purpose of his visit, if you have the least doubt as to whether the manager wants to see the caller, ask him.

If the manager is engaged, ask the caller to wait until he is free, telling the caller approximately how long that will be. Unless the unexpected caller is someone the manager is always especially eager to see, it is wise to keep him waiting a few minutes so that he will realize he should have made an appointment. You might limit the unexpected caller's visit by saying, "Mr. Roberts has another appointment in ten minutes, but he will be glad to see you in the meantime."

Perhaps a crowded calendar makes it inconvenient for the manager to see the unexpected caller at that particular time. Explain the situation to the caller, assuring him that a visit from him at any time other than the present would be most welcome. Offer to make a future appointment if the manager is interested.

A caller the manager does not want to see. When you know that the manager is not interested in the purpose of the visit or is too busy to see the caller, you might say:

"I wish I could be more helpful to you, Mr. King, but Ms. Evans is concerned with some emergencies and will be for some time; and for that reason, she has to limit her engagements to matters directly connected with her business affairs. It will be some time before this situation changes and the only thing I can suggest is that you take your matter up with her in writing."

A caller soliciting a contribution. When a caller states that his business is to solicit a contribution, you might say, when applicable: "Unfortunately, the demands on Mr. Lewis are so numerous that he is forced to limit his contributions to those charitable causes to which he has contributed for years, and he's just not able to add to that list. I'm sure you can understand his situation."

A caller who is a friend of the manager. When a friend of the manager calls to see him, announce the visitor and escort him to the manager's office. If he has called without an appointment and the manager is out, do everything possible to make him comfortable (offering newspapers, cigarettes, and the like) until the manager arrives. If he is not expected, express his regret at not seeing the caller and ask if the caller can return at another time. If the visitor is someone important who has never before called at the office, you might take him into the manager's office and show him any interesting mementos the manager has. However, never ask a visitor to wait in the manager's office for him, unless the manager has told you to do so.

Do everything you can to impress upon the manager's friend that he is most welcome, but at the same time never be *overly* friendly.

A caller whom you refer to another person in the organization.   When you find that the purpose of a caller's visit involves a matter that should be taken up with another person in the organization, you might say:

"I'm sorry, Mr. Bean, but that's something handled for Mr. Johnson by Mr. Smith. I'll be glad to make an appointment for you; or if he's not busy now, I know he'll be happy to see you at once."

Or: "I wonder if you could take this matter up with Mr. Smith of our Sales Department. He's more familiar with the matter than Mr. Johnson and can be of more help to you."

If Mr. Bean agrees to see Mr. Smith, as he probably will, call Mr. Smith on the phone and explain the situation. Then say, "Mr. Smith will be glad to see you now, Mr. Bean. Will you go down to the fourth floor and tell the receptionist that Mr. Smith is expecting you? He may have to keep you waiting a few minutes, but not long." Or, if necessary, tell Mr. Bean, "I'm very sorry, Mr. Bean, but Mr. Smith can't see you this morning. He asked if you'll come in tomorrow at eleven o'clock."

If the caller objects because he cannot see the manager personally, tell him that the instructions are made by the manager and you have to abide by them.

Calls by office personnel.   In many business organizations today, top officials keep an "open door" to the office personnel. The secretary must usually make the appointment; but if the open-door policy prevails, the secretary does not inquire about the purpose of the appointment.

Always treat officers and executives of the company with deference and respect, but it is not necessary to stand up every time an officer enters your office. However, you should offer him a chair if he has to wait, just as you would any other caller.

Occasionally you can save the manager time and trouble and, at the same time, do a favor to a young, new employee who wants to see him. In an appropriate situation you might say, "What's on your mind, Joe? Anything I can do?"

If Joe hedges, "Why don't you sit down and tell me about it? Maybe I can help."

Joe tells you about it.

Then you might say, "I'll tell you what I'll do, Joe. I'll talk to Mr. Abbott about this, and then we'll let you know what can be done."

Or, you go in to Mr. Abbott and say: "Joe Brown, a new member of the Mailing Department, has a little problem on which he wants your advice. He's told me about it; and if you'll see him for a minute, I think you can help him over a hurdle."

Joe Brown sees Mr. Abbott.

Or, you might say to Joe: "Joe, it wouldn't be wise to take that up with Mr. Abbott. It really would be going over the head of your immediate superior, and that's never good policy. Why don't you tell Ms. Edwards (the immediate superior) all about it? I'm sure she'll want to do anything she can to straighten things out for you."

If Joe does not want to confide in you, do not urge him to.

Interrupting conferences.   Try to avoid interrupting a conference, but if it is essential to enter a room where the manager is in conference, do so quietly and unobtrusively.

Type on a slip of paper any message that must be delivered to someone in the conference room. If you want instructions, type the questions. The manager can then handle the matter with a minimum of interruption.

If it is essential to announce a caller to the manager while he is occupied with another, simply take the visitor's card to him or type the name on a slip of paper.

When a visitor overstays his appointment, call the manager on the telephone and notify him of another appointment. In some offices the manager has a concealed bell that he can ring unobtrusively when he wishes to terminate a conference. The secretary can then enter the room and remind him of his next appointment.

Telephone calls for the visitor.   When there is a telephone call for a visitor, ask the person calling if it is possible for you to take the message. If so, type the message on a sheet of paper, addressing it to the visitor, and also type your name, the date, and the time at the bottom of the sheet. No visitor should be required to decipher strange handwriting.

If the person calling insists upon speaking to the visitor, go into the conference room, and, with a glance that takes in both the manager and the visitor, apologize for the interruption: "Pardon me for interrupting. Mr. Howard (looking at the visitor), Mr. Davis is on the phone and wants to speak to you. Do you care to take it here?" (indicating which telephone he should use). If he says yes, the call is put through. Often, however, the visitor says that he will call back, in which case you give the message to the person calling and type out the telephone number as a reminder for the visitor.

If several people are in conference with the manager and you must deliver a message to one of them, type it out and take it to that visitor, just as you would to the manager. If he is wanted on the phone, also type on the card: "Do you want to take the call in my office?" The visitor can then leave the conference without disturbing the others.

Refreshments. If visitors arrive while you are having coffee, it is usually appropriate to offer them refreshments also. Should they refuse, serve the manager anyway; however, if they must wait in your office, you should postpone having your own refreshments.

Seeing a caller out. You may find it necessary to remind the manager that it is time for his next appointment—a cue to the visitor that it is time for him to leave. Or, if the manager warns you in advance that he will need your assistance in cutting a visit short, you might interrupt politely with a reminder that it is time for the manager to leave or time for him to attend some meeting. As the visitor prepares to leave, help him with his coat and other articles left in your office, and show him to the door, saying "Good-bye" with a pleasant smile. If your building is large and the visitor is a stranger, you should, in most cases, escort him to the elevator or the lobby.

ETIQUETTE IN THE OFFICE

Your daily greetings to co-workers. There is no need to be uncertain about whether you should greet certain people whom you do not know personally—those from another office getting on the elevator with you, a doorman, an elevator operator, or the company president. The courtesy of saying "Good morning" or "Good night" to someone is universally acceptable in business. This courtesy does *not* mean that you should try to promote a conversation with the company president.

Naturally, if someone greets you first in the morning, it is only proper to return the greeting pleasantly.

In most offices it is customary to say "Good morning" when you arrive at your office in the morning. Depending on how the office is arranged, a single greeting may do for everyone or you may greet people individually by name. On leaving the office you probably say "Good night" to the same people you greet in the morning.

Helping a new employee.   A new secretary or any new employee appreciates it when co-workers give him or her a friendly reception and help familiarize him or her with the strange surroundings.

Giving a new employee a helping hand with his or her work also assures that he or she will become productive more rapidly. It also helps the new employee decide that yours is a good company, one with which he or she will stay. But even if there were not these very practical reasons for making a new employee feel at home and for helping him or her get started right in a new job, business etiquette requires it.

Most large companies, and many smaller ones, have an orientation program for new employees, but this program does not take the place of personal friendliness and assistance from an established co-worker.

Introduce a newcomer to co-workers. Make a point of seeing that the new person is properly introduced to the people with whom he or she will be dealing. It will help if he or she is also given some idea of what each person does as he or she is being introduced. Names and faces are then easier to remember and the new worker gets a general idea of how his or her job fits in with others.

Are you a newcomer?   There are also certain rules of etiquette for the newcomer to observe. Here are a few suggestions that may help you get a practical and congenial start on a new job.

Don't brag or show off. It is rude and useless to try to impress oldtimers by telling them how much better your old company handled matters, or to point out mistakes you see them making. Once you have established a working relationship with the other workers and with the manager, your suggestions stand a much better chance of being accepted by them, instead of being resented.

Don't try to get too friendly too soon. Use some restraint in your first few days on a new job. Give those already on the job a chance to make the friendly advances. You not only avoid giving the impression that you are forward, but also avoid forming alliances that you may later regret.

What to do when you are invited to lunch. On your first day a few persons may ask you to have lunch with them. Generally, you are expected to pay for your own lunch, even if your immediate superior is in the group. If your immediate superior invites you to have lunch with him or her alone, generally the superior pays for your lunch.

Use of first names in the office.   Most modern offices are rather informal, and the use of first names among fellow employees is the usual practice. Even in such offices, there are situations where it is improper not to use a title (Mr., Mrs., Miss, Ms.) and the last name.

The basic and most important rule is simple: You may follow the practice that has been established in your particular office.

Addressing your supervisor. You should never address your immediate supervisor by first name unless the superior has informed you specifically that it is all right to do so. Even then, you should use a title in the presence of visitors. (The supervisor should extend that same courtesy to you.)

Addressing executives. You should never address a person of executive rank by first name, unless he or she tells you to do so. Addressing executives by title is the only practice that is accepted as conventional etiquette despite the informality that might exist in the office.

Addressing older men and women. It is not unusual for an older employee to prefer to be addressed by title by younger co-workers. Even if others in the office refer to an older employee by first name, it is best to wait before you take the same liberty if you are new in the office.

General principles of etiquette in taking refreshments.   Having a cup of coffee is an established practice in American business, and a few cautions are in order.

1. Be neat. Coffee crumbs, coffee stains, cluttered ashtrays, cigarette ashes, and unwashed coffee cups are unsightly.
2. Observe common table manners when eating and drinking at your desk.
3. Don't let your refreshments interfere with business. The excuse for a cup of coffee is that it increases efficiency, but the practice of taking refreshments at work can be harmful to business if not used with discretion. If a co-worker, a business caller, or an executive comes to your desk while you are having your coffee, you should give your full attention to the caller, and you should never keep a visitor waiting while you finish eating or drinking.
4. Don't "stretch" your pause for refreshments with a second cup of coffee, extra helping of food, or even chewing gum.
5. Do not pause while you are drinking coffee to attend to personal grooming at your desk unless you are clearly alone. Application of makeup, combing of hair, filing of nails, and so on, are most properly attended to in the restroom.

When you get coffee for the manager.   You may be expected to get coffee for the manager in the morning. A good plan regarding payment is for the manager to give you a weekly or monthly "kitty," or fund, for coffee money. You, of course, should keep a strict accounting of what you spend. Such a plan—which you may have to suggest tactfully—will avoid any danger of spending your own money because the manager is forgetful.

Etiquette in office lines.   In many business situations, employees must line up and await their turn. Rules of etiquette not only should prevail in these situations, but *must* be followed. Getting on and off elevators; lining up in the cafeteria or lunchroom; waiting for the drinking fountain; punching the time clock, morning and after-noon—to mention a few of these situations. The same rule applies to all: Take your place in line and wait patiently for your turn.

Time clocks, which are often a necessary evil because of wage and hour laws, create a double problem. Latecomers must rush down the hall, without regard for their own safety or that of others, to punch the clock just before it changes from 9:00 to 9:01. In the afternoons, the rush for first place in the line to punch out is not only a breach of etiquette but is a violation of company rules.

Etiquette promotes safety in the parking lot.   Many employees tend to forget their manners, as well as their own safety and that of others, in a wild dash to get to work on time or to be the first one out of the parking lot. If you calmly continue working for five or ten minutes after quitting time, you will find that you get out of the parking lot easily, and just as soon as if you had rushed down to join the car jam.

Don't help a grapevine of gossip grow.   A grapevine is a trail of office gossip passed from one employee to another by word of mouth. The smart secretary regards grapevine news with caution. If you hear through this source something that seems to be important news and that directly affects you and your job, directly question the manager about it. *Never* spread grapevine information. Passing on unfounded rumors can lead to unfortunate consequences and can involve you in embarrassing situations.

Remember that a rumor can have serious consequences when it gets outside the company. Even when you have no reason to doubt what you hear, avoid making office matters public. Discussing the matter with a close friend in a restaurant is the same as making the news public, because you never know who may overhear you.

What to do about personal borrowing and lending.   In the area of personal borrowing and lending, a breakdown of scrupulous courtesy can cause irreparable ill-will among those in the office who must work together. In general, it is advisable *not* to borrow if you can possibly avoid it.

If you must borrow, be sure to make it a practice to return what you have borrowed as quickly as possible. Delays lead to forgetfulness and to accidents or actual loss of things—with the inevitable disagreeable feeling on the part of the individual who was kind enough to lend you his belongings.

Borrowing money. From a practical standpoint, discretion, responsibility, and trustworthiness rank above courtesy when borrowing money—without them, there is no courtesy in the transaction. Do not borrow money, even very small sums, from co-workers or people who do business with your company if you can possibly avoid it. If you must borrow lunch money, for example, be sure you return it promptly.

Borrowing a large sum of money from a co-worker or someone doing business with the company is frowned upon in all business organizations. Even if a friend, out of kindness, offers you a loan, don't accept it. Banks, not friends or business associates, are for lending.

If a co-worker has been remiss in returning a loan to you, you show far more courtesy and good manners by reminding him tactfully of the debt than by nursing a secret annoyance. Never mention the debt to others. If it is a sizable sum, your only recourse is to go to a high official of the company and ask for his cooperation in recovering the loan. And then you are brewing trouble. Be wise—*neither a borrower nor a lender be.*

Handling personnel problems. Every office, large or small, is a potential trouble spot where human relations are concerned. Even in the highly automated office where tasks involve person-machine contact more that person-to-person interface, there are personnel problems that may confront the secretary. There are two principal types of difficulties that arise where others are concerned: Most problems arise among fellow workers—conflicts or disagreements that may set one person at odds with another, or individual troubles that may prompt one person in need to seek help from another.

Avoiding serious conflicts. How do you handle a situation where you and another worker are in strong disagreement? First, you should remember that it is necessary to continue working each day with your co-workers. Arguments seldom solve anything. The sensible route is to take time to listen and try to understand the other side—before it becomes a conflict. If you still disagree, do not change your opinion, but do not let it anger you that someone else has a different viewpoint. If you are in charge, you are entitled to put your decision into effect if it concerns office procedures. If it is a matter of concern to your employer, let him render the final decision. The important thing to remember is that patience, understanding, and a friendly attitude will go a long way in preventing disagreements from becoming battles.

Dealing with the problems of others. One of the most difficult situations arises when a secretary either is asked for personal help, or is in a situation where it seems necessary to offer assistance. If the person in trouble is a co-worker, and possibly a good friend as well, the secretary will doubtless feel compelled to offer help and comfort. There is a dangerous point that may be reached. A good rule to remember is that you never really help someone by covering for his or her errors or problems. If someone has a drinking problem, for instance, or some emotional problem affecting his or her work, do not play doctor or psychologist, and do not help him or her hide it from your employer. Rather, help the person find professional guidance outside—quickly.

If the individual with a problem is your employer, and you are asked to offer suggestions, do the same thing. Otherwise, if the problem is extremely serious and is clearly jeopardizing the company's welfare, you should carefully consider advising the manager's immediate superior that a threatening problem exists. If the problem is minor, or at least not a threat to the company, what you do depends upon how much it disturbs you. You can try to ignore it or ask for a transfer to another office.

Every situation that presents itself is different in some way, and your response will have to be dictated by the seriousness of it and your own involvement. Certainly, you should not seek out individuals with problems and attempt to involve yourself as an amateur psychiatrist or counselor.

How to train and work with new employees. Some secretaries are asked by their managers to interview and train new full- or part-time employees. For example, your manager may feel it is time to add a clerk-typist who will assist you in many of your duties. Your office, or the personnel office in a large company, will advertise and arrange for the interviews.

Interviewing. You must plan ahead for the interviews in order to find out what you want to know about the applicant and also to provide information to the applicant—all within the time set aside for the meeting. These are the basic steps involved:

1. Set a mutually convenient time.
2. Prepare a detailed, written description of the company and the job, listing specific tasks the applicant will have to perform.
3. Devise skills tests if applicable, such as a typing test, when prepared tests are not available.
4. Draw up a list of specific questions you wish to ask (your company may have a standard application form but this list is necessary in addition) and take notes throughout the interview.
5. Make certain that the applicant is comfortable and at ease, and try to encourage her or him to volunteer information and indicate relative interest in skills and job duties.
6. Summarize and type the results, and present them to the manager, along with any recommendations or comments you have, after all the interviews are completed.

Once the new worker is hired, the job orientation and training begins. Of course, the new employee should be made to feel at home and acquainted with not only the immediate office, but general company policy and facilities as well.

Training will require (1) careful instruction and explanation of duties—presented at a pace the employee can digest, and (2) practice sessions where actual tasks are first completed under your direct supervision, often with step-by-step explanations as work proceeds. It will become evident when direct, constant supervision can be relaxed.

Once the worker is functioning alone—with the exception of occasional questions—you should still check his or her work occasionally for errors and general quality, as well as for efficiency and overall performance. If further guidance or discipline is required, do not hesitate to provide it. Remain alert to dissatisfaction and encourage open communication that will prevent such problems.

It is important throughout the worker's employment to provide motivation. An employee who has no incentive to do better probably will not. Job satisfaction is essential in any position.

In spite of all your efforts to find and select the right candidate and give proper training, there is always the chance that the person will not work out. The employee may be unable to adjust to the work pace or may be unable to produce work of adequate quality. If further training will not solve the problem, you will be forced to advise the manager, and he or she may ask you to discharge the employee. It will be necessary to tell the person as gently as possible that she or he is being released. You could indicate that she or he may wish to pursue further training or education, or that she or he would be more suited for a different type of job or office. Be as tactful, but direct, as possible, and wish her or him well upon leaving.

Basic office etiquette check-up. Use the following situations to test yourself on your understanding of basic office etiquette. Each incident could provoke a variety of responses, but the ones given are recommended as the most appropriate and most consistent with proper etiquette.

1. If a talkative client is making small talk with you when an important businessperson enters the office to keep an appointment, but the client does not notice the businessperson, what should you do? Try to draw the conversation to a close gracefully, without appearing to silence the

talk. If you abruptly cut into his conversation, you will embarrass both persons.

2. If a new woman appears each day dressed more gaudily than before, what should you do? Nothing, unless she asks for your advice. Then you might suggest outfits that you think would be especially becoming to her. Or, if you see another employee wearing an outfit that you think would be becoming to her, you might remark about it and tell her that it would also look good on her.

3. If the manager finds an error in a report prepared by a typist working under you, and if he asks who did it, what should you do? Tell him, but add that it is your responsibility. If the error is indicative of a recurring problem, this may be an opportunity to discuss corrective steps.

4. If a slow assistant prevents you from completing reports quickly, what should you do? Do not "tattle." Find out why she is slow and help her along. If that does not solve the problem, get another assistant.

5. If the manager makes a mathematical error in a report, and you discover the correct figure, what should you do? If it is a minor error, correct it, but avoid any reference to it at all. If it is important, show him your change, and ask if he would mind checking it.

6. If a foolish rumor circulates about a woman in the office, and you believe she is rather nice, although you do not know her very well, what should you do? If it is only foolish and not dangerous, ignore it and let it die a natural death. Rumors fade quickly if they are not fed.

SOCIAL AMENITIES
LEFT TO THE SECRETARY

Reserving theater tickets.   The secretary's chief responsibility when the manager entertains at the theater is reserving the tickets. That is a difficult chore unless the tickets are ordered far in advance. On short notice, a ticket agency may be helpful. An account at an agency simplifies the problem somewhat. Establish a contact at the agency and make all purchases through the same person. An additional charge by the agency is added to the original cost of each ticket. Many hotels also have information on and facilities for the purchase of theater tickets, tours, and other forms of entertainment.

Sending tickets through the mail.   If for any reason you send tickets through the mail to anyone, always include the numbers of the seats in your letter of transmittal. This information on the carbon copy of your letter is useful if the tickets are lost.

Information for your employer.   When you give the theater tickets to your employer, enclose them in an envelope with the following information typed on it:

1. Day of week and date of performance
2. Curtain time
3. Name and address of theater
4. Name of show
5. Seat numbers

SOCIAL CARDS

Personal visiting cards.   Visiting cards should be of medium-to-heavy white card stock. The appropriate size of a card is 3 by 1½ inches. The engraving should be in black; Roman lettering is in good taste. When ordering for an executive, be sure to order some matching envelopes so that they may be sent with flowers or gifts.

Initials should be avoided as much as possible and, in any case, one given name must be written in full. It is better to write out the entire name. *Mr., Mrs., Ms.,* and *Dr.* are the only abbreviations that should be used before the name. If the name is very long, *senior* or *junior* may be abbreviated and capitalized, but it is preferable to write the word out in lower-case letters. It is a matter of choice whether an address is engraved on the personal visiting card. If used, the house address appears in the lower right-hand corner. (See pages 206-208 for social amenities for business calling cards.) Stationery stores and printers have samples of card stocks and typefaces.

HOLIDAY PRESENTS
AND CARDS

The secretary's extra holiday duties.   Your calendar has a notation (see page 32) to bring holiday lists to your employer's attention. The time depends upon shopping conditions in your locality. For example, about six weeks before Christmas is the average time. Many secretaries assist in the selection of cards, and address and mail them. Some secretaries are asked to make suggestions as to presents, to shop for some of them, and to wrap and mail them.

Holiday present list.   Figure 27 is a suggested form to use in bringing

Name	Gift yr. before last	Gift last yr.	Amt. spent	Suggestion	Amt. to spend?
CHRISTMAS LIST (Mr. Hambro)				19–	
Mr. & Mrs. Nelson	cocktail glasses	silver bowl	$30	hurricane lamps	
Allen Pierce	humidor	manicure kit	$18	leather pouch	

FIGURE 27   CHRISTMAS LIST

the list of Christmas presents to your employer's attention. The form is self-explanatory. The employer makes additions or deletions, approves the presents suggested by you or decides on something else, and indicates the price range. To avoid duplication, you should keep a card record for those people to whom your employer gives presents at other times of the year as well as at Christmas.

Wrapping and mailing.   Appropriate Christmas cards, in preference to visiting cards, are usually sent with Christmas presents. When you plan to have a store gift-wrap and mail presents, take the cards with you when you do your shopping.

If a present is to be mailed, comply with the request of the post office and mail early. This is especially important if the packages are to be sent abroad.

Money presents.   All executives have a certain number of people to whom they give presents of money each Christmas. Make a list of those to whom the manager gives money and ask him to indicate the amount. The list usually includes household servants, elevator operators, doormen, janitor, and building superintendent (but not the building manager) of apartment house and office building; letter carriers; any others who perform services throughout the year and are not tipped. The amount given household servants is usually based on salary and length of service; the amount given apartment house employees, on the rent; the amount given others, on length of service. Some executives also give presents of money to relatives and members of their family.

If the amount of money is small, $20 or less, use crisp, new bills; for a larger amount, write a check. No matter what the amount or to whom it is given, insert it in a Christmas envelope printed for that purpose.

Card lists. Keep an alphabetical list of the names and addresses of people to whom the manager sends holiday cards. If he or she sends his or her own cards to some people and sends cards jointly with his or her spouse to others, keep separate lists. The manager may also have a select list to whom he or she sends cards that he or she prefers to sign. In addition, you may have to keep a separate list of customers or clients who receive company or firm cards.

When a card is received from someone who is not on the list, add the name below the regular list so that the next year the manager can decide whether or not he wishes to add that person to his list. If he or she makes new contacts during the year, add them to the list, indicating where the manager made the contact. Your employer will cross out any names of persons to whom he does not wish to send cards.

It is important to note changes of address. Many of the addresses will be in your address book; you should compare your list with them before addressing the cards. As cards are received, it is advisable to compare addresses shown on the envelopes with the ones on your list.

Check the names on the list as you address the cards. The same list can be used for several years if there are not many additions.

Other holidays. In addition to Christmas there are holidays that are celebrated about the same time by other denominations, such as Hanukkah. It is important that you are aware of the days and knowledgeable of the various customs.

BIRTHDAYS AND WEDDING ANNIVERSARIES

Birthdays. Keep a card record of those who receive presents on other occasions as well as at Christmas. The record should show the present given on each occasion and the approximate cost. The manager will want to know what presents he has given a particular person at Christmas and on other occasions as well as on previous birthdays before he makes a decision about another birthday present.

Birthday presents with birthstones are always appropriate. (See page 531 for a list of birthstones.)

Wedding anniversaries. Presents on wedding anniversaries follow a tradition—each anniversary is associated with a different substance or jewel (see page 527 for a list). Merchants' associations may revise the list from time to time.

DONATIONS

How to handle requests for donations. Records of donations or contributions must be kept (1) to support the income tax deduction and (2) for your employer's information. Here we are concerned with the use of the records from a nontax viewpoint. Chapter 22 suggests the form of records for tax purposes.

At certain times of the year, numerous organizations make drives for donations. It is usually advisable to accumulate the requests in a folder and give a batch of them to your employer at an opportune time. He gets a better perspective of the demands being made on him than if he receives the requests singly. If the request comes from a new organization, try to find out something about it and present the details to your employer. Never destroy a request for a donation unless your employer has told you that he is not interested in it. Some persons, particularly those in public positions, make a practice of responding, at least in a small way, to nearly every request. See page 302 for a letter regretting inability to make a donation.

The secretary's record of donations. When your employer is considering whether to make a certain donation, he or she is interested in knowing (1) the amount donated to a specific organization the preceding year and (2) the total amount of donations for the current year. Note on each request, before giving it to your employer, the amount donated the previous year. Give the running record of donations for the current year, described on page 483 to your employer with each request.

At the end of the year, make an alphabetical list of organizations to which contributions have been made (see Figure 60, page 483).

When your employer makes a pledge payable in installments, enter the due dates on your calendar or in your card tickler (see page 33).

HOW TO BE USEFUL
AT TIME OF BEREAVEMENT

Expressions of sympathy.   Sympathy to the family of a deceased friend or acquaintance is usually expressed by (1) flowers, (2) a letter of sympathy, (3) mass cards, or (4) contributions.

Flowers. It is customary to send flowers to a bereaved family, except to an Orthodox Jewish family. It is appropriate to send them fruit baskets. A visiting card, with the engraved name struck out in ink and bearing a few words of sympathy, may accompany the flowers. Usually, however, the secretary orders the flowers by phone and the florist supplies the card, on which he writes the name of the person sending the flowers. The florist will ask you the name of the deceased, where the funeral is to be conducted, and the date and time of the service.

Flowers are appropriate at a memorial service—as for someone lost at sea—or when the deceased is to be cremated.

Cut flowers are not appropriate for a funeral service. Some kind of floral piece, a spray or a wreath, is preferable.

Letters of condolence. Letters of condolence are sent to a family of any faith. See page 297 for such letters.

Mass cards. Mass cards may be sent to a Roman Catholic family by a Catholic or a non-Catholic. You may obtain them from any priest. It is customary to make an offering to the church at the time of asking for the card. Although a Roman Catholic might ask a priest to say a mass for a non-Catholic, it is not in good taste to send a mass card to a non-Catholic family.

Charitable contributions. Many families request that, instead of flowers, friends send contributions to charities or other organizations in which the deceased was interested. The organization sends the family a notice of the contribution. Your employer may wish to write a short note to the family of a close friend or relative and tell them that he is sending a donation in their name even though the gift is later announced by the organization.

Acknowledging flowers and mass cards. In case of the death of a member of the manager's family, write descriptions of floral pieces on the back of each accompanying card. Keep a separate file of mass cards and letters. Arrange all in alphabetical order. Make a separate notation of people who have sent both flowers and mass cards and of those who have written and also sent flowers or mass cards. Prepare two lists (see Figure 28).

List No. 1

FLOWERS

Name and Address (Alphabetical)	Kind of Flowers	Remarks
Brown, Mr. and Mrs. R.S. (Catherine and Bob) 275 E. 86th St. New York NY 10017	Spray, calla lilies	See Mass list
Jones, Mrs. A. (Mary) 79 W. Adams St. Boston MA 03201	Iris, white stock	Also wire from Mr. Jones (Tom)

LIST FOR ACKNOWLEDGMENT OF FLOWERS

List No. 2

MASSES

Name and Address (Alphabetical)	Particular form of card; how many masses	Remarks
Brown, Mr. and Mrs. R.S. (Catherine and Bob)	Society for the Propagation of the Faith	See Flowers list
Murphy, Thomas E. (Tom) 44 Fifth Ave. New York NY 10017	6 masses	

LIST FOR ACKNOWLEDGMENT OF CARDS

FIGURE 28

There is a difference of opinion as to whether good taste permits a typed acknowledgment or an engraved acknowledgment card. If there are comparatively few acknowledgments to write, undoubtedly the manager should write them in longhand. However, in the case of a prominent person, when hundreds of people send flowers, mass cards, and letters, the task of acknowledging each by a handwritten letter is too formidable. Engraved acknowledgment cards may be used to acknowledge letters of sympathy, flowers, and mass cards from persons who are unknown to the bereaved, but should not be sent to close personal friends.

Also make a list of the names and addresses of those who performed outstanding services, such as doctors, nurses, priest, rabbi, or minister, editorial writers, and the like. Your employer may want to send letters of appreciation to them.

From these lists it is simple to handle the acknowledgments. The first column gives you the proper salutation (Dear Mary, or the like); from the information in the second column, you can make a special comment in your acknowledgment of the type of flowers or mass card; the column headed *Remarks* gives you any other information you need. A thank-you letter should also be sent to those who sent memorial contributions to organizations. The notices from the organizations tell who made the contributions.

The employer will select from the lists the friends to whom he or she wishes to write in longhand; he or she will dictate acknowledgments to some of the others. The secretary will draft and type acknowledgments to the remainder of the names on the lists.

THE MANAGER'S BUSINESS CALLING CARDS

All executives who call on clients or customers or who make business calls for any reason carry business cards. You should be aware of, and able to make suggestions about, the social amenities for business calling cards. How do they differ from a social visiting card? What is the wording for them? Are they sent with presents from the manager to customers or clients?

The proper size for a manager's business calling card.   The business calling card is usually 3½″ by 2″ (which is larger than a social visiting card).

The arrangement of the wording on a business card.   On the executive level a business card often has the manager's name in the middle of the card and his or her title and the firm name in the lower left-hand corner, either one above the other. The address is then in the lower right-hand corner. If the business is in a large city, the street address and the city are used, but the state may be left out. If the company offices are in a small town, the name of the state is written on the same line as the town, no street address being necessary. Some very prominent executives omit their title from the card; only the executive's name and the name of the company appear on it. Some managers omit their telephone numbers.

A conservative type style, such as block or Roman, is popular, engraved in black on quality parchment or white card stock.

Initials and abbreviations, although not correct on social calling cards, may be used on business cards. However, the word *Company* should be written out unless the abbreviation "Co." is part of the registered name of the firm. The title "Mr." does not precede the manager's name on a business card as it does on a social card.

On business cards of company representatives below the executive level, the firm name is usually imprinted or engraved in the center of the card and the individual's name, title, and department in the lower left corner. The address and the telephone number may be in the lower right-hand corner. Sometimes, the person's name and title will be centered and the firm name will be in the left-hand corner and the firm address in the right-hand corner.

Cards used by salespersons or other representatives to advertise a company or a product frequently carry a trademark or emblem or an eye-catching design. The printing or engraving may be done partly in color. A calendar or advertising matter may appear on the back of the card. The telephone number is always on a card of this type.

Doctors and dentists frequently put their office hours on their cards.

A woman's business card.   The business card used by a woman is the same as a man's, with the exception that her title—Miss, Ms., or Mrs.—may, but need not, precede her name. A married woman should never use *Mrs.* in conjunction with her given—or first—name. For instance, if Dorothy Maxwell Hudson is vice-president of a department store and is married to Donald Hudson, the rules of etiquette require that she be addressed as *Mrs. Donald Hudson,* never *Mrs. Dorothy Hudson.* This custom poses a problem for a career woman who uses her married name. If she insists on observing the rules of etiquette she has one of two choices: (1) She can use her maiden name in business—say *Miss or (Ms.) Dorothy Maxwell*—and be *Mrs. Donald Hudson* the rest of the time. Or (2) she can use her given name and married name without *Miss, Ms.,* or *Mrs.*—*Dorothy Hudson.* Many women who reach the executive level long after marriage prefer using their married name without a title; this form is acceptable.

A woman doctor may use either her maiden name or her married name combined with her first name and her title. For instance, when Dr. Laura Rogers marries John Edwards, she may call herself *Dr. Laura Rogers.* On her professional cards she may use either *Laura Rogers, M.D.* or *Laura Edwards, M.D.*

Is it correct to send a business card with a present? An executive should not enclose a business card with a present, even though the present is going to a client or customer. The giving of a present is presumably a social gesture, and therefore a social card should be enclosed. This rule is honored more in the breach than in the observance. However, presidents or board chairpersons of large corporations often have a special card printed for enclosure with Christmas presents. It mentions the company name and the name of the executive sending the present, but in no way resembles a business card.

The exception to this rule of etiquette is the card enclosed with a present sent to a new business. In such cases, a business card is entirely correct.

A final tip to the secretary. Do not forget to put a reorder reminder with the manager's business calling cards. It usually takes ten days or two weeks (perhaps longer) to get engraved cards, even though you have the engraver's plate on hand. Until you have been working for the manager long enough to know his or her wishes, you should get approval before reordering. But don't let him or her run out of business calling cards. Stationery stores and printers have a wide selection of card stock and typefaces, if you are ordering for the first time. Rules concerning business card style have relaxed in recent years. Raised offset printing, for instance, is becoming increasingly popular and acceptable. Also, the traditional arrangement of copy is no longer adhered to as strictly.

How to Write Good Letters

PART 2

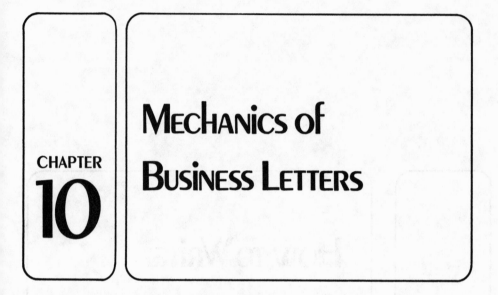

CHAPTER

10

Mechanics of Business Letters

This chapter presents the correct forms of the structural parts of letters. It also tells you how to select and order letterheads that will improve the appearance of your letters. The forms to use in writing and speaking to persons holding official or honorary positions are listed for your use in chapter 11.

Styles of letter setups. The standard styles in which letters are set up are:

1. Full block (Figure 29).
2. Block (Figure 30).
3. Semiblock (Figure 31).
4. Official (Figure 32).

Letters written in these styles are reproduced in the following pages. Read each of the letters for an explanation of its distinguishing characteristics.

Punctuation. Either mixed or open punctuation are most frequently used in the structural parts of a letter.

Mixed punctuation is the most popular style used in today's business letter. With this style you omit punctuation marks after the dateline, after the end of each line of the inside address, and after the signature lines. However, you do use a colon after the salutation and a comma after the complimentary close.

Open punctuation means the omission of punctuation marks after the dateline, each line of the address, the complimentary close, and each line of the signature. This style is used most often with the full-block letter style.

Where and how to type the dateline. The position of the dateline on the page depends to some extent on the style of letter used and the length of the letter. The dateline is usually typed from two to four spaces below the letterhead, or even more if the letter is a very short one. It should be flush with either the right- or left-hand margin, depending on the style of the letter.

The following suggestions should be kept in mind when typing the dateline.

1. Date the letter the day it is dictated, not the day it is typed.
2. Type the date conventionally, all on one line.
3. Do not use *d, nd, rd, st,* or *th* following the day of the month.
4. Do not abbreviate or use figures for the month.

Prentice-Hall, Inc.
Englewood Cliffs, N.J. 07632

Telex No. 13-5423

July 16, 19--

Ms. Sheila Jones
The Modern School for Secretaries
12 Harrington Place
Greenpoint NJ 07201

Dear Ms. Jones:

You have asked me to send you examples of letter styles being used in offices throughout the country.

This letter is an example of the full-block style of letter, which has been adopted as a standard at Prentice-Hall. We have reproduced it in our <u>Employee Manual</u> so that everyone will be familiar with the form and the instructions for its use.

Since Prentice-Hall is a leading exponent of modern business methods, we naturally use the most efficient letter form. This style saves time and energy.

As you see, there are no indentations. Everything, including the date and the complimentary close, begins at the extreme left. This uniformity eliminates several mechanical operations in typing letters.

Our dictaphone typists always use this form unless the dictator instructs otherwise. The dictator is at liberty to alter the form if a change is desirable for business reasons.

Since the dictator's name is typed in the signature, it is not considered necessary to include his initials in the identification line.

Sincerely,

Martha Scott
Correspondence Chief

hc

FIGURE 29 FULL BLOCK STYLE

The distinguishing feature of the full block style of letter is that all the structural parts of the letter begin flush with the left margin. There are no indentations. The dictator's initials are not included in the identification line. Open punctuation is used in the address and signature.

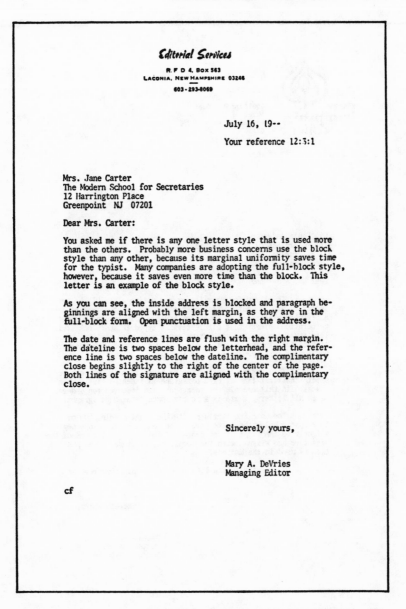

FIGURE 30   BLOCK STYLE

The distinguishing feature of the block style of letter is that the inside address and the paragraphs are blocked, flush with the left-hand margin. The salutation and attention line, if any, are aligned with the inside address. The date and reference line are flush with the right-hand margin. The typed signature is aligned with the complimentary close. Open punctuation is used.

new
hampshire
college

2500 North River Road
Manchester
New Hampshire
03104
Tel. 603-668-2211

July 16, 19--

Ms. Paula Anderson
The Modern School for Secretaries
12 Harrington Place
Greenpoint NJ 07201

Dear Ms. Anderson:

   Thank you for your letter requesting a semiblock style
letter to add to your correspondence manual. Most companies have
a definite preference as to letter style. Some leading business
corporations prefer that all letters be typed in semiblock style.
This style combines an attractive appearance with utility. Many
private secretaries, who are not usually concerned with mass production of correspondence, favor it.

   This style differs from the block form in only one re-
spect--the first line of each paragraph is indented five or ten
spaces. In this example the paragraphs are indented ten spaces.
As in all letters, there is a double space between paragraphs.

   The dateline is flush with the right margin, two or
four spaces below the letterhead. The complimentary close begins
slightly to the right of the center of the page. All lines of the
signature are aligned with the complimentary close. Open punctuation is used in the address.

   No identification line is used in this example.

              Very sincerely yours,

              Nancy Davis
              Chairperson, Business
              Education Department

cf

FIGURE 31   SEMIBLOCK STYLE

The distinguishing feature of a semiblock style of letter is that all structural parts of the
letter begin flush with the left-hand margin, but the first line of each paragraph is
indented five or ten spaces. All lines of the typed signature are aligned with the
complimentary close. The date is typed in the conventional position. Open punctuation is
used.

The National Secretaries Association

(INTERNATIONAL)

2440 PERSHING RD. • SUITE G 10 CROWN CENTER • KANSAS CITY, MISSOURI 64108 • 816—474-5755

Doris B. DiPalermo
EXECUTIVE DIRECTOR

July 16, 19-*

Dear Miss Kennedy:

Every correspondence manual should include a sample of the official style. It is used in many personal letters written by executives and professional persons, and looks unusually well on the executive-size letterhead.

The structural parts of the letter differ from the standard arrangement only in the position of the inside address. The salutation is placed two to five spaces below the dateline, depending upon the length of the letter. It establishes the left margin of the letter. The inside address is written block form, flush with the left margin, from two to five spaces below the final line of the signature. Open punctuation is used in the address.

The identification line, if used, should be placed two spaces below the last line of the address, and the enclosure mark two spaces below that. Because the dictator's name is typed in the signature, it is not necessary for the letter to carry an identification line. The typist's initials may be on the carbon of the letter, but not on the original.

Sincerely yours,

Leslie Thomas
Correspondence Secretary

Miss Janice Kennedy
The Modern School for Secretaries
12 Harrington Place
Greenpoint NJ 07201

1975-76 INTERNATIONAL BOARD OF DIRECTORS

Frances B. Jakes *International President* 3503 East Main Street Murfreesboro, TN 37130	**Lois J. Wilkinson, CPS** *International President-Elect* 13625 Ridgeland Drive Seminole, FL 33542	**Lillian E. Billmeier, CPS** *First Vice President* 1212 Woodcrest Lane, Apt. 4 East Lansing, MI 48823	**Connie McCauley** *Second Vice President* 18550 Hatteras St., Apt. 45 Tarzana, CA 91356	**Dorothy T. Robinson, CPS** *International Secretary* 3116 Laredo Drive Fort Worth, TX 76116	**Beverly H. Hamby, CPS** *International Treasurer* 13718 Camara Lane Houston, TX 77024
Jean Wright, CPS *Director, Great Lakes District* 1211 Devonshire Drive Champaign, IL 61820	**Kay Palazey, CPS** *Director, Northeast District* 35 Colonial Lake Drive Trenton, NJ 08638	**Nancy DeMars, CPS** *Director, Northwest District* 1919 Washburn Avenue North Minneapolis, MN 55411	**Joyce K. Walsh, CPS** *Director, Southeast District* 1014 Hammond Drive North Augusta, SC 29841	**Ann Michele** *Director, Southwest District* 1709 Lead S. E., Apt. 1 Albuquerque, NM 87106	

FIGURE 32 OFFICIAL STYLE

The distinguishing feature of the official style of letter is that the inside address is placed below the signature, flush with the left-hand margin, instead of before the salutation. The identification line and enclosure notations, if any, are typed two spaces below the last line of the address. Open punctuation is used. This style is especially appropriate for personal letters in business.

5. Do not spell out the day of the month or the year, except in very formal letters.

Right	*Wrong*
September 15, 19___	September 15th, 19___
	9/15___
	Sept. 15, 19___
	September fifteenth, nineteen hundred and

INSIDE ADDRESS

What the inside address contains.   The inside address contains the name of the addressee and the address, including the postal zip code number. In addressing an individual in a company, the inside address contains both the individual's name and that of the company. It may also contain the individual's business title.

Where to type the inside address.   Begin the inside address at the left-hand margin of the letter, not less than two spaces, nor more than 12, below the dateline. The exact position of the first line of the address depends on the length of the letter. The inside address should not extend beyond the middle of the page. In the block style of address, carry over part of an extremely long line to a second line. Indent the carry-over line three spaces. It is preferable to single space the address even if the body of the letter is double-spaced.

> The Mississippi Electrical Power
> and Light Company
> 148 West Tenth Street
> Jackson MS 39201

In the official style (Figure 32), place the inside address in the lower left-hand corner of the page, even with the left-hand margin of the letter and two spaces below the signature.

How to type the inside address.   1. The inside address should correspond exactly with the official name of the company addressed. If *Company, Co., The, Inc.,* or *&* is part of the company's official name, use the form shown by the company title.

2. Do not precede the street number with a word or a sign, or with a room number.

Right	*Wrong*
70 Fifth Avenue	No. 70 Fifth Avenue
	# 70 Fifth Avenue
70 Fifth Avenue, Room 305	Room 305, 70 Fifth Avenue

Use *post-office box number* in preference to street address, if you know it.

3. Spell out the numerical names of streets and avenues if they are numbers of 12 or under. When figures are used, do not follow with *d, st,* or *th.* Use figures for all house numbers except *One.* Separate the house number from a numerical name of a thoroughfare with a space, a hyphen, and a space. Authorities give different rules for writing addresses, but the following are standard, approved forms.

> 23 East Twelfth Street
> 23 East 13 Street
> One Fifth Avenue
> 2 Fifth Avenue
> 234 - 72 Street

4. Never abbreviate the name of a city, unless the abbreviation is standard—for example, *St. Louis, St. Paul.* Do abbreviate the names of states, territories, and United States possessions. Use the abbreviations published by the U.S. Postal Service (see chapter 5). Formerly, the best practice was to write out the names of states, territories, etc.

5. The postal zip code follows the state and is not separated from the state by a comma, nor is there a comma in the zip code number. Use two spaces between the last letter of a state name and the first digit of the postal zip code.

6. Even if there is no street address, put the city, state, and zip code on the same line. Formerly, the approved practice was to put the city and state on separate lines when there was no street address.

7. Do not abbreviate business titles or positions, such as president, secretary, and sales manager. *Mr., Mrs., Miss,* or *Ms.* precedes the individual's name even when the business title is used.

If a person's business title is short, place it on the first line; if it is long, place it on the second line.

Mr. James E. Lambert, President	Mr. George F. Moore
Lambert & Woolf Company	Advertising Manager
1005 Tower Street	Price & Patterson
Cleveland OH 44900	234 Seventh Avenue
	New York NY 10023

The modern trend is to omit the business title, particularly if it makes the address run over four lines. For example, *Advertising Manager* would be omitted in the preceding address.

8. In addressing an individual in a firm, corporation, or group, place the individual's name on the first line, and the company's name on the second line. When addressing a letter *to the attention* of such individual, place the attention line two spaces below the address.

9. Do not hyphenate a title unless it represents a combination of two offices.

10. When writing to the officer of a company who holds several offices, use only the title of the highest office, unless letters from him are signed differently.

11. If a letter is addressed to a particular department in a company, place the name of the company on the first line and the name of the department on the second line.

Forms of address.   (For the correct forms of address to those who hold official or honorary positions see the chart in chapter 11.)

1. Always precede a name by a title, unless initials indicating degrees (see 2.) or *Esquire* (see 4.) follow the name. The use of a business title or position or of *Sr., Jr., 2nd, III,* and the like after a name does not take the place of a title.

Right	*Wrong*
Mr. Ralph P. Edwards, III, President	Ralph P. Edwards, III, President

2. Initials or abbreviations indicating degrees and other honors are sometimes placed after the name of the person addressed. Use only the initials of the highest degree; more than one degree may be used, however, if the degrees are in different fields. Usually one lists the degree pertaining to the person's profession first, for example, *John Jones, LL.D., Ph.D.,* if he is practicing attorney by profession. A scholastic title is not used in combination with the abbreviation indicating that degree, but another title may be used in combination with abbreviations indicating degrees.

Right	*Wrong*
Dr. Robert E. Saunders (*preferred*)	Robert E. Saunders, A.B.,
or	A.M., Ph.D.
Robert E. Saunders, Ph.D.	

Right	*Wrong*
Dr. Ralph Jones (*preferred*) or Ralph Jones, M.D.	Dr. Ralph Jones, M.D.
The Reverend Perry E. Moore, D.D., LL.D.	

To a professor

Right	*Wrong*
Professor Robert E. Saunders	Professor Robert E. Saunders, Ph.D.

3. *Messrs.* may be used in addressing a firm (but not a company) of men, or men and women, when the names denote individuals. Do not use *Messrs.* as a form of address for corporations or other business organizations that bear impersonal names.

Right	*Wrong*
American Manufacturing Company	Messrs. American Manufacturing Company
Messrs. Marvin, Tobin, and Smart	Messrs. Marvin, Tobin, and Smart, Inc.
James Marshall & Sons	Messrs. James Marshall & Sons

4. *Esquire* or *Esq.* may be used in addressing prominent attorneys or other high-ranking professional men who do not have other titles. *Mr.* does not precede the name when *Esquire* or *Esq.* is used. In fact, no other title is used with *Esquire* or *Esq.* There is no feminine equivalent of *Esquire*. Do *not* use *Esquire* in addressing a woman attorney.

Right	*Wrong*
Honorable Richard P. Davis	Honorable Richard P. Davis, Esq.
Allison D. Wells, Esquire	Mr. Allison D. Wells, Esquire
Nathan Rogers, Jr., Esq.	Mr. Nathan Rogers, Jr., Esq.

Note: The title *Esq.* is commonly used in England and in her colonies. There it is the proper title to use in addressing the heads of business firms, banking executives, doctors, and the like.

Correct in England
Robert E. Meade, Esq., M.D.
Laurence D. Goode, Esq., M.D.

Forms for addressing women.   1. *Firm composed entirely of women.*

In addressing a firm composed of women either married or unmarried, use *Mesdames* or *Mmes.*

2. *Unmarried woman.* Use *Miss* or *Ms.* when you are addressing an unmarried woman or when you do not know whether she is married or unmarried.

3. *Married woman.* Socially a married woman is addressed by her husband's full name preceded by *Mrs.* In business, she may be addressed either by her husband's name or by her given name and her married name, preceded by *Mrs.* Use the form she prefers if you know it.

4. *Widow.* Socially a widow is addressed by her husband's full name preceded by *Mrs.* In business either her husband's full name or her given name and her married name, preceded by *Mrs.,* is correct. Use the form that she prefers if you know it.

5. *Divorcee.* If a divorcee retains her married name, the title *Mrs.* is preferable to *Miss.* If she uses her maiden name, she may use either *Miss* or *Mrs.* In business she may be addressed by her given name combined with her married name or by both her maiden and married names. Follow the form she prefers if you know it. Socially she is addressed by her maiden name combined with her married name.

As a general rule in items 3, 4, and 5 above, use *Mrs.* when you are addressing a married woman, a widow, or a divorcee, unless you know that she prefers *Ms.*

When Husband's Name Is Retained		When Maiden Name Is Used
Business	*Social*	*Business and Social*
Mrs. Margaret Weeks	Mrs. Barkley Weeks	Mrs. Margaret Barkley
Mrs. Margaret Barkley Weeks		Miss Margaret Barkley
Ms. Margaret Barkley Weeks		Ms. Margaret Barkley
Ms. Margaret Weeks		

6. *Wife of a titled man.* Do not address a married woman by her husband's title. Address her as *Mrs. Robert E. Adams* or *Mrs. R. E. Adams.* If she is addressed jointly with her husband, the correct form is *Dr. and Mrs. Robert E. Adams, Judge and Mrs. Irving Levey.*

7. *Professional women.* Address a woman with a professional title by her title followed by her given and last names. A married woman may use her maiden name in practicing her profession if she prefers.

When writing to a professional woman and her husband jointly, as husband and wife and in social correspondence, you may use or drop the woman's title. Traditionally, the woman's title is dropped, even if the husband and wife are both doctors, thus, *Dr.* and *Mrs.* John Williams. However, as more women are entering professional fields and value the use of their titles, the following alternatives may be used: *Dr.* John Williams and *Dr.* Mary Williams (traditional), *Dr.* Mary Williams and *Dr.* John Williams, *Drs.* John and Mary Williams (traditional), *Drs.* Mary and John Williams. When a professional woman is married to a man without a title, the following alternatives may be used: *Mr.* and *Mrs.* John Williams (traditional), *Dr.* Mary Williams and *Mr.* John Williams (the titled person preceding the untitled person), *Dr.* Mary and *Mr.* John Williams. If possible, follow the style preferred by the man and woman as shown in previous correspondence with them.

8. *Man and woman.* When writing to a man and woman in their individual capacities, address them by their respective titles, placing one name under the other.

Mrs. Jay S. Russell
Mr. Adam L. Matthews

When you do not know whether an addressee is a man or a woman, use the form of address appropriate for a man. For the correct form of addressing women holding honorary or official positions, see the chart in chapter 11.

SALUTATIONS

Where to type the salutation.   Type the salutation two spaces below the inside address, flush with the left-hand margin. If an *attention line* is used, type the salutation two spaces below the attention line.

How to type the salutation.   1. Capitalize the first word, the title, and the name. Do not capitalize *dear* when *my* precedes it, but do capitalize *my*, thus *My dear Mr. Jones.*
2. Use a colon following the salutation. A comma is used only in social letters, particularly those written in longhand.

Forms of salutation.   The preferred practice today is to use an informal salutation, whether or not the letter writer is acquainted with the person to whom he is writing. Thus, *Dear Mr. . . . . ,* instead of the more formal *My dear Mr. . . . . . .* and the antiquated *My dear Sir.* (See the chart in chapter 11 for the correct salutation to use when addressing people in honorary or official positions.)
1. Never use a designation of any kind after a salutation.

Right	*Wrong*
Dear Mr. Roberts:	Dear Mr. Roberts, C.P.A.:

2. Never use a business title or designation of position in a salutation.

Right	*Wrong*
Dear Mr. Adams:	Dear Secretary:
	Dear Secretary Ames:

3. If the letter is addressed to a company to the attention of an individual, the salutation is to the company, not to the individual.

4. Follow a title with the surname:

Right	*Wrong*
Dear Professor Ames:	Dear Professor:

5. The salutation in a letter that is not addressed to any particular person or firm, such as a general letter of recommendation, is *To Whom It May Concern.* Note that each word begins with a capital.

6. The salutation in a letter addressed to a group composed of men and women is, preferably, *Ladies and Gentlemen;* to a married couple, *Dear Mr. and Mrs. Marsh.* As in 7, Forms for addressing women, several alternative salutations may be used for professionals who are husband and wife and for a professional woman married to an untitled man: Dear *Dr.* and *Mrs.* Marsh (traditional, even if Mrs. Marsh is also a doctor), Dear *Drs.* Marsh (if both are doctors), Dear *Dr.* and *Mr.* Marsh (if he is untitled; the professional person is mentioned first).

Forms of salutation in letters addressed to women.   1. Do not use *Miss* as a salutation unless it is followed by a name.

Right	*Wrong*
Dear Miss Brown: (*preferred*)	Dear Miss:
Dear Ms. Brown:	
Dear Madam:	

2. If the letter is addressed to a firm of women, the salutation is *Ladies* or *Mesdames.* Do not use "Dear" or "My dear" with either of these salutations.

3. The salutation to two women with the same name is:

> Dear Mesdames Smith (*if married*)
> Dear Misses Smith (*if unmarried*)
> Dear Miss Smith and Mrs. Smith *or* Ladies
> (*if one is married and the other is not*)

BODY OF THE LETTER

How to type the body.   1. Single space unless the letter is very short. Single space a short letter if half-sheet letterheads are used.

2. Double space between paragraphs.

3. When the block style is used, begin each line flush with the left-hand margin of the letter.

4. When the semiblock style is used, indent the first line of each paragraph five to ten spaces.

5. Always indent paragraphs when a letter is double-spaced.

How to set up enumerated material in the body of the letter.

1. Indent five spaces from each margin of the letter—more if necessary to center the material.

2. Precede each item with a number, followed by a period. Or the number may be enclosed in parentheses.

3. Begin each line of the indented material two spaces to the right of the number.

4. Single space the material within each item, but double space between items.

How to write dates.   Usually in the body of the letter the date is written thus: *March 5.* When the day precedes the month, it is permissible to write the day out or to use the figure with the ordinal abbreviation. For example, *fifth of March,* or *5th of March.*

COMPLIMENTARY CLOSE

Where to type the complimentary close.   Type the complimentary close two spaces below the last line of the letter. Begin it slightly to the right of the center of the page, except in the full block style. It should never extend beyond the right margin of the letter. In letters of more than one page, at least two lines should be on the page with the close.

How to type the complimentary close.   1. Capitalize only the first word.

2. Follow the complimentary close with a comma. This is the better practice even when open punctuation is used in the inside address.

Forms of complimentary close. As with salutations, the preferred practice today is to use a warm, friendly, complimentary close. Thus: *Sincerely, Sincerely yours, Cordially, Cordially yours.* When writing to a company, *Sincerely yours* is preferable to *Cordially yours.* (See the chart in chapter 11 for the correct complimentary close to use in letters to persons in official or honorary positions.)

SIGNATURE

What the signature contains. The signature to a business letter usually consists of the typed name of the company, the signature of the writer, and the typed name of the writer and his business title. Some authorities recommend using the firm name when the letter is contractual. (For the use of *I* or *we* in letters, see page 333.) The modern trend and the approved practice is to omit the firm name, except in a signature to formal documents. The typed name of the writer can be omitted if it appears on the letterhead.

The inclusion in the signature of the writer's business title or position indicates that he is writing the letter in his official capacity. Thus, if an officer of a company writes a letter on firm stationery about a purely personal matter, his position is not included in the signature.

Firms of attorneys, certified public accountants, and the like frequently sign letters manually with the firm name, particularly if the letter expresses a professional opinion or gives professional advice.

Where to type the signature. When the firm name is included in the signature, type it two spaces below the complimentary close, the writer's name four spaces below the firm name, and the writer's position either on the same line or on the next line. When the firm name is not included, type the writer's name and position four spaces below the complimentary close.

When the inside address is typed in block form, align the signature with the first letter of the complimentary close. The lines of the signature should be blocked, unless an unusually long line makes this arrangement impractical. No line of the signature should extend beyond the right-hand margin of the letter.

How to type the signature.   1. Type the firm name in capitals, exactly as it appears on the letterhead.

2. Type the signature exactly as the dictator signs his name.

Right	*Wrong*
Richard P. Miller	*Richard P. Miller*
Richard P. Miller	R. P. Miller
President	President

3. Business titles and degree letters follow the typed signature. No title precedes either the written or typed signature except *Miss* or *Mrs.*

Forms of signature for women.   1. An *unmarried woman* may precede her typed signature with *Miss* in parentheses, or omit it.

Eleanor Davis	*Eleanor Davis*
(Miss) Eleanor Davis	Eleanor Davis

2. A *married woman* may indicate in her signature the title to be used in addressing her. She may precede her typed signature with *Mrs.* in parentheses, or she may type her married name in parentheses beneath the pen-written signature. The latter form is compulsory for social usage.

Eleanor Davis	*Eleanor Davis*
(Mrs.) Eleanor Davis	(Mrs. John R. Davis)

3. A *widow* signs her name as she did before her husband's death.

4. Assuming that a divorcee does not use her maiden name, she signs her given name, with or without the initial of her maiden name, and her former husband's surname. The typed signature is the same as the written signature, and may be preceded by *Mrs.* in parentheses. Or the typed signature may combine her maiden name with her former husband's surname.

Right	*Wrong*
Eleanor M. Davis	*Eleanor M. Davis*
(Mrs.) Eleanor M. Davis	(Mrs. John R. Davis)
Eleanor M. Davis	
(Mrs. Montgomery Davis)	

Secretary's signature.   When you sign your employer's name to a letter, place your initials immediately below it.

> Yours very truly,
>
> *Hiram R. Jones* M.B.
> Hiram R. Jones
> President

When you sign a letter in your own name as secretary to your employer, do not include his initials unless another person in the organization has the same name. Always precede your employer's name by a title.

Right	*Wrong*
Elizabeth Mason	Secretary to Mr. R. S. Nelson
Secretary to Mr. Nelson	Secretary to R. S. Nelson

MISCELLANEOUS STRUCTURAL PARTS OF LETTERS

Attention line.   Strictly business letters addressed to a firm are often directed to the attention of an individual by the use of an attention line, in preference to addressing the letter to the individual. This practice marks the letter as a business rather than a personal letter and ensures that it will be opened promptly should the person to whom it is directed not be available.

Type the attention line two spaces below the address. The word *of* is not necessary. The attention line has no punctuation and is not underscored. When a letter addressed to a firm has an attention line, the salutation is *Gentlemen* because the salutation is to the firm, not the individual. It is permissible to direct the letter to the attention of an individual without including his given name or initials, if they are unknown.

Preferable	Attention Mr. Walter R. Richardson
Permissible	Attention Mr. Richardson

Subject line.   Subject lines are a convenience to both the writer and the reader. They make it unnecessary for the writer to devote the first paragraph of his letter to a routine explanation of the subject of the letter; they facilitate the distribution of mail to various departments; they also expedite subject filing.

Center the subject line two spaces beneath the salutation. If the full-block style of letter (Figure 29) is used, type the subject line flush with the left-hand margin. Never place the subject line before the salutation. It is part of the body of the letter, not of the heading.

Sometimes the subject line is preceded by *In re* or *Subject.* The better practice is to omit these words, except in letters about legal matters. In these letters *In re* is customarily used. No punctuation follows *In re;* a colon follows *Subject.* The important words in a subject line are capitalized. The last line may be underlined, but the modern trend is to omit the underlining.

Reference line.   If a file reference is given in an incoming letter, include a reference line in your reply, whether requested or not. Place your own reference beneath the incoming reference.

When letterheads include a printed reference notation, such as *In reply please refer to,* type the reference line after it. Otherwise, type the reference line about four spaces beneath the date.

> Your File 3476   April 20, 19. .
> Our File 2785   *or*
>   Our Order 846 D

Identification line.   The identification line shows who dictated the letter and who typed it. The only purpose of the identification line is for reference by the business organization *writing* the letter. The dictator's name is typed in the signature. Unless company rules require otherwise, type nothing but your initials in the identification line and do not show them on the original of the letter.

If your company requires the usual identification line, type the initials of the dictator and the stenographer flush with the left-hand margin, on a line with the last line of the signature. If the official style of letter is used (Figure 32), the identification line is typed two spaces below the address. When the person who signs the letter has not dictated it, type his initials first and follow with those of the dictator and the transcriber.

Enclosure mark.   When a letter contains enclosures, type the word *Enclosure* or the abbreviation *Enc.* flush with the left-hand margin one or two spaces beneath the identification line. If there is more than one enclosure, indicate the number. If the enclosures are of special importance, identify them. If an enclosure is to be returned, make a notation to that effect.

RPE: es	RPE: es	RPE: es
Enclosure	Enc. 2	Enc. Cert. ck. $2,350
		Mtge.——Nelson to Jones

RPE: es
Enc. Policy 35 4698-M (to be returned)

"Personal" notation.   A letter or envelope should not be marked "Personal" or "Confidential" as a device to catch the attention of a busy manager. These words should be used only when no one but the addressee is supposed to see the letter. Type the word *Personal* or *Confidential* four spaces above the address, which is at the top of the letter. You may underline the notation to make it more noticeable.

Mailing notation.   When a letter is sent by any method other than regular mail, type a notation of the exact method on the envelope, in the space below the stamps and above the address. Make a similar notation on the carbon copy of the letter.

Carbon copy distribution notation.   When a carbon copy is to be sent to another person, type the distribution notation flush with the left-hand margin, below all other notations. If space permits, separate it from the other notations by two spaces.

SRE: ng
Enclosure
Copy to Mr. S. A. Williams

The abbreviation *c.c.* may be used instead of *Copy to.*

Blind copy notation. Type the carbon copy notation in the upper left-hand portion of the letter *on the carbons only.* This indicates that the addressee of the letter does not know that a copy was sent to anyone.

Postscript.   When it is necessary to add a postscript to a letter, type it two spaces below the identification line or the last notation on the letter. Indent the left margin of the postscript five spaces from the left margin of the letter. You may include or omit the abbreviation "P.S." Use "P.P.S." with a second postscript. Type the dictator's initials after the postscript.

Heading on second page.   If the letter runs to two or more pages, use a plain sheet, without a letterhead, but of the same size and quality of paper as the letterhead. Of course, your company might have special stationery for the continuation pages. The heading should contain the name of the addressee, the number of the page, and the date, and the margins should be exactly the same as those for the first sheet. Leave spaces between the heading and the body of the letter.

Mr. R. H. Smith   2.   September 12, 19—

You should have at least two lines of the body of the letter, exclusive of complimentary close, signature, etc., on the continuation sheet.

There is no need to use the word "continued" at the bottom of the first page. The fact that no signature appears at the end of the page makes it obvious that another page follows.

ENVELOPES

Figures 33 and 34 show acceptable and commonly used styles of address on envelopes, They also show the correct placement of the attention line and personal and special delivery notations.

```
Prentice-Hall, Inc.
Englewood Cliffs, N.J.  07632



                                                    FIRST CLASS MAIL

         PERSONAL
                    Mr. R. S. Jackson, President
                    Northern Manufacturing Company
                    25 West 79 Street
                    Milwaukee  WI   12345
```

FIGURE 33   ENVELOPE SHOWING CORRECT PLACEMENT OF PERSONAL NOTATION

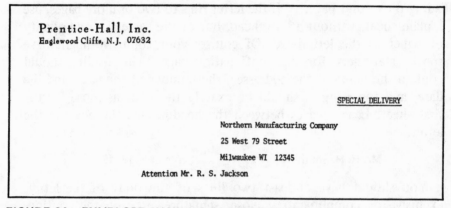

Prentice-Hall, Inc.
Englewood Cliffs, N.J. 07632

SPECIAL DELIVERY

Northern Manufacturing Company

25 West 79 Street

Milwaukee WI   12345

Attention Mr. R. S. Jackson

FIGURE 34   ENVELOPE SHOWING CORRECT PLACEMENTS OF ATTENTION LINE AND SPECIAL DELIVERY NOTATION

The items in the envelope address are the same as those in the inside address (see page 216). It is important that you cooperate with the U.S. Postal Service and use the official post office abbreviation of the state, followed by the zip code, in the outside address (see chapter 5).

The name of a foreign country is written in capitals in an address on the envelope, but with only initial capitals in the inside address.

HOW TO SELECT
AND ORDER STATIONERY

Letterhead sizes.   Common use has standardized 8½" by 11" as the most practical size for business letterheads. Envelopes, files, and business machines are all geared most efficiently to this size. It is referred to as "letterhead size," although letterheads in other sizes are used. The executive size (7 ¼" by 10 ½") is frequently selected for the personal stationery of executives. Other variations in size are 8" by 10 ½" and 7 ½" by 10".

Continuation sheets.   Continuation sheets are frequently referred to as "second sheets." Technically, the reference is inaccurate. Second sheets are papers used for making multiple copies of letters and other documents.

Continuation sheets should be of the same size and quality as the letterhead. Some firms print their name and address in small type at the top of the continuation sheet, near the left-hand margin. Order them when you order the letterheads. Comparatively few letters run to more than one page, but the percentage varies with the office. After you have placed two or three orders for stationery, you will be able to judge fairly accurately the proportion of continuation sheets to letterheads.

Executive letterheads.   Letterheads for the personal use of top executives possess dignity to impress the reader. Their chief characteristic is simplicity, attained by black (color has become acceptable in recent years) engraved copy on pure white paper of heavy substance and high quality. In addition to the company letterhead, the full name of the office is engraved at the left margin, with the title of the office he holds directly underneath it. The size of the sheet is sometimes smaller than standard letterhead.

An executive may use his or her business letterheads for all correspondence except answers to formal invitations, letters of condolence, or answers to letters of condolence from personal friends. For these purposes, he should use writing paper engraved with his residence address or with both his name and residence address. The stationery is usually the Monarch size, 7½" by 10½".

Envelopes.   Envelopes should be of the same quality as the letterhead. The most popular sizes for business are:

No. 6-3/4	3-5/8 by 6-1/2 (in.)
Monarch	3-7/8 by 7-1/2
No. 9	3-7/8 by 8-7/8
No. 10	4-1/8 by 9-1/2

No. 6¾, 9, and 10 fit 8½ by 11 letterheads. The Monarch size is used with a letterhead size 7¼ by 10½, the executive size stationery. Another size, the No. 5 Baronial, 4¼ by 5-1/8, is also sometimes used by business executives for personal stationery.

How to select paper for letterheads.   Good paper enhances the effectiveness of a letterhead. The features to consider in selecting paper for a business letterhead are (1) appearance and feel, (2) workability, (3) permanence, and (4) cost.

Appearance and feel. These are the foremost standards by which letterhead papers are evaluated. High-grade papers have good bulk, crispness, and crackle like a new bank note.

Workability. Workability determines the ease of use, economy of operation, and quality of workmanship in the office and in the pressroom. In the office, the workability of the paper is judged by its ability to reproduce clearly defined characters, to withstand erasures, and to permit a smooth, flowing signature. In the pressroom, workability means the adaptability of paper to the various printing processes.

Permanence. Strength and durability are prime requisites of good letterheads and envelopes.

Cost. The difference in price between a cheap bond and paper of the highest quality is a considerable amount when quoted by the ream, but the difference in the cost of a letter written on the highest quality paper is very little more than the same letter written on the cheapest of business letter paper.

How to judge the quality of paper. The quality of paper may be judged by its appearance and use characteristics.

Weight. Paper weight is measured by the ream, which consists of 500 sheets, 17″ by 22″. There are 2,000 business letterheads in a ream. When we speak of "substance 16" letterhead, we mean that 2,000 sheets, 8½″ by 11″, weigh 16 pounds. The weight of the ream may be 20 pounds, 24 pounds, or even more. Figure 35 indicates the most practical weights for various uses.

Weight of Paper	
Use	*Substance Weight (In order of preference)*
Executive letterheads	24, 20
Company letterheads	24, 20
Personal or semibusiness letterheads	24, 20
Airmail letterheads	13, 9
2nd page letterheads	Same as letterhead
Branch office and salesperson's letterheads	20, 16
Circular or form letters	20, 24
Hotel, fraternal or club letterheads	24, 20

Courtesy Hammermill Paper Company

FIGURE 35   CHART SHOWING WEIGHTS OF PAPER FOR VARIOUS USES

Content. Paper used for business purposes is made of wood pulp, cotton fiber, or from a combination of the two.

Most letterhead paper is made from chemically treated wood pulp. It is manufactured in a range of grades and qualities to meet the various demands of business.

At one time watermark rag content paper, and later 100 percent cotton content paper, was considered synonymous with the best quality paper. Today, in the commercial field, fine quality paper is not confined to cotton and rag but also includes the better grades of wood pulp.

Grain. All paper has a "grain," or chief fiber direction. It comes from the process by which the paper is made. In letterheads the grain should be parallel to the direction of the writing.[1] The sheets hug the typewriter platen better and provide a smoother, firmer surface for the type impression. Erasing is easier with the grain parallel to the platen, and paper always folds easier *with,* rather than against, the grain. There is today a growing demand for paper with the grain perpendicular to the writing to meet the requirements of the small printing presses used in many offices.

Every sheet of paper has a "felt" side and a "wire" side. The "felt" side of the paper is the "top" side, the side from which the watermark (the design made by the roller) can be read. The letterhead should be printed on the felt side.

How to order stationery. Get a written quotation that specifies the weight and content of paper and the kind of engraving or printing that will be on it.

In placing your order, specify:

1. The quantity in sheets
2. The weight
3. The content
4. The grain
5. That the letterhead shall be printed on the "felt" side of the paper
6. The size
7. The color
8. The previous order number if a repeat order
9. The supplier's reference number if an initial order. Include a sample with your order if possible.

---

[1]Letterheads to be used with one of the duplicating processes are an exception.

Forms of Address for Official or Honorary Positions

The chart in this chapter gives the correct forms of written address, salutation, and complimentary close for letters to persons holding official or honorary titles, whether of high or low rank. It also gives the correct form of referring to those persons in a letter and the correct form to use in speaking to, or informally introducing, them. (The form of informal introduction and the form of reference to a person are usually similar. Where they differ, the form of reference is shown in parentheses.)

To facilitate usage, the forms of addresses are presented in nine groups:

You should make every effort to learn the name of the person addressed, as well as his or her title. Use the name in writing, except in those few instances where the name is omitted in the chart. If you know the person's title only, address him by the title prefaced by *The.* For example, *The Lieutenant Governor of Iowa.* The formal salutation would be *Sir* or *Madam.*

When a person is acting as an official, the word *acting* precedes the title in the address, but not in the salutation or spoken address. For example, *Acting Mayor of Memphis, Dear Mayor Blank.*

A person who has held a position entitling him to be addressed as *The Honorable* is addressed as *The Honorable* after retirement. The title itself, such as Senator or Governor, is not used in the address or salutation. Even a former president is called *Mr.* An exception to this practice is the title of *Judge.* A person who has once been a judge customarily retains his title even when addressed formally. Retired officers of the armed forces retain their titles, but their retirement is indicated, thus, *Lieutenant General John D. Blank, U.S.A., Retired.*

In many cases the name in the address is followed by the abbreviation of a scholastic degree. If you do not know whether the addressee has the degree, you should not use the initials. Nor should a person be addressed by a scholastic title unless he or she actually possesses the degree that the title indicates.

The wife of an American official does not share her husband's title. She is always addressed as *Mrs. Blank.* When they are addressed jointly, the address is, for example, *Ambassador and Mrs. Blank.* Nor does a husband share his wife's title. When they are addressed jointly, if he does not have a title, the traditional address is *Mr. and Mrs. J.W. Blank,* regardless of any high-ranking title she may hold. Alternatives to the traditional address that include her title if her husband is untitled are: *Ambassador* Ruth Blank and *Mr.* J. W. Blank (the titled person preceding the untitled person), *Ambassador* Ruth and *Mr.* J. W. Blank, *Ambassador* and *Mr.* Blank. (See page 220 for guides to addressing a husband and wife when both are doctors and when the wife is a doctor and the husband is not.)

Women in official or honorary positions are addressed just as men in similar positions, except that Madam replaces Sir, and Mrs., Miss, or Ms. replaces Mr. Ms. may be substituted for *Miss* or *Mrs.* in cases where the marital status of the woman is unknown or where the woman has stipulated that she prefers the title *Ms.*

Note: In the following chart, Correct Forms of Address, the form of address for a man is used throughout, except where not applicable. To use the form of address for a woman in any of these positions, use the substitution *Madam* for *Sir,* and *Mrs., Miss,* or *Ms.* for *Mr.* Thus, Dear *Madam; Mrs.* Blank, Representative from New York; The Lieutenant Governor of Iowa, *Miss* Blank; The American Minister, *Ms.* Blank. The *Mr.* preceding a title becomes *Madam;* thus, *Madam* Secretary, *Madam* Ambassador. Use *Esquire* or *Esq.* in addressing a man, where appropriate; never use *Esquire* in addressing a woman.

Correct Forms of Address

UNITED STATES GOVERNMENT OFFICIALS

Personage*	Envelope and Inside Address (Add City, State, Zip)	Formal Salutation	Informal Salutation	Formal Close	Informal Close	1. Spoken Address 2. Informal Introduction or Reference
The President	The President The White House	Mr. President	Dear Mr. President:	Respectfully yours,	Very respectfully yours, Very truly yours, or Sincerely yours.	1. Mr. President 2. Not introduced (The President)
Former President of the United States[1]	The Honorable William R. Blank (local address)	Sir:	Dear Mr. Blank:	Respectfully yours,	Sincerely yours,	1. Mr. Blank 2. Former President Blank *or* Mr. Blank
The Vice-President of the United States	The Vice-President of the United States United States Senate	Mr. Vice-President:	Dear Mr. Vice-President	Very truly yours,	Sincerely yours,	1. Mr. Vice-President *or* Mr. Blank The Vice-President
The Chief Justice of the United States Supreme Court	The Chief Justice of the United States The Supreme Court of the United States	Sir:	Dear Mr. Chief Justice:	Very truly yours,	Sincerely yours,	1. Mr. Chief Justice 2. The Chief Justice
Associate Justice of the United States Supreme Court	Mr. Justice Blank The Supreme Court of the United States	Sir:	Dear Mr. Justice:	Very truly yours,	Sincerely yours,	1. Mr. Justice Blank *or* Justice Blank 2. Mr. Justice Blank

*See page 236 for appropriate substitutions for women in these positions.

[1] If a former president has a title, such as *General of the Army*, address him by it.

237

UNITED STATES GOVERNMENT OFFICIALS *continued*

Personage*	Envelope and Inside Address (Add City, State, Zip)	Formal Salutation	Informal Salutation	Formal Close	Informal Close	1. Spoken Address 2. Informal Introduction or Reference
Retired Justice of the United States Supreme Court	The Honorable William R. Blank (local address)	Sir:	Dear Justice Blank:	Very truly yours,	Sincerely yours,	1. Mr. Justice Blank *or* Justice Blank 2. Mr. Justice Blank
The Speaker of the House of Representatives	The Honorable William R. Blank Speaker of the House of Representatives	Sir:	Dear Mr. Speaker: *or* Dear Mr. Blank:	Very truly yours,	Sincerely yours,	1. Mr. Speaker *or* Mr. Blank 2. The Speaker, Mr. Blank (The Speaker *or* Mr. Blank)
Former Speaker of the House of Representatives	The Honorable William R. Blank (local address)	Sir:	Dear Mr. Blank:	Very truly yours,	Sincerely yours,	1. Mr. Blank 2. Mr. Blank
Cabinet Officers addressed as "Secretary"2	The Honorable William R. Blank Secretary of State The Honorable William R. Blank Secretary of State of the United States of America (if written from abroad)	Sir:	Dear Mr. Secretary:	Very truly yours,	Sincerely yours,	1. Mr. Secretary *or* Secretary Blank *or* Mr. Blank 2. The Secretary of State, Mr. Blank (Mr. Blank *or* The Secretary)
Former Cabinet Officer	The Honorable William R. Blank (local address)	Dear Sir:	Dear Mr. Blank:	Very truly yours,	Sincerely yours,	1. Mr. Blank 2. Mr. Blank

Postmaster General	The Honorable William R. Blank The Postmaster General	Sir:	Dear Mr. Postmaster General:	Very truly yours,	Sincerely yours,	1. Mr. Postmaster General *or* Postmaster General Blank *or* Mr. Blank 2. The Postmaster General, Mr. Blank (Mr. Blank *or* The Postmaster General)
The Attorney General	The Honorable William R. Blank The Attorney General	Sir:	Dear Mr. Attorney General:	Very truly yours,	Sincerely yours,	1. Mr. Attorney General *or* Attorney General Blank 2. The Attorney General, Mr. Blank (Mr. Blank *or* The Attorney General)
Under Secretary of a Department	The Honorable William R. Blank Under Secretary of Labor	Dear Mr. Blank:	Dear Mr. Blank:	Very truly yours,	Sincerely yours,	1. Mr. Blank 2. Mr. Blank
United States Senator	The Honorable William R. Blank United States Senate	Sir:	Dear Senator Blank:	Very truly yours,	Sincerely yours,	1. Senator Blank *or* Senator 2. Senator Blank
Former Senator	The Honorable William R. Blank (local address)	Dear Sir:	Dear Senator Blank:	Very truly yours,	Sincerely yours,	1. Senator Blank *or* Senator 2. Senator Blank

*See page 236 for appropriate substitutions for women in these positions.

[2] Titles for cabinet secretaries are Secretary of State; Secretary of the Treasury; Secretary of Defense; Secretary of the Interior; Secretary of Agriculture; Secretary of Commerce; Secretary of Labor; Secretary of Health, Education, and Welfare; Secretary of Housing and Urban Development; Secretary of Transportation.

UNITED STATES GOVERNMENT OFFICIALS *continued*

Personage*	Envelope and Inside Address (Add City, State, Zip)	Formal Salutation	Informal Salutation	Formal Close	Informal Close	1. Spoken Address 2. Informal Introduction or Reference
Senator-elect	Honorable William R. Blank Senator-elect United States Senate	Dear Sir:	Dear Mr. Blank:	Very truly yours,	Sincerely yours,	1. Mr. Blank 2. Senator-elect Blank *or* Mr. Blank
Committee Chairman— United States Senate	The Honorable William R. Blank, Chairman Committee on Foreign Affairs United States Senate	Dear Mr. Chairman:	Dear Mr. Chairman: *or* Dear Senator Blank:	Very truly yours,	Sincerely yours,	1. Mr. Chairman *or* Senator Blank *or* Senator 2. The Chairman *or* Senator Blank
Subcommittee Chairman— United States Senate	The Honorable William R. Blank, Chairman, Subcommittee on Foreign Affairs United States Senate	Dear Senator Blank:	Dear Senator Blank:	Very truly yours,	Sincerely yours,	1. Senator Blank *or* Senator 2. Senator Blank
United States Representative or Congressman[3]	The Honorable William R. Blank House of Representatives The Honorable William R. Blank Representative in Congress (local address) (when away from Washington, DC)	Sir:	Dear Mr. Blank:	Very truly yours,	Sincerely yours,	1. Mr. Blank 2. Mr. Blank, Representative (Congressman) from New York *or* Mr. Blank

Former Representative	The Honorable William R. Blank (local address)	Dear Sir: *or* Dear Mr. Blank:	Dear Mr. Blank:	Very truly yours,	Sincerely yours,	1. Mr. Blank 2. Mr. Blank
Territorial Delegate	The Honorable William R. Blank Delegate of Puerto Rico House of Representatives	Dear Sir: *or* Dear Mr. Blank:	Dear Mr. Blank:	Very truly yours,	Sincerely yours,	1. Mr. Blank 2. Mr. Blank
Resident Commissioner	The Honorable William R. Blank Resident Commissioner of (Territory) House of Representatives	Dear Sir: *or* Dear Mr. Blank:	Dear Mr. Blank:	Very truly yours,	Sincerely yours,	1. Mr. Blank 2. Mr. Blank
Directors or Heads of Independent Federal Offices, Agencies, Commissions, Organizations, etc.	The Honorable William R. Blank Director, Mutual Security Agency	Dear Mr. Director (Commissioner, etc.):	Dear Mr. Blank:	Very truly yours,	Sincerely yours,	1. Mr. Blank 2. Mr. Blank
Other High Officials of the United States, in general: Public Printer, Comptroller General	The Honorable William R. Blank Public Printer The Honorable William R. Blank Comptroller General of the United States	Dear Sir: *or* Dear Mr. Blank:	Dear Mr. Blank:	Very truly yours,	Sincerely yours,	1. Mr. Blank 2. Mr. Blank

*See page 236 for appropriate substitutions for women in these positions.

[3]The official title of a "congressman" is *Representative*. Strictly speaking, senators are also congressmen.

UNITED STATES GOVERNMENT OFFICIALS *continued*

Personage*	Envelope and Inside Address (Add City, State, Zip)	Formal Salutation	Informal Salutation	Formal Close	Informal Close	1. Spoken Address 2. Informal Introduction or Reference
Secretary to the President	The Honorable William R. Blank Secretary to the President The White House	Dear Sir: *or* Dear Mr. Blank:	Dear Mr. Blank:	Very truly yours,	Sincerely yours,	1. Mr. Blank 2. Mr. Blank
Assistant Secretary to the President	The Honorable William R. Blank Assistant Secretary to the President The White House	Dear Sir: *or* Dear Mr. Blank:	Dear Mr. Blank:	Very truly yours,	Sincerely yours,	1. Mr. Blank 2. Mr. Blank
Press Secretary to the President	Mr. William R. Blank Press Secretary to the President The White House	Dear Sir: *or* Dear Mr. Blank:	Dear Mr. Blank:	Very truly yours,	Sincerely yours,	1. Mr. Blank 2. Mr. Blank

STATE AND LOCAL GOVERNMENT OFFICIALS

Personage	Envelope and Inside Address	Formal Salutation	Informal Salutation	Formal Close	Informal Close	Spoken Address / Informal Introduction or Reference
Governor of a State or Territory[1]	The Honorable William R. Blank Governor of New York	Sir:	Dear Governor Blank:	Respectfully yours,	Very sincerely yours,	1. Governor Blank *or* Governor 2. a) Governor Blank b) The Governor c) The Governor of New York (used only outside his or her own state)

Position	Address					
Acting Governor of a State or Territory	The Honorable William R. Blank Acting Governor of Connecticut	Sir:	Dear Mr. Blank:	Respectfully yours,	Very sincerely yours,	1. Mr. Blank 2. Mr. Blank
Lieutenant Governor	The Honorable William R. Blank Lieutenant Governor of Iowa	Sir:	Dear Mr. Blank:	Respectfully yours, *or* Very truly yours,	Sincerely yours,	1. Mr. Blank 2. The Lieutenant Governor of Iowa, Mr. Blank, *or* The Lieutenant Governor
Secretary of State	The Honorable William R. Blank Secretary of State of New York	Sir:	Dear Mr. Secretary:	Very truly yours,	Sincerely yours,	1. Mr. Blank 2. Mr. Blank
Attorney General	The Honorable William R. Blank Attorney General of Massachusetts	Sir:	Dear Mr. Attorney General:	Very truly yours,	Sincerely yours,	1. Mr. Blank 2. Mr. Blank
President of the Senate of a State	The Honorable William R. Blank President of the Senate of the State of Virginia	Sir:	Dear Mr. Blank:	Very truly yours,	Sincerely yours,	1. Mr. Blank 2. Mr. Blank
Speaker of the Assembly or The House of Representatives[2]	The Honorable William R. Blank Speaker of the Assembly of the State of New York	Sir:	Dear Mr. Blank:	Very truly yours,	Sincerely yours,	1. Mr. Blank 2. Mr. Blank

*See page 236 for appropriate substitutions for women in these positions.

[1]The form of addressing governors varies in the different states. The form given here is the one used in most states. In Massachusetts by law and in some other states by courtesy, the form is *His (Her) Excellency, the Governor of Massachusetts.*

[2]In most states the lower branch of the legislature is the House of Representatives. The exceptions to this are: New York, California, Wisconsin, and Nevada, where it is known as the Assembly; Maryland, Virginia, and West Virginia—the House of Delegates; New Jersey—the House of General Assembly.

STATE AND LOCAL GOVERNMENT OFFICIALS *continued*

Personage*	Envelope and Inside Address (Add City, State, Zip)	Formal Salutation	Informal Salutation	Formal Close	Informal Close	1. Spoken Address 2. Informal Introduction or Reference
Treasurer, Auditor, or Comptroller of a State	The Honorable William R. Blank Treasurer of the State of Tennessee	Dear Sir:	Dear Mr. Blank:	Very truly yours,	Sincerely yours,	1. Mr. Blank 2. Mr. Blank
State Senator	The Honorable William R. Blank The State Senate	Dear Sir:	Dear Senator Blank:	Very truly yours,	Sincerely yours,	1. Senator Blank *or* Senator 2. Senator Blank
State Representative, Assemblyman, or Delegate	The Honorable William R. Blank House of Delegates	Dear Sir:	Dear Mr. Blank:	Very truly yours,	Sincerely yours,	1. Mr. Blank 2. Mr. Blank *or* Delegate Blank
District Attorney	The Honorable William R. Blank District Attorney, Albany County County Courthouse	Dear Sir:	Dear Mr. Blank:	Very truly yours,	Sincerely yours,	1. Mr. Blank 2. Mr. Blank
Mayor of a city	The Honorable William R. Blank Mayor of Detroit	Dear Sir:	Dear Mayor Blank:	Very truly yours,	Sincerely yours,	1. Mayor Blank *or* Mr. Mayor 2. Mayor Blank
President of a Board of Commissioners	The Honorable William R. Blank, President Board of Commissioners of the City of Buffalo	Dear Sir:	Dear Mr. Blank:	Very truly yours,	Sincerely yours,	1. Mr. Blank 2. Mr. Blank

City Attorney, City Counsel, Corporation Counsel	The Honorable William R. Blank, City Attorney (City Counsel, Corporation Counsel)	Dear Sir:	Dear Mr. Blank:	Very truly yours,	Sincerely yours,	1. Mr. Blank 2. Mr. Blank
Alderman	Alderman William R. Blank City Hall	Dear Sir:	Dear Mr. Blank:	Very truly yours,	Sincerely yours,	1. Mr. Blank 2. Mr. Blank

COURT OFFICIALS

Chief Justice[1] of a State Supreme Court	The Honorable William R. Blank Chief Justice of the Supreme Court of Minnesota[2]	Sir:	Dear Mr. Chief Justice:	Very truly yours,	Sincerely yours,	1. Mr. Chief Justice *or* Judge Blank 2. Mr. Chief Justice Blank *or* Judge Blank
Associate Justice of a Supreme Court of a State	The Honorable William R. Blank Associate Justice of the Supreme Court of Minnesota	Sir:	Dear Justice Blank:	Very truly yours,	Sincerely yours,	1. Mr. Justice Blank 2. Mr. Justice Blank
Presiding Justice	The Honorable William R. Blank Presiding Justice, Appellate Division Supreme Court of New York	Sir:	Dear Justice Blank:	Very truly yours,	Sincerely yours,	1. Mr. Justice (*or* Judge) Blank 2. Mr. Justice (*or* Judge Blank)

*See page 236 for appropriate substitutions for women in these positions.

[1]If his or her official title is *Chief Judge* substitute *Chief Judge* for *Chief Justice*, but never use *Mr.*, *Mrs.*, *Miss*, or *Ms.* with *Chief Judge* or *Judge*.

[2]Substitute here the appropriate name of the court. For example, the highest court in New York State is called the Court of Appeals.

COURT OFFICIALS *continued*

Personage*	Envelope and Inside Address (Add City, State, Zip, or City, Country)	Formal Salutation	Informal Salutation	Formal Close	Informal Close	1. Spoken Address 2. Informal Introduction or Reference
Judge of a Court[3]	The Honorable William R. Blank Judge of the United States District Court for the Southern District of California	Sir:	Dear Judge Blank:	Very truly yours,	Sincerely yours,	1. Judge Blank 2. Judge Blank
Clerk of a Court	William R. Blank, Esquire Clerk of the Superior Court of Massachusetts	Dear Sir:	Dear Mr. Blank:	Very truly yours,	Sincerely yours,	1. Mr. Blank 2. Mr. Blank

[3]Not applicable to judges of the United States Supreme Court.

UNITED STATES DIPLOMATIC REPRESENTATIVES

American Ambassador	The Honorable William R. Blank American Ambassador[1]	Sir:	Dear Mr. Ambassador:	Very truly yours,	Sincerely yours,	1. Mr. Ambassador *or* Mr. Blank 2. The American Ambassador[2] (The Ambassador *or* Mr. Blank)
American Minister	The Honorable William R. Blank American Minister to Rumania	Sir:	Dear Mr. Minister:	Very truly yours,	Sincerely yours,	1. Mr. Minister *or* Mr. Blank 2. The American Minister, Mr. Blank (The Minister *or* Mr. Blank)

		Sir:	Dear Mr. Blank:	Very truly yours,	Sincerely yours,	
American Chargé d'Affaires, Consul General, Consul, or Vice Consul	William R. Blank, Esquire[3] American Chargé d'Affaires ad interim (or other title)	Sir:	Dear Mr. Blank:	Very truly yours,	Sincerely yours,	1. Mr. Blank 2. Mr. Blank
High Commissioner	The Honorable William R. Blank United States High Commissioner to Argentina	Sir:	Dear Mr. Blank:	Very truly yours,	Sincerely yours,	1. Commissioner Blank or Mr. Blank 2. Commissioner Blank or Mr. Blank

[1] When an ambassador or minister is not at his or her post, the name of the country to which he or she is accredited must be added to the address. For example: *The American Ambassador to Great Britain.* If he or she holds military rank, the diplomatic complimentary title *The Honorable* should be omitted, thus *General William R. Blank, American Ambassador (or Minister).*

[2] With reference to ambassadors and ministers to Central or South American countries, substitute *The Ambassador of the United States* for *American Ambassador* or *American Minister.*

[3] Do not use *Esquire* to refer to a woman in this position.

FOREIGN OFFICIALS AND REPRESENTATIVES

		Excellency:	Dear Mr. Ambassador:	Very truly yours,	Sincerely yours,	
Foreign Ambassador[1] in the United States	His Excellency,[2] Erik Rolf Blankson Ambassador of Norway	Excellency:	Dear Mr. Ambassador:	Very truly yours,	Sincerely yours,	1. Mr. Ambassador or Mr. Blank 2. The Ambassador of Norway (The Ambassador or Mr. Blank)

*See page 236 for appropriate substitutions for women in these positions.

[1] The correct title of all ambassadors and ministers of foreign countries is *Ambassador (Minister) of* _____ (name of country), with the exception of Great Britain. The adjective form is used with reference to representatives from Great Britain—*British Ambassador, British Minister.*

[2] When the representative is British or a member of the British Commonwealth, it is customary to use *The Right Honorable* and *The Honorable* in addition to *His (Her) Excellency,* wherever appropriate.

FOREIGN OFFICIALS AND REPRESENTATIVES *continued*

Personage*	Envelope and Inside Address (Add City, State, Zip, or City, Country)	Formal Salutation	Informal Salutation	Formal Close	Informal Close	1. Spoken Address 2. Informal Introduction or Reference
Foreign Minister[3] *in the United States*	The Honorable George Macovescu Minister of Rumania	Sir:	Dear Mr. Minister:	Very truly yours,	Sincerely yours,	1. Mr. Minister *or* Mr. Blank 2. The Minister of Rumania (The Minister *or* Mr. Blank)
Foreign Diplomatic Representative with a Personal Title[4]	His Excellency,[5] Count Allesandro de Bianco Ambassador of Italy	Excellency:	Dear Mr. Ambassador:	Very truly yours,	Sincerely yours,	1. Mr Ambassador *or* Count Bianco 2. The Ambassador of Italy (The Ambassador *or* Count Bianco)
Prime Minister	His Excellency, Christian Jawaharal Blank Prime Minister of India	Excellency:	Dear Mr. Prime Minister:	Respectfully yours,	Sincerely yours,	1. Mr. Blank 2. Mr. Blank *or* The Prime Minister
British Prime Minister	The Right Honorable Godfrey Blank, K.G., M.C., M.P. Prime Minister	Sir:	Dear Mr. Prime Minister: *or* Dear Mr. Blank:	Respectfully yours,	Sincerely yours,	1. Mr. Blank 2. Mr. Blank *or* The Prime Minister
Canadian Prime Minister	The Right Honorable Claude Louis St. Blanc, C.M.G. Prime Minister of Canada	Sir:	Dear Mr. Prime Minister: *or* Dear Mr. Blanc:	Respectfully yours,	Sincerely yours,	1. Mr. Blanc 2. Mr. Blanc *or* The Prime Minister

	Address	Salutation	Salutation	Complimentary Close	Complimentary Close	In Speaking
President of a Republic	His Excellency, Juan Cuidad Blanco President of the Dominican Republic	Excellency:	Dear Mr. President:	I remain with respect, Very truly yours, *(formal general usage)* Sincerely yours, *(less formal)*	Sincerely yours,	1. Your Excellency 2. Not introduced (President Blanco *or* the President)
Premier	His Excellency, Charles Yves de Blanc Premier of the French Republic	Excellency:	Dear Mr. Premier:	Respectfully yours,	Sincerely yours,	1. Mr. Blanc 2. Mr. Blanc *or* The Premier
Foreign Chargé d'Affaires (de missi)6 in the United States	Mr. Jan Gustaf Blanc Chargé d'Affaires of Sweden	Sir:	Dear Mr. Blanc:	Respectfully yours,	Sincerely yours,	1. Mr. Blanc 2. Mr. Blanc
Foreign Chargé d'Affaires ad interim in the United States	Mr. Edmund Blank Chargé d'Affaires ad interim7 of Ireland	Sir:	Dear Mr. Blank:	Respectfully yours,	Sincerely yours,	1. Mr. Blank 2. Mr. Blank

*See page 236 for appropriate substitutions for women in these positions.

[3]The correct title of all ambassadors and ministers of foreign countries is *Ambassador (Minister) of* _____ (name of country), with the exception of Great Britain. The adjective form is used with reference to representatives from Great Britain—*British Ambassador, British Minister.*

[4]If the personal title is a royal title, such as *His (Her) Highness, Prince*, etc., the diplomatic title *His (Her) Excellency* or *The Honorable* is omitted.

[5]*Dr., Señor Don,* and other titles of special courtesy in Spanish-speaking countries may be used with the diplomatic title *His (Her) Excellency* or *The Honorable.*

[6]The full title is usually shortened to *Chargé d'Affaires.*

[7]The words "ad interim" should not be omitted in the address.

THE ARMED FORCES/THE ARMY

Personage*	Envelope and Inside Address (Add City, State, Zip)	Formal Salutation	Informal Salutation	Formal Close	Informal Close	1. Spoken Address 2. Informal Introduction or Reference
General of the Army	General of the Army William R. Blank, U.S.A. Department of the Army	Sir:	Dear General Blank:	Very truly yours,	Sincerely yours,	1. General Blank 2. General Blank
General, Lieutenant General, Major General, Brigadier General	General (Lieutenant General, Major General, or Brigadier General) William R. Blank, U.S.A. [1]	Sir:	Dear General Blank:	Very truly yours,	Sincerely yours,	1. General Blank 2. General Blank
Colonel, Lieutenant Colone	Colonel (Lieutenant Colonel) William R. Blank, U.S.A.	Dear Colonel Blank:	Dear Colonel Blank:	Very truly yours,	Sincerely yours,	1. Colonel Blank 2. Colonel Blank
Major	Major William R. Blank, U.S.A.	Dear Major Blank:	Dear Major Blank:	Very truly yours,	Sincerely yours,	1. Major Blank 2. Major Blank
Captain	Captain William R. Blank, U.S.A.	Dear Captain Blank:	Dear Captain Blank:	Very truly yours,	Sincerely yours,	1. Captain Blank 2. Captain Blank
First Lieutenant, Second Lieutenant[2]	Lieutenant William R. Blank, U.S.A.	Dear Lieutenant Blank:	Dear Lieutenant Blank:	Very truly yours,	Sincerely yours,	1. Lieutenant Blank 2. Lieutenant Blank
Chief Warrant Officer, Warrant Officer	Mr. William R. Blank, U.S.A.	Dear Mr. Blank:	Dear Mr. Blank:	Very truly yours,	Sincerely yours,	1. Mr. Blank 2. Mr. Blank
Chaplain in the U.S. Army[3]	Chaplain William R. Blank, Captain, U.S.A.	Dear Chaplain Blank:	Dear Chaplain Blank:	Very truly yours,	Sincerely yours,	1. Chaplain Blank 2. Captain Blank (Chaplain Blank)

THE ARMED FORCES/THE NAVY

Fleet Admiral	Fleet Admiral William R. Blank, U.S.N. Chief of Naval Operations, Department of the Navy	Sir:	Dear Admiral Blank:	Very truly yours,	Sincerely yours,	1. Admiral Blank 2. Admiral Blank
Admiral, Vice Admiral, Rear Admiral	Admiral (Vice Admiral or Rear Admiral) William R. Blank, U.S.N. United States Naval Academy[1]	Sir:	Dear Admiral Blank:	Very truly yours,	Sincerely yours,	1. Admiral Blank 2. Admiral Blank
Commodore, Captain, Commander, Lieutenant Commander	Commodore (Captain, Commander, Lieutenant Commander) William R. Blank, U.S.N. U.S.S. Mississippi	Dear Commodore (Captain, Commander) Blank:	Dear Commodore (Captain, Commander) Blank:	Very truly yours,	Sincerely yours,	1. Commodore (Captain, Commander) Blank 2. Commodore (Captain, Commander) Blank
Junior Officers: Lieutenant, Lieutenant Junior Grade, Ensign	(Lieutenant, etc.) William R. Blank, U.S.N. U.S.S. Wyoming	Dear Mr. Blank:	Dear Mr. Blank:	Very truly yours,	Sincerely yours,	1. Mr. Blank[2] 2. Lieutenant, etc., Blank (Mr. Blank)

*See page 236 for appropriate substitutions for women in these positions.

[1] *U.S.N.* signifies regular service; *U.S.N.R.* indicates the Reserve.

[2] Junior officers in the medical or dental corps are spoken to and referred to as *Dr.* but are introduced by their rank.

THE ARMED FORCES/THE NAVY *continued*

Personage*	Envelope and Inside Address (Add City, State, Zip, or City, Country)	Formal Salutation	Informal Salutation	Formal Close	Informal Close	1. Spoken Address 2. Informal Introduction or Reference
Chief Warrant Officer, Warrant Officer	Mr. William R. Blank, U.S.N. U.S.S. Texas	Dear Mr. Blank:	Dear Mr. Blank:	Very truly yours,	Sincerely yours,	1. Mr. Blank 2. Mr. Blank
Chaplain	Chaplain William R. Blank Captain, U.S.N. Department of the Navy	Dear Chaplain Blank:	Dear Chaplain Blank:	Very truly yours,	Sincerely yours,	1. Chaplain Blank 2. Captain Blank (Chaplain Blank)

THE ARMED FORCES—AIR FORCE

Air Force titles are the same as those in the Army. *U.S.A.F.* is used instead of *U.S.A.*, and *A.F.U.S.* is used to indicate the Reserve.

THE ARMED FORCES—MARINE CORPS

Marine Corps titles are the same as those in the Army, except that the top rank is *Commandant of the Marine Corps. U.S.M.C* indicates regular service, *U.S.M.R.* indicates the Reserve.

THE ARMED FORCES—COAST GUARD

Coast Guard titles are the same as those in the Navy, except that the top rank is *Admiral U.S.C.G.* indicates regular service, *U.S.C.G.R.* indicates the Reserve.

			Always Formal	Respectfully,	*Always Formal*	
The Pope	His Holiness, The Pope *or* His Holiness Pope ⎯⎯⎯ Vatican City	Your Holiness: Most Holy Father:		Respectfully,		1. Your Holiness 2. Not introduced (His Holiness *or* The Pope)
Apostolic Delegate	His Excellency, The Most Reverend William R. Blank Archbishop of ⎯⎯⎯ The Apostolic Delegate	Your Excellency:	Dear Archbishop Blank:	Respectfully yours,	Respectfully,	1. Your Excellency 2. Not introduced (The Apostolic Delegate)
Cardinal in the United States	His Eminence, William Cardinal Blank Archbishop of New York	Your Eminence:	Dear Cardinal Blank:	Respectfully yours,	Respectfully, *or* Sincerely yours,	1. Your Eminence *or less formally* Cardinal Blank 2. Not introduced (His Eminence *or* Cardinal Blank)
Bishop and Archbishop in the United States	The Most Reverend William R. Blank, D.D. Bishop (Archbishop) of Baltimore	Your Excellency:	Dear Bishop (Archbishop) Blank:	Respectfully yours,	Respectfully, *or* Sincerely yours,	1. Bishop (Archbishop) Blank 2. Bishop (Archbishop) Blank
Bishop in England	The Right Reverend William R. Blank Bishop of Sussex (local address)	Right Reverend Sir:	Dear Bishop:	Respectfully yours,	Respectfully,	1. Bishop Blank 2. Bishop Blank
Abbot	The Right Reverend William R. Blank Abbot of Westmoreland Abbey	Dear Father Abbot:	Dear Father Blank:	Respectfully yours,	Sincerely yours,	1. Father Abbot 2. Father Blank

*See page 236 for appropriate substitutions for women in these positions.

CHURCH DIGNITARIES/CATHOLIC FAITH *continued*

Personage*	Envelope and Inside Address (Add City, State, Zip)	Formal Salutation	Informal Salutation	Formal Close	Informal Close	1. Spoken Address 2. Informal Introduction or Reference
Canon	The Reverend William R. Blank, D.D. Canon of St. Patrick's Cathedral	Reverend Sir:	Dear Canon Blank:	Respectfully yours,	Sincerely yours,	1. Canon Blank 2. Canon Blank
Monsignor	The Right (or Very)[1] Reverend Msgr. William R. Blank	Right Reverend and Dear Monsignor Blank: *or* Very Reverend and Dear Monsignor Blank:	Dear Monsignor Blank:	Respectfully yours,	Sincerely yours,	1. Monsignor Blank 2. Monsignor Blank
Brother	Brother John Blank 932 Maple Avenue	Dear Brother:	Dear Brother Blank:	Respectfully yours,	Sincerely yours,	1. Brother Blank 2. Brother Blank
Superior of a Brotherhood and Priest[2]	The Very Reverend William R. Blank, M.M. Director	Dear Father Superior:	Dear Father Superior:	Respectfully yours,	Sincerely yours,	1. Father Blank 2. Father Blank
Priest	*With scholastic degree:* The Reverend William R. Blank, Ph.D. Georgetown University	Dear Dr. Blank:	Dear Dr. Blank:	Respectfully,	Sincerely yours,	1. Doctor (Father) Blank 2. Doctor (Father) Blank
	Without scholastic degree: The Reverend William R. Blank St. Vincent's Church	Dear Father Blank:	Dear Father Blank:	Respectfully,	Sincerely yours,	1. Father Blank 2. Father Blank

	Envelope	Salutation	Salutation	Closing	Closing	Informal Address
Sister Superior	The Reverend Sister Superior (*order, if used*)³ Convent of the Sacred Heart	Dear Sister Superior:	Dear Sister Superior:	Respectfully,	Respectfully, *or* Sincerely yours,	1. Sister Blank *or* Sister St. Teresa 2. The Sister Superior *or* Sister Blank (Sister St. Teresa)
Sister	Sister Mary Blank St. John's High School	Dear Sister:	Dear Sister Blank:	Respectfully,	Sincerely yours,	1. Sister Blank 2. Sister Blank
Mother Superior of a Sisterhood (Catholic or Protestant)	The Reverend Mother Superior, O.C.A. Convent of the Sacred Heart	Dear Reverend Mother: *or* Dear Mother Superior:	Dear Reverend Mother: *or* Dear Mother Superior:	Respectfully,	Sincerely yours,	1. Reverend Mother 2. Reverend Mother
Member of Community	Mother Mary Walker, R.S.M. Convent of Mercy	Dear Mother Walker:	Dear Mother Walker:	Respectfully,	Sincerely yours,	1. Mother Walker 2. Mother Walker

*See page 236 for appropriate substitutions for women in these positions.

¹Dependent upon rank. See the *Official (Roman) Catholic Directory.*

²The address for the superior of a Brotherhood depends upon whether or not he is a priest or has a title other than superior. Consult the *Official Catholic Directory.*

³The address of the superior of a Sisterhood depends upon the order to which she belongs. The abbreviation of the order is not always used. Consult the *Official Catholic Directory.*

CHURCH DIGNITARIES/JEWISH FAITH

Personage*	Envelope and Inside Address (Add City, State, Zip, or City, Country)	Formal Salutation	Informal Salutation	Formal Close	Informal Close	1. Spoken Address 2. Informal Introduction or Reference
Rabbi	*With scholastic degree:* Rabbi William R. Blank, Ph.D. *or* *Without scholastic degree:* Rabbi William R. Blank	Sir:	Dear Rabbi Blank: *or* Dear Dr. Blank:	Respectfully yours, *or* Very truly yours,	Sincerely yours,	1. Rabbi Blank *or* Dr. Blank 2. Rabbi Blank *or* Dr. Blank
		Sir:	Dear Rabbi Blank:	Respectfully yours, *or* Very truly yours,	Sincerely yours,	1. Rabbi Blank 2. Rabbi Blank

CHURCH DIGNITARIES/PROTESTANT FAITH

Archbishop (Anglican)	The Most Reverend Archbishop of Canterbury *or* The Most Reverend John Blank, Archbishop of Canterbury	Your Grace:	Dear Archbishop Blank:	Respectfully yours,	Sincerely yours,	1. Your Grace 2. Not introduced (His Grace *or* The Archbishop)
Presiding Bishop of the Protestant Episcopal Church in America	The Most Reverend William R. Blank, D.D., LL.D. Presiding Bishop of the Protestant Episcopal Church in America Northwick House	Most Reverend Sir:	Dear Bishop Blank:	Respectfully yours,	Sincerely yours,	1. Bishop Blank 2. Bishop Blank

	Envelope	Formal Salutation	Informal Salutation	Formal Close	Informal Close	Speaking to or Introduction
Anglican Bishop	The Right Reverend The Lord Bishop of London	Right Reverend Sir:	My dear Bishop:	Respectfully yours,	Sincerely yours,	1. Bishop Blank 2. Bishop Blank
Methodist Bishop	The Very Reverend William R. Blank Methodist Bishop	Reverend Sir:	My dear Bishop:	Respectfully yours,	Sincerely yours,	1. Bishop Blank 2. Bishop Blank
Protestant Episcopal Bishop	The Right Reverend William R. Blank, D.D., LL.D. Bishop of Denver	Right Reverend Sir:	Dear Bishop Blank:	Respectfully yours,	Sincerely yours,	1. Bishop Blank 2. Bishop Blank
Archdeacon	The Venerable William R. Blank Archdeacon of Baltimore	Venerable Sir:	My dear Archdeacon:	Respectfully yours,	Sincerely yours,	1. Archdeacon Blank 2. Archdeacon Blank
Dean[1]	The Very Reverend William R. Blank, D.D. Dean of St. John's Cathedral	Very Reverend Sir:	Dear Dean Blank:	Respectfully yours,	Sincerely yours,	1. Dean Blank or Dr. Blank 2. Dean Blank or Dr. Blank
Protestant Minister	*With scholastic degree:* The Reverend William R. Blank, D.D., Litt.D. *or* The Reverend Dr. William R. Blank	Dear Dr. Blank:	Dear Dr. Blank:	Very truly yours,	Sincerely yours,	1. Dr. Blank 2. Dr. Blank
	Without scholastic degree: The Reverend William R. Blank	Dear Mr. Blank:	Dear Mr. Blank:	Very truly yours,	Sincerely yours,	1. Mr. Blank 2. Mr. Blank

*See page 236 for appropriate substitutions for women in these positions.

[1]Applies only to the head of a Cathedral or of a Theological Seminary.

CHURCH DIGNITARIES/PROTESTANT FAITH *continued*

Personage*	Envelope and Inside Address (Add City, State, Zip)	Formal Salutation	Informal Salutation	Formal Close	Informal Close	1. Spoken Address 2. Informal Introduction or Reference
Episcopal Priest (High Church)	*With scholastic degree:* The Reverend William R. Blank, D.D., Litt.D. All Saint's Cathedral *or* The Reverend Dr. William R. Blank	Dear Dr. Blank:	Dear Dr. Blank:	Very truly yours,	Sincerely yours,	1. Dr. Blank 2. Dr. Blank
	Without scholastic degree: The Reverend William R. Blank St. Paul's Church	Dear Mr. Blank: *or* Dear Father Blank:	Dear Mr. Blank: *or* Dear Father Blank:	Very truly yours,	Sincerely yours,	1. Father Blank *or* Mr. Blank 2. Father Blank *or* Mr. Blank

COLLEGE AND UNIVERSITY OFFICIALS

President of a College or University	*With a doctor's degree:* Dr. William R. Blank *or* William R. Blank, LL.D., Ph.D. President, Amherst College	Sir:	Dear Dr. Blank:	Very truly yours,	Sincerely yours,	1. Dr. Blank 2. Dr. Blank

Person	Formal Salutation	Informal Salutation	Formal Close	Informal Close	Signature
Without a doctor's degree: Mr. William R. Blank President, Columbia University	Sir:	Dear President Blank:	Very truly yours,	Sincerely yours,	1. Mr. Blank 2. Mr. Blank *or* Mr. Blank, President of the College
Catholic priest: The Very Reverend William R. Blank, S.J., D.D., Ph.D. President, Fordham University	Sir:	Dear Father Blank:	Very truly yours,	Sincerely yours,	1. Father Blank 2. Father Blank
University Chancellor Dr. William R. Blank Chancellor, University of Alabama	Sir:	Dear Dr. Blank:	Very truly yours,	Sincerely yours,	1. Dr. Blank 2. Dr. Blank
Dean or Assistant Dean of a College or Graduate School Dean William R. Blank School of Law *or (If he holds a doctor's degree)* Dr. William R. Blank, Dean (Assistant Dean) School of Law University of Virginia	Dear Sir: *or* Dear Dean Blank:	Dear Dean Blank:	Very truly yours,	Sincerely yours,	1. Dean Blank 2. Dean Blank *or* Dr. Blank, the Dean (Assistant Dean) of the School of Law
Professor Professor William R. Blank *or (If he holds a doctor's degree)* Dr. William R. Blank *or* William R. Blank, Ph.D. Yale University	Dear Sir: *or* Dear Professo (Dr.) Blank:	Dear Professor (Dr.) Blank:	Very truly yours,	Sincerely yours,	1. Professor (Dr.) Blank 2. Professor (Dr.) Blank

*See page 236 for appropriate substitutions for women in these positions

259

COLLEGE AND UNIVERSITY OFFICIALS *continued*

Personage*	Envelope and Inside Address (Add City, State, Zip)	Formal Salutation	Informal Salutation	Formal Close	Informal Close	1. Spoken Address 2. Informal Introduction or Reference
Associate or Assistant Professor	Mr. William R. Blank *or* *(If he holds a doctor's degree)* Dr. William R. Blank *or* William R. Blank, Ph.D. Associate (Assistant) Professor Department of Romance Languages Williams College	Dear Sir: *or* Dear Professor (Dr.) Blank:	Dear Professor (Dr.) Blank:	Very truly yours,	Sincerely yours,	1. Professor (Dr.) Blank 2. Professor (Dr.) Blank
Instructor	Mr. William R. Blank *or* *(If he holds a doctor's degree)* Dr. William R. Blank *or* William R. Blank, Ph.D. Department of Economics University of California	Dear Sir: *or* Dear Mr. (Dr.) Blank:	Dear Mr. (Dr.) Blank:	Very truly yours,	Sincerely yours,	1. Mr. (Dr.) Blank 2. Mr. (Dr.) Blank

Chaplain of a College or University	The Reverend William R. Blank, D.D. Chaplain, Trinity College *or* Chaplain William R. Blank Trinity College	Dear Chaplain Blank: *or* *(If he holds a doctor's degree)* Dear Dr. Blank:	Dear Chaplain (Dr.) Blank:	Very truly yours,	Sincerely yours,	1. Chaplain Blank 2. Chaplain Blank *or* Dr. Blank

UNITED NATIONS OFFICIALS[1]

Secretary General	His Excellency, William R Blank Secretary General of the United Nations	Excellency:[2]	Dear Mr. Secretary General:	Very truly yours,	Sincerely yours,	1. Mr. Blank *or* Sir 2. The Secretary General of the United Nations *or* Mr. Blank
Under Secretary	The Honorable William R. Blank Under Secretary of the United Nations The Secretariat United Nations	Sir:	Dear Mr. Blank:	Very truly yours,	Sincerely yours,	1. Mr. Blank 2. Mr. Blank

*See page 236 for appropriate substitutions for women in these positions.

[1] The six principal branches through which the United Nations functions are The General Assembly, The Security Council, The Economic and Social Council, The Trusteeship Council, The International Court of Justice, and The Secretariat.

[2] An American citizen should never be addressed as "Excellency."

UNITED NATIONS OFFICIALS *continued*

Personage*	Envelope and Inside Address (Add City, State, Zip, or City, Country)	Formal Salutation	Informal Salutation	Formal Close	Informal Close	1. Spoken Address 2. Informal Introduction or Reference
Foreign Representative (with ambassadorial rank)	His Excellency, William R. Blank Representative of Spain to the United Nations	Excellency:	Dear Mr. Ambassador:	Very truly yours,	Sincerely yours,	1. Mr. Ambassador *or* Mr. Blank 2. Mr. Ambassador *or* The Representative of Spain to the United Nations (The Ambassador *or* Mr. Blank)
United States Representative (with ambassadorial rank)	The Honorable William R. Blank United States Representative to the United Nations	Sir: *or* Dear Mr. Ambassador:	Dear Mr. Ambassador:	Very truly yours,	Sincerely yours,	1. Mr. Ambassador *or* Mr. Blank 2. Mr. Ambassador *or* The United States Representative to the United Nations (The Ambassador *or* Mr. Blank)

*See page 236 for appropriate substitutions for women in these positions.

CHAPTER

12

Valuable Aids for Good Letter Writing

The aim of a business letter is to make a personal contact in the simplest way possible—to *talk* to the reader in words of everyday speech. We do not all have the genius that makes an outstanding letter writer, but we can improve the style and effectiveness of our own letters by studying those written by the masters. Careful planning and highly developed techniques make those letters outstanding. The purpose of this chapter is to help you to develop techniques that will improve the quality and persuasiveness of your letters.

Methodical planning of a letter. Plan the letter as a whole before beginning to write the first paragraph. A simple procedure follows:

1. Read carefully the letter you are answering and underscore in red or blue pencil the main points in it.
2. Tell yourself the purpose of the letter.
3. Jot down an outline of what your answer should contain.
4. Get all the facts.
5. Try to visualize your reader and adapt the letter to him.

Nine suggestions about language. The language of a business letter should be natural, just as though you were talking to the reader. Here are nine suggestions that will help you write letters in simple, straightforward language:

1. Never use stilted or trite phrases.
2. Avoid unnecessary words or phrases.
3. Do not use two words with the same meaning for emphasis.
4. Avoid favorite words or expressions.
5. Do not use big words.
6. Use different words to express various shades of meaning.
7. Use short sentences.
8. Avoid words that antagonize.
9. Use the positive approach.

Each of these suggestions is discussed in the following paragraphs.

Stilted and trite phrases. The primary requisite of good letter writing—as of any writing—is the avoidance of stilted or worn-out expressions. To illustrate the improvement that results when stilted or trite phrases are eliminated, consider the following example of a business letter as originally written and then as rewritten:

Stilted and Verbose

Dear Sir:

Replying to your kind favor of the 15th inst. in which you inform us that the enameling sheets ordered by you have not come to hand, beg to advise we have checked up on this shipment and find same left our factory March 10 and should have reached you March 13. For your information wish to state that we are now tracing through the express company. If the shipment does not arrive by March 19, kindly wire us collect, and we will duplicate same.

Regretting the inconvenience caused you, we are,

Yours truly,

Clear and Straightforward

Dear Mr. Bradley:

Your letter of March 15 reached us this morning.

The shipment of enameling sheets left our factory on March 10, and should have been delivered to you not later than March 13. We have asked the express company to trace the shipment immediately.

If you do not receive the sheets by March 19, please wire us collect, and we will start another shipment at once.

We are very sorry that this delay occurred and assure you that we will do everything possible to expedite delivery.

Sincerely yours,

TRITE TERMS TO BE AVOIDED

Here is a list of expressions that are stilted or trite and hence are not in good usage.

Acknowledge receipt of. Use *We received.*

Advise. Used with too little discrimination and best reserved to indicate actual advice or information. Often *say* or *tell* is better.

Poor: We wish to *advise* that your order has been shipped.
Better: We are pleased to *tell* you that your order has been shipped.

And oblige. A needless appendage.

Poor: Kindly ship the enclosed order *and oblige.*
Better: Please ship the enclosed order *immediately.*

As per; per. Correctly used with Latin words: *per annum* and *per diem.*

Allowable: 5 dollars *per* yard.
Better: 5 dollars *a* yard.
Poor: As *per* our telephone conversation.
Better: *In accordance with* our telephone conversation.

Poor: *Per* our agreement.
Better: *According to* our agreement.

At all times. Often used with little meaning. Better to use *always.*

Poor: We will be pleased to talk with you *at all times.*
Better: We will *always* be pleased to welcome you at our office.

At this time. Also unnecessary in most cases. Try *at present* or *now.*

Poor: We wish to advise that we are out of stock of handkerchiefs #1000 *at this time.*
Better: We are out of stock of handkerchiefs # 1000 *at present.*

At your convenience; at an early date. Trite, vague, and unnecessary in most cases. Be specific.

Indefinite: Please notify us *at an early date.*
Better: Please let us know *by return mail* (or *within ten days;* or *by the first of next month).*
Vague: We would appreciate hearing from you *at your convenience.*
Better: We would appreciate hearing from you *by return mail* (or *by the tenth of _____*).

Beg. Avoid such expressions as *beg to state, beg to advise, beg to acknowledge,* and so on.

Poor: In answer to yours of the 10th inst., *beg to state.* . . .
Better: In answer (or response; or reply) to your letter of May 10, *we are pleased.* . . .

Contents carefully noted. Contributes little to a business letter.

Poor: Yours of the 5th received and *contents carefully noted.*
Better: The instructions outlined in your letter of June 5 have been followed in every detail.

Duly. Needless and unnecessary.

Poor: Your request has been *duly* forwarded to our executive offices.
Better: We have forwarded your request to our executive offices.

Enclosed please find. Needless and faulty phraseology. The word *please* has little meaning in this instance. And the word *find* is improperly used.

Poor: *Enclosed please find* sample of our # 1989 black elastic ribbon.
Better: *We are enclosing* (or *we enclose*) a sample of our #1989 black elastic ribbon.

Esteemed. Too flowery and effusive.

> Poor: We welcomed your *esteemed* favor of the 9th.
> Better: Thank you for your letter of April 9.

Favor. Do not use the word *favor* in the sense of letter, order, or check.

> Thank you for your *letter* (not *favor*) of October 5.

Have before me. A worn-out expression.

> Poor: I *have before me* your complaint of the 10th.
> Better: *In answer* (or *response;* or *reply*) to your letter of November 10. . .

Hereto. Often needless.

> Poor: We are attaching *hereto* a copy of our contract covering prices on linoleum.
> Better: We are attaching *to this letter* a copy of our contract covering prices on linoleum.

Herewith. Often redundant.

> Poor: We enclose *herewith* a copy of our booklet.
> Better: We are pleased to enclose a copy of our booklet.

In re. Avoid. Use *regarding* or *concerning.*

> Poor: *In re* our telephone conversation of this morning. . . .
> Better: *Supplementing* (or *confirming;* or *about*) our telephone conversation of this morning . . . .

In the event that. Use *if* or *in case.*

> Poor: *In the event* that you are in the city Thursday. . . .
> Better: *If* you are in the city Thursday. . . .

Line. Do not use in place of *merchandise* or *line of goods.*

> Poor: Our salesman, Mr. Whitman, will gladly show you our *line.*
> Better: Our salesman, Mr. Whitman, will gladly show you our *merchandise* (or *line of goods*).

Our Miss Becker. Use *our representative, Miss Becker,* or just *Miss Becker.*

> Poor: *Our Miss Becker* will call on you next Tuesday, May 10.

Better: *Our representative, Miss Becker,* will call on you next Tuesday, May 10.

Please. Use *please* for requests.

Recent date. Vague and unbusinesslike. Better to give the exact date.

Vague: Your letter of *recent date.*
Definite: Your letter of *June 2.*

Same. A poor substitute for one of the pronouns *it, they,* or *them.*

Poor: Your order of the 5th received. Will ship *same* on the 10th.
Better: Thank you for your order of March 5. We expect to be able to ship *it* to you by the 12th of this month.

State. Often too formal. Better to use *say* or *tell.*

Poor: We wish to *state.* . . .
Better: We are pleased to *tell* you. . . .

Take pleasure. A trite expression. Use *are pleased, are happy,* or *are glad.*

Poor: We *take pleasure* in announcing our fall line of shoes.
Better: We *are pleased* to announce our fall line of shoes for women.

Thanking you in advance. Discourteous and implies that your request will be granted.

Poor: Kindly mail me any information you may have for removing crabgrass. *Thanking you in advance* for the favor, I remain
                                        Yours truly,
Better: I would appreciate any information you may have for removing crabgrass.
                                        Very truly yours,

Under separate cover. Rather meaningless. Better to be specific and give the method of shipping.

Poor: We are sending you *under separate cover* a copy of our pamphlet, "How to Grow Lawns."
Better: We are pleased to send you by *third-class mail* a copy of our pamphlet, "How to Grow Lawns."

Valued. Too effusive and suggestive of flattery. Better to omit.

Poor: We appreciate your *valued* order given to our salesman, Mr. McCall.
Better: We appreciate your order given to our salesman, Mr. McCall.

Wish to say; wish to state; would say. All are examples of needless, wordy phraseology. Simply omit.

> Poor: Referring to your letter of the 10th, *wish to say* that we cannot fill your order before the first of December.
>
> Better: In response to your letter of March 10, we regret we cannot fill your order before December 1.

Unnecessary words and phrases. Many letter writers add unnecessary words to their phrases because of an erroneous idea that the padding gives emphasis or rounds out a sentence. For example, letter writers frequently speak of "*final* completion," "*month of* January," or "*close* proximity." The completion must be final or it is not complete; January must be a month; incidents in proximity must be close. Here is a list of some padded phrases frequently used in business letters. The italicized words are *totally* unnecessary and should be omitted.

> It came *at a time* when we were busy.
> Leather depreciates *in value* slowly.
> During *the year of* 19___. . . .
> It will cost *the sum of* one hundred dollars.
> At a meeting *held* in Philadelphia. . . .
> We will ship these shoes *at a* later *date.*
> In about two weeks' *time.* . . .
> *In order* to reach our goal. . . .
> The mistake *first* began owing to a misunderstanding.
> A *certain* person by the name of Bill Jones. . . .
> The *close* proximity of these two incidents. . . .
> It happened at *the hour of* noon.
> We see some good in both *of them.*
> In *the city of* Columbus. . . .
> The body is made *out* of steel.
> During the *course of the* campaign. . . .
> *Perhaps* it may be that you are reluctant.
> Our uniform *and invariable* rule is. . . .
> Somebody *or other* must be responsible.
> We are now *engaged in* building a new plant.
> By *means of* this device we are able. . . .

Two words with the same meaning. Some letter writers think that if one word does a job, two words add emphasis. Actually, the second word makes the thought less effective. Here are a few examples of "doubling."

sincere and good wishes
the first and foremost
appraise and determine the worthwhile things
our experience together and contacts in a civic
deeds and actions
feeling of optimism and encouragement
we refuse and decline
unjust and unfair manner
advised and informed
at once and by return mail
immediately and at once
we demand and insist
right and proper consideration
assume obligation or responsibility

Favorite words and expressions. Avoid acquiring favorite words or expressions. They become habitual and your letters sound cut and dried.

L.E. Frailey in his *Handbook of Business Letters*[1] describes how an insurance company overworked the word "records." One letter would say, "According to our records, the grace period will expire next Monday," and then next, "The enclosed is for your records." A skillful letter writer would simply say, "The grace period will expire next Monday," and "The enclosed copy is for you."

Big words versus one-syllable words. Some people think that a large vocabulary of big words marks them as learned; but simple, short words do the best job. This statement does not mean a large vocabulary is not an asset. The more words a writer has, the more clearly and forcibly he can express himself, but he never uses words of many syllables unless there is a reason for it. Why, in a business letter, say "ultimate" when you mean "final," or "prerogative" when you mean "privilege," or "transpire" when you mean "occur."

Test your percentage of one-syllable words. Take five letters that you have written recently and count the words, leaving out names of people and places. Then count all the one-syllable words. Divide the smaller number (one-syllable words) by the larger number (all the words) and you have your percentage. If it is 60 or under, add some one-syllable words to your vocabulary and drop a few of the many-syllable ones.

---

[1]Prentice-Hall, Inc., Englewood Cliffs, N.J.

Various shades of meaning.   Use different words to express various shades of meaning. This is how a large vocabulary is helpful. The writer with an adequate vocabulary writes about the *aroma* of a cigar, the *fragrance* of a flower, the *scent* of perfume, the *odor* of gas, instead of the *smell* of all of these things. There is a reason for using words of more than one syllable here.

Sentence length.   Since the aim of a business letter is to transfer a thought to the reader in the simplest manner with the greatest clarity, avoid long, complicated sentences. Break up overlong, stuffy sentences by making short sentences of dependent clauses. Here is an example (101 words):

> Believing the physical union of the two businesses to be desirable and in the best interests of the stockholders of each corporation, the Boards of Directors have given further consideration to the matter and have agreed in principle upon a new plan that would contemplate the transfer of the business and substantially all of the assets of the A Company to B in exchange for shares of common stock of B on a basis that would permit the distribution to the A Company stockholders of one and one-half shares of B common stock for each share of A Company common stock.

Rewritten in four sentences, this becomes:

> The Boards of Directors of both companies thought a merger desirable and in the best interests of the stockholders. They finally agreed on a new plan. The business and substantially all assets of the A Company will be transferred to B in exchange for B common stock. A Company stockholders will get one and one-half shares of B common stock for each share of A Company common stock.

Words that antagonize.   Words that carry uncomplimentary insinuations are not only tactless but they often defeat the purpose of your letter. Never use a word that might humiliate or belittle the reader. Here are some expressions *to avoid* in letters:

claim	inferior
complaint	mistake
defective	neglect
dissatisfied	poor
error	trouble
failure	unfavorable
inability	unsatisfactory

Positive approach.   Always use a positive approach in letters. The following examples show how much more forceful and effective a positive approach is than a negative one.

Negative We cannot quote you a price until we have seen the specifications.

Positive We will be glad to quote you a price just as soon as we have seen the specifications.

Negative We cannot ship these goods before August 8.

Positive We will ship the goods on or shortly after August 8.

FOR A BETTER LETTER BEGINNING

The opening of any letter must get the reader's attention immediately. (See Figure 36.) Here are seven concrete suggestions that will help you develop the technique of starting a letter, even a routine letter, in a natural and interesting manner.

1. **Make the opening short.**   Long paragraphs are uninviting; therefore, the opening should always be short.

2. **Avoid pointless, dull, or stilted openings.**   Participial phrases and stilted expressions bore the reader and exhaust him before he reaches the point of the letter.

Boring and Artificial	*Natural*
Replying to your letter of July 9 in which you request that we send you samples of our WEAREVER fabrics, we are asking. . . .	Thank you, Mr. Edwards, for your request for samples of our WEAR-EVER fabrics.
In accordance with the authority contained in your letter of April 9th, the records of this office have been amended to show the date of your birth as January 4, 1943, instead of January 4, 1945.	After getting your letter of April 9, we corrected our records to show the date of your birth as January 4, 1943, instead of January 4, 1945.
It is with the deepest regret that I must decline your kind invitation to speak at the luncheon meeting of the Secretarial Association to be held on April 18.	As much as I dislike doing so, I must decline your invitation to speak at the Secretarial Association's luncheon on April 18.

3. Go straight to the point.   Beating about the bush does not capture the reader's attention. Start talking, just as if you were taking your part in a conversation. This does away with the practice of restating the contents of a letter that you are answering.

When to use a restatement. A brief restatement sometimes makes it easier for your correspondent to find the letter in his files. Or, the restatement might relieve him of having to refer to the copy of his letter. In these cases a brief restatement is desirable. Your guide should be: Does the restatement serve any useful purpose?

Let us analyze this restatement.

> In reply to yours of the 15th in which you state that you would be interested in receiving more complete information as to our STEADY-HEAT Oil Burner, as you are considering installing a burner in your home, we are enclosing a booklet. . . .

The reader knows that he is considering installing a burner and knows that he wrote for information about the Steady-Heat burner. He can see that a booklet is enclosed. And the date he wrote the letter is of no interest. Why not open the letter with:

> This booklet, "Better Heat with Steady-Heat," gives you the information you requested about the STEADY-HEAT burner.

4. Include the reader's name.   The use of the reader's name in the opening sentences personalizes a routine letter. There is no discourtesy in the use of a person's name even in the first letter that is written to him. The use of the name in the illustrations under point 5 make those opening sentences more interesting to the reader. When overdone, however, the use of the name sounds too familiar. Do not use the name more than once in a short letter of two or three paragraphs.

5. Use a pleasant phrase.   Use any appropriate statement that may start an agreeable reaction in the reader's mind. Even if you are going to disagree with him later, don't put the bad news in the first sentence. This device is particularly helpful in adjustment letters. Here are three pleasant opening sentences:

> Your letter is appreciated, Mrs. Adams.
> You are very patient, Mrs. Jones.
> Your interest in better businesss letters, Mr. Johnson, makes writing to you a real pleasure.

6. Refer to a previous contact.   Take advantage in your opening of a previous contact with your reader, either by letter or in person. Reference to a mutual interest or contact requires no particular skill, but it tends to get a letter off to a good start.

> It was a pleasure indeed to have such a fine visit with you during my eastern trip last week.
>
> Thanks to you, Mr. Barrett, my stay in Cleveland proved a most delightful one.

7. "Who, What, When, Where, and Why."   When you have good news that you know will interest an individual or group, follow newspaper style and tell your reader who, what, when, where, and why in the opening. This technique is particularly effective in sales or promotion letters. Here is an illustration:

> June—the vacation month [*when*] —and motoring America takes to the highways [*why*]. Wherever you may be planning to go this summer [*where*], our new travel information bureau [*who*] will be very glad to assist you [*what*].

Additional techniques used by the experts.   The experts devote considerable time and effort to developing techniques that help them write attention-capturing openings. Some additional techniques they have developed are:

1. Use of a question
2. Statement of an unusual or not commonly known fact
3. Interesting story
4. Quotation
5. Reference to a famous name

FOR A BETTER ENDING

The closing of your letter frequently influences the reader to do what you ask—or it might have the opposite effect. The closing should add something definite to the letter or it should not be there. (See Figure 36.) Here are four techniques that will help you to write closings that add to the persuasiveness of your letters.

1. Avoid stilted or formal endings.   Here is the last paragraph of a letter soliciting club memberships. The job was finished—and it was a good job—with the first paragraph. But, the writer weakened the

	Openings	Closings
Appreciation	It was generous of you to give me so much of your time yesterday, and I appreciate your fine cooperation.	Thank you again for your help. We will be ready to serve you in every way possible.
Appreciation for messages of congratulations	I appreciate your words about my efforts to guide the recent Credit Management program.	Thanks again for your thoughtful note.
Replying to requests for information, booklets, and samples	The information requested by you concerning the STEADY-HEAT Oil Burner is in the enclosed booklet.	When we can be of further assistance to you, do not hesitate to write us.
Congratulations	It was a pleasure to read in this morning's paper of your appointment yesterday to a place on the Supreme Court bench.	You have my sincere congratulations added to all the others that you must have been receiving.
Complaints	Unfortunately my last case of mayonnaise reached me in damaged condition.	I shall keep the damaged case until I receive further instructions from you.
Adjustments or answering complaints	We are glad that you notified us promptly that some of your books were damaged in transit.	We very much regret the delay and hope that it will not cause you serious inconvenience.
Asking a favor	I know you must be busy with vacation time nearly here, but I have a favor to ask, which I hope is not too great an imposition.	
To Applicants	We appreciate the interest shown by your application for a position on the Prentice-Hall sales staff.	The best of luck to you, both in finding the right job and in making the most of it.

FIGURE 36   CHART SHOWING OPENINGS AND CLOSINGS FOR VARIOUS TYPES OF LETTERS

appeal of his selling paragraph because he could not resist the temptation to add a conventional sentence in the closing paragraph, which follows:

> Thanking you for your kind consideration of the advantages of membership in our organization, and trusting you will see your way clear to acceptance of this invitation, we remain. . . .

2. **Suggest only one action.** Tell the reader the *specific* action that you expect him to take. If he is given a choice of several things to do, he will probably do nothing. Concentrate on *one* action and do not mention others.

In the following closings, the alternative suggestions tend to confuse the reader; the specific suggestions are impelling and produce action.

Alternative Suggestions	*Specific Suggestions*
Write us a letter, telegraph, or send the enclosed card right now.	Send the enclosed card right now.
If it is convenient for you to see me, please drop me a note or call me at 356-4920.	When it is convenient for you to see me, please call me at 356-4920.
Please mail this payment to arrive at our office within five days. Or if you don't feel able to do that now, send us a postdated check for the same amount.	Please mail this payment to arrive at our office within five days, which would be by Saturday.

3. **Use dated action.** If you expect the reader to take a certain action in the future, use *dated action.* That is, tell the reader that you expect the action by a given date, or within a certain number of days, not "in the near future."

The experience of an insurance company illustrates how an indefinite date can weaken a letter. The company had difficulty getting reports from examining physicians. The letters asked the doctors to return the report blanks "as soon as possible," but the company found that on an average it had to write 3.7 follow-up letters to each physician. The company then switched to dated action and called for the return of the blanks by a specific date. As a result, the average number of follow-up letters for each report was reduced to 2.1.

Here are two examples of dated-action closings:

For us to handle this claim promptly for your patient, we need your preliminary report by the *end of this week.*

An *immediate reply* will enable us to complete the draft of the contract by Friday.

4. Use positive words.   Negative words anywhere in a letter weaken it because they show the writer's lack of confidence in himself. They are doubly harmful in the closing. "Hope," "may," "if," and "trust" tend to defeat the purpose of any business letter. Compare the following negative closings with the positive revisions.

Negative	*Positive*
If you will O.K. the card, we will gladly send you a copy of the bulletin. *Trusting* you will do this. . . .	Your copy of this interesting bulletin is waiting for you. Just O.K. and mail the card.
Now is the time when our customers are stocking for summer business. We *trust* you will join them by placing your requirements on the order blank enclosed.	Now is the time when our customers are stocking for summer business. You can join them by placing your requirements on the order blank enclosed.
If you would like to have our salesman call with samples, please so advise.	Ted Mead, a fellow you are going to like, will be around next Monday morning to show you samples and service your order.

FORM LETTERS

Use of form letters.   Keep a file of form letters and form paragraphs to be used in recurring situations that require almost the same letter. They are entirely satisfactory when no attempt is being made to slant the letter toward a particular reader. Often they are better than an individually composed letter because more time and thought is given to their preparation. Rewrite form letters from time to time to keep them current and up to date.

The secretary is concerned with two types of form letters: (1) model forms, and (2) processed forms.

Model form letters and paragraphs.   A list of routine letters that the secretary writes and examples of them are given in chapter 13. These letters may be used as models. Make copies of those you are likely to need and keep them in your form letter file. Analyze your correspondence to see what other types of model letters you need. Select one you have already written to meet the need and correct and improve it to conform with the principles explained in this chapter. Then place it as a model in your form letter file.

You will find, also, that model paragraphs can be used in many letters. For example, if you answer, instead of merely acknowledge, a letter received in your employer's absence, your opening paragraph could be the same in each letter. Place the paragraph in your form letter file. Be careful not to use the same opening paragraph in frequent letters to the same person.

When to use processed form letters. Situations that can be covered by mechanically processed form letters vary with the secretary's position. The factors that determine which letters might be mechanically processed are (1) frequency of use, (2) purpose of the letter, and (3) the probable reaction of the recipient. Difference of opinion exists as to the effectiveness of form letters, but if properly handled and personalized, there can be no logical objection to them. When the letter is purely routine or when the recipient is interested only in the information it contains, a mechanically processed letter can be used to advantage. Obviously, form letters save time and money.

How to personalize processed form letters. Form letters are often prepared by one of the duplicating processes, such as stencil, spirit, offset, or copier. The appearance and layout of form letters processed in this manner will be improved if you type in the dateline, the inside address, the salutation, and the complimentary close. In doing this it is important to match as closely as possible your typewriter ribbon's color and impression with the type on the electronically prepared form letter.

Automated typewriters are also available that will type letters at high speed. Some of these machines, such as the magnetic tape models, produce individually typed, personalized form letters, combining a standard letter body with the individual names and addresses. Revisions and corrections are easily and quickly edited into the tape, and letter-perfect copy is produced with a minimum of time and effort.

Whether form letters are prepared by one of the duplicating processes or by automatic typewriter, these simple steps will help to personalize the letter:

1. Use a good quality paper.
2. Sign the letter with pen and ink.
3. Seal the envelope.
4. Send the letter by first-class mail.
5. Use postage stamps rather than a meter stamp.

INTEROFFICE MEMORANDA

Interoffice memoranda are those exchanged among the various offices, departments, and divisions within a corporation. Some companies have specially printed stationery; others use inexpensive stationery without a letterhead; others use a special size of stationery for interoffice memos.

The format of interoffice memoranda.   Interoffice memoranda do not have salutations and complimentary closes. Otherwise, there is no special way to write or arrange memos. Within a company, there should be consistency; otherwise there is likely to be confusion. Any of the following forms is practical:

```
(Date)
TO:       Mr. L. Smith
FROM:     R. E. Brown
SUBJECT:  Format for Interoffice Memoranda
```
Or
```
(Date)
TO:
FR:
RE:
```
Or
```
(Date)
Mr. L. Smith
(Body of Memo)
R. E. Brown
```

When you send copies of the same memorandum to various people, address it this way:

```
Mr. S. Brown
Mrs. C. Smith
Ms. R. Jones
```

Make four copies of the memo (one for your own file) and check the name on each of the first three copies to which that copy is to go.

The letters *F.Y.I.* or *fyi* (For Your Information) after the name of a person receiving a copy of the memorandum indicate that the copy is sent to him merely to keep him informed.

Routing a memorandum.   If you wish a *single* copy of a memorandum to go successively to each of several persons, address it this way:

1. Mr. S. Brown
2. Mrs. C. Smith
3. Ms. R. Jones

If you wish the memorandum to come back to the manager, include his or her name as number 4. Each person receiving the memorandum will strike out his own name, write the date on which he read the memorandum and took action, and check the next name.

Unless the material is confidential, do not use envelopes. If the memorandum is going out of the office to a salesperson in the field, enclose it with other material going to the salesperson.

Model
Business Letters

Incoming letters can be divided into three categories: (1)
those you can answer over your own signature, (2) those you
can prepare for the manager's signature, and (3) those that
the manager must write himself. Your judgment in selecting
the letters that you will prepare should be guided by experience in your job, your grasp of the problems covered in the
letter, your knowledge of the facts, and the extent to which
the manager expects you to use your initiative in handling
correspondence.

LETTERS WRITTEN
OVER THE SECRETARY'S SIGNATURE

Letters the secretary signs.   As in all situations, the manager's wish is
the principal factor in deciding which letters you might sign. If he or
she expects you to use your own judgment, the determining factor is
consideration for the recipient of the letter. A writer who expects his
letter to be answered by the manager might be offended if it is
passed to a subordinate. In this case it would be poor business
procedure for you to write the letter over your signature. However, if
the recipient is interested only in the information given in answer to
his letter, write the letter over your own signature.

Letters written by the secretary in the manager's absence.   Letters that
you usually write over your signature when the manager is away
include:

    1. Acknowledgments and apologies
    2. Appointments
    3. Information

Letters routinely written by the secretary.   Letters that you usually
write over your signature include:

    1. Reservations
    2. Adjustments in accounts
    3. Orders and follow-ups

    A pattern and models for each type of letter follow. The signature
is the same in each case:

(your name)
Secretary to *(your employer)*

LETTERS WRITTEN
IN THE MANAGER'S ABSENCE

**Acknowledgment of correspondence received during the manager's
absence.**   Acknowledgment of a letter received during the manager's absence is a business courtesy. These letters fall into two

classes: (1) an acknowledgment without answering the letter, and (2) an acknowledgment that also answers the letter.

Acknowledgment without answer. The pattern for these letters is simple:

1. Say that your employer is out of the city or away from the office.
2. Give the expected date of his return.
3. Assure the writer that his message will receive attention when your employer returns.
4. If the delay may cause inconvenience to the writer, add a note of apology.

Do not refer to an illness or other difficulties when explaining the manager's absence from the office, unless the addressee knows the circumstances. Say, "Because of Mr. Peters' absence from the office, he will not be able to attend...."

Dear Mr. Stevenson:

Since Mr. James is away from the office this week, I am acknowledging your letter of August 5 concerning the Denver project. I will bring this to his attention as soon as he returns, and I'm certain he will contact you promptly.

Please accept my apologies for this unavoidable delay.

Sincerely yours,

Dear Mr. Ames:

Your letter of August 14 arrived the day after Mr. Tauber left on a two-week business trip. Since you indicated that it does not require an immediate answer, I will hold it for prompt attention on his return.

Sincerely yours,

Dear Ms Parker:

Thank you for contacting Mr. King about the new tax forms. He is attending a convention in Philadelphia this week and will return to the office next Monday. I will bring your letter about the new tax forms to his attention at that time.

Sincerely yours,

Acknowledgment that also answers. The important factor in answering, as well as acknowledging, a letter during the manager's absence is to *know the facts.* Here is a suggested pattern:

1. Identify the incoming letter.
2. Say that the manager is away.
3. State the facts that answer the letter.

4. If appropriate, or desirable, say that the manager will write when he returns.

Dear Mr. Frederick:

Your letter reminding Mr. Stone of his promise to speak before the ABC Club at lunch on Tuesday, December 20, arrived during his absence from the office.

He will return on Monday and I will bring your thoughtful letter to his attention then. I know that he is looking forward to speaking at the luncheon.

Sincerely yours,

Dear Ms. Florio:

Thank you for asking to see Mr. French about office equipment.

He will be out of the office for the next month. However, Mr. Rhinesmith is responsible for all company purchases, and you may wish to contact him.

Mr. Rhinesmith's office is in Room 512 and he is usually available every morning from 10:00 to 12:00. If you want to call him for an appointment, his extension number is 560.

I will see that he has this correspondence so you may refer to it when you call.

Sincerely yours,

Dear Mr. Roberts:

Your letter asking Ms Ainsworth to speak before the ABC Club of Jackson on January 14 arrived a few days after she left town on a business trip.

However, after checking her schedule for January 14, I see that she is to make a special report to the Board of Directors on that day and, therefore, it will be impossible for her to address the members of your club.

I know that Ms. Ainsworth will nevertheless appreciate your kind invitation and will write to you as soon as she returns to Nashville.

Sincerely yours,

Letters concerning appointments.   Here is the pattern that a letter arranging an appointment should follow:

1. Refer to the purpose of the appointment.
2. Suggest, or ask the person to whom you are writing to suggest, the time, the place, and the date.
3. Ask for a confirmation of the appointment.

These letters fall into three groups: the manager asks for an appointment; you ask someone to come in to see the manager, or you reply to a letter asking the manager for an appointment.

The manager asks for appointment.   *You want to fix the time.*

Dear Mr. Green:

Mr. Stone is attending a convention in Chicago next week. While he is there, he would like to discuss with you the revision of your book on tax reports.

Will it be convenient for him to call on you Tuesday afternoon, June 1, at two o'clock?

Sincerely yours,

You have to let the other person fix the time.

Dear Mr. Roberts:

Ms. Gorman is returning from Washington on Friday of this week and would like to discuss with you the results of her sessions with the Labor Committee.

Will you please ask your secretary to telephone me and let me know when it will be convenient for you to see Ms. Gorman?

Sincerely yours,

You ask someone to come in to see the manager.   *You want to fix the time.*

Dear Mr. Morris:

Mr. Brown would like to know if it would be possible to see you on Monday, February 27, at two o'clock at his office, Room 201, to complete arrangements for the rental of your summer cottage.

Please let me know whether this time is convenient.

Sincerely yours,

You have to let the other person fix the time.

Dear Mrs. Elwood:

The papers in connection with the trust that you are creating for your daughter are now complete, except for your signature. Mr. Brown would like to know if you could come to his office early next week to sign them. Please telephone me to arrange a convenient time for you.

Sincerely yours,

Reply to letter asking your employer for an appointment.   *You fix a definite time.*

Dear Mr. Smith:

Mr. Brown will be glad to see you on Monday, December 27, at two o'clock in his office, Room 201, to discuss with you the program for the annual convention.

Sincerely yours,

You want to let the other person fix the time.

Dear Mr. Edwards:

Mr. Brown will be glad to see you sometime during the week of March 3 to talk over the installation of the elevator in his residence at 20 West 20 Street.

If you will telephone me, we can arrange a time that will be convenient for you and Mr. Brown. The number is 353-9200.

Sincerely yours,

The manager signs the letter.

Dear Mr. Boyd:

I will be happy to talk with you when you are in Minneapolis next week. Would it be convenient for you to come to my office at ten o'clock, Thursday morning, November 5? I believe this hour would give us the best opportunity to discuss your project without interruption.

It will be a pleasure to see you again.

Cordially yours,

You have to say "no" politely.

Dear Mr. Thomas:

Ms. Brown has considered very carefully all that you said in your letter of December 21. If there were any possibility that a meeting with you would be helpful, she would be glad to see you. However, she does not believe that would be the case, and has asked me to let you know and to thank you for writing.

Sincerely yours,

Letters that process information.   Letters that concern information received or requested include those that (1) supply information about such things as products and services, (2) acknowledge the receipt of information, and (3) answer inquiries about such things as delivery dates and prices. These letters should cover the following:

1. Identify the incoming letter and acknowledge any information received.
2. State that the manager is away.
3. Provide the information requested, if possible.
4. Advise the writer that the manager will contact him upon his return.

Request for information.

Dear Ms. Jones:

This will acknowledge receipt of your letter of January 25, addressed to Mr. Smith, concerning the proposed plant expansion.

Mr. Smith will be out of town until February 3, but I know that he will give your request his immediate attention as soon as he returns.

Cordially,

Information received.

Dear Mr. King:

Thank you for sending information about your July sales presentation to Mr. Harris. He will be away from his office until June 24, but I will see that this is called to his attention as soon as he returns.

Sincerely,

Supply information.

Dear Mr. Jackson:

In Ms. Cole's absence I am replying to your request for information about our Model ABC office copier.

This copier is in stock and available at $525. A brochure describing its many new features is enclosed.

I hope this will be of some help to you until Ms. Cole returns next Monday, September 20. She will be happy to call you then to answer any further questions you have.

Sincerely,

Omission of enclosures.

Dear Mr. Pearson:

Since Mr. Symonds is out of town this week, I am acknowledging your letter of April 12 to him. You mentioned that you were including the proposed plans for the new tennis courts; however, they were not enclosed.

Mr. Symonds will not be able to discuss this matter with the Board of Trustees unless he has the plans. As they are meeting early next week, could you please send them by the next mail?

Sincerely,

LETTERS WRITTEN ROUTINELY BY THE SECRETARY

Letters making plane reservations. The points to cover in a letter making a plane reservation are:

1. Name and position of person desiring reservation
2. Flight and date on which space is desired
3. Schedule of flight
4. Air credit card number (if any)
5. Confirmation

Gentlemen:

Mr. Edward P. Case, president of Case Motor Company, would like to reserve space to Los Angeles on Jet Flight 26 out of Chicago on Saturday, November 24. Our schedule shows that this flight leaves at 9:45 a.m., Central Standard Time, for Los Angeles, and arrives at 2:45 p.m., Pacific Standard Time. Mr. Case is holder of air travel card 72910.

Please confirm reservation by wire immediately.

Sincerely yours,

Letters making hotel reservations. When you write for hotel reservations for your employer, include the following information:

1. Accommodations desired
2. Name of person for whom reservation is requested
3. Date and time of arrival
4. Probable date of departure
5. Request for confirmation

Gentlemen:

Please reserve for Ms. Jane Bergman a living room and bedroom suite, beginning Friday, January 5. Ms. Bergman will arrive the afternoon of the fifth and plans to leave the afternoon of the tenth.

Please confirm this reservation by wire.

Sincerely yours,

Gentlemen:

Please reserve for Mr. Richard L. Brown a moderately priced single room with bath for August 10 to August 15. Mr. Brown plans to arrive about noon on Wednesday, August 10. Please confirm this reservation and tell me what the rate will be.

Sincerely yours,

Letters calling attention to an error in an account. In calling attention to an error in an account, avoid giving the impression that you are complaining. Keep the tone of your letter pleasant and remember not to use words that antagonize (see list on page 271). These letters fall into four classes: (1) when the amount of an item is incorrect; (2) when the total is incorrect; (3) when returned merchandise has not been credited; (4) when an item not purchased is charged to the account. (The illustrations here relate to personal accounts but can be adapted to business accounts.)

When the amount of an item is incorrect. Here is a workable outline that covers the necessary points:

1. Give the name and number of the account.
2. Describe the incorrect item, and tell how it is incorrect.
3. State your version of what the item should be, giving any documentary information you may have.
4. Ask for a corrected statement *or* enclose a check for the correct amount and ask that the error be rectified on the account.

Gentlemen:

The September statement of Mr. Northrup's account shows a charge of $15.00 for dinner for two on the evening of August 15. Evidently this charge should have been posted to someone else's account as Mr. Northrup was out of town that evening.

I have deducted $15.00 from the total amount of the statement and am enclosing Mr. Northrup's check for $50.80.

Sincerely yours,

When an item not purchased is charged to the account. These letters should include the following points:

1. Name and number of the account
2. Description of the item charged in error, including the price and the date charged
3. Any additional pertinent information that you have
4. A request that the charge be investigated
5. A request for a corrected statement

Gentlemen:

The June statement of Mrs. Robert Walker's account, no. 14825, shows a charge of $5.85 on May 15 for three pairs of hose. Mrs. Walker charged three pairs of hose for $5.85 on May 10 and three pairs for the same amount on May 20, but she did not charge any hose on May 15. The six pairs that she bought were properly charged to her account.

Naturally, Mrs. Walker is concerned that someone might have used her account without her permission. Would you please investigate and let her know what happened?

Sincerely yours,

When returned merchandise has not been credited. Follow the same pattern as when the amount of an item is incorrect.

Gentlemen:

On May 4 Mrs. Robert Walker, whose account number is 15836, returned for credit a shower curtain that she purchased from you on May 2. The price was $27.50, including tax.

Mrs. Walker's June statement does not show this credit. A credit slip was given to her but, unfortunately, it has been misplaced. Mrs. Walker would appreciate it if you would verify the credit and send her a corrected statement.

In the meantime, I am enclosing Mrs. Walker's check for $146.25, which is the amount of the statement less the price of the returned merchandise.

Sincerely yours,

Letters of adjustment of travel card accounts. Many companies and executives now prefer to open travel credit card accounts as the most convenient way to make and pay for travel arrangements and services. The charge for travel tickets, hotel accommodations, car rental, and many other travel services are billed by itemized monthly statement. Where services are involved, the statement is accompanied by *a record of charge* made at the time the service is completed. This record of charge shows the date and items of purchase, the signature of the purchaser, and the name and address of the service establishment.

Always check the items of the record of charge signed by the manager against the itemized monthly statement received. Also make certain that any travel ticket cancellations have been properly credited to the account. Letters that you will need to write usually fall into three classes: (1) when the amount of an item is incorrect; (2) when the total is incorrect; (3) when a ticket cancellation has not been credited.

When the amount of an item is incorrect.

1. Give the name, the company, and the account number in which the travel card is issued.
2. Describe the incorrect item, and tell how it is incorrect.
3. State what the item should be, giving any documentary information that you have.
4. Ask for a corrected statement *or* enclose a check for the correct amount and ask that the error be rectified on the next statement.

Gentlemen:

Account 365-809-112

A.D. Brock

Parker Publishing Company

Your statement of June 17 charges Mr. Brock's account for dining services at the Princess Hotel in Bermuda during the week of May 8 for $112.67.

According to record of charge, the total should be $102.67, or $10 less than the statement shows.

Enclosed is Mr. Brock's check for this month's statement, minus $10.00. Please credit Mr. Brock's account in full.

Sincerely yours,

When a ticket cancellation has not been credited.

1. Give the name, the company, and the account number in which the travel card is issued.
2. Give the date, point of departure and destination of the original reservation.
3. Tell how and when it was canceled.
4. State the amount that has been incorrectly charged.
5. Ask for a corrected statement, or enclose a check for the correct amount and ask that the error be rectified on the next statement.

Gentlemen:

Account 711-298-067-A

Alfred R. Ace

Winston Motors, Inc.

Your statement of August 15 to Mr. Ace includes a charge of $33 for a flight from New York to Washington. We originally scheduled this flight by telephone and received the tickets and your letter of confirmation on July 28.

However, on Mr. Ace's instructions, I canceled this flight by telephone on the morning of July 29, and returned the tickets to you in my letter of that date.

Enclosed is Mr. Ace's check for the amount of your August 15 statement, minus the charge for this flight. Please credit Mr. Ace's account in full.

Sincerely yours,

Placing orders.

1. Indicate that your letter represents an order (or request for refund).
2. Give the name and address to which the bill should be sent.

3. List items desired, with all pertinent order data (catalog no., color, etc.).

4. Advise where the order should be sent and indicate if a specific delivery date is desired.

Gentlemen:

Please send the following item, and charge it to our account number 730-01-221163.

One (1) #47321 Easel, Walnut, $25.95

Please deliver to our letterhead address, attention Robert M. Blake. We will need this item by March 25.

Sincerely,

Gentlemen:

On August 5 I placed an order for rental of two overhead projectors to be used at our company's September 6 seminar at the Hotel Franklin. The rental fee was paid in advance by our check no. 7808 for $37.50.

The seminar has since been postponed indefinitely, and we wish to cancel our order. Please acknowledge this cancellation by mail and send us our refund of $37.50.

Sincerely,

Follow-up letters. If correspondence in your follow-up file (see chapter 9) is not answered by the follow-up date, trace the letter for a reply. Your letter should cover the following points:

1. Identify the letter. Identification by date is not sufficient because your correspondent does not know what you are writing to him about.

2. Offer a reason for the recipient's failure to reply, without casting reflection on him.

3. Enclose a copy of your original letter, unless it was very short. If so, simply repeat the contents in your follow-up letter.

Copy of original letter not enclosed.

Gentlemen:

On February 2 we ordered from you 200 copies of your latest bulletin on "Successful Selling Techniques," but we have not yet had an acknowledgment of the order.

Since our first order evidently went astray, please consider this a duplicate.

Sincerely yours,

Copy of original letter enclosed. (As this is a follow-up of a letter requesting a favor, it is written for the manager's signature.)

Dear Mr. Roberts:

In the rush of work you probably have not had time to answer my letter of October 25 about using some of your selling ideas in our Real Estate Service, with credit to you. On the chance that this letter did not reach you, I am enclosing a carbon copy of it.

I would like very much to include your selling ideas in the next supplement of the Service. This will be possible if I have your reply by December 15.

Thanks very much for your cooperation.

Cordially,

LETTERS THE SECRETARY WRITES FOR THE MANAGER'S SIGNATURE

Some managers permit their secretaries to write only routine letters; others expect them to handle nearly all of their correspondence. In the latter case the letters the secretary writes for the employer's signature are limited only by ability and experience on the job. These letters may be divided into two groups, as follows.

1. **Letters about company business.** All of the rules of good letter writing described in chapter 12 are applicable here. Obviously, letters vary too widely with particular businesses to permit inclusion here of patterns and examples.

One type of letter that you may send out in the company's name is the letter announcing to a firm or a customer that a donation is being given in its name to a hospital or charity in place of the usual Christmas gift. This is a custom in many corporations or companies.

Dear Mr. Jones:

On behalf of this company, I am happy to tell you that we are sending in your name a donation to the Children's Hospital in place of the personal gift we usually send at this season.

May the coming holidays bring to you and yours good health, happiness, and a full share of those things that make this world a better place in which to live.

Cordially yours,

2. **Personal business letters.** Before you acquire the technical knowledge necessary to write letters about the company's business, you

can handle the personal letters that the amenities of business require. The following sections deal with letters of this type.

You will write some letters for the manager's signature without instructions from him or her, and others from a few words of instruction or from marginal notes that he or she makes on the incoming letter.

Style and tone of letters the secretary writes for the manager's signature. Familiarize yourself with the tone and style of the manager's correspondence. Remember that the aim in composing a letter for his signature is to write it exactly as he would have dictated it. Here are three rules:

1. Follow his style as closely as possible without flagrantly disregarding the rules of good letter writing—even if he does so. Thus, if he has a few pet phrases, use them, but if he has a habit of opening his letters with long participial phrases, try a natural opening and probably he will approve it.
2. Adapt the tone of your letter to the tone he uses when he dictates. Thus, if his letters come quickly to the point, compose letters in that tone; if his letters are gentle and courteous, use that tone. It is particularly important to know whether the tone of the letter should convey personal friendship, a formal business relationship, or some other attitude.
3. Use the same salutation and complimentary close that your employer would use. These change with the relationship existing between the writer and the addressee. Thus, if the manager uses "Dear Bob" as the salutation to Senator Robbins, you use the same salutation in letters that you write for his signature.

PERSONAL BUSINESS LETTERS

There are many occasions when business executives and professional persons must write personal letters to business acquaintances. Many managers expect their secretaries to write such letters. The manager indicates the circumstances that prompt the letter, and the secretary writes it without dictation from him. He signs the letter. For example, the manager might say, "Write to Burkett and thank him for luncheon at the University Club." Or he might jot down on the margin of a letter what he wants the secretary to say. Of course, the secretary should follow the manager's style as closely as possible in framing the letters.

The following are patterns that help the secretary compose various types of personal letters, with model letters the secretary can use with slight adaptations.

Checklist of requirements.   An effective personal letter must meet these requirements, in addition to those given in chapter 12, for any letter:

1. Be sure that your letter is opportunely timed. A note of congratulation, a message of condolence, or a letter of appreciation is far more effective if it is written promptly—that is, immediately after the event.
2. Make the tone of your letter personal, so that the message is "tailor-made" for the *individual* reader.
3. Be cordial and friendly, but not gushy.
4. Select a salutation and complimentary close that harmonize with the friendly tone of the letter. Use the reader's name in the greeting unless the letter is addressed to an organization.
5. Write with a sincerity that lends conviction to your message.
6. Have the manager sign the letter. The recipient will value the personal touch of his or her signature.

LETTERS OF APPRECIATION

A letter of appreciation should reflect genuine sincerity and honest gratitude; it should not reflect merely the writer's desire to conform with the rules of etiquette. The tone should be one of friendly informality. The factors that determine the suitable degree of informality are the following:

1. The extent to which the favor, service, or courtesy performed is a personal one
2. The degree of friendship existing between the writer and the recipient
3. The age and temperament of the recipient

For personal favor or service.

Dear John:
   Thank you so much for the ticket to the Annual Retailers' Convention and Forum. The exhibits were extremely interesting, and I particularly enjoyed the forum sessions.
   It was thoughtful of you to remember me. My sincere thanks for your kindness.
                                        Cordially,

For assistance to company, club, or association.

Dear Ms. Noble:

It was generous of you to spend so much time with our organization yesterday. The material you brought and the suggestions you made will be of great help in our new organization plans in the Personnel Department.

We all appreciate your cooperation. My sincere thanks for your valuable help.

Sincerely yours,

For hospitality.

Dear Ned:

I want to thank you for your hospitality during my two-week stay in Chicago. I count the evenings spent in your home as highlights of my stay in your city.

Your personal knowledge of the Merchandise Mart and the time you spent with me in the Mart greatly enhanced the pleasure and fruitfulness of my trip.

Thank you again for your kindness.

Sincerely,

For message of sympathy.

Gentlemen:

The members of this organization appreciate your kind expression of sympathy upon the sudden death of our treasurer, Mr. Thomas Thornhill.

We feel keenly the loss of one whose ability and sterling personal qualities have meant so much in the growth of this firm.

Please accept our sincere thanks for both your sympathetic message and your splendid tribute to Mr. Thornhill.

Sincerely,

For message of congratulation about a speech.

Dear Andy:

That was a fine letter you wrote me about my talk in Milwaukee last week, and I appreciate it ever so much.

Speaking to the members of your organization was a most enjoyable experience, and I am very glad that my remarks contributed in some small way to the success of your meeting.

Cordially,

For favorable mention in a speech.   (Adapt the letter if mention is in an article or a book.)

Dear Mr. Kennedy:

Thank you for the generous remarks you made in your speech before the Dry Goods Association yesterday about my part in the association's activities.

Coming from one of your high standing among the businessmen of the state, the compliment was especially pleasing.

Sincerely,

LETTERS OF CONDOLENCE

In any letter written to express sympathy, sincerity and tact are the most important qualities. Avoid words or sentiments that could distress the reader. Do not philosophize upon the meaning of death or quote scripture or poetry. A letter of condolence and sympathy should not be long and involved. Decision as to the length is based upon (1) the degree of friendship between writer and reader; (2) the situation that prompts the letter; and (3) the tastes and temperament of the reader.

Formerly all letters of condolence were written in longhand, but today such letters to business acquaintances who are not well known to the writer may be typewritten on business letterheads.

In the case of the death of an intimate friend, a handwritten letter, on personal writing paper, is correct. Some executives prefer to write letters of condolence in longhand, whether to a business or social acquaintance. In these cases, you give your employer the paper, the correct address, and perhaps a necessary fact or two.

Upon death.

To a business associate of the deceased:

Dear Mr. James:

It was with deep regret that I learned this morning of the sudden passing of Walter Conroy. I thought of you immediately, for I realize that the death of your good friend and business partner of some twenty years is an irreparable loss to you.

All of us in the furniture business will miss Walter. All of us admired the combination of kindness and honesty that his life represented. But since the loss to you is most direct and personal, I wanted to send you these words of sincere sympathy upon the death of a loyal friend and trusted associate.

Sincerely,

To the widow of an employee:

Dear Mrs. Echols:

It was with a very real sense of loss that I heard today of the death of your husband. I valued his friendship for many years. I don't believe I've ever known another man who was so loved and respected by all who knew him. It was a privilege to know Jack, whose place in our company can never be fully taken by anyone else.

My heartfelt sympathy goes out to you and your family. If there is any way in which I can be of assistance in the weeks ahead, please do not hesitate to call on me.

Sincerely,

Upon personal injury or illness; or property damage.

Dear Clyde:

I have been watching closely the reports in the paper each evening about your progress, and I am delighted at the news of your continued improvement. Tonight's item says that you and the doctors have won the fight, for which your many friends here are very thankful.

I hope you will be feeling more and more like your old self from now on, and that you will soon be returning home.

Sincerely,

Dear Mr. Beckman:

We were extremely sorry to learn that your warehouse was damaged by fire last night.

Perhaps there is some special service that we can perform in this emergency. If there is, please feel entirely free to call on us.

You have been a friend and customer of Maybank Brothers for many years, and we welcome an opportunity to be helpful in any way possible.

Sincerely yours,

LETTERS OF CONGRATULATIONS

The outstanding qualities of an expression of congratulations are (1) brevity, (2) naturalness of expression, and (3) enthusiasm. Trite, stilted phrases indicate a lack of sincerity and destroy the individuality of the letter.

The following illustrations of congratulatory messages are suitable for numerous occasions that occur frequently in business.

Upon professional or civic honor.

Dear Dr. Dodge:

I read with mixed feelings the announcement of your election as president of Norwich University. I am delighted, of course, at this splendid tribute to your ability and achievements; but I am also keenly regretful that it will take you away from Highland. The place you hold in the life of this community will be hard to fill.

The purpose of this letter, however, is to congratulate you upon the high honor that has come to you, and and which you so well deserve. You have my very best wishes for continued success in your new work.

Sincerely yours,

Upon outstanding community service.

Dear Ms. Morrison:

I read with pleasure of your acceptance of the chairmanship of the United Cerebral Palsy Fund Drive in the community.

When a woman as busy as you are makes time to assist in the conduct of the affairs of the town, it's time for the rest of us to take our hats off to the wonderful job she is doing.

Please accept my sincere admiration and every good wish for your success.

Sincerely,

Upon retirement.

Dear Walter:

I have just learned of your forthcoming retirement from Scott Investment Company and want to congratulate you on your record of wise leadership that has given your company the stature it now has.

No man, upon retiring from business, ever took with him as high a degree of respect and good wishes from so many devoted friends and associates.

Sincerely,

To attend a social event.

Dear Mr. Walker:

The Scott-Miller Company will observe its fiftieth anniversary at an informal banquet to be held in the Langley Hotel junior ballroom at seven o'clock.

We hope very much that you will attend as a guest of the company.

Since you have played a substantial part in its progress, your presence on this happy occasion seems particularly appropriate.

The program following the dinner will be varied and entertaining, and we feel sure you will have a most enjoyable evening.

Cordially yours,

To give an address or informal talk.

Dear Mrs. Serenbetz:

The Board of Directors of the National Office Management Association has asked me to extend an invitation to you to be our guest speaker at the monthly association meeting, Monday, December 7, at the Waldorf-Astoria Hotel at 8:00 p.m.

We have had many inquiries from regional members for updated information in connection with the use and misuse of aptitude, vocational, and personality tests used in modern employment practice. We know of your research work in this field, and hope that you will be able to honor us with an acceptance to speak to association members at this time.

I look forward to hearing from you.

Sincerely yours,

LETTERS OF ACCEPTANCE

A personal letter accepting an invitation should convey appreciation and enthusiasm. If the invitation has left certain details—such as time and place—to the convenience of the recipient, the acceptance must deal specifically with these points. Otherwise, a brief note is sufficient.

Accepting invitation to a special event.

Dear Mr. Nash:

I'll be delighted to be a guest of the Rand-Niles Company on the happy occasion of its fiftieth anniversary dinner.

Our association has indeed been a very close one, and I wouldn't miss being with you for anything in the world.

I am looking forward to the event and to being with you with a great deal of pleasure.

Sincerely,

Accepting speaking invitation.

Dear Mr. Scott:

I will be pleased to accept your invitation to speak at the American Business Administrators' annual meeting on March 5 at two o'clock.

What do you think of the topic "The Relationship between Business and the College of Business Administration"? This is simply a suggestion. You have not indicated how long you wish me to speak. Unless I hear from you, I will limit my address to thirty minutes.

I am looking forward to meeting you and the other members of your society.

Cordially yours,

Accepting membership in professional or civic organization.

Dear Ms. Foley:

Your cordial invitation for me to join the American Business Writing Association pleases me very much, and I accept with pleasure.

I realize that your membership includes many recognized authorities on the subject of business writing, both in academic ranks and in business circles. I am highly complimented to have the opportunity to become associated with such a group.

Sincerely yours,

LETTERS OF DECLINATION

Letters of declination should include an expression of regret and an expression of appreciation for the invitation. An explanation of the circumstances that prevent acceptance helps to show that the regret is sincere. The message must combine cordiality with tact.

Declining invitation to banquet, luncheon, or entertainment.

Dear John:

For several weeks I have expected that you would be holding the annual Foundation banquet sometime in June, and I've been keeping my fingers crossed in the hope that I could be present.

Unfortunately, however, June 15 is out of the question for me. I'll be in Boston at that time attending a company sales conference.

My sincere thanks, nevertheless, for your gracious invitation. I hope this year's banquet will be the best yet; and under your capable guidance, I am sure it will be.

Cordially,

Declining a speaking invitation.

Dear Ms. Connors:

It was good of you to invite me to be your guest speaker at the monthly meeting of the National Office Management Association on

March 18. I know I would very much enjoy being with you. However, on that evening, I am scheduled to speak in Boston.

I appreciate your thinking of me. Should another such occasion arise, please call on me. I would be very happy to address the members of your group another time, if I am free.

Sincerely,

Declining invitation to serve on civic or professional committee or board.

My dear Mr. Cavanaugh:

Thank you for your kind letter of March 6, in which you invite me to become a member of your Committee on Professional Standards in Advertising.

I would like very much to accept the invitation. Unfortunately, my present business duties will not permit me to give such an undertaking the time and consideration it deserves. I want you to know, however, that your invitation is deeply appreciated and that you and your associates have my very best wishes.

Yours sincerely,

Declining request to support charitable or other organization.

My dear Mr. Duval:

I have just received your letter of December 15, inviting me to participate in the fund-raising program of the Human Welfare Association, and I appreciate your thought in writing me.

There is no undertaking more deserving of financial aid, nor any to which I would more gladly contribute, than that which you represent. At the same time, I must tell you that all of the funds I have available for such purposes have already been ear-marked and that it just is not possible for me to do what you ask at this time. Later, perhaps—but at the moment I do not feel free to make either a current or future commitment.

Although I am not in a position to lend active support just now, I send you my best wishes for success in the fine work you are doing.

Sincerely yours,

LETTERS OF SEASONAL GOOD WISHES

Written in mid-December, letters of seasonal good wishes emphasize (1) appreciation of the reader's friendship, confidence, and cooperation, and (2) an expression of good wishes for the holiday season and the coming year. Ordinarily the message of seasonal good wishes should not be over 150 words. The tone and content are influenced by the relationship involved, but they should all have the essential qualities of informality, friendliness, and sincerity.

Dear Mr. Ramsey:

The association with you during the past year has been so enjoyable that I want to send you this word of good wishes for a happy and successful 19___.

I hope the coming year will afford more opportunities for pleasant contacts between your firm and mine, and that I will have the pleasure of further visits with you from time to time.

Sincerely,

Dear George:

As we approach the end of 19___, I realize that the enjoyable association with you has contributed much toward making it a very pleasant year for me.

In sending you these words of thanks for your kindness on several occasions, I wish for you the happiest of holiday seasons. May the New Year bring you continued health, happiness, and success!

Sincerely yours,

LETTERS OF INTRODUCTION

The letter of introduction may be prepared for direct mailing to the addressee, or for delivery in person by the one introduced. In the latter case the envelope should be left unsealed as a courtesy to the bearer. When there is sufficient time for the letter to reach its recipient before the arrival of the person introduced, the preferable practice is to send the note directly to the addressee.

The letter is ordinarily written in a spirit of asking a favor. It should include:

1. The name of the person being introduced
2. The purpose or reason for the introduction
3. All relevant and appropriate details, personal or business
4. A statement that any courtesy shown will be appreciated by the writer

The writer's acquaintance with the person introduced and with the recipient of the letter, and also the purpose for which the letter is written, determine its tone. When the writer is introducing one of his personal friends on both social and business bases, the tone is informal. When he is introducing one of his business associates for purely business reasons, the tone is more conservative.

A letter introducing a new sales representative is distinctly promotional in its purpose. It should include a summary of the new representative's qualifications and background for this work, as well as an assurance of his desire to cooperate with the reader.

Introducing a personal friend.

Dear Edward:

My good friend Paul Davison plans to be in Akron next week, and will present this letter to you.

Paul is very much interested in developing a house magazine for Robert Gould & Company of this city, where he is in charge of the Sales Promotion Department. I have told him that you publish one of the finest house organs I have ever seen, and suggested that he drop in for a chat with you.

I know that you and Paul will like each other, and I am sure you can give him some valuable suggestions. I will much appreciate anything you do to assist him, and I know that Paul will be sincerely grateful for your help.

It must be about time for you to make another trip to Cleveland, and I hope you will plan to have lunch with me at the club.

Cordially,

Introducing business or professional associate.

Dear Mr. Bradley:

I am pleased to introduce to you a very good friend of mine, Mr. Arthur Truesdale, chief engineer for the Acme Fisher Company.

Mr. Truesdale is making a careful investigation of the heating and power plants of some of our largest industries preliminary to writing a report on the subject. He tells me that your company has one of the most modern plants in our country and that he would like very much to inspect it.

Because I feel that you both might profit from knowing one another, I am writing this letter. I will appreciate whatever assistance you can give Mr. Truesdale.

Sincerely yours,

MISCELLANEOUS COURTESY LETTERS

Letters of apology.   When there is an adequate and convincing explanation for a situation that requires an apology, a few words can be devoted to the explanation. If no justification exists, a frank admission of that fact usually has a disarming effect upon the reader. Regardless of the circumstances, any situation that requires a letter of apology requires a tone of warmth and friendliness.

Dear Ms. Morton:

I hope you will accept a sincere apology for my absence from the Credit Association meeting yesterday afternoon.

When I told you earlier in the week that I planned to be there, I fully intended to be. But a meeting of our own credit department staff yesterday afternoon lasted much longer than expected, and it was quite impossible for me to get away.

When I see Jim Davis at lunch tomorrow, I will ask him to bring me up to date on yesterday's developments.

Sincerely yours,

Letters explaining delayed action.   When definite action on a letter of inquiry or request cannot be taken immediately, a note of acknowledgment is a business courtesy. When this situation arises because the addressee is out of town, the secretary acknowledges the incoming letter. (See page 282.) When the situation arises because the addressee needs time in which to prepare the information or material requested, the reply (1) explains the reason for the delay and (2) indicates approximately how long the delay will be.

Dear Mr. Hanley:

Your letter of February 18 has been read with much interest.

I will be glad to send you whatever information I have on mailing-list testing that is relevant to your problem. You are quite right that I have been interested in this aspect of promotional work for some time, and I have accumulated a considerable amount of material.

It happens that I must leave this evening on a business trip to Boston and Providence, and I will be away from the office for the next three or four days. As soon as I return, I will check over the mailing-list material and send you anything that I think may prove helpful.

Cordially yours,

Dear Bill:

Just a short note to tell you that I have received your letter of April 24. May I have a few days to think this over?

You will hear from me further within the week, and I hope it will be possible for me to be helpful to you.

Sincerely yours,

Letters granting requests. A friendly acknowledgment expressing pleasure in granting a request builds good will. Even if the request can be granted without the necessity of a letter, a cordial message is advisable. The letter should convey to the recipient the pleasure the writer feels in granting the request.

For information.

Dear Ms. Boardman:

I am glad to send you the address of Barton & Green, Inc. Their central office is located at 314 Fifth Avenue, New York City; their warehouse address is 211 Varick Street, New York City.

If there is any other way in which I can cooperate as your project develops, by all means let me know.

Cordially yours,

For booklet, pamphlet, or magazine.

Dear Mr. Milliken:

We are glad to send you with our compliments the booklet "A Dozen Ways to Build Business." Your copy is being mailed today in a separate folder.

Your interest in this publication is appreciated, and we hope the booklet will prove useful to you.

Cordially yours,

How to Write Correctly

PART
3

CORRECT WORD USAGE

This chapter contains an alphabetical list of troublesome words, phrases, and grammatical constructions, with explanations and examples of correct usage.

Necessary rules of grammar are included to avoid repeating the rules under each word to which they apply. Thus, the correct usage of a collective noun is not repeated under **audience, council,** and other collective nouns. Instead, reference is made under several collective nouns to the topic **Collective Nouns.** The grammatical rules, or topics, are listed alphabetically under an appropriate heading.

It is necessary to understand the nature of a grammar problem in order to find the solution to it. To help you in your search, we preface the alphabetical list beginning on page 312 with a short chart of the parts of speech and rules of grammar. You can glance through the chart and find an example similar to your problem. Then, under that heading in the alphabetical list, or under one to which you are referred, you will have your solution.

Example: If you wonder whether to say "surer" or "more sure" the brief explanation under **ADJECTIVE** indicates that your problem is one of comparison of adjectives. Turn to **Adjectives** in the alphabetical list and you will find your answer.

Definition	Example
NOUN—May be preceded by *a* or *the.* Most nouns can be made plural (1,4) and most can show possession (2). Nouns occur as subjects of a sentence (1,3,5), as objects of verbs (6) or prepositions (4), and as predicate nouns (7) after certain verbs. A noun is often defined as the name of any person, place, or thing.	The *letters* (1) were perfect. The *secretary's* (2) *supervisor* (3) was pleased with the perfect *letters* (4). The *secretary* (5) typed the *letter* (6). She was an outstanding *secretary* (7).
PRONOUN—Used in place of a noun. *I, we, you, he, she, it, they* are personal pronouns used as subjects (1,6,7) or predicate nouns (2). *Me, us, you, him, her, it, them* are personal pronouns used as objects (4). *Who* (3,8) and *whom* (objects—5) are relative pronouns used to refer to persons or animals; *which* to animals or things; *that* to persons, animals, and things.	*It* (1) is *she* (2) *who* (3) will help *them* (4). To *whom* (5) do *you* (6) wish to speak? May *I* (7) ask *who* (8) is calling?

Definition	Example
ADJECTIVE—Usually adds *er* or *est* to mean more or most or may be preceded by *more* or *most*. Adjectives modify nouns or pronouns.	strong, stronger, strongest intelligent, more intelligent, most intelligent
ADVERB—Often, but not always, is recognized by *ly* ending. As with adjectives, adverbs can add *er* or *est* or may be preceded by *more* or *most, less* or *least*. Adverbs are used to modify verbs (1,2,5), adjectives (3), and other adverbs (4).	She did the work *quickly* (1). He searched the files more *thoroughly* (2) the second time. It was an *unusually* (3) busy day. The report was *exceptionally* (4) *well* (5) written.
VERB—May add *ing* and be preceded by *to*. Many verbs add *ed, d,* or *t* to show past time. Verbs show action or state of being. A verb must always agree with its subject in number and person. Problems occur (1) when two or more subjects are joined by *and* (see Compound Subject); (2) when two or more subjects are joined by *or, nor,* and the like (see Alternate Subject); (3) when a noun or phrase intervenes between the subject and the verb (see Intervening Noun or Phrase).	Each student and teacher *was* (1) given a chance to speak. Neither poverty nor haste *is* (2) a good excuse for untidiness. The president, as well as the employees, *is* (3) interested in profit sharing.
PREDICATE NOMINATIVE—A noun or pronoun following an intransitive verb (one that does not take an object), thereby helping to complete the predicate. Mistakes occur (1) when the objective instead of the nominative case of a pronoun is used; (2) with singular subject and plural predicate nominative, or *vice versa*.	It was *I* (1) who called you. The answer to our office problems *is* [not *are*] (2) better-trained secretaries.

Definition	Example
SUBJUNCTIVE MOOD (OR MODE) —Expresses an idea as desirable, supposable, conditional, and the like. It is used to express contrary-to-fact conditions and unfulfilled wishes, and in *that* clauses after verbs expressing necessity and demand.	I wish I *were* [not *was*] in her position. Is it essential that he *have* [not *has*] a witness?
SEQUENCE OF TENSES—The purpose of changing the tense in a sentence is to indicate a change of time. The forms of the verbs should indicate which event came first and which came later.	She endorsed the check her employer *had given* [not *gave*] her. [The check was given to her *before* she endorsed it.]
GERUND—A verbal nouns; i.e., a word derived from a verb and used as a noun. A gerund always ends in *ing*. Errors occur from confusion between gerunds and active participles, which also end in *ing*. If a noun or pronoun precedes a gerund, it must be in the possessive case.	*Your* [not *you*] *buying* the house was a good investment. The *girl's typing* could be improved.
PARTICIPLE—A verbal adjective; i.e., a word derived from a verb and modifying a noun or pronoun. The active participle ends in *ing* and is often confused with the gerund, which also ends in *ing*. The participle must *modify* a noun or pronoun; if it does not, it is *dangling*. It cannot be used as a noun or pronoun, as is the gerund.	[Dangling] When typing the reports, extra care was used. [*Typing* does not modify a noun or pronoun.] When *typing* the reports, the *secretary* used extra care. The *girls typing* in that room are experts.

Definition	Example

INFINITIVE—Formed by the use of *to* before a verb. A common error is to place a word or words between *to* and the verb, resulting in a *split infinitive.*

Wrong: He promised *to* firmly *hold* our position.
Better: He promised *to hold* our position firmly.

PREPOSITION—A word used to show the relationship of a noun or pronoun to some other word in the sentence. It is not grammatically incorrect to place a preposition at the end of a sentence; it is better to end a sentence with a preposition than to use an awkward construction. It is incorrect to place an unnecessary preposition at the end of the sentence.

Wrong: Which office are we going *to*?
Better: *To* which office are we going?

If a word causes trouble in more than one sense, the various troublesome points are numbered 1, 2, 3, etc. (See **between.**) No attempt has been made to point out all uses of the words listed. Only those uses that cause confusion or trouble are included. Problems involving meaning or spelling should be looked up in the dictionary.

INDEX TO ALPHABETICAL LISTING OF RULES OF GRAMMAR

a, an (indef. arts.) Use *an* before all words beginning with a vowel except those beginning with the sound of *y* or *w,* and before words beginning with a silent *h.* In all other cases, use *a.*

> *an* attitude
> *an* era
> *an* ideology
> *an* obligation
> *an* understanding
> *an* hour
> *an* honorable discharge
> *a* humble workman
> *a* historical novel
> *a* unit
> *a* eulogy
> *a* one-sided affair

about (prep.) 1. Never use the combination *at about.* If you are being precise, use *at;* if you are approximating, use *about.*

2. If a sentence indicates an approximation or estimate, *about* is redundant.

> He will be here *about* [approximately] nine o'clock and will leave *at* [precisely] noon.

> The program will begin *about* [not *at about*] 8:30.

above. Preferably used as an adverb or preposition rather than as an adjective or noun.

Permissible: The *above* outline.

Preferable: The outline given *above.*
Preferable: The foregoing [or preceding] outline.

accede (vb.) When followed by a preposition, use *to.*

accompany (vb.) Use *by* when a person accompanies another. Use *with* when the reference is to some intangible thing.

> He was accompanied *by* his wife.
> The angry tones were accompanied *with* a pounding on the desk.

according (adj.) Follow by preposition *to.*

> According *to* your decision, I will . . . .

adapt, adopt (vbs.) *Adapt* means to make fit or suitable, to adjust; *adopt* means to take as one's own, to accept formally.

> Many companies *adapted* their plants to the needs of an expanding economy.
> The company *adopted* the suggestions made.

addicted to, subject to. *Addicted to* means devoted to persistently, as to a bad habit or indulgence; *subject to* means liable to or conditional upon.

> Jones is *addicted to* alcohol.
> Jones is *subject to* [liable to] colds.

This arrangement is *subject to* [conditional upon] approval by Mr. Jones.

adept (adj.) When followed by a preposition, use *in.*

adequate (adj.) When followed by a preposition, use *for* when enough is meant; *to* when commensurate is meant.

That amount is adequate *for* [enough] her living expenses.

That amount is not adequate *to* [commensurate] the demands made on her.

Adjectives. Adjectives modify nouns and pronouns. They have three degrees for comparison purposes: positive, comparative, and superlative. Adjectives of one syllable form the comparative by adding *-er* and superlative by adding *-est.*

slow, slow*er,* slow*est*

Some adjectives of two syllables form the comparative and superlative by adding *-er* and *-est* while others use *more* and *most.*

happi*er,* happi*est*
more helpful, *most* helpful

When you are in doubt as to how to compare an adjective, consult an unabridged dictionary.

Comparison to indicate less or least of a quality is accomplished by using the words *less* and *least* before the adjective.

helpful, *less* helpful, *least* helpful

Adjectives of more than two syllables always form the comparative and superlative with *more* and *most.*

industrious, *more* industrious, *most* industrious

Some adjectives are compared irregularly, such as:

good, well, *better, best*
bad, *worse, worst*

Avoid double comparisons such as *more slower, more faster,* etc. Be sure to use the comparative when you have just two to compare and the superlative for three or more. Don't say, "Jack is the best editor of the two." Say, "Jack is the better."

Adverbs. Adverbs modify verbs, adjectives, and other adverbs.

1. Avoid using an adjective for an adverb. A common error is the misuse of an adjective to modify another adjective.

He submitted a *really* [not *real*] good report to the president. ["Good" is an adjective and must be modified' by the adverb "really," not by the adjective "real."]

The requirements of the position are those that an *ordinarily* [not *ordinary*] intelligent man should have. ["Intelligent" is an adjective and must be modified by the adverb "ordinarily," not by the adjective "ordinary."]

2. Frequently a verb is used, not primarily for its own meaning, but to link the subject to a word following the verb that specifies a quality or condition of the subject. In such a case, this word should be an adjective, not an adverb.

The report sounded *strange* [not *strangely*] to me in view of the circumstances. ["Strange" modifies "report," not "sounded."]

When the word following the verb

does *not* qualify the subject, but qualifies the action of verb, it should be an adverb. Note that the same verb can take both constructions. *See also* **Predicate Nominative.**

His laugh sounded *hollowly* through the room.

3. Some adverbs have two forms, either of which is correct.

slow, slow*er,* slow*est*
or
slow*ly, more* slow*ly, most* slow*ly*

The *-ly* form is preferable unless the emphasis is on the degree or manner of action rather than on the action.

He struggled *slowly* back to consciousness. [The emphasis is on the struggling back to consciousness.]
Drive *slow* around the curve. [The emphasis is on the slowness with which the car is driven.]

Most common adverbs that have two forms are listed in alphabetical position in this Correct Word Usage list.

adverse, averse (adjs.) *Adverse* means in opposition, unfavorable; *averse* means having a dislike for. *Adverse* refers chiefly to opinion or intention; *averse* to feeling or inclination.

His report was *adverse* to the interest of labor.
He is *averse* to criticism from others.

advise, inform (vbs.) Use *advise* in the sense of counsel, warn; use *inform* in the sense of acquaint, tell, communicate knowledge to.

I will *advise* him not to accept the contract as it now stands.
I will *inform* [not *advise*] him that the contract is full of loopholes.

affect, effect. 1. The word *affect* is not used as a noun, except as a technical psychological term; *effect,* used as a noun, means result.

The *effect* [not *affect*] of a sarcastic business letter is to harm business.

2. These two verbs are totally different in meaning. *Affect* means to influence, to concern, to change; *effect* means to cause, produce, result in, bring about.

Passage of this bill will *affect* [influence, concern] the entire country.
Passage of this bill can be *effected* [brought about] by cooperation of all parties.
The change of climate may *affect* [alter, have an influence upon] his recovery.
The change of climate may *effect* [cause, result in] his recovery.

3. *Affect* is also used in the sense of assuming or pretending.

He *affects* [not *effects*] a blustery manner to hide his shyness.
He *affected* [not *effected*] ignorance of the matter to avoid a fight.

ago (adj.) When a qualifying clause is used after *ago,* begin the clause with *that,* not with *since.*

The measure was passed a year *ago.* [No qualifying clause.]
It is over ten years *ago,* as well as I remember, *that* [not *since*] the stores were consolidated.

agree (vb.) You agree *with* a person, *to* a proposal, *on* a plan.

I agree *with* you.
He agreed *to* the suggestion.

The union will not agree *on* a compensation plan.

Also, a thing may agree with another thing.

The photograph *agrees* with the painting.

agreeable (adj.) Usually followed by *to*, but may be followed by *with* when used in the sense of in conformity, or in accordance.

The plan is agreeable *with* [in accordance with] my understanding of what is expected of us.

Agreement of Verb with Subject. A verb should always agree with its subject in number and person. The rule is simple, but the number of the subject is not always clear. Mistakes sometimes occur when two or more subjects are joined by *and* (*see* **Compound Subject**); when two or more subjects are joined by *or, nor,* and the like (*see* **Alternate Subject**); when a noun or a phrase intervenes between the subject and the verb (*see* **Intervening Noun**) and when a verb is followed by a predicate nominative (*see* **Predicate Nominative**).

alike (adj.) Do not precede by *both.*

Wrong: They are *both alike.*
Right: They are *alike.*

all. 1. When used as a noun, *all* is either singular or plural, depending upon the meaning.

All *is* [meaning everything] forgiven.

All *are* [meaning several people] forgiven.

2. When used with a pronoun, *all* is a noun and is followed by *of.*

Number *all of* them.

When used with a noun, *all* is, properly, an adjective; *of* is not needed.

Number *all* the sheets.

all right. This expression should always be written as two words.

Are you *all right?*
It will be *all right* to ship the goods on the tenth.

allusion, illusion, delusion. An *allusion* is a reference to something; an *illusion* is a false image; a *delusion* is a false concept or belief.

In his speech he made an *allusion* [reference] to the president's last news conference.

The mirrors gave the *illusion* [false image] of a larger room.

The company's accounting system creates a *delusion* [false concept] about its profits.

Alternate Subject. 1. Two or more singular subjects in the third person joined by *or, nor, and not, but, either . . . or,* or *neither . . . nor* take singular verbs in the third person.

Either the sales manager *or* the advertising manager *obtains* [not *obtain*] these data.

Neither power *nor* wealth *is* [not *are*] a substitute for health.

Not only the typing *but* also the spelling *was* [not *were*] poor.

2. If two or more subjects differing in number or person are joined by *or, nor, and not, but, either . . . or, neither . . . nor,* the verb agrees with the subject nearer it. It is often wise to recast the sentence to avoid awkwardness.

Neither the boy *nor* the *men were* [not *was*] able to work the problem.
Either the girls *or* the *supervisor has* [not *have*] to work late.
I understand *you or Mr. Jones was* [not *were*] to meet the train.
He said that *he and not I have* [not *has*] been chosen.

among (prep.) *See* **between,** 2.

Amounts. Words stating amount (time, money, measurement, weight, volume, fractions) take a singular verb.

Five days *is* the usual work week.
Three feet *is* the correct measurement.
Five yards *is* what I ordered.
Three quarters of a pound *is* enough.
Ten dollars *is* more than I expected.

and (conj.) Frequently misused to connect two verbs when the second verb should be an infinitive.

Wrong: Come *and* visit me.
Right: Come *to visit* me.
Wrong: Try *and* finish the chapter.
Right: Try *to finish* the chapter.

anger (n.) Anger *at* that which hurts or annoys, *toward* a person.

angry (adj.) Angry *at* a thing, *with* a person.

annoyed. Annoyed *with* a person, *by* that which annoys.

I am annoyed *with* her.
I am annoyed *by* her carelessness.

anxious, eager. *Anxious* is frequently misused for *eager.* To be *anxious* is to be worried; to be *eager* is to anticipate enthusiastically.

I am *eager* [not *anxious*] to hear the new director's address.

He is *anxious* [worried] about the outcome of the election.

anyone (pron.), **any one.** 1. Singular, followed by a singular verb and singular pronoun.

Anyone who *is* [not *are*] interested in *his* [not *their*] work *makes* [not *make*] a point of getting to work on time.

2. Of the two forms *anyone* and *any one,* the first is correct when *anybody* can be substituted in the sentence with no change in meaning. In other uses, *any one* is the correct form.

If we send *anyone,* it should be Mr. Jones.
If we send *any one* of the salesmen, it should be Mr. Jones.
Any one of the manuscripts is worthy of publication.

any time. Never written as one word.

anywhere (adv.) Always written as one word.

apropos (adv.) Means with respect to something; usually used with *of.*

Apropos of our recent talk.

apt, liable, likely (to do something). These words are frequently confused. *Apt* suggests an habitual tendency; *liable* usually means exposed to a risk or unpleasantness. When the sense is simple probability, use *likely.*

Businessmen are *apt* [have a tendency] to dictate letters carelessly.

A businessman who dictates letters carelessly is *liable* to lose [exposed to the danger of losing] his customers. [*Note:* Some authorities condemn "liable to do something" altogether, allowing only the prepositional instead of the infinitive phrase—"A businessman is liable to the loss . . . . "]

He is *likely* to [probably will] vote against the bill.

as. 1. Use *as . . . as* in affirmative statements; *so . . . as* in negative statements and in questions implying a negative answer.

This window display is *as* attractive *as* the last one.

This window display is *not so* attractive *as* the last one.

Could any ambitious young man be *so* foolish *as* to turn down the offer? [Implying a negative answer.]

2. Use *as* to express comparison when a clause containing a verb follows. *See also* **like**, 2.

Copy the report exactly *as* [not *like*] it is written.

3. An explanatory *as* clause should be placed before the main sentence. The exception to this rule is an *as* clause that states a fact necessarily known to the reader.

Wrong: The minority abandoned its position, *as* the opposition showed no sign of yielding.

Right: As the opposition showed no sign of yielding, the minority abandoned its position.

Right: I need not read the fifth clause, *as* you are familiar with it.

As it overworked when used as a substitute for *for, since, because.*

4. Avoid using *as to* in lieu of a simple preposition such as *of, about, among, upon.*

She has no conception *of* [not *as to*] the proper performance of her duties.

The witness testified *about* [not *as to*] the defendant's early life.

audience (n.) *See* **Collective Nouns.**

averse. Not to be confused with *adverse. See* **adverse.**

aversion (n.) Aversion *to* a person, *for* acts or actions.

bad, badly. Use the adjective *bad* when it refers to the subject and is simply joined to the subject by the verb. When the verb denotes action, use the adverb *badly* to modify the action. *See* **Adverbs,** 2.

He looks *bad.* [Describes "he."]

He was injured *badly* in the accident. [Describes how he was injured.]

He writes *badly.* [Describes how he writes.]

He feels *bad* about the incident. [Describes "he." *See* **feel.**]

He behaves *badly* when he is disappointed. [Describes how he behaves.]

balance (n.) Frequently misused for "rest" or "remainder." *Balance* is a financial term and should be used only in reference to the difference between two amounts.

She gave the *balance* of the money to the Red Cross.

We expect to ship the *remainder* [not *balance*] of the order next week.

The *rest* [not *balance*] of the audience enjoyed the program.

The *balance* of the account. . . .

The *remainder* of the week. . . .

because (conj.) Frequently incorrectly used instead of *that* after *The reason . . . is . . . .*

Wrong: Her reason for quitting her job is *because* she does not earn enough money.

Right: Her reason for quitting her job is *that* she does not earn enough money.

Right: The reason the goods were delayed was *that* [not *because*] they were shipped to the wrong zone number.

beside(s). *Beside* means by the side of, close to; *besides* means additionally, in addition to.

The letter is on his desk, *beside* [close to] the file.

Besides [in addition to] these two bills, there are several others.

We have these two bills and several others *besides* [in addition].

between (prep.) 1. Use the objective case after *between*.

Between you and *me* [never *I*].

2. Use *between* when reference is made to only two persons or things; use *among* when reference is made to more than two.

The friendliness *between* [not *among*] the British Foreign Minister and the American Secretary of State promoted harmony.

The friendliness *among* [not *between*] British, American, and Israeli delegates promoted harmony.

3. Do not use *each* or *every* after *between* or *among* when *each* or *every* has a plural sense.

Wrong: Almost all the audience went into the lobby *between each* scene.

Right: Almost all the audience went into the lobby *between* scenes.

Wrong: It is essential that harmony prevail *between every* department.

Right: It is essential that harmony prevail *among* the departments.

biannual, biennial (adjs.) 1. *Biannual*

means twice a year, though not necessarily at six-month intervals; *biennial* means once in two years.

The association holds *biannual* conferences. [Two conferences a year.]

Congressmen are elected *biennially*. [Every two years.]

2. *Biannual* is distinguished from *semiannual* in that *semiannual* implies an interval of six months.

3. *Biannually*, *biennially* are the adverbial forms.

biweekly, bimonthly (adjs., advs.) *Biweekly* means once every two weeks or twice a week; *bimonthly* usually means once every two months. These expressions are confusing. It is clearer to use *once every two weeks, once every two months. See* **semimonthly, semiweekly.**

blame (vb.) Blame a person *for* something; do not blame something *on* a person.

Wrong: Blame the present difficulty *on* the administration.

Right: Blame the administration *for* the present difficulty.

Wrong: The blame for the accident is *on* him.

Right: The blame for the accident is his.

both (adj., pron., and conj.) 1. Pl., followed by plural verb and plural pronoun.

2. *Both* is unnecessary with the words *between, alike, at once, equal(ly)*, and should be omitted unless the omission of the other words is preferable.

Wrong: Both the Democrats and the Republicans are *equally* anxious to prevent the spread of communism. [Omit either "both" or "equally."]

Wrong: They are *both alike* in their zeal for perfection. [Omit "both."]

bring, take (vbs.) These words are opposites. *Bring* implies *coming* with some person or thing to another place; *take* implies *going* with some person or thing to another place.

I will *bring the book* [with me] when I come to your office this afternoon.

I will *take* the book *to* him when I go to his office this afternoon.

Please *bring* the book *with* you the next time you come to my office.

Please *take* the book *to* him the next time you go to his office.

but (conj.) 1. When used in the sense of *except,* some writers incorrectly consider *but* as a preposition and follow it with the objective case. The case after *but* varies according to its usage. When *but* and the word that follows it occur at the end of the sentence, the word after *but* is in the objective case.

Everyone *but she* [not *her*] enjoyed the entertainment. [She did not enjoy it.]

No one wanted to make the change *but* me. [I wanted to make it.]

I told no one *but him* [not *he*] about the change. [I told him about it.]

2. A common error is the use of *but* after a negative.

Wrong: I *cannot but* object to the title.
Right: I *can* but object to the title.
Wrong: There *are not but* ten shopping days left before Christmas.
Right: There are *but* ten shopping days. . . .

When *but* is used in the sense of *except,* it may follow a negative, of course.

Nobody but he went.

He accepted *none* of the shipment *but the* short coats.

3. *But what* is correctly used only when *except* could be substituted for *but.* The use of *but what* for *but that* is a colloquialism.

Right: He said nothing *but what* [or, *except what*] any honorable person would have said.

but that. 1. A common error is the use of *but that* instead of *that* to introduce a clause after *doubt* (either the verb or the noun "doubt").

I do not doubt *that* [not *but that*] the shipment will reach you tomorrow.

There is no doubt *that* [not *but that*] the shipment will reach you tomorrow.

2. *But that* is not interchangeable with *that.* Notice the difference in meaning in the following sentences.

It is impossible *that* the signatories to the United Nations Charter will sanction the move. [They will not sanction.]

It is impossible *but that* the signatories to the United Nations Charter will sanction the move. [Sure to sanction.]

It is not impossible *that* the signatories to the United Nations Charter will sanction the move. [May sanction.]

3. *Unnecessary negative.* When *but that* has a negative implication, the subsequent use of *not* is incorrect.

Wrong: How do you know *but that*

the apparent friendliness of our competitor may *not* be an attempt to learn more about our new project?

Right: How do you know *but that* the apparent friendliness of our competitor may be an attempt . . . ?

cabinet (n.) When used to mean a "body of advisors," cabinet is a **Collective Noun.**

can, could. 1. *Could* is the past tense of *can*. Remember this when using *can* or *could* in sentences with other verbs. *See* **Sequence of Tenses.** Use *can* with verbs in the present, perfect, and future tenses; use *could* with verbs in the past and past perfect tenses.

> I give
> I have given ⎫ what I *can.*
> I will give ⎭
>
> I gave
> I was giving ⎫ what I *could.*
> I had given ⎭

2. Use *could*, not *can*, when *would* is used in the main clause.

He *would* stop in Cincinnati on his way west if he *could* [not *can*] arrange to meet you there.

He said that he *would* recommend that the agency change its specifications so that we *could* [not *can*] get some of the business.

Even if the company *could* [not *can*] ship the order by Monday, the material *would* not reach the factory soon enough.

3. A common error is the misuse of *could* for *might* in conditional sentences. *Could* expresses ability, *might* expresses permission or possibility. *See* **can, may.**

If you have not bought the stock,

you *might* [not *could*] as well forget about it.

If the certificate fails to make provision for the issuance of stock in series, it *might* [not *could*] subsequently be amended to include that provision. [The thought is that the certificate *would perhaps* be amended; there is no question that it *can* be amended.]

can, may. *Can* denotes ability or power; *may* denotes permission.

Can you [will you be able to] make shipment next week?

May we [will you give us permission to] make shipment next week?

I *can* [it is possible for me to] go to Alaska by plane. *May* I? [Do I have your permission?]

canvas (n.) *Canvas* means a heavy cloth.

canvass (vb.) *Canvass* means to scrutinize, discuss, solicit. Not to be confused with *canvas.*

capital, capitol (ns.) *Capital* is a city that is the seat of the government; *Capitol* is the building in which Congress meets, or a building in which a state legislature meets. State capitols may be spelled either upper or lower case, but the United States Capitol is spelled with an upper-case C.

Washington DC is the *capital* of the United States.

I hope the repairs to the *Capitol* are completed when we visit Washington.

The *capitol* at Albany is being repaired.

Capital has several other meanings but they do not cause confusion.

careless (adj.) Careless *about* appearance and dress; *in* the performance of an action; *of* others.

class (n.) Pl., *classes.* 1. A Collective Noun when used in the sense of a group of students.

2. For correct usage in the sense of "kind or sort" *see* kind.

coincident (adj.) When followed by a preposition, use *with.*

Collective Nouns. Collective nouns are singular if the writer is referring to the group as such, plural if he is referring to the individual persons or things of which the group is composed. The number of the verb and pronoun depends upon whether the collective noun is used in the singular or plural.

The council *is* insisting on *its* right to enforce the regulation. [Meaning the council as a unit.]

The council *are* disagreeing as to *their* authority to enforce the regulation. [Meaning that the members disagree among themselves.]

In some cases it is a matter of discretion whether the singular or plural sense should be used, but after the choice is made, the verbs and pronouns must all agree. It is incorrect to use a singular verb in one sentence and begin the next sentence with a plural pronoun, or *vice versa.*

Wrong: The Democratic party *has* elected *their* candidate as mayor for the last four terms. However, *they* have not had a majority in the City Council for several years.

Right: The Democratic party *has* elected *its* candidate as mayor for

the last four terms. However, *it* has not had a majority in the City Council for several years.

Right: The Democratic party *have* elected *their* candidate as mayor for the last four terms. However, *they* have not had a majority in the City Council for several years.

committee (n.) *See* **Collective Nouns.**

common, -er, -est (adj.) Preferable to *more common, most common.*

common, mutual (adjs.) 1. *Common* refers to something that is shared alike by two or more individuals or species, as *common fear* of war, *common trait* of character. *Mutual* refers to something that is reciprocally given and received, as *mutual agreement, mutual respect.* Careful writers do not use *mutual* when *common* is the correct word.

Wrong: mutual effort, *mutual* sorrow.
Right: common effort, *common* sorrow.

2. *Mutual* can also be used in the sense of "having the same relationship to each other."

mutual [or *common*] foes
mutual [or *common*] friends

compare to, compare with. If it is desired to suggest a similarity or to state that a similarity exists, use *to.* If it is desired to indicate specific similarities or differences, use *with.*

The speaker compared the new law *to* a plague. [The speaker merely suggested a similarity.]

The speaker compared the British law *with* the American statute. [The speaker made a detailed comparison.]

complacent (adj.), -ency (n.); complaisant (adj.), -ance (n.) A *complacent* person is pleased with himself or with things that affect him personally. A *complaisant* person is anxious to please by compliance or indulgence.

Don't let your *complacency* about your work keep you from knowing your shortcomings.

If Congress were in a more *complaisant* mood, the president might be able to push the law through.

complement, compliment (ns., vbs.) 1. *Complement* is that which is required to complete or make whole; *compliment* is an expression of admiration.

This department has its full *complement* [quota] of workers. [Noun]

A gold clip on your dress will *complement* [complete] your costume. [Verb]

His *compliments* on my article were gratifying. [Noun]

The president *complimented* him on the showing made by his department. [Verb]

2. The noun *complement* is followed by the preposition *of;* the verb *compliment* is followed by *on.*

complementary, complimentary (adjs.) 1. The distinction in meaning is the same as that between *complement* and *compliment. See above.*

Practical experience is *complementary* to theoretical training.

Two *complementary* colors mixed together make a third color.

His review of the book was not *complimentary.*

Complimentary remarks about a person's work are always appreciated.

2. The preposition *to* is used with *complementary; about* or *concerning* with *complimentary.*

compliance (n.) When followed by a preposition, use *with.*

comply (vb.) When followed by a preposition, use *with.*

Compound Personal Pronouns. Formed by adding *-self* (sing.) or *-selves* (pl.) to some personal pronouns.

1. They are used to call attention to the subject and to emphasize a noun or pronoun.

Right: He hurt *himself* more than anyone else by his attitude.

Right: The *president himself* made a report to the employees.

2. A common error is the use of a compound personal pronoun in place of the objective case of the pronoun.

Wrong: Best regards from George and *myself.*

Right: Best regards from George and *me.*

3. Another common error is the omission of a possessive pronoun when a word is joined to a compound personal pronoun. Test the sentence by omitting the compound personal pronoun.

Wrong: He hurt *himself and family* by his attitude. [The absurdity of "He hurt family" is obvious.]

Right: He hurt *himself and his* family by his attitude.

Compound Subject. 1. Two or more subjects joined by *and* take a plural verb.

Personal power, progress, *and* success *depend* [not *depends*] upon many things.

A good quality of stationery *and* neat typing *make* [not *makes*] a good impression upon the recipient of the letter.

2. If the compound subject consists of two nouns referring to the same person or thing, the verb is singular.

The vice-president and treasurer of the company *is* out of the city. [When both offices are filled by the same person.]

The vice-president and the treasurer of the company *are* out of the city. [When separate individuals fill the two offices.]

3. When *each, every, many a,* and the like modify the complete subject, the verb is singular.

Each (or *Every*) officer and member *was* [not *were*] present.

Many a man and woman *has* [not *have*] voted for him.

Compound Terms. This name applies to two or more short words written together, or joined by a hyphen, or written separately but expressing a single idea. Thus, *editor-in-chief, businessman,* and *attorney general* are all compounds. The authorities differ as to whether many compounds should be written as one word. The approved forms of many compound pronouns and other troublesome compound terms are included in this list in their proper alphabetical position. The following rules are a guide to writing other compounds.

1. *Plurals.* Form the plural of a compound word by adding *-s* to the most important noun in the compound. Thus, *editors-in-chief, sons-in-law, attorneys general.* (*See also* **Plurals of Compound Terms,** chapter 15.)

2. *Consistency.* Be consistent. When there is a choice, decide whether you wish to hyphenate two or more words, to write them as one word, or to write them as separate words. Follow the form you choose consistently. If your company has a style manual, you should follow it.

3. *Meaning.* An invariable rule is to use the form that conveys the proper meaning. Although your dictionary might show two or more words joined together or hyphenated, the meaning might differ from the meaning of the same words used separately, sometimes to the point of absurdity.

The *take-off* was smooth.
We will *take off* from LaGuardia Airport.
They have a *hothouse.*
They have a *hot house.*
He is very *matter-of-fact.*
As a *matter of fact,* I did go.

4. *Usage.* Do not hyphenate or join words together for the sole reason that they are frequently used together. Wait until the authorities accept them in compounded form.

5. *Adjectives.* Hyphenate two or more words used as an adjective, such as *two-story* house, *short-term* loan, *no-par* stock, *above-mentioned* law, *well-known* politician. Do not hyphenate color variations used as an adjective, such as *navy blue* dress, *light grey* paint.

6. Fractions. Hyphenate fractions when the numerator and the denomi-

nator are both one-word forms, such as *one-third, three-fourths, one-hundredth.*

7. *Nationalities.* Hyphenate two or more words to indicate that the person or thing shares in the qualities of both, as *Anglo-American, Sino-Japanese, Latin-American* (but not Latin America), *Scotch-Irish.*

8. *Coined phrases.* Hyphenate coined phrases, such as *middle-of-the-road, pay-as-you-go, drive-it-yourself, ready-to-wear.*

9. *Adverbs.* Do not use a hyphen to connect an adverb and an adjective. Do not use a hyphen to connect an adverb ending in -*ly* and a past participle in such phrases as a *happily married couple, a brilliantly lighted house.*

10. *Titles.* Do not hyphenate titles such as *rear admiral, Chief of Staff,* but do hyphenate *secretary-treasurer* and other coined compounds. Also hyphenate *ex-president, president-elect,* and *vice-president-elect.*

concur (vb.) Concur *in* a decision, opinion, belief; concur *with* a person.

conducive (adj.) When followed by a preposition, use *to.*

conform (vb.) When followed by a preposition, use *to* or *with.*

connect (vb.) Objects, places, or people are connected *with* one another *by* certain means.

Gimbels used to be connected *with* Saks *by* a bridge.

connection. The phrase *in this connection* is never good usage; the phrase *in connection with* is generally considered trite and is overworked. There is no grammatical objection to it when it is the proper phrase to use, but a substitution is generally preferable. Try *about* as a substitute.

conscious, aware. *Conscious* emphasizes inner realization; *aware* emphasizes perception through the senses.

He became *conscious* of the reason for his failure.

He was *aware* of staleness of the air in the room.

consensus (n.) An erroneous expression frequently used is *consensus of opinion. Consensus* means agreement in matter of opinion; therefore, the expression is clearly redundant.

Wrong: The *consensus of opinion* at the board meeting was . . . .

Right: The *consensus* at the board meeting was . . . .

consist (vb.) Followed by *of* to indicate the material; *in* to define or show identity.

Margarine consists *of* [the materials] vegetable oils and coloring.

The sinking fund method consists *in* [may be defined as] the payment of a sum . . . .

His greatest asset consists *in* [is] his ability to understand.

contemptible, contemptuous (adjs.) *Contemptible* means despicable, deserving of being despised. *Contemptuous* means scornful.

The effort to bring pressure to bear on him was *contemptible* [despicable].

His comments on the report were *contemptuous* [scornful].

continual, continuous (adjs.) *Con-*

tinual means occurring in close succession, frequently repeated; *continuous* means without stopping, without interruption. The same distinction applies to the adverbs *continually* and *continuously.*

Continual [frequent] breakdowns in the factory delayed production.

The machinery has been in *continuous* operation [without stopping] for 60 hours.

He is *continually* [frequently] asking for favors.

He drove *continuously* [without stopping] for six hours.

correct (adj.) Not comparable. If anything is correct, it cannot be *more* correct. *More nearly correct* is allowable.

correlative (adj.) When followed by a preposition, use *with.*

could. *See* **can, could.**

council, counsel, consul. *Council* applies to a board or assembly and to the meeting of such a body; *counsel* applies to deliberation or advice, as an attorney. *Counsel* may be either a verb or a noun, but *council* is always a noun. *Consul* (n.) is a government representative looking after his country's interest in a foreign country.

credible, credulous, creditable (adjs.) *Credible* means believable; *credulous* means easily imposed upon, believing too easily; *creditable* means praiseworthy.

He is not a *credible* witness.

The readers are indeed *credulous* if they believe the editorial completely.

His summation of the case was highly *creditable.*

damage, injury (ns.) *Injury* is the broad, general term; *damage* is especially an injury that impairs value or involves loss. *Injury* is impairment of utility or beauty and applies generally to persons, feelings, reputation, character, and sometimes to property. *Damage* applies to property only.

The *damage* to the *house* is extensive, but it does not compare with the the *injury* to the *landscape.*

He collected insurance for *injury* to his *back* and for *damage* to his *car.*

He will never live down the *injury* to his *reputation.*

data (n.) Plural and takes a plural verb and plural adjective pronoun. The singular form, *datum,* is now seldom used.

We have proved that *these* [not *this*] *data are* [not *is*] reliable.

dates from. The correct expression is *dates from,* not *dates back to.*

defect (n.) Defect *in* a concrete object; defect *of* an intangible quality, such as judgment or character.

The failure to pick up speed is a defect *in* the *machine.*

The defect *of* his *character* is impatience.

depositary, depository (ns.) *Depositary* is applied to the person or authority entrusted with something for safekeeping. It may also be used to apply to the place where something is deposited or stored. *Depository* is applied only to the place where something is deposited or stored.

depreciate (vb.) Do not follow by the words *in value.* If anything has depreciated, its value is less.

did (vb.) Sometimes misused in place of *has* or *have*. *Did* represents past action; *has* or *have*, action continuing to the present moment. The misuse usually occurs with *yet* or *already*.

Did you listen to Town Meeting yesterday? [Past action].

Have you heard the results of the election *yet*? [not *did you hear*].

Wrong: I *did* not hear the results of the election *yet*.

Right: I *have* not heard the results of the election *yet*.

differ (vb.) Used in the sense of unlikeness, *differ* is followed by *from;* used in the sense of disagreeing in opinion, by *with*.

My sales campaign *differs from* [not *with*] yours.

I *differ with* [not *from*] you as to the value of your sales campaign.

different. Do not use to show separate identity that has already been established.

Three secretaries [not three *different* secretaries] asked for a Christmas vacation.

different from. This is the correct form; *different than* is rarely used.

My sales plan is different *from* (not *than*) yours.

direct. 1. The adverb form is *direct* or *directly*.

2. *Direct* is not comparable. If anything is direct, it cannot be *more* direct. *More nearly direct* is allowable.

disappointed (adj.) *Disappointed* with a thing or object; otherwise, *disappointed in*.

I am disappointed *with* the car.

I am disappointed *in* the outcome of the election.

I am disappointed *in* him.

disinterested, uninterested (adjs.) *Disinterested* means impartial, without selfish motive or thought of personal gain. *Uninterested* means not interested or enthusiastic.

The teacher did not state the case in a *disinterested* [impartial] manner.

He seems *uninterested* [lacking in interest] in his work.

dissent (vb.) When followed by a preposition, use *from*.

do (vb.) 1. Principal parts, *do, did, [has, had or have] done. See* **Irregular Verbs.**

2. For the misuse of *did* for *has* or *have, see* **did.**

double entendre. This is the accepted form; it is considered a French expression and treated like a foreign phrase.

Double Negatives. The use of two negatives to express a negative thought is wrong. Some double negatives, such as *don't want no, doesn't need none, wouldn't never,* are too obviously wrong for discussion. The insidious double negatives occur with words that convey a negative idea, such as *hardly, barely, scarcely, but, but that,* rather than with words that are definitely negative in form, such as *no, more, never. See* **hardly,** 1; **scarcely; but; but that,** 3; **not.**

due to. Often misused for *owing to*. *Due* is an adjective and must be attached to a noun or pronoun, whereas *owing to* is now considered a compound preposition. *Due to* means *caused by.* Test your sentence by substituting *caused by* for *due to.*

Wrong: The labor movement is losing prestige *due to* the methods of some of its leaders. [There is no noun for "due" to modify. The prestige was not *caused by* the methods.]

Right: The labor movement is losing prestige *owing to* the methods of some of its leaders. ["Methods" is the object of the compound preposition "owing to."]

Right: The success of the firm was *due to* [caused by] the ability of its president. [The "success" was caused by the "ability."]

Right: The firm succeeded *owing to* [not *due to*] the ability of its president.

each. 1. When used as a subject, *each* invariably takes a singular verb and pronoun even when followed by *of them.*

Each of the reports made by the committees *was* [not *were*] a tribute to the late president.

Each of the companies filed *its* [not *their*] reports promptly.

Each carries [not *carry*] *his* [not *their*] share of the load.

2. When *each* immediately follows a plural noun or pronoun the verb is plural.

The officers *each take* [not *takes*] an oath.

3. When *each* refers to a preceding plural noun or pronoun, the number of a subsequent noun or pronoun depends upon whether *each* comes before or after the verb. Use the plural when *each* precedes the verb; the singular when *each* follows the verb.

The employees *each have their* own assignments. [Precedes the verb.]

The employees *are* responsible *each* for *his* own assignment. [Follows the verb.]

4. For the use of *each* after *between* or *among, see* **between, 3.**

each other, one another. 1. *Each other* should be used when only two things are referred to, and *one another* when more than two are referred to.

Wrong: Smith and I see *one another* often.

Right: Smith and I see *each other* often.

Wrong: It will be interesting for the four of us to see *each other* again.

Right: It will be interesting for the four of us to see *one another* again.

2. The possessive of *each other* is *each other's*; of *one another, one another's.*

They did not spare *each other's* [not *each others'*] feelings.

They did not spare *one another's* [not *one anothers'*] feelings.

economics (n.) Usually plural in form but singular in meaning; hence, takes singular verbs and singular pronouns. *See* **-ics.**

Economics *is* [not *are*] of prime importance to every student of commerce. Several courses in *it* [not *them*] are required.

effect. *See* **affect.**

either (conj.) 1. Singular, followed by singular verb. The use of a plural verb after *either* is a common error.

Either of these sales plans *is* [not *are*] excellent.

2. Use *either* to designate one of

two persons or things; *any one* to designate one of three or more.

You may choose *either* of the [two] new typewriters or *any* one of the [three] old typewriters.

either . . . or. The construction after correlatives should be the same; for example, if *either* is followed by a verb, *or* must be followed by a verb. The misplacement of *either,* a common error, frequently results in an unbalanced construction after the correlatives.

Wrong: You *either are required* to register by the 15th *or to drop* the course. [*Either* is followed by a verb and *or* by an infinitive phrase.]

Right: You are required *either to register* by the 15th *or to drop* the course.

Wrong: You must *either* go today, *or* you must wait until next week.

Right: Either you must go today, *or* you must wait until next week.

Right: You must *either go* today *or wait* until next week.

else. 1. A common error is to combine *else* with *but.*

Wrong: It was nothing *else but* selfishness on his part.

Right: It was nothing *but* selfishness on his part.

2. The possessive of *somebody else* is *somebody else's,* of *everyone else, everyone else's,* and so on for *anyone else, no one else.*

emigrate, immigrate (vbs.) *Emigrate* means to go *from* one's own country to another for the purpose of living there. *Immigrate* means to go *into* a country or place for the purpose of living there. *Emigrate* is followed by the preposition *from; immigrate* by *to.*

Thousands of Jews *emigrated from* [left] Germany and *immigrated to* [moved to] Israel.

eminent, imminent (adjs.) *Eminent* means prominent, distinguished, and is applied to persons. *Imminent* means impending, threatening, close at hand, and is applied to events.

He is an *eminent* lecturer.

A struggle for power between the two nations is *imminent.*

(*See also* **immanent, imminent.**)

equally as. Often incorrectly used for *equally . . . with, equally* by itself, or *as* by itself.

Wrong: The Republicans are equally *as* guilty as the Democrats.

Right: The Republicans are *as* guilty as the Democrats.

Right: The Republicans are *equally* guilty *with* the Democrats.

Wrong: The trouble in the Western cities is *equally as* alarming.

Right: The trouble in the Western cities is *equally* alarming.

-ever. Compounds of *-ever—however, whichever, whoever, whatever—* are not interrogatives. A common error, particularly in speech, is to use these compounds as interrogatives with the thought that they add emphasis to the question.

Wrong: However did you find out?
Right: How did you find out?
Wrong: Whoever told you that?
Right: Who told you that?

every (adj.) Always singular. Followed by singular verb and singular pronouns.

Every large company in the industry *files its reports* [not *file their reports*] with the trade association.

Everyone was [not *were*] trying to better *his position* [not *their positions*].

Every one of the students who participated in the demonstration put *himself* [not *themselves*] in the position of insubordination.

Every one but he *was* [not *were*] at the meeting.

everybody (pron.) Write as one word. Always singular. *Everyone* is preferred.

every one, everyone. 1. Write as one word only when *everybody* is meant. Thus, *every one* is always written to refer to objects; also if *of* is used, the expression must be written as two words.

Everyone [*everybody*] should attend the meeting.

Every one of the department heads attended the meeting.

All of the drawings are excellent; *every one* [of the drawings] deserves a prize.

2. *See* **every** for the correct number of verb and pronoun to use after *every one* or *everyone*.

everywhere (adv.) Always written as one word. *Every place* is commonly misused for *everywhere*. *See* **place.**

expect (vb.) Expect *of* a person; otherwise, expect *from*.

The company expects loyalty *of* its employees.

faced (vb.) When followed by a preposition, use *by* or *with*.

farther, further. Use *farther* to refer to

distance; *further* to refer to time, quantity, or degree.

Philadelphia is *farther* from Washington than from New York.

We went *further* into the matter.

This distinction is rapidly disappearing and *further* is more widely used.

fatal (adj.) Not comparable. If anything is fatal, it cannot be *more* fatal. "More nearly fatal" is allowable.

feel (vb.) Followed by a predicate adjective and not by an adverb (see **Adverbs,** 2), unless used in the sense of touching physically.

I do not feel *well*. [Predicate adjective modifying "I."]

He telephoned and said that he still feels very *bad* [not *badly*]. [Predicate adjective modifying "he."]

The doctor felt the bruise *tenderly*. [Adverb describing how the doctor touched the bruise.]

I felt *sick* when I heard the news. [Predicate adjective modifying "I."]

few (indef. pron.) 1. Either singular or plural, depending upon the meaning.

A few *is* enough.

Many are called, but few *are* chosen.

2. *See* **less** for distinction between *less* and *fewer*.

final (adj.) Not comparable. If anything is *final* it cannot be *more* final. "More nearly final" is allowable.

firstly (adv.) In formal enumerations, the use of *first, second, third,* or *firstly, secondly, thirdly, lastly* is a matter of personal preference. However, use *firstly*, not *first*, with *secondly, thirdly, lastly*.

formally, formerly. *Formally* means in a formal manner; *formerly* means previously.

He was *formally* initiated into the club.

He was *formerly* president of this company.

former (adj.) Correct when used to designate the first of two persons or things; incorrect when used to designate the first of three or more.

Right: Smith and Jones were at the convention; the *former* gave an interesting talk.

Wrong: Smith, Jones, and Brown were at the convention; the *former* gave an interesting talk.

Awkward: Smith, Jones, and Brown were at the convention; *the first-named* gave an interesting talk.

Better: Smith, Jones, and Brown were at the convention; *Smith* gave an interesting talk.

Fractions. *See* **Amounts.** For use of hyphen in writing fractions, *see* **Compound Terms, 6.**

-ful. The correct plural of words ending in *-ful*, such as *spoonful, handful*, is *-fuls: spoonfuls, handfuls* [not *spoonsful, handsful*]. *See also* **Compound Terms, 1. Plurals.**

full (adj.) 1. Not comparable. If anything is full, it cannot be fuller. "More nearly full" is allowable.

2. The adverb form is *full* or *fully*. *See* **Adverbs, 3.**

further. Widely used instead of *farther*. *See* **farther.**

Future Tense. The *future tense* expresses action that will take place in the future. A common error is the use of the future tense, instead of the future perfect tense, to express action *completed* before a time in the future.

Right: She *will finish* the book next month. [Simple future.]

Wrong: She *will finish* the book *before* the end of the month. [Completed action.]

Right: She *will have finished* the book *before* next month. [Future perfect expressing completed action.]

Wrong: Next month *I will be* his secretary ten years.

Right: Next month, *I will have been* his secretary ten years.

Right: I *will write* the letter tomorrow. [Simple future.]

Right: I *will have written* the letter by that time. [Future perfect.]

generally, usually. Use *generally* in a general sense or as a whole; use *usually* when you mean in the majority of cases.

It was *generally* believed that the market would rise.

The market is *usually* erratic in a presidential election year.

Gerunds. A gerund is a verbal form ending in *-ing* and used as a noun.
1. Possessive nouns, possessive pronouns, or prepositions precede gerunds.

I do not approve of *your* [not *you*] reading the book.

I had not heard of the *company's* [not company] buying the building.

2. A gerund may take an object or be completed in meaning by a predicate noun or adjective.

Recording test data required . . . .
Recording is simple.
Recording is the final step.

3. The gerund is identical in form with the active participle and is often confused with it. Notice in the following examples that the use of the gerund with a possessive gives the sentence a meaning entirely different from that given by the use of a participle.

I do not approve of the *girl's reading* the book. [Gerund]

I do not approve of the *girl reading* the book. [Participle]

4. If a verb has a noun form, use the noun form instead of the gerund.

Poor: Accepting the position was an ill-advised move.

Better: Acceptance of the position was an ill-advised move.

good (adj.) *See* **well.**

goods (n. pl.) Always takes a plural verb and plural pronouns.

The goods *were* [not *was*] damaged in transit before *they* [not *it*] *were* delivered.

government (n.) In the United States, *government* is construed as singular; in Great Britain, as plural.

Her Majesty's government *are* sending *their* representatives at once.

The United States government *is* sending delegates also.

group (n.) *See* **Collective Nouns.**

guarantee, guaranty. For the verb, always use *guarantee*. Business convention has established a specialized use of *guaranty* as a noun, which is illustrated in such expressions as *contract of guaranty, act of guaranty*.

However, *guarantee* is never wrong, even in these expressions. A safe rule to follow is: When in doubt, use *guarantee*.

habitual (adj.) When followed by a preposition, use *with.*

had (vb.) *Had . . . have* is sometimes carelessly used in inverted sentences when only *had* is required.

Wrong: Had I *have* been on the jury, I would have acquitted him.

Right: Had I *been* on the jury, I would have acquitted him.

An incorrect use of *had have* occurs when the sentence has not been inverted.

Wrong: If I *had have* been on the jury, I would have acquitted him.

Right: If I *had been* on the jury, I would have acquitted him.

had better. An idiomatic expression that requires care in usage. Error results from following *had better* by the perfect tense of a verb without the use of *have.*

Wrong: He *had better seen* a doctor while he was in New York.

Right: He *had better have seen* a doctor while he was in New York.

Right: He *had better see* a doctor while he is in New York.

Wrong: He *had better stayed* in New York another week.

Right: He *had better have stayed* in New York another week.

hardly (adv.) 1. This word conveys a negative idea and should not be used with a negative. The error usually occurs when the speaker or writer decides to modify a negative statement.

Wrong: There is *no* company *hardly*

that does not have an employee benefit plan.

Right: There is *hardly any* company that does not have an employee benefit plan.

Wrong: The company *cannot hardly* take that attitude.

Right: The company *can hardly* take that attitude.

2. *Hardly* is used only in the sense of *scarcely.* The adverb of *hard,* meaning firm or solid, is the same as the adjective—*hard.* The following sentences illustrate how the use of *hardly* changes the meaning of a sentence.

His salary as president of the company is *hard* earned.

His salary as president of the company is *hardly* earned.

he. Nominative case of third person singular pronoun. 1. For misuse of *he* instead of *him, see* **Pronouns,** 1.

2. For use after forms of the verb *to be (am, is, are, was, were), see* **Predicate Nominative,** 2.

heavy. The adverb forms are *heavy, heavier, heaviest,* or *heavily, more heavily, most heavily. See* **Adverbs,** 3.

help. Should not be followed by *but* when used in the sense of avoid.

Wrong: I cannot *help but* feel that you are unwise.

Right: I cannot *help feeling* that you are unwise.

her. Objective case of *she.* 1. For use as an object, see **Pronouns,** 1.

2. For misuse of *her* instead of *she* after forms of the verb *to be (am, is, are, was, were), see* **Predicate Nominative,** 1.

him. Objective case of *he.* 1. For use as an object, see **Pronouns,** 1.

2. For misuse of *him* instead of *he* after forms of the verb *to be (am, is, are, was, were), see* **Predicate Nominative,** 1.

himself. *See* **Compound Personal Pronouns.**

hope (n.) Sometimes incorrectly used in the plural after *no.*

We have no *hope* [not *hopes*] of receiving payment.

hope (vb.) When *hope* is used in the passive voice, the indefinite pronoun *it* is always the subject. The error usually occurs when *it* is omitted from the parenthetical expression *it is hoped,* especially in a clause introduced by *what.*

Wrong: This region is now experiencing *what is hoped* will be a short cold spell.

Right: This region is now experiencing what, *it is hoped,* will be a short cold spell. ["What" is the subject of "will be" and not of "is hoped."]

Right: It was hoped by all that he would win.

Hyphen. For use of the hyphen in compound terms, *see* **Compound Terms.**

I. Nominative case of first person singular pronoun. 1. For use of *I* instead of *me, see* **Pronouns,** 1.

2. For use after the forms of the verb *to be (am, is, are, was, were), see* **Predicate Nominative,** 1.

3. Avoid use of the editorial *we* instead of *I* in a letter written on behalf of a company. Use *I* when referring to the writer individually and *we* when referring to the company. *I* and *we* may be used in the same letter.

I [the writer] will look after this order and you can be sure *we* [the company] will ship it tomorrow.

-ics. A few English words end in -ic—music, rhetoric, logic, magic—but the normal form is *-ics*. Words ending in *-ics* are sometimes treated as singular and sometimes as plural.

Singular when used strictly as the name of a science or study:

Politics [the science of] *is* most interesting.

Singular when used with a singular noun complement:

Politics is a *game* at which more than two can play.

Athletics is the chief *attraction* at the school.

Plural when used loosely and when denoting qualities, usually preceded by *his, the, such:*

Such politics never *win* an election.
The acoustics in the new building *are* faulty.

Plural when denoting practice or activity:

Superb *tactics were* responsible for our victory.
Athletics are necessary for every normal boy.

identical (adj.) When followed by a preposition, use *with* or *to*.

if. 1. Often misused in place of *whether.*

Wrong: I am not sure *if* I can ship the goods on that date.
Right: I am not sure *whether* I can ship the goods on that date.

2. Avoid the use of *if and when.* Only in rare cases is *if and when* really better in a sentence than *if* or *when.*

Wrong: If and when the voters in this country elect a Communist to high office, they can expect curtailment of free speech.
Right: If the voters in this country elect a Communist . . . .
Wrong: He told the union members that *if and when* the Republicans gain control of the Senate they will. . . .
Right: He told the union members that *when* the Republicans gain control. . . .
Right: He told the union members that *when, or if,* the Republicans gain control . . . . [The writer expects the condition to be realized but has his doubts.]

ignorant (adj.) When used in the sense of uninformed, follow by *in;* in the sense of unaware, by *of.*

He treats her as if she were *ignorant in* the subject.
I was *ignorant of* his interest in the matter.

ill (adj.) When followed by a preposition, use *with.*

immanent, imminent (adjs.) *Immanent* means indwelling, inherent. *Imminent* means impending, threatening, close at hand.

Honesty and fairness are *immanent* in the president's character.
The passage of the bill is *imminent.*

immigrate (vb.) See **emigrate.**

impatient (adj.) Impatient *at* actions or characteristics; *with* persons.

imply, infer (vbs.) *Imply* means to suggest, insinuate, express vaguely. *Infer* means to draw from, deduce from, gather from, or conclude from.

Your letter *implies* that I have tried to evade payment of the bill.

I *infer* from your letter that you cannot grant an extension of time.

impossible. Not comparable. If anything is impossible it cannot be *more* impossible. "More nearly impossible" is allowable.

in, into, in to. 1. *In* denotes position or location; *into* denotes action, motion from without to within.

The sport coats that were advertised yesterday are *in* the Junior Miss department.

He was *in* the sales department but is now *in* the advertising department.

Put this folder *in* [not *into*] the file drawer before locking it. [The folder itself is passive and takes no action.]

We went *into* the room.

2. Do not use *into* for the words *in to* (adverb and preposition).

He went *in to* the meeting. [You cannot go *into* the meeting.]

He took her *in to* [not *into*] dinner.

inasmuch. Always written as one word.

infer. *See* **imply.**

inferior (adj.) Should be followed by *to*, not *than*.

Their products are always *inferior* from every point of view *to* [not *than*] ours.

Infinitives. 1. *Tense.* Use the present infinitive, not the perfect, after past conditions, such as *would have liked, would have been possible.*

It *would have been possible* to *reduce* [not *to have reduced*] the cost at that time.

2. *Split infinitives.* The infinitive sign *to* and the verb naturally go together; it is best not to split the infinitive by placing a word or words between *to* and the verb.

Wrong: The company agrees *to substantially increase* the salaries.

Right: The company agrees *to increase* the salaries substantially.

Wrong: To really be understood, it should be read carefully.

Right: To be really understood, it should be read carefully. ["To be" is the infinitive, not "to be understood."]

Split infinitives are preferable to ambiguity.

Right: We tried to get the states *to at least repair* the roads. [If "at least" is placed anywhere else in the sentence, the meaning is not clear.]

Split infinitives are preferable to awkwardness.

Awkward: Efforts *to unite firmly* bolters from the party were a failure.

Improved: Efforts *to firmly unite* bolters from the party were a failure.

3. *Series of infinitives.* If qualifying words separate infinitive phrases, repeat *to* in each phrase; if no qualifying words intervene, do not repeat *to.*

To punish and [*to*] *expose* the guilty is one thing; *to help* the unfortunate is another.

It is improper for the debtor *to take* an unearned discount and then *to refuse* to pay the difference.

inform. *See* **advise.**

ingenious, ingenuous (adjs.) *Ingenious* means clever, skillful; *ingenuous* means frank, innocent, trusting.

He concocted an *ingenious* [clever] plan to avoid the law.

He is very *ingenuous* [trusting, easily fooled] for a man of his age and background.

insofar. One word or three separate words. One word is preferred.

Intervening Noun or Phrase. The intervention of a noun between the subject and the verb will sometimes cause trouble if the intervening noun is different in number from the subject. Remember that the verb agrees with the subject, not the intervening noun.

Celluloid used as handles on umbrellas and canes *is* [not *are*] of high quality.

A phrase coming between a subject and a verb can sometimes cause trouble. The verb agrees with the subject of the main sentence, not with the subject of the phrase.

The *community,* as well as the owners of the land, *is* interested in development.

Intransitive Verbs. *See* **Transitive Verbs.**

investigation. When followed by a preposition, use of.

Irregular Verbs. Almost all verbs form the past and perfect tenses by adding *-ed* to the present—thus, *look, looked, looked; ship, shipped, shipped.*

However, many verbs are irregular, and there is no rule for the formation of the past and perfect tenses. Form the perfect tenses by adding the auxiliaries [*has, have* or *had*] to the past participle. Thus, I *do,* I *did,* I *have done.*

Where the past participle differs from the past tense, it is incorrect to use the past participle of the verb without an auxiliary. It is also incorrect to use an auxiliary with the past tense form of that verb.

I did [never *I have did*]
I have done [never *I done*]

its, it's. *Its* is the possessive form of the impersonal pronoun *it. It's* is a contraction of *it* and *is* or *it* and *has* and is incorrectly used as a possessive.

The company has expanded greatly in recent years; *its* [not *it's*] success is attributable to *its* [not *it's*] founders.

It's [*it is*] too bad that the books will not be ready for delivery by September.

It's [*it has*] been three months since we received that order.

jury (n.) *See* **Collective Nouns.**

kind (n.) Pl., *kinds.* The explanation here applies also to *class, sort, type, size, breed, brand, quality, variety, species,* and similar words. 1. The singular form is modified by *this* and *that,* not *these* and *those.*

This [not *these*] kind does not grow readily; *that* [not *those*] does grow readily.

2. The expression *kind of* is followed by a singular noun unless the plural idea is particularly strong. The common error is inconsistency.

The *kind of position* [not *positions*] that appeals to me doesn't interest her.

The company has numerous positions open. What *kind of positions* are they?

Wrong: The *kind of position* I prefer *are those* that offer a lot of money.

Right: The *kind of positions* I prefer *are those* that offer a lot of money.

Right: The *kind of position* I prefer *is one that* offers a lot of money.

3. It is incorrect to follow *kind of* by *a.*

Wrong: What *kind of a* position do you want?

Right: What *kind of* position do you want?

4. After the plural form *kinds of*, a singular or a plural noun may be used.

The *kinds of* writing that *are* the most lucrative are novels and inspirational books.

The *kinds of* books that they publish *are* novels and textbooks.

latter, last (adjs.) 1. The word *latter* may be used to designate the second of two persons or things previously mentioned, but should not be used where more than two have been mentioned.

Right: We are now conducting a special sale of suits and overcoats; the *latter* [not *last*] are particularly good value.

Wrong: We are now conducting a special sale of hats, suits, and overcoats; the *latter* are particularly good value.

Awkward: We are now conducting a special sale of hats, suits, and overcoats; the *last* are particularly good value.

Better: We are now conducting a special sale of hats, suits, and overcoats; the *overcoats* are particularly good value.

2. Do not use the expression *the latter part of*. The correct expressions are *toward the end of, the last part of.*

Wrong: The book will be published *the latter part of* next month.

Right: The book will be published *toward the end of* next month.

Right: The book will be published *the last part of* next month.

lay, lie (vbs.) There is no excuse for confusing *lay* and *lie*. *Lay* means to put or set down, place, deposit; *lie* means to rest, be in a certain position or location. *Lay* takes an object; *lie* confines the action to the subject. Principal parts, *lay: lay, laid, laid, laying*. Principal parts, *lie: lie, lay, lain, lying*. The common error is the use of *lay* or one of its principal parts for *lie* or one of its principal parts. Thus, *lay* is used incorrectly in place of *lie*. Remember that you must lay *something* down.

lay, laid, laid, laying

You *lay* the *book* on the table, and it *lies* there.

You *laid* the *book* on the table yesterday, and it *lay* there until Mary picked it up.

I *lay* the *letters* in the same place on his desk each morning.

I *laid* the *letters* on his desk before I left the room.

The brickmason *has laid* the *stones* in an irregular pattern.

The brickmason *is laying* the *stones* in an irregular pattern.

lie, lay, lain, lying

I *lie* [not *lay*] in the sun for an hour every day.

I *lay* [not *laid*] in the sun for an hour yesterday. [Past tense.]

The book has *lain* [not *laid*] there for a month.

The book is *lying* [not *laying*] here where you laid it.

lead (vb.) Principal parts, *lead, led, led. See* **Irregular Verbs.**

less. Use *less* only in the sense of a smaller amount. Apply *less* only to things that are measured by amount and not by size, quality, or number.

He has *less* [a smaller amount] assets than liabilities.

The staff in the New York office is *smaller* [not *less*] than that in the Chicago office.

Fewer [not *less*] industrial accidents occurred this year than last.

liable. *See* **apt.**

like. 1. Commonly misused in place of *such as* when the meaning is *for example.*

In his factory are a number of useful machines, *such as* [not *like*] cutters and stamps.

2. Use *like* as a preposition; *as* as a conjunction. *Like* takes an object; *as,* or *as if,* introduces a clause.

Their product is not *like ours* in quality. [No verb follows "like."]

To increase sales, reduce the price *as* [not *like*] our competitors *do.*

You are *like me* in your desire for perfection. [No verb follows "like."]

He treats her *as if* [not *like*] she were ignorant.

I wish I could think *as* [not *like*] he (does). [The verb is understood.]

likely. *See* **apt.**

live (vb.) Live *in* a town, *on* a street, *at* a certain address, *by* means of a livelihood.

He lives *in* New York *on* Tenth Street.

He lives *at* 231 West Tenth Street.

He lives *by selling* family heirlooms.

loan, lend. Many authorities object to any use of *loan* as a verb. It is best to use the word only in connection with formal banking transactions—for example, placing a loan through a banker. For general purposes, use *lend.* Never use *borrow* to mean *lend.*

Will you *lend* [not *loan*] me ten dollars?

He *lent* [not *loaned*] me ten dollars.

The bank *loaned* the money at six percent interest.

Lend [not *borrow*] me a quarter, please.

loose. Adjective meaning unfastened. Frequently confused with *lose* (verb) meaning to misplace.

majority (n.) 1. Relates to the greater of two parts regarded as parts of a whole.

Wrong: A *majority* of his *time is* devoted to his personal work. [There is only one "time."]
Right: A *major part* of his *time is.* . . .
Right: A *majority* of my *hours are.* . . . [A greater number of the hours.]
Wrong: A *majority* of the *month was* spent on research. [There is only one "month."]
Right: A *majority* of the past six *months were* spent on research. [More than half of the months.]

2. *Plurality.* In a contest, *majority*

means more than half the votes cast, whereas *plurality* means more votes than any other candidate received but less than half the votes cast.

Smith received a *plurality* but not a *majority* of the votes. There were 21,000 votes cast, and Smith received only 10,000. Jones received 7,000, so Smith's *plurality* was 3,000. A majority is necessary for election.

3. *Number. Majority* is singular or plural depending upon the sense in which it is used. Thus in 1, *majority* is plural, followed by a plural verb. More than one hour and more than one month is meant. In 2, *majority* means the greater number of votes as a whole and takes a singular verb.

The *majority* [the majority as a whole] *is* against the new bill.

A *majority* [the larger number as individuals] *are* against the new bill.

many a. Always takes a singular verb, even if followed by a compound subject.

Many a newspaper and magazine *has* [not *have*] published his work.

mass (n.) 1. Do not capitalize.

2. A *mass* is offered or celebrated, not held.

mathematics. See **-ics.**

may. See **can.**

may, might (vbs.) 1. When expressing possibility in a simple sentence, these words are usually interchangeable. See 2 below.

I suggest that we settle the question now; otherwise it *may* [or *might*] cause trouble several years hence.

We *may* [or *might*] decide to order a different make.

2. *Might* is the past tense of *may.* In using *may* or *might,* observe the **Sequence of Tenses** if *might* is not required by 3, 4, or 5. With the present, perfect, and future tenses, use *may;* with the past or past perfect, use *might.*

I give   }   you the information
I have given }   that you *may* under-
I will give   }   stand the situation.

I gave   }   you the information
I was giving }   that you *might* un-
I had given   }   derstand the situa-
                tion.

As we *have seen,* it *may be wise* to allow the debtor additional credit.

I *have not heard* what happened this morning, but he *may have persuaded* her to adopt his view.

The president *said* that we *might have* a holiday.

The instructions *were* that, come what *might,* the task should be completed by the end of September.

3. *Might* is conditional. It is used in the main clause of a conditional sentence whether the condition is expressed or implied.

Anyone *might* learn the facts from the report [if he read it] .

If the product is successful, it *might be* necessary to increase the size of the plant. [The increase is conditional upon success.]

If the certificate fails to make provision for the issuance of stock in series, it *might* subsequently be amended to include that provision.

4. *Might* is used in the sense of *would perhaps* in a conditional statement.

With a little persuasion, Mr. Brown *might* [would perhaps] agree to that arrangement.

5. *Might* is used in the subjunctive to express a supposition.

He acts *as if* the company *might* try to take advantage of his lack of legal knowledge.

He spoke *as though* he *might* sever his connections with the company.

6. *May* is used in prayer and benedictions. The subjunctive *might* denotes wish without expectation of fulfillment.

May God bless you.

7. *See* **can, could,** 3 for the misuse of *could* for *might* in conditional sentences.

me. Objective case of I. 1. For use as an object, *see* **Pronouns,** 1.

2. For misuse of *me* instead of *I* after forms of the verb *to be (am, is, are, was, were), see* **Predicate Nominative,** 1.

might. *See* **may.**

monopoly (n.) When followed by a preposition, use *of.*

Mood (mode). The mood of a verb expresses the attitude of the speaker. *See* **Subjunctive Mood.**

more than one. Always takes singular noun and verb, although the meaning is plural.

More than one *defendant is* involved.

most, almost. *Most* is used with an adjective to express the superlative degree. Do not use *most* for the adverb *almost.*

He is the *most eager* of the boys.

Almost [not *most*] all the senators voted against the bill.

Apart from the fact that *most* is not a substitute for *almost,* in many constructions it changes the meaning of the sentence when it is used incorrectly.

I am *most ready* to go. [More ready than others.]

I am *almost ready* to go. [Nearly ready to go.]

mutual. *See* **common.**

myself. *See* **Compound Personal Pronouns.**

Negatives. 1. For comparative negative, *see* **as,** 1.

2. *See* **Double Negatives.**

neither. 1. Singular, followed by singular verb. The use of a plural verb after *neither* is a common error.

Neither of these plans *is* [not *are*] satisfactory.

2. Use *neither* to designate between one of two persons or things; *none* or *no* instead of *neither* to designate one of three or more.

He decided that *neither* of the [two] plans suggested was satisfactory. [The word "two" is unnecessary.]

He decided that *none* of the [five] plans was satisfactory.

No report submitted to date covers the subject adequately.

Authorities do not agree about this distinction. Good writers occasionally use *neither* in relation to more than two.

neither ... nor. 1. It is always incorrect to use *or* with *neither.*

2. The construction after correlatives should be parallel. The misplacement of *neither* frequently results in unbalanced construction after the correlatives.

Wrong: The plan *neither meets* the approval of the president *nor of* the treasurer. ["Neither" is followed by a verb and "nor" by a prepositional phrase. "Meets the approval" is common to both the president and the treasurer.]

Right: The plan meets the approval *neither of* the president *nor of* the treasurer.

Right: The plan meets the approval of *neither* the president *nor* the treasurer.

news (n.) Plural in form but singular in meaning.

The news *is* good.

nobody (pron.) Always written as one word. *No one* is preferred.

none (indef. pron.) Either singular or plural, depending on the meaning.

We asked for volunteers, but *none* of them *was* willing to go.

I want *none* of them to go unless *they* want to.

no ... or. When *no* precedes the first word or phrase in a series and is applicable to each, connect the words or phrase with *or,* not *nor.*

No man, woman, *or* child can be happy without friends. [No man, no woman, no child.]

Several of the families had *no* fuel to burn *or* money with which to buy it. [No fuel, no money.]

not. *Not* is often superfluous in a subordinate clause after a negative in the main clause. In each of the following sentences, the bracketed *not* should be omitted.

Nobody knows how much time may [not] be wasted in argument.

It would not surprise me if they had [not] cut expenses.

Do you think there might [not] be some other cause at work here?

Not is correct when its use is necessary to convey the intended meaning, but usually a better construction is the substitution of *no* for *not.*

Right: Is it impossible for you to realize that the merger might *not* be consummated?

Better: Is it impossible for you to realize that *no* merger might be consummated?

Wrong: He does not believe that there are *not* extenuating circumstances.

Right: He does not believe that there are *no* extenuating circumstances.

nowhere. Always written as one word. 1. Do not add an *s* to *nowhere;* there is no such word as *nowheres.*

2. *No place* is commonly misused for *nowhere.*

I have gone *nowhere* [not *no place*] today.

number (n.) Followed by a singular verb when used collectively; by a plural verb when used distributively.

A *number* of company rules and regulations [as a group, not specific] *discourages* employee initiative.

A *number* of the company's rules

and regulations [certain of the group] *discourage* employee initiative.

odds (n. pl.) Always takes a plural verb.

The odds *are* against him.

off. Never follow *off* by *of.*

He gave me 10 per cent *off* [not *off of*] the list price.

Omission of Words. Words may be omitted from a sentence if they can be supplied *clearly and exactly* from a parallel portion of the sentence. A common error, however, is the omission of a word that cannot be clearly and exactly supplied.

1. In two clauses, if one subject is singular and the other plural, do not omit the verb.

Wrong: The *sky was* clear and the *stars* bright.
Right: The *sky was* clear and the *stars were* bright.

2. Do not omit part of a verb phrase if it is different in form from the corresponding part of the parallel verb phrase.

Wrong: The company always *has* and always *will give* recognition where it is due.
Right: The company always *has given* and always *will give* recognition where it is due.

3. Do not omit an article, a personal or relative pronoun, or a preposition that is necessary to the grammatical completeness or to the clear understanding of a sentence.

Wrong: He wrote to the chairman and president. [If two persons are involved.]

Right: He wrote to the chairman and *the* president.
Wrong: I have great sympathy but no confidence in that class of people.
Right: I have great sympathy *for,* but no confidence in, that class of people.
Better: I have great sympathy for that class of people, but no confidence in them.

4. *See* **Infinitives, 3,** for omission of *to* in a series of infinitive phrases.

oneself (pron.) Formerly *one's self,* but now preferably written as one word.

only (adv., adj.) 1. The meaning that the sentence is intended to convey determines the position of the word *only.*

Only his *assistant* has authority to sign the payroll record.

His assistant has authority *only* to *sign* the payroll record, not to prepare it.

His assistant has authority to sign *only* the payroll *record.*

His assistant has authority to sign the payroll *record only.*

Each of these sentences conveys a different meaning. The first states that the assistant, and no one else, has the authority; the second, that the assistant has no authority beyond signing the payroll; the last two, that the assistant has authority to sign the payroll record and nothing else.

No hard and fast rule can be given. The writer must consider carefully the exact meaning that he wishes to convey and place the *only* accordingly. If there is danger of ambiguity or misunderstanding, the construction should be changed to eliminate the *only.* The foregoing explains the orthodox or conventional placement of *only*. It is permissible, however, to choose another position if the change does not obscure the meaning.

Orthodox: In typing manuscript, use *only one side* of the sheet.

Permissible: In typing manuscript, use *one side* of the sheet *only*. [What is there besides the sheet to use?]

2. *Only* is sometimes erroneously used as a conjunction.

Wrong: Your pen is the same as mine *only* that the nib is different.

Right: The *one* [or *only*] difference between your pen and mine is the different nib.

oral (adj.) *Verbal* is often misused for *oral. See* **verbal.**

over. The expression *over with* is erroneous. The *with* is superfluous.

Our annual sale is now *over* [not *over with.*]

owing to. *See* **due to.**

Participles. 1. *Dangling participles.* A participle or participial phrase used as an adjective must modify a definite noun or pronoun within the sentence.

Wrong: When *writing* this book, an attempt was made to organize the material to best advantage. [What does "writing" modify?]

Right: When *writing* this book, the *author* attempted to organize the material to best advantage.

Wrong: The study showed that while *advancing* the cause of one group, another *group* was injured by the new law. ["Advancing" wrongly modifies "group."]

Right: The study showed that while *advancing* the cause of one group, the new law injures another group.

Right: The study showed that the new law *advanced* the cause of one group but injured another.

Exceptions: Certain participles may indicate a general rather than a specific action—an action in which no particular actor is implied. They do not then need a noun or pronoun to modify and are not dangling. Some participles that may be used in this manner are *allowing, coming, granting, considering, speaking, talking, learning, owing.*

Allowing for interruptions, the work will be completed by the end of the year.

Generally *speaking,* our products are superior to theirs.

In *learning* to write, it is well to study the works of great authors.

2. *Misplaced participles.* The misplacement of a participial modifier can result in a meaningless sentence.

The classic example is, "I saw the new file *cabinet walking* up the stairs."

Right: Walking up the stairs, *I* saw the new file cabinet.

Past Tense. 1. Use the simplest past tense to express action that was completed at some time before the time a statement is made.

The report concerns events that *occurred* many years ago.

He *had* [not *has had*] practical ideas on every phase of the problem.

2. Avoid substitution of the past tense for the present perfect or past perfect tenses.

Wrong: I *was filing* when he returned, but I *was typing* the report before that time.

Right: I *was filing* when he returned, but I *had been typing* the report before that time. [Past perfect.]

Wrong: Since Mr. Scott *was elected* president of the club, the members *enjoyed* better socials.

Right: Since Mr. Scott *was elected* president of the club, the members *have enjoyed* better socials. [Present perfect.]

3. In dependent clauses, a *permanently true* fact is usually put in the present tense, even when the main verb is in the past tense. This rule does not apply to independent clauses or sentences with one verb.

We *were taught* in school that "Hamlet" *is* Shakespeare's greatest tragedy.

"Hamlet" *was* Shakespeare's greatest tragedy.

San Francisco *was* the birthplace of the United Nations.

people (n.) 1. Singular in form but plural in meaning. The plural *peoples* is used when more than one race or nation is referred to.

The *peoples* of France and Italy. . . .

2. *Persons, people.* When referring to a number of individuals, use *persons.* When referring to a group, use *people.*

Six *persons* were in the room.

Do you know the *people* who live next door?

The American *people* are democratic.

perfect. Not comparable. If anything is perfect, it cannot be *more* perfect. "More nearly perfect" is allowable.

Perfect Tenses. The perfect tenses are formed by adding the auxiliaries *has, have, had* to the past participle. Only the illiterate use the past participle as a verb without an auxiliary.

Present perfect tense:
have (has) looked
have (has) taken
Past perfect tense:
had looked
had taken
Future perfect tense:
shall (will) have looked
shall (will) have taken

place (n.) Must be used as the subject or as the object of a verb or preposition. *Place* is commonly misused with *any, every, no, some* after an intransitive verb. The adverbs *anywhere, everywhere, nowhere, somewhere* are usually better.

Wrong: Are you going *any place* this afternoon?

Right: Are you going *anywhere* this afternoon?

Wrong: I have looked *every place* for the letter.

Right: I have looked *everywhere* for the letter.

Right: I have *no place* to go. [Object of the transitive verb "have."]

Right: I have *nowhere* to go.

Right: He is located in *some place* in the West. [Object of preposition "in."]

Right: He is located *somewhere* in the West.

plurality. *See* **majority,** 2.

Possessives. 1. *Compound nouns and proper names.* The possessive is formed by adding *'s* to the word nearest the object possessed.

attorney *general's* argument
John Brown, *Jr.'s* office
John Brown, *II's* office
Mr. Mason of *Consolidated's* staff
notary *public's* seal
aide-de-*camp's* promotion

Use the *of* phrase to form the plural possessive of a compound noun.

arguments *of* the attorneys general
seals *of* notaries public
promotions *of* aides-de-camp

2. *Awkward or sibilant sounds.* Drop the *s* and add only an apostrophe to form the possessive when the use of *'s* would cause a hissing or an awkward sound.

Moses' rod
Kansas' son
for *conscience'* sake
for *goodness'* sake
for *appearance'* sake
for *convenience'* sake

3. *Words ending in s.* The singular possessive of words ending in *s* is formed by adding *'s*; the plural possessive by adding only the apostrophe.

Mr. *Jones's* car
the *Joneses'* car
Misses *Smiths'* reception
James's position
bus's motor

The use of the apostrophe without the *s* still prevails in poetic or biblical expressions.

Jesus' life
Achilles' heel
Mars' Hill

4. *Words ending in* ss. If a word ends in *ss*, form the possessive by adding an apostrophe.

the *witness'* testimony
the *princess'* wedding
Strauss' waltzes

5. *"Of" phrase.* An *of* phrase may be used to show possession. When the thing possessed is a specific number or group belonging to the possessor, the *'s* also is used, thus forming a double possessive.

In his book he tried to imitate a novel *of* James *Street's.*
That remark *of* the *commentator's* aroused. . . . [A specific remark.]
Those investments *of* his *father's* are. . . . [Specific investments.]

When the thing possessed is not restricted or limited to a specific number or group, the *'s* is not used.

In his book he tried to imitate the novels *of* James *Street.*
The remarks *of* the *commentator* aroused. . . . [Generally speaking.]
The investments *of* his *father* are. . . . [Generally speaking.]

6. *Appositives and explanatory words.* Whenever possible, avoid the use of appositives or explanatory words with the possessive case. If the object possessed is named, the word nearest the object takes the possessive. If the object is not named and the appositive or explanatory words end the sentence, the first noun takes the possessive form. When in doubt,

change the construction of the sentence and use the *of* phrase.

Right: His guardian, *Mr. Nelson's,* control of the money. . . .
Better: Control of the money *by his guardian, Mr. Nelson,* . . .
Right: The reception was held at her *aunt's,* Mrs. Mason.
Right: In his writings, he tries to imitate his father, *James Ludlow's,* novels.
Better: In his writings, he tries to imitate the novels *of his father,* James Ludlow.

When the appositive is restrictive and, therefore, not set off by commas, the awkward construction does not arise.

The defendant *Adams's* defense

When the explanatory words are parenthetical, and especially when they are enclosed in parentheses, the construction *must* be changed to avoid the possessive.

Awkward: Mrs. *Ball's* (formerly *Miss Brown*) estate is. . . .
Awkward: Mrs. *Ball,* formerly *Miss Brown's,* estate is. . . .
Awkward: Mrs. *Ball's,* formerly *Miss Brown's,* estate is. . . .
Better: The estate *of Mrs. Ball,* formerly *Miss Brown,* is. . . .

7. *Inanimate objects.* An inanimate object cannot actually possess anything. It is usually better to show relationship by the use of the *of* phrase. However, usage has attributed possession to some inanimate objects, especially those expressing time or measure.

one day's vacation
two weeks' pay

one additional day's pay
five dollars' worth
a month's delay
three months' delay
six pounds' weight

The italicized expressions are plural. Notice that the apostrophe follows the *s* instead of preceding it. Many of these expressions form compound adjectives and can be hyphenated instead of written as possessives.

a *one-day* vacation
a *three-month* delay
a *six-pound* weight
a *three-ounce* bottle

practical, practicable (adjs.) *Practicable* means feasible, capable of being put into practice; *practical* means useful or successful in actual practice. *Practical* may be used with reference to either persons or things, but *practicable* can be used only with reference to things.

Jones is a *practical* man. [A doer rather than a theorist.]
The scheme is *practical.* [It will be successful when it is carried out.]
The scheme is *practicable.* [It can be carried out.]

precedence (n.) When followed by a preposition, use *of.*

The vice-president has *precedence of* the secretary of state.

precedent (n.) When followed by a preposition, use *of* or *for.*

precedent (adj.) When followed by a preposition, use *to.*

preclude. An erroneous expression is *preclude the possibility of.* Since *pre-*

clude means to render impossible, the absurdity of the expression is obvious.

Wrong: In an effort to *preclude the possibility of* a misunderstanding. . . .

Right: In an effort to *preclude* a misunderstanding. . . .

Predicate Nominative. A noun or pronoun following an intransitive verb (one that does not take an object), thereby completing, or helping to complete, the predicate is a *predicate nominative.* As its name implies, a predicate nominative is always in the nominative case. A predicate nominative is also called a "complement." All complements, however, are not predicate nominatives.

1. Forms of the verb *to be* (*am, is, are, was, were*) do not take an object but are followed by a predicate nominative. A common error is the use of the objective case of a pronoun (*me, us, her, him, them*) as a predicate nominative. The phrase *It wasn't me* is a colloquialism and not too important. It is technically incorrect, however, and should be avoided in writing.

It was *I* [not *me*] to whom you spoke.

It was *he* [not *him*] who delivered the papers.

I am *she* [not *her*].

2. A verb agrees with its subject and not with the predicate nominative. Difficulty is caused by the use of a singular subject and plural predicate nominative, or vice versa.

A valuable *by-product* of training conferences *is* the numerous *opportunities* afforded for management to observe the trainees' reactions. ["By-product" is the subject of "is"; "opportunities" is the predicate nominative.]

Progressive *interviews are* a useful *form* for training personnel. ["Interviews" is the subject of "are"; "form" is the predicate nominative.]

Preposition at the End. It is not grammatically incorrect to place a preposition at the end of a sentence; it is better to end a sentence with a preposition than to use an awkward construction. It is incorrect to place an unnecessary preposition at the end of the sentence.

Wrong: Where is the book *at*? [Preposition unnecessary]

Right: Where is the book?

Awkward: Prepositions sometimes follow the nouns *with* which they are coupled.

Better: Prepositions sometimes follow the nouns they are coupled *with*.

Prepositional Idioms. In this book the correct usage is given under the word to be used. For example, what preposition follows *angry*? Look under **angry.**

prescribe, proscribe. The word *prescribe* means to order as a rule or course to be followed or, in medicine, to order as a remedy. The word *proscribe* means to denounce or condemn a thing as dangerous, to outlaw.

Present Tense. 1. Use the present tense to indicate action that is taking place at the present time.

He told me that the company's home office *is* [not *was*] located in New York. [The office is still located in New York.]

2. The present tense is used idiomatically to express future action.

Congress *adjourns* [for *will adjourn*] next week.

My vacation *starts* [for *will start*] next Friday.

3. Use the progressive form, not the simple present, to express action in progress.

Wrong: St. Vincent's Hospital, where he *is treated*, has the most modern equipment.

Right: St. Vincent's Hospital, where he *is being treated,* has the most modern equipment.

Wrong: When I write in the morning, as I *write* now, I compose with more facility than in the evening.

Right: When I write in the morning, as I *am writing* now, I compose with more facility than in the evening.

presently (adv.) Meaning soon, before long. A common error is the use of *presently* when *at present* is meant.

We expect to complete the book *presently* [soon.]

At present [not *presently*] we are working on your book.

principal, principle. The word *principle* is a noun only and cannot be used as an adjective. *Principle* means a fundamental or general truth, a rule. *Principal* is used in all other cases. As a noun, *principal* has a variety of meanings; as an adjective, it means chief, main, most important.

We have always acted on the *principle* [fundamental truth] that honesty is the best policy.

An agent may bind his *principal* to contracts entered into within the scope of his authority.

The loan, including *principal* and interest, amounted to $350.

The New England states have been our *principal* source of business during the past five years.

The *principal* of the school.

proceeds (n. pl.) Used in the plural and takes a plural verb.

Pronouns. 1. *As objects.* When a pronoun is used as an object, it is always in the objective case. A common error is the use of the nominative case of the first and third person pronouns (*I, we, he, she, they*) instead of the objective case (*me, us, him, her, them*), especially when the pronoun is joined to another object. (The second person pronoun, *you,* causes no trouble because the nominative and objective cases, singular and plural, have the same form.) Test the sentence by omitting the first object. The omission will show the absurdity of the use of the nominative instead of the objective.

Wrong: We received a letter inviting my wife and *I* to spend the weekend in the country. [Inviting . . . . I?]

Right: We received a letter *inviting* my wife and *me* to spend. . . .

Wrong: Mr. Smith, let's you and *I* discuss the matter from every viewpoint. [Let . . . I?]

Right: Mr. Smith, let's you and *me* discuss the matter from. . . .

Wrong: I know you and *he* to be my friends. [I know . . . he to be?]

Right: I know you and him to be my friends.

2. *After forms of the verb* to be (am, is, are, was, were). *See* **Predicate Nominative**, 1.

prove (vb.) Principal parts, *prove, proved, proved.* The use of *proven* for *proved* is increasing in the United States but is not considered good usage.

provided, providing. 1. Some writers use *providing* as a conjunction in place of *provided,* but many authorities do not sanction this.

Correct: I will give you the order *providing* you agree to my price.
Better: I will give you the order *provided* you agree to my price.

2. It is preferable not to use *that* after *provided* except where it is accepted usage in formal documents.

quality (n.) Pl., *qualities. See* **kind.**

quarter. When referring to the time of day, the correct expression is *a quarter to* not *a quarter of.*

reason. When a sentence begins with *The reason is* or *The reason why . . . is,* the clause giving the reason should begin with *that* and not with *because.*

Wrong: Her *reason is because* she does not have the money.
Right: Her *reason is that* she does not have the money.
Wrong: The *reason why* the goods were delayed *was because* they were not shipped.
Right: The *reason why* the goods were delayed *was that* they were not shipped.

reconcile (vb.) When followed by a preposition, use *with* or *to.*

regard. Do not use *regards* in place of *regard* in the expressions *in regard to, with regard to.*

regardless. There is no such word as *irregardless.* Misuse perhaps is caused by confusion with the word *irrespective,* which means "without respect to" and is correct. *Regardless* takes the preposition *of.*

We should acknowledge all orders *regardless* [not *irregardless*] of the amount involved.

relation (ship) (n.) When followed by a preposition, use *of, to,* or *with.*

The relation *of* these parts is not clear.
The relationship *of* the beneficiary *to* the insured is not close.
Our strained relations *with* Russia are a source of worry.

resentment (n.) Resentment *at* or *for* an action, *against* a person.

My resentment *against* him was *at* [or *for*] his rudeness to me.

retroactive (adj.) When followed by a preposition, use *to.*

Retroactive *to* May 15th.

riches (n. pl.) Always plural and takes a plural verb.

right. 1. The adverb form is *right* or *rightly. See* **Adverbs**, 3.

2. *Right* is not comparable. If anything is right, it cannot be *more* right. "More nearly right" is allowable.

round. *Round* is not comparable. If anything is round, it cannot be *more* round. "More nearly round" is allowable.

same (adj.) Do not use as a pronoun.

Businesspersons especially are guilty of the misuse of *same.*

Wrong: We will repair the spring and ship *same* to you.

Right: We will repair the spring and ship *it* to you.

scarcely (adv.) This word carries a negative idea and should not be used with a negative.

Wrong: There is *scarcely no* time left in which to fill the order.

Right: There is *scarcely any* time left in which to fill the order.

Wrong: We could *not scarcely* ship the goods before August.

Right: We could *scarcely* ship the goods before August.

seem. Followed by a predicate adjective and not by an adverb. *See* **Adverbs,** 2.

semimonthly, semiweekly (adjs., advs.) Since *semi* means half, *semiweekly* means twice a week and *semimonthly* means twice a month.

Sequence of Tenses. When two or more verbs are used in the same sentence, the time relation, or *sequence of tenses,* is important and sometimes troublesome.

1. Remember that the purpose of changing the tense in a sentence is to indicate a change in time.

I *remember* I *owe* him a debt of gratitude. [The whole situation is in the present.]

I *remembered* I *owed* him a debt of gratitude. [The whole situation is in the past.]

I *remember* I *owed* him a debt of gratitude. [Implication: The debt is no longer owed.]

2. If you are writing in the past tense and wish to refer to a preceding event, you must use the past perfect tense.

He *pledged* the bonds he *had bought* [not *bought*] last week.

3. After the future tense in a main clause, use the present tense in a dependent clause.

The chairman *will open* the meeting as soon as the speaker *arrives.*

4. A fact that is *permanently true* is usually put in the present tense, even when the main verb is in the past tense.

Even then men *knew* that tides *are caused* [not *were caused*] by the moon.

As a child she *was taught* that honesty *is* [not *was*] the best policy.

5. The perfect participle expresses an action that has been completed at the time indicated by the main verb. A common error is the use of the present participle instead of the perfect.

He completed the report on schedule, *having worked* [not *working*] unusually long hours.

He will complete the report on schedule, *having worked* [not *working*] unusually long hours.

set (vb.) *See* **sit.**

shall (should); will (would). *Should* is the past tense of the auxiliary verb *shall; would,* of the auxiliary *will.* Traditionally, *shall* and *should* are used in the first person *(I shall),* and *will* and *would* in the second and third persons *(he will, they will)* to express simple futurity. To express determination, the order is traditionally reversed *(I will, he shall, they shall)*. However, *will* and *would* are often preferred in all persons in contemporary popular American usage *(I will)* as sounding less stuffy.

she. Nominative case of third person singular pronoun. 1. For misuse of *she* instead of *her, see* **Pronouns, 1.**

2. For use after forms of the verb *to be (am, is, are, was, were), see* **Predicate Nominative, 1.**

since. 1. Do not use *since* to begin a clause after *ago.* Begin the clause with *that.* This error is more apt to occur when a parenthetical expression follows *ago.*

It is over ten years *ago,* as well as I remember, *that* [not *since*] the stores were consolidated.

2. Be certain that a phrase introduced by *since* is correctly attached to the sentence and is not a dangling participial phrase. *See* **Participles, 1.**

Wrong: Since preparing the report, new figures are available. ["Preparing" is a dangling participle.]

Right: Since I prepared the report, new figures are available.

Right: Since the preparation of the report, new figures are available.

sit, set (vbs.) There is no excuse for confusing these words. *Sit* means to rest when the subject rests. *Set* means to place an object. *Sit* never takes an object, *set* always does. Principal parts, *sit: sit, sat, sat, sitting.* Principal parts, *set: set, set, set, setting.*

He *sits* at his desk.

He *sat* at his desk from ten to eleven.

He *has sat* there for two hours.

He *is sitting* at his desk.

I *set* the thermos on his desk every morning.

I *have set* the thermos on his desk every day for a month.

I *set* the thermos on his desk yesterday, as usual.

I *am setting* the thermos on the table.

The thermos *sat* on the table for a week. [Past of *sit.*]

The thermos *has sat* there for a week. [Present perfect of *sit.*]

size (n.) Pl., *sizes.* 1. *See* **kind.**

2. *Size* is a noun; *sized,* an adjective. Either noun or adjective may form a compound adjective.

medium-size house or
medium-sized house
large-size dresses or
large-sized dresses
different-size dogs or
different-sized dogs

3. Since *size* is a noun and not an adjective, it is incorrect to omit the *of* in these and similar expressions: that size *of* machine, that size *of* paper.

so. For the correct use of *so . . . as, see* **as, 1.**

some. For misuse of *some place, see* **place.**

somebody, someone (prons.) 1. Always write *somebody* as one word. *Someone* is preferred. Write *someone* as one word when it is equivalent to *somebody;* otherwise, it is two words.

He will appoint *someone* of outstanding ability.

If *some one* person is designated to head the project. . . .

2. Singular, followed by singular verb and pronoun.

I know *someone* [or *somebody*] *was* [not *were*] here while I was away, because *he* [not *they*] left *his* [not *their*] briefcase.

some time, sometime, sometimes (advs.) 1. Either *some time* or *sometime* may be used instead of *at some time,* meaning a point of time not specified. There is no distinction. The trend is to omit *at* and use *sometime.*

Right: I expect to be there *at some time* in August.

Right: I expect to be there *some time* in August.

Preferred: I expect to be there *sometime* in August.

2. Use *some time* when referring to an indefinite lapse of time. It is incorrect to use *sometime* in this sense.

It will take *some time* to prepare the report.

3. *Sometime* may be used as an adjective to describe a former state. It is equivalent to *at one time having been.*

Dr. Evatt, *sometime* Minister of Australia. . . .

4. *Sometimes,* written as one word, means at several indefinite times; on some occasions.

Sometimes she works late.

somewhere. 1. Always written as one word. *Some place* is commonly misused for *somewhere. See* **place.**

2. There is no such word as *somewheres.*

sort (n.) Pl., *sorts. See* **kind.**

species. 1. Singular or plural.

The species *is* . . .

These species *are.* . . .

2. For correct usage in the sense of *kind* or *sort, see* **kind.**

Split Infinitives. *See* **Infinitives, 2.**

spoonful (n.) Pl., *spoonfuls.* But see **Plurals of compound terms** in chapter 15.

stationary, stationery. *Stationary* means standing still; *stationery* means writing materials.

Some loading platforms are *stationary,* but others move.

Don't forget to order the office *stationery.*

straight. 1. The adverb form is *straight. Straightly* is rare.

2. *Straight* is not comparable. If anything is straight, it cannot be *more* straight. "More nearly straight" is allowable.

subject to. *See* **addicted to.**

Subjunctive Mood. Although the trend is away from the subjunctive mood, correct usage still requires the subjunctive in some cases.

1. Use the subjunctive mood to express a condition contrary to fact. Contrary-to-fact statements are generally introduced by *wish* or *if.*

I *wish* I *were* [not the indicative *was*] in a position to attend to the matter [but I am not].

If the company *were* [not the indicative *was*] in a sound financial position, a merger would not be necessary. [The company is not in a sound financial position.]

If I *were* [not the indicative *was*] you, I would not accept the offer.

I *wish* their relationship *were* [not the indicative *was*] more harmonious.

Many clauses introduced by *if* do not express impossible or contrary-to-fact conditions, but merely a condition or a doubt. In those clauses, the subjunctive is not generally used.

If optimism *does* [not the subjunctive *do*] not get out of hand, there will be no sudden collapse.

If he *is* [not *be*] in town I am sure he will call you. [Doubt implied.]

If he *was* [not *were*] at the meeting, we did not see him [but it is possible he was there].

2. Use the past subjunctive to express a supposition or condition in clauses introduced by *as if, as though.*

He looks *as if* he *were* [not *is* or *was*] ill.

The motor sounds *as though* a spark plug *were* [not *is* or *was*] missing.

It appears *as if* he *did* [not *does*] realize the necessity.

3. Use the subjunctive in *that* clauses when the main verb expresses importance, necessity, demand, recommendation, order, and the like.

We demanded that he *vacate* [not the indicative *vacates*] the premises.

He gave instructions that the office *be* closed early.

It is essential that the orders *be* shipped tomorrow.

The requirement is that he *remain* [not the indicative *remains*] abroad for two years.

He recommended that a Department of Welfare *be* established.

Note that in each of the foregoing examples *should* could be inserted before the italicized verbs.

4. Use the subjunctive in formal writing to express a motion, resolution, or ruling.

Mr. Edwards moved that the secretary *be* instructed to. . . .

Resolved: That the Certificate of Incorporation *be* amended. . . .

The Court ruled that the plaintiff *receive* [not the indicative *receives*] damages in the sum of $10,000.

such. 1. Do not use *which, who, that,* or *where* with *such.* The correct combination is *such . . . as.* Frequently the better usage is to omit *such* or change *such* to *the, that, those,* and the like.

Wrong: Some people give only *such* things for *which* they have no need.

Right: Some people give only *such* things *as* they do not need.

Right: Some people give only *those* things for *which* they have no need.

Wrong: We shipped immediately *such* parts of the machinery *that* were in stock.

Right: We shipped immediately *such* parts of the machinery *as* were in stock.

Better: We shipped immediately *those* parts of the machinery *that* were in stock.

2. Do not use *such as* in place of *as* to introduce a prepositional phrase.

Wrong: Radios that you have previously purchased from us, *such as in* your last shipment, are out of stock.

Right: Radios that you have previously purchased from us, *as in* your last shipment, are out of stock.

suitable (adj.) *Suitable for* a use or purpose; *to* an occasion or requirements.

The machine is suitable *for* that work.

The machine is suitable *to* the requirements of your office.

An informal invitation is suitable *to* the occasion.

superior (adj.) Should always be followed by *to*, not *than*.

It is superior from every point of view *to* [not *than*] the other material.

surround (vb.) When followed by a preposition, use *by*.

tactic (n.) Pl., *tactics*. Commonly used in the plural.

Tense. Tense indicates the time of action expressed by a verb. For correct usage in sentences that cause difficulty, look under the different tenses. *See* **Sequence of Tenses** for correct usage when a sentence has more than one verb expressing action at different times.

than. 1. Never use after *more and more*.

Wrong: The Supreme Court has granted *more and more* powers to the federal government *than* was originally intended. [Delete "and more" to make the sentence correct.]

2. *See* **different from.**

thanks (n. pl.) Always takes a plural verb.

that (conj.) Use only one *that* to introduce a single clause. A common error is the use of a second *that* when a phrase or clause intervenes between *that* and the clause it introduces.

I hope *that* (when you have reconsidered the matter) *that* you will cooperate. [Omit the second "that."

The first "that" introduces "you will cooperate."]

that, which (rel. prons.) Use *that* to introduce a defining or restrictive clause; use *which* to introduce a nondefining, nonrestrictive clause, a comment, or an additional thought.

Statutory requirements *that* fix a definite number of days for notice must be followed. [Only certain requirements are referred to.]

The proposed amendments, *which* improve the practicability of the measure, were adopted unanimously. [The clause introduced by "which" is an additional thought.]

them. Objective case of *they*. 1. For use as an object, *see* **Pronouns**, 1.

2. For misuse of *them* instead of *they* after forms of the verb *to be (am, is, are, was, were)*, *see* **Predicate Nominative**, 1.

there. Often used to introduce a clause in which the verb precedes the subject. The number of the verb is not affected *by there*, but depends on the number of the subject. Contrast this construction with **Predicate Nominative, 2.**

There *are* not sufficient *data* available. [Plural subject.]

There *is* a *mass* of data available. [Singular subject.]

they. Nominative case of third person plural pronoun. 1. For misuse of *they* instead of *them*, *see* **Pronouns**, 1.

2. For use after the forms of the verb *to be (am, is, are, was, were)*, *see* **Predicate Nominative**, 1.

time card (n.) Two words. *See* **Compound Terms**, 2 and 4.

time clock (n.) Two words. *See* **Compound Terms,** 2 and 4.

toward(s). Either is correct, but the use of *toward* is more prevalent. *Towards* is the accepted British form.

Transitive, Intransitive Verbs. The action of a transitive verb goes from the doer to a receiver, from a subject to an object. The action of an intransitive verb either does not include an object, is limited to the subject, or the intransitive verb shows no action at all.

He opened the door. [Transitive]

He sings beautifully. [Intransitive, action limited.]

He is a good painter. [Intransitive, no action.]

trust (vb.) Trust *in* a person, *to* a quality, trust a person *with* something.

I trust *in* you.

I trust *to* his discretion.

I trust you *with* this secret.

try (vb.) Often erroneously followed by *and* with a verb in place of an infinitive.

Try *to come* [not *and come*] to New York.

Try *to solve* [not *and solve*] the problem.

type (n.) Pl., *types.* 1. *See* **kind.**

2. The noun *type* should not be used as an adjective. It is incorrect to omit the *of* in these and similar expressions: type *of* machine, type *of* building, type *of* person.

uninterested. *See* **disinterested.**

unique. *Unique* is not comparable; it means the only one of its kind. You should not say "*most* unique," "*more* unique" or "*very* unique."

unquestioned, unquestionable (adjs.) *Unquestioned* refers to that which has not been questioned; *unquestionable,* that which cannot be sensibly questioned.

The statement was *unquestioned.* His loyalty is *unquestionable.*

us. The objective case of *we;* sometimes misused for *we.*

Wrong: They are not as efficient as *us* from the standpoint of accuracy.

Right: They are not as efficient as *we* [are efficient] from the standpoint of accuracy.

Wrong: The production department is no more at fault than *us* for the delay.

Right: The production department is no more at fault than *we* [are at fault] for the delay.

valuables (n. pl.) Always used in the plural and takes a plural verb.

variety (n.) Pl., *varieties. See* **kind.**

verbal (adj.) Relates to either written or spoken words. *Verbal* is used often carelessly in place of *oral* with reference to spoken words. To avoid confusion, use *oral* to mean spoken words and *written* to mean written words.

A contract, whether written or *oral* [not *verbal*] is binding.

He gave *oral* [not *verbal*] instructions.

A few *verbal* changes [changes in words] are necessary.

Verbs. For agreement of a verb with its subject, *see* **Compound Subject; Alternate Subject; Intervening Noun or Phrase; Predicate Nominative.** *See also* **Irregular Verbs.**

very, very much. 1. These words are overworked. Although they are acceptable modifiers, excessive use of them destroys the force of the words modified. *I am pleased* is as emphatic as *I am very much pleased.* Rather than using *very* or *very much,* selecting a stronger word is often the best alternative.

2. Those who insist on using *very* and *very much* should observe correct usage. These terms are not interchangeable. The problem is whether to use *very* or *very much* before a passive participle. Use *very* when the passive participle has the force of an adjective.

A *very delighted* crowd heard the news.

Use *very much* (or *much*) when the passive participle is used in the predicate with verbal force.

I was *very much* [or *much*] delighted at the result of the game.

I will be *very much* [or *much*] inconvenienced by the delay.

Exception: A passive participle that, although used as a verb, has lost its verbal force by common usage is preceded by *very.*

I am *very* [not *very much*] tired of hearing about the matter.

Voice. The quality of a transitive verb that shows when the subject is acting (active voice) or being acted upon (passive voice). Voice is ordinarily not troublesome.

1. Do not mix the voices by shifting from active to passive.

Wrong: The jurors *deliberated* for forty-eight hours before they *were discharged.*

Right: The jurors *deliberated* for forty-eight hours before the judge *discharged* them.

2. The passive voice is less emphatic than the active.

Weak: The manuscript *was rejected* by the publisher.

Better: The publisher *rejected* the manuscript.

wait on. Do not use in place of *wait for.*

We have been waiting *for* [not *on*] her.

wake (vb.) Principal parts, *wake, waked* or *woke,* [has, had or have] *waked. See* **Irregular Verbs.**

way. Do not use *ways* in place of the singular *way.*

Wrong: This year's sales are quite a *ways* ahead of last year's.

Right: This year's sales are quite a *way* ahead of last year's.

Better: This year's sales are *considerably* ahead of last year's.

we. Nominative case of first person plural pronoun. 1. For misuse of *we* instead of *us, see* **Pronouns,** 1.

2. For use after forms of the verb *to be* (*am, is, are, was, were*), *see* **Predicate Nominative,** 1.

3. For the correct use of *we* or *I* in letters, *see* **I,** 3.

4. *We* is frequently misused for *us* in apposition to a noun in the objective case.

Wrong: It is advisable for *we* citrus growers to organize an association.

Right: It is advisable for *us* citrus growers to organize an association.

well, good. *Well* may be either an

adjective or an adverb, but is usually an adverb except when it refers to a state of health. *Good* is always an adjective.

He *did* the job *well.* [Adverb, describing how he did the job.]

He looks *well.* [Predicate adjective, referring to state of health.]

The *situation* looks *good* to me. [Predicate adjective, describing the situation.]

The upswing in the stock market is a *good indication* that prosperity is still with us. [Adjective, modifying "indication."]

what. May be either singular or plural. In the singular, *what* stands for *that which* or *a thing that.* In the plural, *what* stands for *those* [persons] *who* or *those* [things] *that.*

Singular: What *is* saved in price *is* likely to be lost in service and goodwill.

Singular: The reports show not only what *has* been done during the period covered, but also what will be done.

Plural: My reasons for refusing the order *were* what I considered sufficient. ["Reasons" is the plural antecedent of "what."]

If *what* is singular in the beginning of the sentence, it remains singular. A common error is to make the second verb agree with a plural predicate nominative. In each of the following examples, *what* is definitely established as singular because it is followed by a singular verb. The second verb must also be singular, although it is followed by a plural predicate nominative, which is the complement to *what.*

What *is* needed *is* [not *are*] houses at prices that the people can afford.

What *seems* to be needed *is* [not *are*] stringent regulations.

What *causes* the delay *is* [not *are*] the three transfers.

In each of the following examples, *what* is used in the plural sense. Test the sentence by substituting *those* [things] *that* for *what.*

He is attempting to show by the chart *what appear* [not *appears*] to be the reasons for the decrease in sales. [Meaning "those reasons that."]

The company sold at discount only what *were* [not *was*] considered refrigerators of second quality. [Meaning "only those refrigerators that were considered."]

when. 1. Do not use *when* to define a word.

Wrong: A sentence is *when* you have a complete thought.

Right: A sentence is a complete thought.

2. *Where* is frequently misused for *when. Where* should introduce an adverbial clause of place; *when,* of time.

When [not *where*] a proxy is given limited power, he must act within the limitations.

A surplus exists *when* [not *where*] there is an excess in the aggregate value of assets over liabilities and capital.

Where the company is building. . . .

where. 1. Sometimes misused in place of *that.*

I see in the paper *that* [not *where*] the corporation has declared a dividend.

2. *Where* should be used to introduce an adverbial clause of place, not of time. *See* when, 2.

3. Do not use *where* to define a word.

Wrong: Perjury is *where* a person voluntarily violates an oath.
Right: Perjury is the voluntary violation of an oath.

which. For use of *that* as a relative pronoun instead of *which, see* that, which.

while. When used most precisely, *while* means "during the time that" or "as long as."

who, whom (prons.) *Who* is the nominative case and is used as the subject; *whom* is the objective case and is used as the object of a verb or preposition.

He is the client for *whom* I prepared the contract. [Object of "for."]
Mr. Adams is the person *who* has charge of sales. [Subject of "has."]
Who has charge of sales? [Subject of "has."]

Whom do you wish to see? [Object of "to see."]
Mr. Edwards is the candidate *who* I believe will win. ["Who" is the subject of "will win"; "I believe" is parenthetical.]
Mr. Edwards is the candidate *whom* I favor. ["Whom" is the object of "favor."]

will. See shall.

would. See shall.

2. When an indirect object follows *write*, without a direct object, precede the indirect object by *to*. If a direct and indirect object follow, *to* is not necessary.

Wrong: I will write *you* [indirect object] as soon as I can.
Right: I will write *to you* as soon as I can.
Right: I will write *you* [indirect object] a *letter* [direct object] as soon as I can.

wrong. The adverb forms are *wrong, wrongly. See* Adverbs, 3. *Wrong* is not comparable. If anything is wrong it cannot be *more* wrong.

yourself. Pl., *yourselves. See* Compound Personal Pronouns.

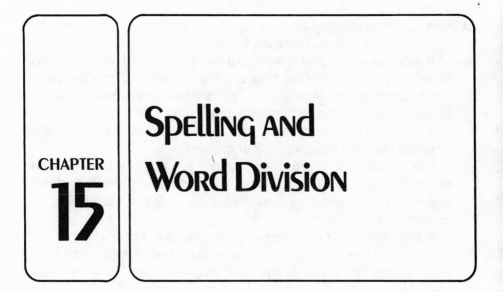

CHAPTER 15

Spelling and Word Division

When you have a doubt about how to spell a word, *look it up* in a standard dictionary. Do not ask someone how to spell it; if you look it up, you are more apt to remember it. *Never* guess at how to spell a word.

Good spellers spell from a mental picture of the word; that is why careful reading is the surest method of improving your spelling. A few rules that will help you are given here; but most of them have exceptions, and you simply have to memorize words that give you trouble. (See the helpful *mnemonics* on page 367.)

Plurals.   Ordinarily the plural is formed by adding *s;* in some cases by adding *es,* as in *classes, churches, boxes.*

Words ending in o. All words ending in *o* preceded by a vowel form the plural by adding *s,* as in *folios, trios, studios.* Generally, words ending in *o* preceded by a consonant form the plural by adding *es,* as in *potatoes, heroes;* a few form the plural by adding *s,* as in *solos, dynamos, memos.* Some have both forms, as in *cargoes,* or *cargos, mottoes* or *mottos, zeros* or *zeroes.*

Words ending in y. Words ending in *y* preceded by a vowel form the plural by adding *s,* for example, *attorneys, days;* but words ending in *y* preceded by a consonant change the *y* to *i* and add *es,* as in *ladies, berries, countries, counties.*

Words ending in f or fe. Some nouns ending in *f* or *fe* change the *f* to *v* and add *s* or *es;* some do not; some have both forms. There is no way to distinguish the groups. For example, *roof* becomes *roofs, chief, chiefs,* but *loaf* becomes *loaves* and *leaf, leaves.* When in doubt, consult the dictionary.

Abbreviations. The plural of an abbreviation is usually formed by adding *s,* as in *mfrs., mos., nos.*

The plurals of some abbreviations are formed by repeating the abbreviation.

> p., pp.—page, pages   v., vv.—verse, verses.

Figures, letters. Add *'s,* as in *p's and q's, size 6's, Ph.D.'s* if *s* alone would be confusing. In other cases letters and numbers form the plural by adding *s* alone, as in *YWCAs* or *1970s.*

Plurals of compound terms.   In general, the plural of a compound term is formed by making the most important word plural. The most important word is the word telling what the principal is. Following this general rule, military titles for the most part form the plural by adding *s* to the second word, which is usually the most important. However, *sergeant major* forms the plural on the first word since the rank is really a form of *sergeant,* not major. Civilian titles usually add the *s* to the first word, since the first word usually tells what the person is. Thus:

notaries public (they are *notaries,* not *publics*)

major *generals* (they are *generals,* not *majors*)
adjutants general (they are *adjutants* (assistants), not *generals*)

Examples of forming the plural of a compound term by making the most important word plural:

adjutants general	*governors* general
aides-de-camp	judge *advocates*
ambassadors at large	lieutenant *colonels*
assistant *attorneys* general	*notaries* public
attorneys general	*presidents*-elect
bills of lading	*rights*-of-way
brigadier *generals*	*sergeants* at arms
brothers-in-law	*sergeants* major
comptrollers general	*surgeons* general
deputy *chiefs* of staff	trade *unions*
general *counsels*	vice *chairmen*

1. When both words are of equal importance, both words take the plural form.

coats of arms   *men employees*   *women drivers*

When no word is of importance in itself, the last word takes the plural form.

forget-me-*nots*   jack-in-the-*pulpits*   pick-me-*ups*

2. When a noun is compounded with a preposition, the noun takes the plural form.

hangers-on   *listeners*-in   *passers*-by   by-*products*

3. When neither word in the compound term is a noun, the last word takes the plural form.

also-*rans*   go-*betweens*   sell-*outs*   take-*offs*   strike-*overs*

4. Compound nouns written as one word form their plurals regularly. Words ending in *-ful* are the only ones that cause any trouble.

cup*fuls*   tablespoon*fuls*   bucket*fuls*

When it is necessary to convey the meaning that more than one container was used, write the compound as two words and add *s* to the noun.

5 *cups* full   2 *tablespoons* full   4 *buckets* full

Combinations of i and e.   Learn the following rhyme and you will not be likely to make a mistake in combining *i* and *e*.

> The *i* before *e*
> Except after *c,*
> Or when sounded like *a*
> As in *neighbor* and *weigh*

Exceptions: either, neither, seize, weir, weird, sheik, leisure, plebeian, financier, specie, conscience.

Doubling the final consonant.   Nothing causes quite as much trouble as not knowing when to double a consonant before adding a suffix to a word. This is the rule:

Double the consonant before (1) a suffix beginning with a vowel if (2) the word ends in a single consonant (3) preceded by a single vowel and if (4) the accent falls on the last syllable of the word. (For the purpose of this rule, words of *one syllable* are considered "accented" on the last syllable.)

Confusion arises because *all* of these conditions must be met before the consonant can be doubled. The suffix *must* begin with a vowel. The word must end in a *single* consonant preceded by a *single* vowel. The accent must fall on the *last* syllable of the word.

Consonant *not* doubled:

commit, commitment (suffix does not begin with a vowel)
desert, deserting (word does not end in a *single* consonant)
appeal, appealed (final consonant not preceded by a single vowel)
offer, offered (accent does not fall on the last syllable)
occur, occurred (all conditions are met)
bag, baggage (all conditions are met)

Exceptions: Unfortunately, even this very workable rule has a few exceptions. Most of the exceptions are derivatives in which the syllabication changes and the accent of the main word is thrown back upon the first syllable: *de fer'—def'er-ence; re fer'—ref'er-ence; pre fer'—pref'er-ence.* (But the *r* is doubled when adding *ed* or *ing* to *defer, prefer,* or *refer.*) Other frequently used exceptions are *infer—inferable; transfer—transferable.*

Words ending in silent e.   *Suffixes beginning with a vowel.* Words ending in a silent *e* generally drop the *e* before a suffix beginning with a vowel. *See also* **Suffixes: -able, -ous.**

bride, bridal	argue, arguable
guide, guidance	owe, owing
ice, icing	judge, judging
use, usable, using	sale, salable (*variant,* saleable)

Exceptions:

dye	singe
eye	tinge
hoe	toe
shoe	

Suffixes beginning with a consonant. Words ending in silent *e* generally retain the *e* before suffixes beginning with a consonant, unless another vowel precedes the final *e*.

pale, paleness	excite, excitement
hate, hateful	due, duly
argue, argument	

Exceptions:

abridgment	nursling
acknowledgment	wholly
judgment	

Words ending in -ie.   Words ending in *ie* drop the *e* and change the *i* to *y* before adding the *ing*.

die, dying
lie, lying

Suffixes: -able, -ous.   Words ending in *e* preceded by *c* or *g* do not drop the final *e* before the suffixes *-able* or *-ous*, but do drop the final *e* before the suffix *-ible*.

service, serviceable	manage, manageable
courage, courageous	advantage, advantageous
deduce, deducible	convince, convincible

The -able, -ible difficulty.   If a word has an *-ation* form, it always takes the suffix *-able* instead of *-ible.* Thus, *application, applicable; reparation, reparable.* However, many words that do not have an *-ation* form also take the suffix *-able,* which is far more common than the suffix *-ible.* There is no rule distinguishing the groups.

The following list includes some common -*ible* adjectives. It does not include other forms of the same word made by adding a prefix. For example, *credible* is included in the list, but *incredible* is not.

accessible	discussible,	invincible
adducible	discussable	irascible
admissible	dismissible	irresistible
apprehensible	distensible	legible
audible	divertible	negligible
avertible	divisible	omissible
coercible	edible	ostensible
cohesible	educable	perceptible
collapsible	educible	perfectible
collectible,	eligible	permissible
collectable	exhaustible	persuasible,
combustible	expansible	persuadable
compatible	expressible	pervertible
comprehensible	extendible,	plausible
compressible	extensible	preventible,
conductible	fallible	preventable
contemptible	feasible	producible
contractible	flexible	reducible
convertible	forcible	remissible
corrigible	gullible	reprehensible
corruptible	ignitible,	repressible
credible	ignitable	responsible
deducible	impassible	reversible
deductible	impressible	sensible
defensible	includible,	suggestible
depressible	includable	suppressible
descendible	incontrovertible	susceptible
destructible	indefeasible	suspendible
diffusible	indefectible	tangible
digestible	indelible	terrible
dirigible	inducible	vendible
discernible	intelligible	visible
	invertible	

Words ending in -sede, -ceed, or -cede.   Only one word in our language ends in -*sede*—*supersede*. Only three end in -*ceed*—*proceed, exceed, succeed*. All the others end in -*cede*. Remember, also, that *proceed* changes its form in *procedure*.

Suffixes: -ance or -ence.   When the suffix is preceded by *c* having the sound of *k*, or *g* having a hard sound, use *-ance*, *-ancy*, or *-ant;* when *c* has the sound of *s*, or *g* the sound of *j*, use *-ence*, *-ency*, or *-ent*.

convalescence	indigent
significant	extravagant
negligence	

If the suffix is preceded by a letter other than *c* or *g* and you are in doubt about the spelling, consult the dictionary.

Suffixes: -ise or -ize.   There is no rule governing the use of *-ise* or *-ize*. The words in the following list, and their derivatives and compounds, are spelled with *-ise*. The preferable American spelling for all other words is *-ize*.

advertise	despise	incise
advise	devise	merchandise
apprise	disguise	premise
arise	enterprise	reprise
chastise	excise	revise
circumcise	exercise	supervise
comprise	exorcise	surmise
compromise	franchise	surprise
demise	improvise	

Words ending in c.   When a word ends in *c*, insert a *k* before adding a suffix beginning with *e*, *i*, or *y*.

picnic, picnicking, picnicked
traffic, trafficker, trafficking

Words ending in y preceded by a consonant.   Words ending in *y* preceded by a consonant generally change the *y* to *i* before any suffix except one beginning with *i*.

modify	modifying	modifier	modification
lonely	lonelier	loneliness	
worry	worrisome	worried	

Exceptions: 1. Adjectives of one syllable have two forms in the comparative and superlative.

dry: drier, driest	shy: shier, shiest	spry: sprier, spriest
or	or	or
dryer, dryest	shyer, shyest	spryer, spryest

2. Adjectives of one syllable usually retain the *y* before *ly* and *ness*.

> shyly, shyness
> dryly, dryness
> spryly, spryness

3. The *y* is retained in compounds of *-ship* and *-like* and in derivatives of *lady* and *baby*.

> secretaryship ladylike ladyfinger babyhood

The prefixes: dis- and mis-.   Words formed by adding the prefix *dis-* are frequently misspelled because of doubt about whether the combined form has one *s* or two. If the word to which the prefix is added begins with *s*, the combined form has two *s's;* otherwise, the combined form has only one *s*. The same word applies to the prefix *mis-*.

dis-	appoint	disappoint
dis-	appear	disappear
dis-	satisfy	dissatisfy
mis-	spell	misspell
mis-	apply	misapply
mis-	print	misprint

SPECIAL SUGGESTIONS FOR BOOSTING YOUR EFFICIENCY IN SPELLING

Helpful mnemonics for accurate spelling.   One of the easiest ways to learn to spell a certain word is to make up a phrase that will call the correct spelling to mind. This device to aid the memory is called a *mnemonic*. A silly phrase or a little rhyme will often make a word stick in your mind even better than a sensible rule does.

Don't scorn this method. Anything that helps you to be a better speller is worthwhile. There are some old favorites in the following list. You can easily think up others for the words that give you trouble. Keep a list of these words and the little phrase or rhyme close at hand on your desk. Each time you must look up the spelling of a word, add the word to your list together with your own little phrase or jingle; the next time that word comes up, look at the list instead of in the dictionary. You will be amazed at how quickly you will learn to spell the words on the list.

Helpful Mnemonics

A superinten*dent* collects *rent*.

All right is the opposite of *all wrong*. [There is no word "alright" just as there is no word "alwrong."]

Only *a rat* would sep*arat*e friends.

Perhaps he is only *a* comp*arat*ive *rat*.

A fri*end* sticks to the *end*.

My button is lo*ose*. [You can see it dangling.] If I am not careful I will *lose* it and then it will be *lost*. Or—You g*oose*, your button is l*oose!*

Cut me a *piec*e of *pie*.

An apartment *lease* brings *peace* from rent *increase*.

A l*etter* is written on station*ery*. You st*a*nd still when you are station*a*ry.

The princip*al* p*a*rt is the m*ain* p*a*rt.

The paral*l*el lines are in the center of the word. [You can think of the two l's as parallel lines if you stretch your imagination a little.]

Super*sede* is the only word in the English language that ends in *-sede*.

She is irresist*i*ble when wearing *li*pstick.

An *able* man is depend*able* and indispens*able*.

These few examples will give you the idea. Think up your own for other words and use them.

DIVISION OF WORDS

Division of words at the end of a line.   To avoid a ragged right-hand margin, it is sometimes essential to divide a word at the end of a line, but divide *only* when necessary. Try not to have two successive lines with a divided word at the end, and never have more than two. Never divide the last word on a page except in legal documents where the word is sometimes divided to show continuity. Try to avoid dividing the last word in a paragraph.

The correct division of a word depends first of all on the breakdown of the word into syllables. American dictionaries syllabicate according to pronunciation, and not according to derivation. If you do not know the proper division into syllables for a word, look up the word in the dictionary. There are, however, a few simple rules in addition to the rule of syllables that govern the division of a word.

Rules for the division of words at the end of a line.

1. Never divide words pronounced as one syllable.

through   drowned   gained

2. Never divide a four-letter word.

only   into

3. Never separate one-letter syllables at the beginning of a word from the rest of the word.

around   alone

4. Divide a word with a one-letter syllable within the word after the one-letter syllable, except in the case of the suffixes *-able* or *-ible*.

busi-ness   sepa-rate   medi-cal   con-sider-able   reduc-ible

> *Note:* There are many words ending in *-able* or *-ible* in which the *a* or *i* does not form a syllable by itself. These words are divided after the *a* or *i*.
>
> pos-si-ble   char-i-ta-ble   ca-pa-ble

5. Do not carry over a two-letter syllable at the end of a word.

caller   deeded   pur-chaser

6. Avoid separating two-letter syllables at the beginning of a word from the rest of the word.

eli-gi-ble   begin-ning   atten-tion   redeemed
(But re-deemed is preferable to redeem-ed.)

7. When the final consonant in a word is doubled before a suffix, the second consonant belongs with the letters following it.

run-ning   occur-ring

8. Do not carry over to the next line single or double consonants in the root word.

call-ing   forc-ing   divid-ing   fore-stall-ing

9. When two consonants occur within a word, divide the word between the consonants.

gram-mar   expres-sive   moun-tain   foun-da-tion

10. The following suffixes are not divisible:

-cial	-sion	-ceous
-sial	-tion	-tious
-tial	-gion	-geous
-cion	-cious	-gious

11. Avoid dividing a compound hyphenated word except where the hyphen naturally falls.

father-in-law   self-applause

12. Do not divide abbreviations.

Ph.D.   **YWCA**   **C.O.D.**

13. Avoid dividing numbers. If it is necessary to divide, divide on a comma and retain the comma.

$1,548,-345,000

14. Divide dates in the body of a letter between the day and the year, not between the month and the day.

. . . . September 19,
19___ . . . .

15. Do not separate the initials of a name and avoid separating initials, titles, or degrees from the name; also avoid dividing proper names.

SPECIAL SUGGESTION FOR BECOMING A WORD-DIVIDER EXPERT

A little best-seller called *Word Finder*, 4th ed., Anderson, Straub, and Gibson,[1] is a secretary's indispensable aid to the accurate division of words. The book lists about 15,000 words and shows the correct division and pronunciation of each. You can quickly locate the word you want because no text of meaning or explanation interferes with the alphabetical sequence of the words.

COMMONLY MISSPELLED WORDS

Certain words are more troublesome than others, and special

---

[1]Published by Prentice-Hall, Inc., Englewood Cliffs, New Jersey 07632.

attention is required to avoid misspellings. This list[2] contains 500 of such problem words, listed by frequency of spelling error.

occurrence	siege	correspondents	efficiency
negligible	acknowledgment[6]	vicinity	judgment[7]
permissible	ascertain	forfeit	occasion
liaison	allotment	analyze	inconvenience
acquiesce	criticize	omission	canceled[8]
questionnaire	illegible	laboratory	concurred
clientele	inasmuch as	license	itinerary
develop	livelihood	expedite	calendar
likable	deficit	advisory	convenience
collateral	consensus	bankruptcy	withhold
supersede	criticism	commitment	justifiable
forcible	adequate	repetition	prejudice
conscientious	vendor	gauge	recipe
etiquette	irrelevant	hazardous	simultaneous
deductible	privilege	participant	apparel
catalog[3]	phase	psychology	defendant
aggravate	benefited	maintenance	definitely
equipped	cancellation	occurred	conscious
harass	advantageous	congratulate	unnecessary
accede	guarantee	grievance	deferred
allotted	legitimate	imperative	interrupted
all right	influential	environment	reimburse
discrepancy	consistent	definite	convenient
accessible	jeopardize	acquaintance	disappoint
mischievous	personnel	council	opportunity
percent[4]	indispensable	usable	exaggerate
existence	recurrence	negotiate	leisure
interfere	vacuum	deteriorate	competitor
occurring	possession	attorneys	annoyance
parallel	precede	edition	unanimous
regrettable	accompanying	mortgage	procedure
salable[5]	eligible	counsel	undoubtedly

[2]Compiled by the Dictation Disc Company, 240 Madison Avenue, New York, New York 10016.

[3]"catalogue" acceptable.

[4]"per cent" acceptable

[5]"saleable" acceptable

[6]"acknowledgement" acceptable.

[7]"judgement" acceptable.

[8]"cancelled" acceptable.

oblige
accessory
emphasize
conceivable
omitted
substantial
inquiry
patronage
conscience
effect
noticeable
appreciable
accommodate
price list
stationery
applicable
correspondence
indebtedness
preliminary
stationary
precision
preferable
accumulate
concession
excellent
familiarize
loose
lose
remittance
courteous
pamphlet
recognized
itemized
persuade
accidentally
apologize
except
recommend
similar
eliminate
endeavor
manufacturer
miscellaneous
permanent

proceed
anxious
affidavit
enthusiasm
restaurant
amendment
announcement
mileage
ninety
attendance
separate
referring
bulletin
legible
thorough
dependent
embarrass
preferred
representative
strictly
surprise
advisable
foreign
formerly
partial
brochure
dissatisfied
emphasis
respectively
nevertheless
offense
fascinate
pursue
approximate
principle
intelligence
acquire
advertisement
enterprise
analysis
allowable
basis
brilliant
menus

accrued
hesitant
customer
decision
extension
grateful
reference
argument
exercise
management
seized
recently
sufficient
architect
vehicle
confidential
controversy
courtesy
anticipate
bureau
fulfillment
superintendent
deceive
personal
practical
practically
referred
minimum
overdue
particularly
complement
tariff
appropriate
debtor
freight
serviceable
sincerity
writing
receive
whether
advertising
especially
merchandise
preference

assessment
inducement
visible
immediately
incidentally
receipt
applicant
commission
succeed
excellence
excessive
independent
quantity
quite
specialize
letterhead
modernize
volunteer
physician
achievement
beginning
confident
difference
equipment
admirable
original
recognize
essential
facilities
casualty
magazine
voluntary
incurred
altogether
fourth
schedule
extraordinary
beneficiary
capitol
premium
prominent
prosecute
ridiculous
tragedy

unfortunately	necessary	responsibility	forty
volume	shipment	statistics	handled
across	adapt	ultimately	length
appearance	pleasant	yield	ordinary
too	maximum	affect	organization
bargain	salary	planning	warehouse
bookkeeper	significant	adjustment	controlling
expenditure	throughout	advise	initial
responsible	depositors	businessman	somewhat
satisfactorily	professor	campaign	address
successful	subscriber	capital	current
concede	survey	defense	accuracy
neighborhood	temporary	desirable	believe
securities	urgent	governor	coming
announce	acceptance	paid	committee
assured	allowance	permitted	their
describe	article	previous	there
absence	envelope	probably	really
exceed	experience	purchase	submitted
advice	respectfully	secretary	installment
annual	circumstances	choice	someone
available	concern	choose	worthwhile
delegate	extremely	it's	comparison
development	financial	requirement	reasonable
economical	genuine	appraisal	enclose
efficient	individual	competent	expense
practice	occupant	compromise	shipping
principal	response	identical	organize
career	valuable	impossible	route
column	beneficial	library	until
hardware	continuous	manuscript	various
height	emergency	medical	wholesale
inventory	furthermore	offering	compelled
quiet	hoping	creditor	consequence
comparable	intention	decide	director
compliment	memorandum	devise	employee
endorsement	accordance	favorite	associate
investor	among	already	appointment
corporation	assistance	arrangement	appliance
disappear	cannot	usually	assignment
intercede	consignment	explanation	cordially
ninth	renewal	February	pleasure
apparent	attention	finally	accept
description	realize	knowledge	agreeable

almost	eagerly	client	official
business	forward	coverage	remember
budget	government	favorable	supervisor
busy	typing	device	transferred
conference	authorize	friend	weather

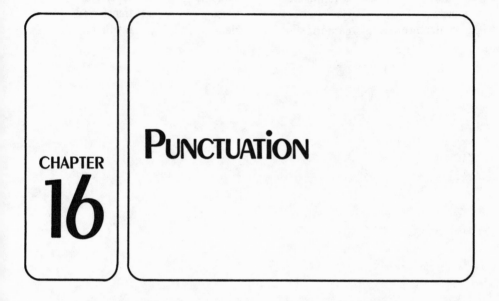

Punctuation

The sole purpose of punctuation is to make the structure and meaning of the written word clear to the reader. Punctuation in moderation adds emphasis and strength to the writer's words, but it is not a panacea for a poorly constructed sentence. Sentences that are difficult to punctuate or that require the use of a great many commas are usually weak, and the writer should express such sentences differently.

A few conventions of punctuation are arbitrarily applied in certain situations. Such conventions, or rules, are called *mechanics*. This chapter treats the most important marks of punctuation and mechanics in the following order:

Comma	Interrogation Point
Period	Quotation Marks
Semicolon	Apostrophe
Colon	Hyphen
Dash	Parentheses or Brackets
Exclamation Point	Leaders and Ellipses

COMMA—
THE SECRETARY'S TROUBLEMAKER

Many secretaries—probably following in the footsteps of their employers—tend to overwork the comma. The trend in good usage is to curtail the use of the comma and omit it in many cases where its use was formerly mandatory.

Appositives. Use a comma to set off an appositive; that is, an expression that explains or gives additional information about a preceding expression.

The president of our company, *Mr. Edwards,* is in Europe.

But do not separate two nouns, one of which identifies the other.

The *conductor Bernstein* returned to America today.
The *witness Jones* testified that he saw the defendant.

Cities and states. Use a comma to separate the name of a city from the name of a state.

Brown Company of Auburn, *New York* has reduced turnover 50 percent.

Compound predicates. Compound predicates are not usually separated by commas.

The total number of children in high school is increasing *and* will continue to increase for several more years.

Compound sentences. Use a comma to separate the two main clauses joined by the conjunctions *but, and, or, for, neither, nor* or *either.* The comma precedes the conjunction.

We appreciate very much your order of July 16, *but* we are unable to accept it because of our established merchandising policy.

The comma may be omitted before *and* if the clauses are short and closely connected in thought.

The radios were shipped yesterday *and* the television sets will be shipped tomorrow.

Dash and comma.   Do not use a dash and comma together.

Dates.   Separate the day of the month from the year by a comma. The trend is to omit the comma after the month if no day is given, and after the year, unless the construction of the sentence requires punctuation.

> . . . . payable March 12, 19___ to stockholders.
> . . . . .as of March 19___, the stockholders . . .

Ellipsis.   Use a comma to indicate that one or more words, easily understood, have been omitted. (A construction of this type is known as an *ellipsis.*)

> The employer contributed 60 percent; the employees, 40 percent.

Essential and nonessential phrases and clauses.   A restrictive phrase or clause is one that is essential to the meaning of the sentence and is not merely descriptive or parenthetic; it should not be set off by commas. A nonrestrictive phrase or clause is one that adds an additional thought to the sentence but is not essential to the meaning of the sentence; it should be set off by commas.

> The lawyer *who argued the case* is a close friend of the defendant.
> Mr. Ransome, *who argued the case,* is a close friend of the defendant.
> The rule against lateness, *which has been in effect many years,* is strictly enforced.

Inseparables.   A frequent error is to separate words that belong together and are interdependent, such as a verb from its subject or object or predicate nominative, or a limiting clause from its antecedent.

In the following examples the commas in brackets should be omitted.

> The rapid advancement of the company to its present enviable position in the publishing world [,] is attributable largely to the acumen and energy of its founders. [The comma separates the subject "advancement" from its verb "is."]
> The revision combines with the first edition's thoroughness [,] a constructive viewpoint, a wide range of practices, and up-to-date methods. [The comma separates the verb "combines" from its objects "viewpoint," "range," and "methods."]
> The leeway allowed the defendants in this trial, as in all others [,] where

justice prevails, is in sharp contrast to the treatment accorded defendants in totalitarian countries. [The "where" starts a limiting relative clause modifying "others." *See* **Essential and nonessential phrases and clauses.**]

Introductory words. (*See also* **Parenthetical words and phrases.**) Use a comma to separate an introductory word from the rest of the sentence.

Yes, the meeting will be held as scheduled.

Names. Do not use a comma between a name and *of* indicating place or position.

Brown Company *of* Auburn, New York
Mr. Edwards *of* Robinson & Co.
Mr. Nash *of* counsel

Place a comma between a name and *Inc., Sr., Jr., 2nd, III,* etc.

Lever Brothers, *Ltd.*   Mr. R. G. Jones, *Sr.*

Numbers. Use a comma when writing figures in thousands, *but not* in street, room, post office box, postal zip codes, and telephone numbers.

$15,800.65   3,800   1381 Vinton Avenue   39201
P.O. Box 4671   553-3521

Oh. Use a comma after *oh* if other words follow it.

Oh, he returned the manuscript yesterday.

Parentheses and comma. Use a comma after a closing parenthesis if the construction of the sentence requires a comma. Never use a comma *before* a parenthesis or an expression enclosed in parentheses.

Our incorporators' meeting (the first meeting of our stockholders), which is required by law, will be held November 15.
Our incorporators' meeting (the first meeting of our stockholders) will be held November 15.

Parenthetical words and phrases. Use commas to set off parenthetical words or phrases like *I believe, for example, however,* unless the connection is close and smooth enough not to call for a pause in reading.

> *Furthermore,* credit obligations may be paid out of capital items.
> The economic condition of the country, *I believe,* is gradually improving.
> He was *perhaps* busy at the time.
> That make of car is not expensive and *therefore* appeals to potential customers in the low-income brackets.

Participial phrases.   Do not separate a participle from the noun it modifies when the noun is not the subject and the expression is not closely connected with the rest of the sentence. In transcribing, the natural tendency is to strike a comma where the virgules appear in the following sentences, necessitating an erasure.

> The operators/ *having agreed to arbitrate,* the union called off the strike.
> The evidence/ *being merely circumstantial,* the jury acquitted him.

Phrases with a common element.   Place a comma before a word or words that are common to two or more phrases but are expressed only after the last phrase. In the following examples the commas in brackets are frequently *omitted in error.*

> The report was documented with references to many, if not all [,] of the recent court decisions on the question of interlocking directorates. [The words "of the . . . " are common to "many" and to "all."]
> The sales manager's reports are clearer, more concise, more instructive [,] than those of the advertising manager. [The words "than those . . . " are common to "clearer," "more concise," and "more instructive."]
>
> *Note:* If the phrases are connected by a conjunction, the comma is omitted.
> . . . are clearer, more concise, and more accurate than those . . .

Quotations.   Set off direct quotations by commas.

> His reply was, "I am not interested in the matter."
> "I am not interested in the matter," he replied.

But if a question mark is needed at the end of the quotation, do not use a comma.

> "What is the lowest price you can quote?" he inquired.

Quotation marks and comma.   Place the comma on the *inside* of quotation marks.

When he spoke of "overtime," I thought he meant over 35 hours.

Series.   Separate words and phrases in a series by a comma. A comma is preferred but may be omitted before the conjunction connecting the last two members of a series; however, be consistent in your usage. (See the use of a semicolon in a series, page 381.)

Thus, we speak of buying goods on credit, of a merchant's credit [,] *and* of making a payment by credit.

Its membership comprises manufacturers and wholesalers of silverware, watches, diamonds [,] *and* semiprecious stones.

But do not use a comma between two (not a series) parallel constructions joined by a conjunction.

This amount is equal to the covered loss less (1) the coinsurance deduction *and* (2) the normal loss.

He can ask for changes in the estimate *or* for a completely revised estimate.

PERIOD— THE MOST FAMILIAR PUNCTUATION MARK

Sentences.   Place a period at the end of a declarative or imperative sentence.

The contract was signed last week. [Declarative]
Hold the shipment until next month. [Imperative]

Initials and abbreviations.   Place a period after initials and abbreviations. There are a few exceptions to this rule, which are indicated in the list of abbreviations in chapter 18. Preferably, the periods are omitted between initials standing for federal agencies.

Ph.D.   C.O.D.   ibid.   Chas.   Thos.   R. E. Smith   CAA

Outlines.   Place a period after each letter or number in an outline or itemized list unless the letter or number is enclosed in parentheses.

Omissions.   Omit the period after:

Contractions (*ass'n, sec'y*)
Roman numerals, except in an outline (*Vol. II, George V*)
Sums of money in dollar denominations, unless cents are added (*$50, $50.25*)

Shortened forms of names and words in common use (*Ed, Will, ad, memo, percent, photo*)

Letters identifying radio stations (*WOR, NBC*)

Periods and parentheses.   When an expression in parentheses comes at the end of a sentence and is part of the sentence, put the period outside the parentheses; if the parenthetical expression is independent of the sentence and a period is necessary, place the period within the parentheses.

> The creditor can get a judgment against him and garnishee his wages (see section 15).
>
> The creditor can get a judgment against him and garnishee his wages. (The law of garnishment is discussed in section 15.)

But do not use a period when a complete declarative or imperative sentence is enclosed in parentheses *within another sentence.*

> The honorary chairman of the board (he retired from active duty several years ago) addressed the Quarter-Century Club.

Periods and quotation marks.   Always place the period *inside* quotation marks.

> Please explain what you meant by the expression "without reservation."

SEMICOLON—
THE COMPROMISE BETWEEN
PERIOD AND COMMA

Compound sentences.   A semicolon may be used to separate the parts of a compound sentence when the comma and conjunction are omitted.

> The adjustment has been made; the file has been closed.

Long, involved clauses.   Use a semicolon to separate long, involved clauses.

> A low rate of interest usually reflects easy conditions and a rather inactive industrial situation; a high rate indicates money stringency and industrial activity.

Punctuated clauses.   Use a semicolon to separate clauses that are punctuated by commas.

> On the other hand, if the turnover is low in comparison with the normal figure, it shows just the opposite; that is, it indicates weaker sales policy, and poorer purchasing ability and stock control than the average.

Series.   In enumerations use semicolons to separate the items unless they are short and simple; also, to separate items that contain commas. (See the use of a comma in a series, page 379.)

> The three classes of long bills are (1) bills drawn in ordinary business operations; (2) long bills arising from the making of foreign loans; (3) finance bills.
>
> The most important of these services are published by Moody's Investors Service, Inc.; Standard & Poor's Corporation; and Fitch Publishing Co., Inc.

Before a conjunctive adverb.   Use a semicolon before an adverb that serves the purpose of a conjunction. The conjunctive adverbs are *accordingly, also, besides, consequently, furthermore, hence, however, indeed, likewise, moreover, nevertheless, otherwise, similarly, so, still, therefore, thus.*

The trend is to omit the comma after a conjunctive adverb preceded by a semicolon. In the following examples the commas in brackets are not only unnecessary but are unwanted:

> He telephoned that he did not plan to leave until next week; therefore [,] I did not consider it necessary to send the report to him by airmail.
>
> He told his secretary he did not wish to be disturbed; consequently [,] she did not announce the chairman of the board, whom she did not recognize.
>
> He will attend the meeting; indeed [,] he will be the main speaker at the meeting.

Quotation marks and semicolon.   Place the semicolon *outside* quotation marks.

Parentheses and semicolon.   Use a semicolon after a closing parenthesis if the construction of the sentence requires a semicolon. Never use a comma or semicolon before a parenthesis or an expression enclosed in parentheses.

COLON—
ITS FOUR IMPORTANT USES

Introduction to lists, tabulations. The most frequent use of the colon is after a word, phrase, or sentence that introduces lists, a series, tabulations, extracts, texts, and explanations that are in apposition to the introductory words.

> The following is an extract from the report:
> These conditions must exist:

But do not use a colon to introduce a series of items that are the direct objects of a preposition or verb or that follow a form of the verb *to be*.

> *Wrong:* The requirements of a good secretary *are:* ability to take rapid dictation and to transcribe it rapidly and accurately; ability to spell correctly and to use the dictionary to the best advantage; familiarity with . . . [Omit the colon.]
>
> *Note:* A colon may precede a formal tabulation even when the tabulated words or phrases are the objects of a preposition or verb or follow a form of the verb *to be:*
> The requirements of a good secretary are:
>> Ability to take rapid dictation and to transcribe it rapidly
>> Ability to spell correctly and to use the dictionary to the best advantage
>> Familiarity with . . .

Time. Use a colon to indicate clock time.

4:15 a.m.   9:30 p.m.

Footnotes. When reference is made to a publication in a footnote, use a colon to separate the name of the city and state of publication from the name of the publisher.

> Gavin A. Pitt, *The Twenty Minute Lifetime* (Englewood Cliffs, N.J.: Prentice-Hall, Inc., 19___), p. 20.

Bible references. Use a colon to separate the verse and chapter in biblical references.

Matthew 10:4.

Dash and colon.   Do not use a dash with a colon.

DASH—
A USEFUL SUBSTITUTE

Principal use.   The dash is used principally to set off explanatory or parenthetical clauses, to indicate abrupt changes in the continuity of expression, and to set off a thought that is repeated for emphasis.

Series.   A dash may be used before or after a clause that summarizes a series of words or phrases, but a colon is more common *after* such a clause.

> Wage and Hour, Arbitration, Union Contracts—these are only a few of the services in our Complete Labor Equipment.
> Our Complete Labor Equipment includes six services: Wage and Hour, Employee Relations, Union Contracts, Labor Relations, State Labor Law, and Pension and Profit Sharing.

Dash and other punctuation marks.   A dash may be used after an abbreviating period. If the material set off by dashes requires an interrogation or exclamation point, retain the punctuation before the second dash. Do not use a dash with a comma or semicolon. Do not use a dash and colon together before a list of items.

> The check is now O.K.—he made a large deposit.
> The head of the personnel department—is his name Donovan or O'Donovan?—said he thought there would be an opening next week.

EXCLAMATION POINT—
A STRANGER IN THE SECRETARY'S WORK

Exclamatory sentences.   Place an exclamation point after a startling statement or a sentence expressing strong emotion.

> How incredible that he should take that attitude!

Exclamatory words.   Place an exclamation point after exclamatory words.

> Great!

For emphasis.   If not used to excess, an exclamation point is a good device to lend emphasis or to drive home a point. It is used more frequently in sales letters than in any other business correspondence.

> Buy now!
> And over 100 forms!

INTERROGATION POINT—
A QUESTION

Interrogative sentences.   Place a question mark after a direct question but not after an indirect question.

> Have you heard the decision that was made at the conference? [Direct]
> Mr. Rogers asked me, "When will the book be ready for publication?" [Direct]
> Mr. Rogers asked me when the book would be ready for publication. [Indirect]

Requests.   Do not place a question mark after a question that is a request to which no answer is expected.

> Will you please return the signed copy as soon as possible.

Queries.   A question mark enclosed in parentheses may be used to query the accuracy of a fact or figure. Other punctuation is not affected by this use of the question mark.

> The treaty was signed September 5 (?), 1945.

Series of questions.   A question mark is usually placed after each question in a series included within one sentence, and each question usually begins with a capital.

> What will be the significance of man's landing on the moon if man still cannot get along with his fellow man? If man's cultural endeavors have been sacrificed? If world peace is still unstable?

But the question mark may be omitted in a series of questions in a construction like the one in the following example.

> Who is responsible for (a) copyreading the book, (b) the artwork, (c) the production schedule?

Quotation marks with question marks.   *See* **Placement of quotation marks.**

**QUOTATION MARKS—
HOW TO USE THEM**

Direct quotations.   Enclose the exact words of a speaker or writer in quotation marks, but do not enclose words that are not quoted exactly. The quoted material may be a word or several paragraphs in length.

> On the 15th he wrote, "Please consider the contract canceled if the goods are not shipped by the tenth of next month."
> On the 15th he wrote that we should consider the contract canceled if the goods were not shipped by the tenth of next month.
> He wrote that he was "no longer interested" in the proposition.

But do not use quotation marks when the name of the speaker or writer immediately precedes the quoted material or in question-and-answer material.

> Mr. Edwards: In my opinion the machine is worthless.
> Mr. Roberts: Upon what do you base that opinion?

Paragraphs.   When quoted material is more than one paragraph in length, place quotation marks at the beginning of each paragraph but only at the close of the last paragraph.

Definitions.   Use quotation marks to enclose a word or phrase that is accompanied by its definition. (In print, the word would be italicized.)

> The party against whom garnishment proceedings are brought is called the "garnishee."
> "Bankruptcy insolvency" means that a debtor's total assets are less than his total liabilities.

Unique words or trade terms.   Use quotation marks to enclose a word or phrase the first time the term is used in an unusual sense or with a special trade meaning. It is not desirable to use the quotation marks when the term is repeated.

> This "pyramiding" was carried to an extreme in the public utility field.

In "spot" markets, commodities are bought and sold in specific lots and grades with a definite delivery date specified.

Titles and names.   Use quotation marks to enclose the titles of:

Articles
Books, chapters, or parts of books
Brochures, pamphlets
Operas
Paintings
Plays, motion pictures, sketches
Poems
Songs
Television and radio shows

Note: In letters or advertising material, the title of a book may appear in all capitals for emphasis. In printed material, the titles of books, brochures and pamphlets, operas, paintings, plays and motion pictures, and long poems are usually italicized; therefore, in preparing material for the printer, underline these names.

But do not use quotation marks with:

Names of periodicals and well-known publications, such as Who's Who and dictionaries
The Bible or names of its books or other parts of it
Movements of a symphony, concerto, or other compositions, or names of numbered compositions.

Single quotation marks.   Use single quotation marks to enclose a quotation within a quotation.

Last week he wrote, "It is understood that delivery 'must be made on or before the 30th.' "

Placement of quotation marks.   Always place a period or comma inside quotation marks.

The account was marked "paid," but he never received a receipt.
The check was marked "canceled."
Many thanks for sending me a copy of Dr. Jones's book, "The Trade of Nations."

Always place colons and semicolons outside quotation marks.

Turn to the chapter entitled "Consideration for Stock"; the reference is in the first paragraph.

Interrogation and exclamation points come before or after the quotation marks, depending upon the meaning of the text.

Who is the author of "Up the Down Staircase"? [The entire question is not quoted.]

He shouted, "I will never consent to those terms!" [The exclamation is part of the quotation.]

APOSTROPHE— ITS FIVE PRINCIPAL USES

Possessives. Use the apostrophe to indicate the possessive case of nouns. Do *not* use the apostrophe to indicate the possessive case of personal pronouns. (*See also* **Possessives**, chapter 14.)

John's   Davis's   its

Contractions. Use the apostrophe to denote a contraction or omission of letters. Place the apostrophe where the letter or letters are omitted.

it's for *it is*
haven't for *have not*
ass'n for *association*
class of *'64*

But omit the apostrophe in contractions formed by dropping the first letters of a word if the contraction has come into common usage.

phone   plane   though

Letters and symbols. Use the apostrophe to form the plurals of letters and symbols. (*See also* **Figures, letters,** page 360.)

p's and q's   5's   #'s

Words. Use an apostrophe to indicate the plural of a word referred to *as a word*, without regard to its meaning, but use the regularly formed plural if a meaning is attached to the word.

There are three *but's* in the sentence.
The *years* have it.
There are eight *threes* in twenty-four.
There are eight *three's* in the sentence.

Abbreviations.   Use an apostrophe to denote the plural or some other form of an abbreviation. (See also *Figures, letters,* page 360.)

three O.K.'s   O.K.'d   V.I.P.'s

HYPHEN—
A USEFUL AID

Division of words.   Use a hyphen at the end of a line to show that part of a word has been carried over to another line. See chapter 15 for the principles governing the division of words at the end of a line.

Compound terms.   Use a hyphen as a connecting link in compound terms. (*See* **Compound Terms,** chapter 14.)

Series of hyphenated words.   In a series of hyphenated words having a common base, place a hyphen after the first element of each word and write the base after the last word only.

fourth-, fifth-, or sixth-grade pupils

Time.   Use a hyphen to indicate a span of time.

The report covers the fiscal year 1976-77.

PARENTHESES OR BRACKETS—
WHEN TO USE THEM

Brackets.   If your typewriter has a bracket key, use brackets to enclose comments or explanations, to rectify mistakes or quoted material, and to enclose parentheses within parentheses; otherwise, use parentheses for these purposes. If necessary, brackets can be made by using the short diagonal (virgule) and dash keys.

Explanatory expressions.   Use parentheses to enclose parenthetical or explanatory expressions that are outside the general structure of the sentence. Parentheses indicate a stronger separation than do commas or dashes.

The place at which an incorporators' meeting (sometimes called the first meeting of the stockholders) is to be held is determined by statute in most states.

Figures.   Enclose a figure in parentheses when it follows an amount that has been written out in words, and when the American equivalent of foreign currency is given.

> Under the will he received £100,000 ($280,000).
> seven thousand five hundred (7,500) dollars
> seven thousand five hundred dollars ($7,500)
>
> *Note:* If the figure is written before the word "dollars," do not use the dollar sign; if the figure is written after the word "dollars," use the dollar sign. This rule also applies to the percent sign.

Questions and answers.   In testimony (question-and-answer material), use parentheses to enclose matter describing an action and, also, to indicate a person who has not previously taken part in the questions and answers.

> Q. (By Mr. Smith) Will you identify this handkerchief? (handing the witness a handkerchief).

Enumerations.   Enclose in parentheses letters or numbers in enumerations run into the text.

> Stock may be divided broadly into two kinds: (1) common stock and (2) preferred stock.

Single (closing) parentheses.   Parentheses are usually used in pairs, but a single closing parenthesis may be used instead of a period to follow a letter or roman numeral in outlines.

Punctuation in parentheses.   Commas, periods, and similar punctuation marks belong within the parentheses if they belong to the parenthetical clause or phrase. They are outside the parentheses if they belong to the words of the rest of the sentence. *See also* **Periods and parentheses** on page 380.

> The boy ran as if a ghost (and, indeed, he may have been right) were following him.
> He reported the action at once. (He has a strong sense of civic responsibility.)
> He turned in a perfect examination paper. (What an example for the rest of the class!)

LEADERS AND ELLIPSES—
INVALUABLE AIDS

Leaders are a row of dots (periods) or short lines (hyphens) to lead the eye across a space in the line of writing to a related figure or words. Their principal use is in statements of account or other tabulations.

Ellipses—How to Use Punctuation Marks to Show Omission. An ellipsis is the omission from a sentence of a word or words that would clarify the construction of the sentence.

Ellipses are the marks used to show an omission from a sentence of a word or words that would complete the construction. The marks may be dots (periods) or asterisks. When you are quoting and want to omit words, use three consecutive asterisks (***) or dots (. . .) to indicate an omission of words. If a period would ordinarily follow the words omitted, you will then have three dots followed by a period (. . . .).

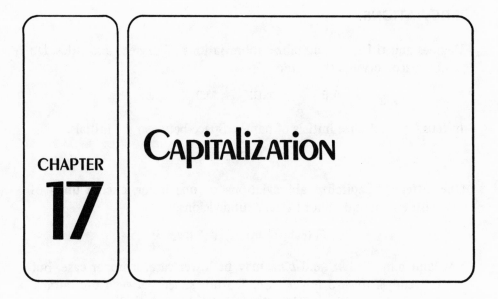

CHAPTER

17

Capitalization

Almost all publications have adopted rules and principles of capitalization appropriate to their special fields and audiences. As a result, the authorities differ widely on the correct usages of capitalization. The trend, however, is toward a more general use of lower-case letters. The rules and principles of capitalization given in this chapter are appropriate for business correspondence and reports.

ABBREVIATIONS

Degrees and titles.   Capitalize abbreviations of degrees and titles. Do not space between the letters.

A.B.   Ph.D.   M.P.   Jr.

Initials.   Capitalize initials of names. Space between the initials.

R. D. Ellis

One letter.   Capitalize abbreviations of one letter, except units of measurement and minor literary subdivisions.

F. (Fahrenheit)   p. 3 (page 3)

a.m. and p.m.   *a.m.* and *p.m.* may be lower case or upper case, but the trend is toward *lower* case. Do not space between the initials. The abbreviation for *meridies* (noon) should be capitalized because it is one initial—*M.* Do not use these abbreviations when the hour is written out, but write *four o'clock in the afternoon* or *three o'clock,* not *three p.m.*

Common abbreviations.   Many common abbreviations may be lower case or upper case, but the trend is toward lower case. Do not space between the letters. (See list of abbreviations in chapter 18).

C.O.D. *or* c.o.d.   F.O.B. *or* f.o.b.   n.b. *or* N.B.

ACTS, BILLS, CODES, AND LAWS

Official title.   Capitalize the official title of specific acts, bills, codes and laws; also capitalize the accepted title by which the law generally known.

Securities Exchange Act
Civil Rights Bill
the National Labor Relations Act

But lower case *bill* or *law* when used with the sponsor's name unless the formal title of the bill is given.

the Thomas bill
the Thomas wage-hour bill

General descriptive terms. Lower case *bill* and *act* when they are standing alone; also abbreviated titles and general descriptive terms designating them.

the securities act
the rent-control bill
the wage-hour bill

Federal, state, and municipal codes. Lower case federal, state, and municipal codes, *but* capitalize the formal title of codes of law.

building code
Code of Criminal Procedure
Code Napoléon

Constitution. Capitalize *constitution* when it refers to the specific constitution of a country or state, *but* lower case it as a general term.

the Constitution (of the United States)
the Constitution of New Jersey
the constitution of a democracy

Amendments to the Constitution. Capitalize amendments to the Constitution when they are referred to by number or by full title, *but* lower case when they are used as general terms or as parts of general descriptive titles.

Eighteenth Amendment
prohibition amendment
Child Labor Amendment
constitutional amendment

AMOUNTS OF MONEY

Checks. In writing checks the amount of money is always written out with each word capitalized.

Legal documents. To ensure accuracy, in legal documents spell out amounts of money and capitalize each word in the amount. For example, Eight Hundred Twenty-Five Dollars ($825).

ARMED SERVICES

Names. Capitalize names of military services, *but* lower case words such as *army* and *navy* when they stand alone, are used collectively in the plural, or are not part of an official title.

United States Army (the army; the armed forces)
United States Navy (the navy)
United States Signal Corps; Signal Corps

United States Marines (the marines)
Red Army (Russian army)

Branches, divisions. Capitalize titles of various branches or divisions.

First Division
Third Army
Company A

Navy Militia
Second Battalion
National Guard

Titles. Capitalize titles of distinction that refer to a specific person, whether the title is standing alone or is followed by a proper name. Lower case other military and naval titles when they are standing alone and are not followed by a proper name.

Chief of Staff
General of the Army; the general
Admiral of the Fleet; the admiral
Admiral Rogers; the admiral
Captain Smith; the captain

the Adjutant General
the Judge Advocate General
the Paymaster General
Commander Roberts; the commander

COURTS AND JUDGES

Full title. Captialize the full title of a court, *but* lower case *court* when it is standing alone or when it is used in a general descriptive sense. Always capitalize references to the Supreme Court, even when the word *Court* is standing alone.

in the federal courts
Judge Mason's court
Supreme Court; the Court
Court of Appeals of New York

a court of appeals
General Sessions
Magistrate's Court
Night Court

Judges, justices. Capitalize titles when they precede a proper name, *but* lower case *chief justice, associate justice, justice, judge, magistrate, surrogate,* and so on when they stand alone, unless they are used in place of a proper name.

> The letter is addressed to *Magistrate* Williams.
> She was appointed *associate justice* of the . . . .
> The *Judge* will reply to your letter as soon as he returns.
> He was elected *surrogate* by a large majority.

Reference to the judge.   Capitalize *court* when it refers directly to the judge or presiding officer.

> The *Court* overruled the objection.
> In the opinion of the *Court.* . . .

Capitalize *Your Honor, His* (or *Her*) *Honor,* when they refer to the Court.

Bar, bench.   Capitalize *bar* and *bench* when they are part of a judicial body, *but* lower case in all other instances.

> American Bar Association;
>   the bar
> Court of King's Bench;
>   the bench

EDUCATION

Names of schools.   Capitalize the names of schools or colleges and their departments, *but* lower case *school, college,* and *department* when they are not part of a name.

Washington Irving High School;
    high school
	Department of Natural History;
	    the history department

Dartmouth; university	College of Liberal Arts;
Public School No. 1; public school	college
	School of Business Administration; business school

Classes.   Capitalize the names of classes of a high school, college, or university, *but* lower case the word when it refers to a member of a class.

> Freshman Class; a freshman
> Sophomore Class; a sophomore
> Junior Class; a junior
> Senior Class; a senior

Degrees, chairmanships.   Capitalize academic degrees, scholastic honors, chairmanships, fellowships, and the like, whether abbreviated or written in full, if the full name is given. Lower case these words when they are not part of a name or title.

> John Smith, Doctor of Philosophy
> John Smith, LL.D.
> degree of Doctor of Laws *or* degree of doctor of laws
> Master of Arts
> Robert Brown Fellowship

Courses, subjects.   Capitalize the names of courses, *but* capitalize the names of subjects only when they are derived from proper names.

> Education II
> Modern History
> I am studying history, Latin, and English.

ENUMERATIONS

Preceded by a colon.   Capitalize the first word in each section of an enumeration that has been formally introduced if the enumerations are in a complete sentence. Lower case brief items that do not make sentences, unless they are itemized.

> A secretary uses the guide under these circumstances: (1) Someone outside the immediate office wants the material. (2) The manager expects to take the material out of the office. (3) The secretary expects . . . .
> She listed the following as her qualifications for the position: (1) initiative, (2) intelligence, (3) tact, (4) . . . .
> Her qualifications for the position are:
>   1. Initiative
>   2. Intelligence
>   3. Tact
>   4. . . . .

Not preceded by a colon.   Lower case enumerations that are not preceded by a colon.

The disadvantage is offset to some extent by (1) the limited liability of shareholders, (2) the marketability of ownership in the company, (3) the continuous . . . .

GEOGRAPHICAL TERMS

Points of compass.   Capitalize names of points of the compass when they refer to a section of the United States, *but* lower case when they denote simple direction or compass points.

the South;	the East;
south of here	toward the east
the Northwest;	traveling in the West;
northwest	a west window

Popular names.   Capitalize popular names of specific localities.

Corn Belt, Cotton Belt
East Side, West Side
the Delta
the Loop (Chicago)
Mississippi Valley (but valley of the Mississippi)
the Continent (continental Europe)

But lower case *ghetto, fatherland.*

Regional terms.   Capitalize regional terms that are part of a precise descriptive title, *but* lower case terms that are merely localizing adjectives.

the Eastern Shore
the South Shore
South Jersey (definite regional term)
northern China (localizing adjective)
western New York (localizing adjective)

Coast.   Capitalize *coast* when it designates a specific locality or stands alone, *but* lower case when it is used with geographic designations.

the Coast (West Coast, U.S.)	Pacific Coast (U.S.)	Gulf Coast (U.S.)
	Jersey coast	East Coast (U.S.)
New England coast		

Divisions of world or country. Capitalize divisions of the world or of a country.

the Old World, the New World   Middle Atlantic states
Far East, Near East   Mountain states
New England states   Orient, Occident

But capitalize *oriental* and *occidental* only when they refer to a person.

He is an *Oriental* with *occidental* manners.

GOVERNMENTAL AND POLITICAL TERMS

Government, administration. Capitalize *government* and *administration* when they are part of a title; otherwise, lower case.

Her Majesty's Government . . . .
The government announces that it is trying to find a solution. . . .
The administration is pushing its legislative program.
The policies of a government that. . . .
Certain government dignitaries. . . .
The government of Tennessee is efficiently administered.

Federal. Capitalize *federal* when it is part of a title and when it identifies a specific government. When *federal* is used as an adjective referring to institutions or activities of the federal government, you may use either lower or upper case (lower case is preferable). Always use lower case when *federal* is used as a general term.

Federal Register (title of publication)
. . . efforts made by the federal government
the federal courts (institution of the government)
the federal principle of government (general)

National. Capitalize *national* when it precedes a capitalized word or when it is part of a title. Lower case when it is used as a general descriptive term. Also lower case *nationals,* meaning the citizens of a country, but capitalize if it refers to a political party. (The word *party* is not capitalized.)

the National Socialist party
national customs

State.   1. Capitalize *state* (or *commonwealth*) when it is part of and follows a name; otherwise, lower case.

New York State
state of Oregon
Commonwealth of Massachusetts
The constitution of a state must not conflict with the Constitution of the
    United States.
The question of states' rights is paramount to many voters.
Our state intervened in the case.

City.   Capitalize *city* when it is part of a name, *but* lower case when it is used in transposed form or when it stands alone.

New York City
city of New York
city of New Orleans
The city is represented by. . . .

County.   Capitalize *county* when it is part of a name, *but* lower case when it is used in transposed form or when standing alone.

Westchester County
county of Richmond
The county is represented by. . . .

District.   Capitalize *district* when it is part of a name, *but* lower case when it is used as a general term or when standing alone.

District of Columbia
Second Congressional District
a congressional district
Third Assembly District

Ward, precinct.   Capitalize *ward* and *precinct* when they are part of a name, *but* lower case when they stand alone.

Third Ward   Fifth Precinct   Ward 4   this precinct

Departments, boards, committees, etc.   Capitalize the full title of governmental departments, boards, committees, commissions, bureaus, and so on, *but* lower case *department, board, committee, commission, bureau,* and the rest when they are used alone in place of the full name.

Police Department	the department
Department of Justice	the bureau
Bureau of Standards	the council
Council Finance Committee	the committee
Foreign Affairs Committee	

Names of legislative bodies.   Capitalize the names of legislative, administrative, and deliberative bodies, both domestic and foreign.

Congress	Board of Estimate
House	House of Lords
Senate (U.S.)	Diet
	City Council

Lower case general or incomplete designations of legislative bodies.

the lower house
state senate (no specific state)
a senate
the national assembly

Legislature.   Capitalize *legislature* when it is part of the name of a specific body. Unless the exact designation is used, there is no need to capitalize *legislature* when it is used with the name of a state.

the Legislature of the U.S.
a legislature
Mississippi Legislature
Arkansas legislature (the exact designation
    is Arkansas General Assembly)

HEADINGS AND TITLES

General rule.   The general rule is to capitalize all important words (nouns, pronouns, verbs, adjectives, adverbs) in headings and titles of books, articles, lectures, reports, and the like, and to lower case articles, conjunctions, and prepositions. (See chapter 3 for the preferred style of writing headings of reports.)

Way of a Gaucho
Valuable Aids in Letter Writing
Selecting and Operating a Business of Your Own
This Is the Way It Was

Infinitives.   The *to* in an infinitive may be capitalized but lower case is preferable.

> How to Build a Better Vocabulary
> How to Establish and Operate a Retail Store

Prepositions.   Prepositions of five or more letters may be capitalized.

> Let's Talk *About* Children

Prepositions that are connected with the preceding verb are usually capitalized.

> Problems *Calling For* Immediate Solution

Break in title.   Articles, prepositions, and conjunctions that immediately follow a marked break in a title, indicated by a colon or dash, are usually capitalized.

> Pick Your Job—And Like It
> Television: The Eyes of Tomorrow

HISTORICAL TERMS

Eras.   Capitalize designations of eras of history and periods in the history of a language or literature.

Dark Ages	Stone Age
Middle Ages	the Exile
Renaissance (*but* lower case in its	the Diaspora
general meaning, such as a	Medieval Latin
renaissance of poetry)	Elizabethan Age
Christian Era	Roaring Twenties

But lower case informal adjectives in such phrases as *early Victorian,* also *twentieth century.*

Important events.   Capitalize the names of important events.

> Missouri Compromise
> World War II
> Peace of Utrecht
> Battle of the Bulge

But lower case *war* unless it is part of the name of a war.

Documents.   Capitalize the names of important historical documents.

> Magna Carta
> Declaration of Independence
> Atlantic Charter

HOLIDAYS, SEASONS, AND FEAST DAYS

Religious.   Capitalize religious holidays and feast days.

> Christmas   Passover
> Christmas Eve   Easter Sunday
> New Year's Eve

Secular.   Capitalize secular and especially designated days and weeks.

> Thanksgiving Day   Memorial Day
> Inauguration Day   Clean-Up Week

But lower case *election day, primary day.*

Seasons.   Lower case names of seasons, unless they are personified.

> autumn
> spring
> summer
> midwinter
> Spring, with her arms full of flowers . . . .

HYPHENATED COMPOUNDS

The capitalization of hyphenated compounds varies among authorities. The style indicated here is favored for use by the secretary. Whatever style you adopt, *be consistent.*

General rule.   Capitalize the parts of a hyphenated word that would be capitalized if the word were not hyphenated.

> No-par stock can be. . . . [first word in a sentence]
> the English-speaking nations
> of Anglo-Saxon descent
> ex-President Johnson

Titles and headings.   Capitalize all parts of hyphenated words in titles and headings, except: (1) when considered as one word; and (2) compound numerals.

> Labor Speed-Up Declining
> Conference of Ex-Senators

Compound numerals.   Lower case the second part of a compound numeral, even in titles and headings.

> Eighty-first Congress Convenes
> One-fifth of Students on Strike
> 261 Sixty-second Street

When considered as one word.   Lower case the second part of a hyphenated word that is considered one word, even in titles and headings.

> Co-author   Anti-inflation   Self-defense

ORGANIZATIONS AND INSTITUTIONS

Official names or titles.   Capitalize the official names of organizations and institutions.

> Young Men's Christian Association
> Prentice-Hall, Inc.
> Ohio University
> Metropolitan Opera
> Independent Order of Odd Fellows; an Odd Fellow
> Southern Railroad

But lower case the common noun when it is used in the plural with two or more names.

> Ohio and Chicago universities
> Southern and Pennsylvania railroads

Terms not part of name or title.   Lower case terms referring to organizations or institutions if those terms are not part of a specific name or title, even when the terms stand for specific organizations or institutions.

parent-teacher associations
chambers of commerce
the chamber of commerce
the railroad
the opera
the company

But in formal writings, such as contracts, capitalize the term that stands for a specific organization or institution.

Pursuant to a resolution of its Board of Directors . . . XYZ Corporation, a corporation duly organized. . . hereinafter called the Corporation, has adopted. . . .

PERSONAL TITLES

General rule.   The general rule is to capitalize all titles or designations preceding names, but to lower case titles following names or used instead of names.

District Attorney Bell
Nurse Smith
the governor
the captain
Mr. Nelson, president of NAM

President.   Capitalize *president* when it precedes a name; otherwise lower case.

President Lincoln will be remembered for . . . .
The president appointed Mr. Fortas to the Supreme Court.
The office of president is a grave responsibility as well as a great honor.
He was elected to the presidency by an overwhelming majority.

National government officials.   Capitalize titles of cabinet members, heads of departments, and government dignitaries when the titles are used with names. The *Speaker* (of the House) is usually capitalized, even when used alone, to avoid ambiguity.

chief justice
ambassador
acting secretary of defense
representative
Speaker (of the House)
senator
under secretary of state

State or municipal officials.   Capitalize the titles of *governor, chief* *executive* (of a state), *lieutenant governor, mayor, borough president,* president of any municipal body, and the like when they are used with proper names. Lower case these titles when they are used as general terms without reference to a specific office or official.

> The policies of Governor Grasso. . . .
> The lieutenant governor is acting in the governor's absence.
> The Republicans nominated him for mayor.
> Mr. Rogers, president of the Board of Aldermen, . . .
> A governor should consider carefully the qualifications of his appointees.

Capitalize the titles of *senator* (state), *assemblyman, alderman,* and the like when they precede names. Lower case when they follow names or are used as general terms.

Capitalize titles of heads of state and city departments, such as *police commissioner, city counsel, commissioner of education, attorney general, sheriff,* and subordinate titles, such as *deputy sheriff, assistant attorney general,* when they precede names. Lower case when they follow a name or stand alone.

> Commissioner Edwards said. . . .
> The assistant attorney general said. . .
> Mr. Lewis, the sheriff, said. . . .

Business and professional titles. Capitalize business and professional titles when they precede a name. Lower case when they follow a name or when they are used instead of the name of a specific office or official.

> the professor
> the doctor
> the president (of XYZ company)
> Edgar Robbins, secretary of XYZ Company

In formal writings, such as contracts and minutes of meetings, titles referring to a specific officer of a specific company or organization may be lower or upper case, but in such writings you must capitalize *company, corporation,* and the like.

Honor or nobility. Capitalize all titles of honor or nobility when preceding a name. Some British titles are also capitalized when used without a personal name. Lower case in all other instances.

Queen Elizabeth
the queen of England
the Duke of York
Princess Royal

the pope
His Excellency
Your Grace

Acting, Under, Assistant.   Capitalize *acting* and *under* when they are part of a capitalized title that precedes a name. Titles that are subordinated by the word *assistant* are not capitalized, except when they precede names.

Acting Secretary of State Brown
Under Secretary of State Brown
the assistant secretary of state

Words in apposition.   When a common noun precedes a name but is separated from it by a comma, the noun does not have the force of a title and is not capitalized.

the secretary, John Smith

Compound titles.   Capitalize all parts of a compound title if any part is capitalized.

Lists of names.   In formal lists, titles and descriptive designations immediately following the names should be capitalized.

POLITICAL PARTIES, FACTIONS, ALLIANCES

Names.   Capitalize names of political parties, factions, and alliances. Do not capitalize *party*.

Democratic party
Democrat(s)
Rightists, Leftists
Socialist

Left Wing, Right Wing (as the
titles of political parties, *but
left wing* of the CIO; *right
wing* of the Democratic party)

Words derived from names.   Lower case words derived from the names of political parties, factions, and alliances.

communism   socialistic   democratic

PROPER NOUNS
AND ADJECTIVES

Names.   Capitalize the names of particular persons, places, and things (proper nouns) and adjectives derived from them.

Common nouns used in names.   Capitalize common nouns and adjectives used in proper names.

the Liberty Bell

Words derived from proper nouns.   Lower case words derived from the proper nouns that have developed a specialized meaning through use.

anglicize	roman (type), *but* Roman numerals
japan (varnish)	bohemian
italicize	manila (envelopes)

Epithets.   Capitalize common nouns and epithets used with, or as substitutes for, proper names.

the Canal (for the Panama Canal)	Peter the Great
the First Lady	Richard Coeur de Lion

QUOTATIONS

Direct quotation.   Capitalize the first word of an *exactly* quoted passage if it is a complete sentence, *but* lower case quoted parts that do not form a complete sentence.

In his report the president said, "A member will not be permitted to remain in service after the normal retirement date without the special consent of the company."

In his report the president said that employees who reach retirement age cannot remain in service without the "special consent of the company."

What did he mean by calling my action "reprehensible"?

Indirect quotation.   Do not capitalize indirect quotations.

In his report the president said that employees will not be permitted to remain in service. . . .

Broken quotation. Do not capitalize the second part of a broken quotation, unless it is a complete sentence.

> "If the order is not received by the first," he wrote, "we will be compelled to cancel it."
> "If the order is not received by the first, we will be compelled to cancel it," he wrote. "We cannot sell the goods after that date."

RELIGIOUS TERMS

Church. Capitalize *church* when it is part of the name of an edifice.

> Central Presbyterian Church
> the Catholic church
> The Methodist church is on Main Street.
> The First Methodist Church is on Main Street.

Church dignitaries. Capitalize the title of a church dignitary when it is used with a name. Lower case in other instances.

> the Reverend John Smith
> the pope
> the mother superior
> Cardinal Spellman
> moderator
> the rabbi
> Father Williams
> I discussed the matter with the deacon.
> The point is, Deacon Jones, that we should. . . .

Deity. Capitalize all names and appellations of the one supreme God and of other deities (e.g. Greek gods). Capitalize the personal pronouns *He, His, Him, Thee, Thou,* and so on when they refer to the Deity only in cases where capitalization avoids ambiguity. Do not capitalize the relative pronouns *who, whom.*

Bible. Capitalize all names for the Bible and other sacred books, whether Christian or not; also capitalize books and versions of the Bible. Do not underscore or use quotation marks.

Denominations. Capitalize the names of all religious denominations.

SPORTS AND GAMES

College colors.   Capitalize *gold, maroon, crimson,* and the like when they designate teams and refer to college colors.

The Crimson Tide triumphed over the Black and Gold.

Games and sports.   Lower case the names of sports and games, except when the names derive from proper names or are trade names.

football (but Rugby)   bridge   Monopoly   going to Jerusalem

Playing fields.   Capitalize the names of playing fields and stadiums.

Yankee Stadium   Madison Square Garden   the Garden   the Bowl

Cups, stakes.   Lower case *cup, stakes, trophy,* and the like when they stand alone and are not part of a specific title.

Belmont Stakes   the Davis Cup   the trophy

MISCELLANEOUS

Foreign names.   Usually articles, prepositions, and conjunctions (such as *du, de, la, le, von, van*) that constitute a part of foreign names are not capitalized unless the name is written without the given name or a title. However, some people with foreign names prefer capitals.

E. I. du Pont de Nemours
Van Wort, the author, is. . . .
Martin Van Buren (preferred spelling)
Ludwig van Beethoven
Dr. de la Bonne

Leagues, treaties, pacts, plans.   Capitalize the names of bodies, except adjectives derived from them or incomplete designations.

United Nations
General Assembly; the assembly
Security Council; the council
the Secretariat
the secretary general (and other similar titles)

Capitalize *treaty* and *pact* or *plan* only when part of a specific title.

the Treaty of Versailles	Nine-power treaty
Versailles treaty	the Marshall Plan
treaty at Versailles	Pact of Paris

Music, drama, paintings.   Capitalize the principal words in titles of plays, hymns, songs, paintings, and the like. Lower case movements of a symphony, concerto, or other musical composition.

Beethoven's Fifth Symphony

Lower case *trio, quartet, quintet,* and so on when they refer to compositions, but capitalize them when they are used in the name of performers.

Alabama Quartet

Nouns with numbers or letters.   Nouns or abbreviations used with numbers or letters in a title are capitalized.

Act IV	Grade 3
Article III	Division IV
Class B	Room 6
	Precinct 4

Peoples, race, and tribes.   Capitalize the names of peoples, races and tribes.

Roman	Aryan
Caucasian	Negroes
Jew, Jewish	Malay

But lower case terms that refer to color or localized designations.

white men   bushmen   black children

Personification.   Personification gives some attribute of a human being to inanimate objects, abstract ideas, or general terms. Capitalize the thing personified when emphasis is desired.

The meeting was called to order by the Chair.
"Low Spirits are my true and faithful companions...." [Thomas Gray]
but   trees whisper   waves roar   winds moan

Planets.   Capitalize the names of the planets and imaginative designations of celestial objects.

> Saturn   Leo   Mars   Milky Way   Big Dipper

But lower case *stars, earth, moon, sun,* unless they are used in connection with other planets that are always capitalized.

> A scientific treatise on the relation of Mars to the Earth. . . .

Poetry.   Capitalize the first word in every line of poetry.

> I bridle in my struggling Muse in vain,
> That seeks to launch into a nobler strain. [Pope]

But some modern poetry is not capitalized in the traditional style. In cases of irregularity, follow copy.

Resolutions.   In resolutions, write every letter in WHEREAS and RESOLVED in capitals; begin *That* with a capital.

Series of questions.   When a series of questions is included in one sentence, each question usually begins with a capital.

> What must a secretary do to advance herself? Should she have a college education? Should she take evening courses? What subjects should she study?

Trade names.   Always capitalize trade names and spell and punctuate them as the manufacturer does.

> Teletype   Kleenex   Coca-Cola   "Q-Tips" Cotton Swabs

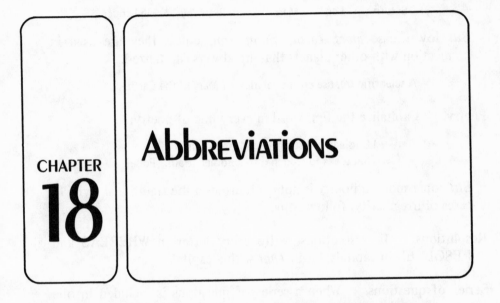

CHAPTER 18

Abbreviations

Abbreviations are used to save space. In ordinary text or in the body of letters, abbreviations are rarely used; this includes abbreviations such as *etc.*, *e.g.*, and *i.e.* However, in texts of technical and legal publications and in footnotes, tables, and bibliographies, many words are commonly abbreviated. Abbreviations are also common in orders, invoices, and shipping instructions.

There is no total agreement among authorities on spelling, capitalization, and punctuation of abbreviations. The important thing, therefore, is to be consistent in use. For instance, both *a.a.r.* and *AAR* are acceptable abbreviations for "against all risks," but only one should be selected and used.

The list presented here is for reference when you do not know a standard abbreviation and when you come across an abbreviation that you cannot interpret. It includes the abbreviations commonly used in an office; there are many other technical abbreviations peculiar to special fields. The list includes only a few of the numerous federal departments, agencies, and bureaus. You can get an alphabetical list of these from the U.S. Government Printing Office, Washington, DC.

The list is arranged alphabetically according to the abbreviation; therefore, if a word has more than one abbreviation, each is listed in its proper alphabetical sequence.

In addition to the general list, other lists of abbreviations are given as indicated:

Abbreviations of academic degrees (page 425).
Abbreviations of months and days (page 425).
Abbreviations of organizations (page 427).
A list of Postal Service abbreviations appears in chapter 5, (page 132).

GENERAL ABBREVIATIONS

A

@ .... at (referring to price)
a .... ampere (*see* amp.)
A-1 .... first-class
a.a. .... author's alterations (printing)
a.a.r., AAR .... against all risks
abst. .... abstract
AC, A.C., a.c. .... alternating current
a/c .... account
A/C .... account current
accum. .... accumulative
A/cs Pay. .... accounts payable
A/cs Rec. .... accounts receivable
a/d .... after date
a.d. .... before the day
ad fin. .... to the end
ad int. .... in the meantime
ad lib., ad libit. .... at one's pleasure;
freely; to the quantity or amount desired
ad loc. .... to, *or* at, the place
ad. val. .... according to value *(ad valorem)* (*see* a/v)
adv. chgs. .... advance charges
advtg. .... advertising
a.f. .... audio frequency
A.F.T.R. .... American Federal Tax Reports
a.g.b. .... a good brand
a-h .... ampere-hour
AM .... amplitude modulation
amd. .... amended
amp. .... ampere(s)
amp-hr. .... ampere-hour
a.n. .... arrival notice (shipping)
anon. .... anonymous
a/o .... account of

A. to O.C. .... attached to other correspondence

A/P .... additional premium; authority to pay

Apd. .... assessment paid

A/R .... all risks; against all risks (marine insurance)

art. .... article

a.s. .... at sight

assmt. .... assessment

A.S.T. .... Atlantic standard time

A/T .... American terms (grain trade)

atm. ... atmosphere(s); atmospheric

at. no. ... atomic number

att. .... attached

attn., atten. .... attention

at. vol. .... atomic volume

at. wt. .... atomic weight

au. .... author

aux. .... auxiliary

A.V. .... authorized version

a/v .... according to value (*ad valorem*)

av., avdp. .... avoirdupois

A/W .... actual weight; all water (transportation)

A.W.G. .... American wire gauge

B

b7d, b10d, b15d .... buyer 7 days to take up, etc. (stock market)

bal. .... balance

b.b. .... bail bond; bill book; break bulk

bbl. .... barrel(s)

B.C. .... before Christ

B/C .... bill of collection

B/D .... bank draft; bar draft (grain trade)

bd.ft. .... board feet

bdl. .... bundle

B/E .... bill of exchange; bill of entry

Bev. .... billion electron volts

B/F .... brought forward (bookkeeping)

bf. .... boldface

b.f. .... board foot or feet

B/G .... bonded goods

B/H .... bill of health

b.h.p. .... brake horsepower

bkpt. .... bankrupt

bkt., bsk. .... basket(s)

B/L .... bill of lading

bl. .... bale(s)

b.m. .... board measure

B/M .... bill of materials

b.o. .... buyer's option; back order

b/o .... brought over

B.O. .... branch office

B/P .... bills payable; bill of parcels; blueprint

B.Pay .... bills payable

b.p.b. .... bank post bill

b.p.d. .... barrels per day

B/R .... bills receivable; builders' risks

B. Rec. .... bills receivable

Bro. .... Brother

Bros. .... Brothers

B/S .... bill of sale; bill of store

Bs/L .... bills of lading

B/St. .... bill of sight

Btu .... British thermal unit(s)

bu. .... bushel(s)

bus. .... business; bushels

B/v .... book value

B.W.G. .... Birmingham wire gauge

bx .... box

C

©, copr. .... copyright

c. .... cent(s); carat; chapter(s)

c/ .... case(s)

C. .... Congress; centigrade

C.A. .... chartered accountant

C/A .... capital account; credit

account; current account; commercial agent; close annealed

ca. .... centare(s); circa

C a/c .... current account

c.a.f. .... cost, assurance, and freight

cal. .... small calories; calendar; caliber

canc. .... cancelled; cancellation

cap. .... capital; capacity

caps .... capital letters

cart. .... cartage

C/B .... cash book

C.B.D. .... cash before delivery

cc. .... cubic centimeter; carbon copy

ccm. .... centimeter(s)

c/d .... carried down (bookkeeping)

cd .... cord

C/D .... commercial dock; consular declaration; certificate of deposit

c. & d. .... collection and delivery

cd.ft. .... cord ft.

cert., ct., ctf. .... certificate; certification; certified

cf. .... compare

c/f .... carried forward (bookkeeping)

c. & f. .... cost and freight

c.f.i. .... cost, freight, and insurance

c.f.o. .... cost for orders

cg. .... centigram(s)

cge.pd. .... carriage paid

cgm. .... centigram(s)

ch. .... chain; chapter; channel (TV); chemical; chart

chap., chaps. .... chapter; chapters

chg. .... charge; change

C.I. .... consular invoice

c.i.f. .... cost, insurance, and freight

cir. .... circa; circuit; circular; circulation; circumference

civ. civil

ck. .... cask(s); check

C/L .... cash letter

c.l. .... carload

c/l .... craft loss

cl. .... centiliter (metric)

clt. .... collateral trust (bonds)

cm. .... centimeter(s)

cm.pf. .... cumulative preferred (stocks)

C/N .... credit note; consignment note; circular note

cn. .... consolidated (bonds)

C/O .... cash order; certificate of origin; case oil

Co. .... company; county

c/o .... carried over (bookkeeping); in care of

c.o.d. .... certificates of deposit (securities)

C.O.D., c.o.d. .... cash, or collect, on delivery

col. .... column

coll.tr., clt. .... collateral trust (bonds)

Comm. .... committee; commission

con. .... continued

consgt. .... consignment

Const. .... Constitution

co-op. .... co-operative

corp. .... corporation; corporal

c.o.s. .... cash on shipment

c-p. .... candle power

C.P.A. .... certified public accountant

CPLS .... certified professional legal secretary

c.p.m., cpm (cps) .... cycles per minute (second)

CPS .... certified professional secretary

C.R. .... class rate; current rate; company's risk; carrier's risk

cr. .... credit; creditor

c/s .... cases

C.S.T. .... central standard time

C.T. .... central time

ctge. .... cartage

ctn. .... carton

ctr. .... center; counter

cu. .... cubic

cu. cm. .... cubic centimeter(s)

cu. ft. .... cubic feet

cu. in. .... cubic inch(es)
cu. mi. .... cubic mile(s)
cum. .... with; cumulative
cum. pref., cu. pf. .... cumulative preferred (stocks)
cur. .... current
cu.yd. .... cubic yard(s)
c.v. .... chief value
cv., cvt. .... convertible (securities)
cv. db. ... convertible debentures (securities)
cv. pf. .... convertible preferred (securities)
C.W. .... commercial weight
c.w.o. .... cash with order
cwt. .... hundredweight(s)

D

d. .... penny
d/a .... days after acceptance
D/A .... deposit account; documents against acceptance; discharge afloat
db .... decibel
d.b.a. .... doing business as (co. name)
dbk. .... drawback
db. rts. .... debenture rights (securities)
dbu .... decibel unit
DC, D.C., d.c. .... direct current
D/C .... deviation clause
D/D .... demand draft; delivered at docks; delivered at destination; dock dues
D/d .... days after date
deb., deben. .... debenture
dec. .... decision; decimal
decim. .... decimeter(s)
def. .... deferred (securities)
deg. .... degree(s)
dep.ctfs. .... deposit certificates
depr. .... depreciation
dept., dpt. .... department
d.f. .... dead freight
D.F.A. .... division freight agent

dg. .... decigram(s)
dia., diam. .... diameter
diag. .... diagram; diagonal
dis. .... discount
dist. .... district
div. .... dividend; division
dkg .... dekagram (metric)
dkl .... dekaliter (metric)
dkm .... dekameter (metric)
dks .... dekastere (metric)
dkt. .... docket
D/L .... demand loan
DL .... day letter (telegraph)
dl .... deciliter (metric)
dld. .... delivered
d.l.o. .... dispatch loading only
D.L.O. .... dead letter office
dls/shr .... dollars per share
dm, decim. .... decimeter(s)
D/N .... debit note
D/O .... delivery order
do. .... ditto (the same)
d.p. .... direct port
D/P .... documents against payment
D/R .... deposit receipt
dr. .... debit; debtor; drawer
dr. ap. .... apothecaries' dram(s)
dr. av. .... dram(s) avoirdupois
D/s .... days after sight
D.S.C. .... distinguished service cross
D.S.M. .... distinguished service medal
D/W .... dock warrant
d.w. .... dead weight
d.w.c. .... dead weight capacity
dwt. .... pennyweight(s)
d.w.t. .... deadweight tons
d. & w.t.f. .... daily and weekly till forbidden
D/y .... delivery

E

ea. .... each
E.A.O.N. .... except as otherwise noted

ed. .... editor; edition(s); education

Ed. Note .... editorial note

EDP .... electronic data processing

E.D.T. .... eastern daylight time

e.e. .... errors excepted

eff. .... effective

e.g. .... for example (*exempli gratia*)

elec. .... electric

e.m.p. .... end of month payment

enc., encl. .... enclosures

end. .... endorse; endorsement

eng. .... engine; engineer; engineering; engraved

e.o. .... ex officio

e.o.d. .... every other day (advertising)

E. & O.E. .... errors and omissions excepted

e.o.h.p. .... except as otherwise herein provided

e.o.m. .... end of month (payments)

Esq. .... esquire

est. .... estate; estimated

E.S.T. .... eastern standard time

e.s.u. .... electrostatic unit

et al. .... and others *(et alii)*

etc. .... and the others; and so forth *(et cetera)*

et seq. .... and the following *(et sequens)*

et ux. .... and wife

et vir. .... and husband

ex .... out of *or* from; without *or* not including

Ex. B.L. .... exchange bill of lading

ex cp. *or* x/cp .... ex coupon

ex d. *or* ex div. .... ex dividend

ex int. .... ex interest

ex n. .... ex new

exp. .... express; expenses; export

ex r. .... ex rights

extrs sess. .... extraordinary session (of a legislature)

ex ship .... delivered out of ship

F

f. .... following (after a numberal)

F., Fahr. .... Fahrenheit

f.a.a. .... free of all average (insurance)

fac. .... facsimile

f.a.c. .... fast as can

F.A.M. *or* F. and A.M. .... Free and Accepted Masons

f.a.q. .... fair average quality; free at quay

f.a.q.s. .... fair average quaity of season

f.b. .... freight bill

fbm. .... fett board measure

f.d. .... free discharge; free delivery; free dispatch

fd. .... fund; funding

f. & d. .... freight and demurrage

Fed. Reg .... Federal Register

ff. .... following (after a numeral); folios

f.f.a. .... free from alongside; free foreign agency

f.i.a. .... full interest admitted

fig.(s) .... figure(s)

f.i.o. .... free in and out

f.i.t. .... free of income tax; free in truck

f.i.w. .... free in wagon

F.L.N. .... following landing numbers

fl. oz. .... fluid ounce(s)

fm. .... fathom(s)

FM .... frequency modulation

fn. .... footnote

F.O. .... firm offer; free overside

f.o. .... for orders; firm offer; full out terms (grain trade)

F.O.B., f.o.b. .... free on board

f.o.c. .... free on car; free of charge

f.o.d. .... free of damage

f.o.f. .... free on field (air mail)

fol. .... folio; following

f.o.q. .... free on quay

f.o.r. .... free on rail
f.o.s. .... free on steamer
f.o.t. .... free on truck
F.P. .... floating (or open) policy; fully paid
f.p.m. .... feet per minute
f.p.s. .... feet per second
F/R .... freight release
f.r.o.f. .... fire risk on freight
frt. .... freight
ft. .... foot *or* feet
f.t. .... full terms
ft/sec. .... feet per second
fur .... furlong
f.v. .... on the back of the page (*folio verso*)
f.w.d. .... fresh-water damage
F.X. .... foreign exchange
F.Y.I. .... for your information (inter-office use)

G

g .... gram (metric)
G/A .... general average (marine insurance)
GAW .... guaranteed annual wage
g.f.a. .... good fair average
G.F.A. .... general freight agent
g. gr. .... great gross
gi. .... gill(s)
GI .... government issue; general issue
gm. .... gram(s)
GNP .... gross national product
G.P.A. .... general passenger agent
g.p.m. .... gallons per minute
gr. .... gram(s); grain; gross
gro. .... gross
gr. wt. .... gross weight
g.s. .... ground speed (aviation)
G.T.C. .... good till canceled, *or* countermanded
G.T.M. .... good this month
G.T.W. .... good this week (becomes void on Saturday)

H

H.B. .... House bill (state)
H.C. .... held covered (insurance); House of Commons
hdqrs. .... headquarters
hdwr. .... hardware
HE .... high explosive
HF .... high frequency
H.F.M. .... hold for money
hg .... hectogram
hhd. .... hogshead(s)
H.L. .... House of Lords
hl .... hectoliter (metric)
hm .... hectometer (metric)
Hon. .... honorable
H.P. *or* hp. .... horsepower
hq. .... headquarters
hr. .... hour(s)
H.R. .... House bill (federal); House of Representatives
H.W. .... high water
H.W.M. .... high-water mark
H.W.O.S.T. .... high-water ordinary spring tide
hyp. .... hypothesis
Hz. .... hertz

I

I.B. .... invoice book; in bond
I.B.I. .... invoice book, inwards
ibid. .... in the same place (*ibidem*)
I.B.O. .... invoice book, outwards
I.C. & C. .... invoice cost and charges
id. .... the same (*idem*)
i.e. .... that is (*id est*)
I.H.P. .... indicated horsepower
imp. gal. .... imperial gallon(s)
in. .... inch(es)
Inc. .... incorporated
in loc. .... in the proper place
ins. .... insurance
Inst. .... institute; institution

int. .... interest
inv. .... invoice
i.p.s. .... inches per second
I.Q. .... intelligence quotient
IRC .... Internal Revenue Code
ital. .... italics
i.v. .... invoice value; increased value

J

j .... joule (electricity)
J/A .... joint account
jg. .... junior grade
jnt. stk. .... joint stock

K

k. .... carat; knot
kc. .... kilocycle(s)
K.D. .... knocked down
kg. *or* kgm. .... kilogram(s)
kilo. .... kilometer(s)
kl. .... kiloliter(s)
km. .... kilometer(s)
kt. .... karat; kiloton
kV .... kilovolts
kVA .... kilovoltampere
kW .... kilowatt(s)
kWh .... kilowatt-hour(s)

L

l. .... line; liter(s)
L .... listed (securities)
L. .... laws
L/A .... letter of authority; landing account; Lloyd's agent
lat. .... latitude
lb. .... pound(s)
l.c. .... lower case; in the place cited
LC .... deferreds (cable messages)
L/C .... letter of credit
l.c.l. .... less than carload lot

l.c.m. .... least common multiple
ldg. .... loading
ldg. & dely. .... landing and delivery
lds. .... loads
L. Ed. .... Lawyers Edition
lf. .... lightface
l.f. .... ledger folio
lge. .... large
lg. tn. .... long ton(s)
lin. ft. .... linear foot
L.I.P. .... life insurance policy
lkg. & bkg. .... leakage and breakage
LL .... leased line (securities)
Ll. & Co.'s .... Lloyd's and Companies
L.M.S.C. .... let me see correspondence
ln. .... lien; loan
loc. cit. .... in the place cited (*loco citato*)
log. .... logarithm
long. .... longitude
lr. .... lire
L.S. .... place of the seal (*locus sigilli*)
LT .... letter message (cables)
l.t. .... long ton
Ltd. .... limited (British)
Lt.-V. .... light vessel
lv. .... leave
L.W. .... low water
l.w.m. .... low-water mark

M

m. .... married; masculine; meter(s)
M .... thousand
M. .... monsieur (*pl.* MM); noon (*meridie*)
ma .... milliampere
m/a .... my account
mar. .... marine; maritime; married
max. .... maximum
max. cap. .... maximum capacity
mb .... millibar
m.c. .... marked capacity (freight cars)
mc .... megacycle

M.C. .... master of ceremonies; member of Congress

M/C .... marginal credit

m.c.p.s. .... megacycles per second; millicycles per second

m/d .... months after date

M/D .... memorandum of deposit

mdse. .... merchandise

M.E. .... Methodist Episcopal

med. .... medium; medicine; medical

m.e.p. .... mean effective pressure

Messrs. .... Misters (Messieurs)

mf .... millifarod (electricity)

mfg. .... manufacturing

mfr. .... manufacturer

mg. *or* mgm .... milligram(s)

mh .... milliheury

M.H. .... main hatch; Medal of Honor

mi. .... mile(s)

min. .... minute(s)

min. B/L .... minimum bill of lading

M.I.P. .... marine insurance policy

misc. .... miscellaneous

mL .... millilambert

Mlle. .... Mademoiselle

mm. .... millimeter(s)

MM .... Messieurs

Mme. .... Madam

Mmes. .... Mesdames

mo. .... month(s)

M.O. .... money order

mol. wt. .... molecular weight

M.P. .... member of Parliament; mounted police; military police

m.p.g. .... miles per gallon

m.p.h. .... miles per hour

mr .... milliroentgen

ms.(s) .... manuscript(s)

M/s .... months after sight

Msgr. .... Monsignor; Monseigneur

mst. .... measurement

M.S.T. .... mountain standard time

mt. .... empty; megaton

Mt., mt. .... mountain

mt.ct.cp. .... mortgage certificate coupon (securities)

mtg. .... mortgage

m.v. .... market value

N

n. .... net; note; number

N. .... north

n/a .... no account (banking)

N/A .... no advice (banking)

NA .... nonacquiescence (by Commissioner of Internal Revenue); not available

natl. .... national

naut. .... nautical

n.b. *or* N.B. .... note well (*nota bene*)

N/C .... new charter; new crop

N.C.O. .... noncommissioned officer

n.c.u.p. .... no commission until paid

N.C.V. .... no commercial value

N.D., n.d. .... no date

N.D. .... Northern District

n.e. .... not exceeding

N.E. .... New England; Northeast

N/E .... no effects (banking)

n.e.s. .... not elsewhere specified

n/f .... no funds (banking)

N.G., ng. .... no good

N.H.P. .... nominal horsepower

N.L. .... night letter (telegraph)

N.L.T. .... night letter cable

N.M. .... night message

n/m .... no mark

No. .... number

n/o .... in the name of (finance)

N/O .... no orders (banking)

N.O.E. .... not otherwise enumerated

N.O.H.P. .... not otherwise herein provided

nol. pros. .... to be unwilling to prosecute (*nolle prosequi*)

nom. .... nominative

nom. std. .... nominal standard

non pros. .... he does not prosecute (*non prosequitur*)

non seq. .... does not follow (*non sequitur*)

n.o.p. .... not otherwise provided for

N.O.S. .... not otherwise specified

N.P. .... no protest (banking)

n/p .... net proceeds

np .... nonparticipating (stocks)

N.P.L. .... nonpersonal liability

n.p.t. ... normal pressure and temperature

n.r. .... no risk; net register

n.r.a.d. .... no risk after discharge

N.S. .... national society; new series

N/S *or* N.S.F. .... not sufficient funds (banking)

n.s.p.f. .... not specially provided for

n.t. .... net ton; new terms (grain trade)

*n*th .... indefinite

nt.wt. .... net weight

nv .... nonvoting (stocks)

O

o/a .... on account of

ob. .... died (*obit*)

O.B./L, ob/l .... order bill of lading

obs. .... obsolete

o/c .... open charter; old charter; old crop; open cover; overcharge; over the counter

o/d .... on demand

o.e. .... omissions excepted

OE .... Old English

Off. Interp. .... official interpretation

O/o .... order of

o.p. .... out of print

O.P. .... open, *or* floating, policy

op. .... opinion

op. cit. .... in the work cited (*opere citato*)

o.r. .... owner's risk (transportation)

o. & r. .... ocean and rail (transportation)

o/s .... out of stock

O/S .... on sample; on sale or return

O.S. .... Old Series

o.s. & d. .... over, short, and damaged (transportation)

o/t .... old terms (grain trade); on truck

o.w. .... one way (fare)

oz. .... ounce(s)

P

p. .... page

p.a. .... by the year (*per annum*); private account

P/A .... particular average; power of attorney; private account; purchasing agent

P.a.C. .... put and call (stock market)

pam. .... pamphlet

part. .... participating (securities)

pat. .... patent

Pat. Off. .... Patent Office

P/Av. .... particular average

PBX, P.B.X. .... private branch exchange (telephone)

p.c. .... percent; post card

P/C .... price current; petty cash; percent

pct. .... percent

P.D. .... port dues; per diem

pd. .... passed; paid

pfd. .... preferred

p. & i. .... protection and indemnity

pk. .... peck(s)

pkg. .... package

p.l. .... partial loss

P. & L. .... profit and loss

p.m. .... afternoon (*post meridiem*)

P.M. .... postmaster; Provost Marshal

pm. .... premium

P/N .... promissory note

P.O.D. .... pay on delivery

P.O.R. .... payable on receipt
P.P. .... parcel post
pp. .... pages
ppd. .... prepaid; postpaid
p.p.i. .... parcel post insured; policy proof of interest
ppt. .... prompt loading
pr. .... pair; price
pref. .... preface; preferred
prin. .... principal
pro tem. .... for the time being (*pro tempore*)
prox. .... proximate; of the next month
PrPro., P.P. .... on behalf of; by proxy
P.S. .... postscript
P/S .... public sale
p.s.f. .... pounds per square foot
p.s.i. .... pounds per square inch
P.S.T. .... Pacific standard time
pt. .... pint(s)
P.T. .... Pacific time
p.w. .... packed weight (transportation)
pwt. .... pennyweight
P.X. .... please exchange; post exchange

Q

q .... quintal (metric)
Q. .... question; query
q.d.a. .... quantity discount agreement
Q.E.D. .... which was to be proved or demonstrated (*quod erta demonstrandum*)
qn. .... quotation
QQ. .... questions; queries
qr. .... quarter
qt. .... quart(s)
q.v. .... which see (*quod vide*)

R

R/A .... refer to acceptor

R/C .... reconsigned
rcd. .... received
R/D .... refer to drawer
r.d. .... running days
re .... in regard to
R.E. .... real estate
recd. rec'd. .... received
ref. .... referee; reference; referred; refund
reg. ... registered; regulation(s)
reg. sess. .... regular session (of legislature)
R.E.O. .... real estate owned (banking)
rep. .... report
res. .... residue; research; reserve; residence; resides; resigned; resolution
retd. .... returned; retained; retired
rev. A/C .... revenue account
revd., rev'd .... reversed
revg., rev'g .... reversing
rf., rfg. .... refunding (bonds)
r.f. .... radio frequency
R.F.D. .... rural free delivery
rfg. .... refunding
rhp .... rated horsepower
R.I. .... reinsurance
r. & l. .... rail and lake (transportation)
r.l. & r. .... rail, lake, and rail (transportation)
rm. .... ream (paper); room(s)
r.m.s. .... root mean square
r. & o. .... rail and ocean (transportation)
R.O.G. .... receipt of goods
rom. .... roman (type)
ROP .... run of paper
rotn. no. .... rotation number
R.P. .... return premium
R/p .... return of post for orders
RP .... reply paid (cable)
r.p.m. .... revolutions per minute
r.p.s. .... revolutions per second
R.R. .... railroad
R.S.V.P. .... please reply (*Respondez, s'il vous plait*)
Rt. .... right(s) (stock)

rva .... reactive volt-ampere

R.V.S.V.P. .... please reply at once

r. & w. .... rail and water (transportation)

Ry. .... railway

S

s .... stere (metric); seconds

S. .... Senate bill (federal); south

s7d, s10d, s15d .... seller 7 days to deliver, etc. (stock market)

s/a .... subject to approval; safe arrival

s.a.n.r. .... subject to approval no risk (no risk until insurance is confirmed)

S.B. .... Senate bill (state); short bill

S/B .... statement of billing (transportation)

s.c. .... small capital letters; same case (legal)

sc., scil. .... namely, to wit (*scilicet*)

S.C. .... salvage charges

s. & c. .... shipper and carrier

s.d. .... without a day being named (*sine die*)

S.D.B.L. .... sight draft, bill of lading attached

S.E. .... southeast

sec., secy., sec'y .... secretary

sec.(s) .... section(s)

seq. .... the following; in sequence

ser. .... series

S.F. .... state senate bill (file); sinking fund

S. & F.A. .... shipping and forwarding

sgd. .... signed

sh. .... share agent

sh.p. .... shaft horsepower

shpt. .... shipment

sh. tn. .... short ton

sic .... so; thus (to confirm a word that might be questioned)

s.i.t. .... stopping in transit (transportation)

sk. .... sack(s)

s.l. .... salvage loss

S/N .... shipping note

S.O. .... seller's option; shipping order; ship's option

soc. .... society

sol. .... solicitor(s)

S.O.L. .... shipowner's liability

Sol.Op. .... solicitor's opinion

SOP .... standard operating procedure

S.P. .... supra protest

s.p.d. .... steamer pays dues

Sp.Op. .... special opinion

sp. term .... special term (of court)

sq. ft. .... square feet

sq. in. .... square inch(es)

sq. mi. .... square mile(s)

sq. rd. .... square rod(s)

sq. yd. .... square yards(s)

ss .... namely

S.S. .... steamship; screw steamer

S. to S. .... station to station

SSE .... south-southeast

SST .... supersonic transport

SSW .... south-southwest

St. .... saint (*pl* SS.)

sta. .... station; stamped (securities)

stat. .... statute(s)

std. .... standard

stg. .... sterling

stk. .... stock

str. .... steamer

supp. .... supplement

supt. .... superintendent

s.v. .... sailing vessel

s.v.p. .... if you please

S.W. .... shipper's weights; southwest

S.W.G. .... standard wire gauge

syn. .... synonymous

T

t. .... metric ton(s)

T.A. .... traffic agent

t.a.w. .... twice a week (advertising)

t.b. .... trial balance

T/C .... until countermanded
T/D .... time deposit
T.E. .... trade expenses
tel. .... telegram; telegraph; telephone
tf. *or* t.f. .... till forbidden (advertising)
T/L .... time loan
t.l.o. .... total loss only (marine insurance)
t.m. .... true mean; trademark
tn. .... ton
T/O .... transfer order
T/R .... trust receipt
tr. .... transpose
T.R. .... tons registered (shipping)
trans. .... transitive; translated; transportation
transp. .... transportation
treas. .... treasurer
T.T. .... telegraphic transfer
TWP .... township
TWS .... timed wire service (telegraph)
TWX .... teletypewriter exchange

U

U. .... university
U/A .... underwriting account (marine insurance)
u.c. .... upper case
u.d. .... as directed
UGT .... urgent (cable)
UHF .... ultrahigh frequency (TV)
u.i. .... as below
ult. .... of the last month (*ultimo*)
univ. .... university
u.p. .... under proof
u.s. .... as above (*ut supra*)
u.t., UT .... universal time
U/w .... underwriter

V

v. .... volt; versus
V. .... value; velocity; volt
va .... volt-ampere (electricity)
V.C. .... valuation clause
v.f., VF .... video frequency (TV)
VHF .... very high frequency (TV)
v.i. .... see below (*vide infra*)
vid. .... see (*vide*)
viz. .... namely *(videlicet)*
vol. .... volume
v.o.p. .... value as in original policy
vs., v.s. .... verse; versus
vt. .... voting (stock)
v.v. .... vice versa

W

w. .... watt (electricity)
W. .... west
w.a. .... with average (insurance)
w/d .... warranted
w.d. .... when distributed (securities)
W.D. .... western district
w.f. .... wrong font (typesetting)
w.g. .... weight guaranteed
wh .... watt-hour (electricity)
whsle. .... wholesale
w.i. .... when issued (stock exchange)
wk. .... week
w.l. .... wave length
W/M .... weight and/or measurement
WNW .... west-northwest
w.o.c. .... without compensation
w.p. .... without prejudice; weather permitting
w.p.p. .... waterproof paper packing
w.r. .... with rights (securities)
W.R. .... warehouse receipt
w. & r. ....water and rail (transportation)
wt. .... weight
W.W., ww .... with warrants (securities)
W/W .... warehouse warrant

X

x-c. *or* x-cp. .... ex coupon
x-d. *or* x-div. .... ex dividend
x-i. *or* x-in. *or* x-int. .... ex interest
x-n. .... ex new
x-pr. .... ex privileges
x-rts. .... ex rights
xw .... ex warrants

Y

yb. .... yearbook
yd. .... yard
yr. .... year

Z

z. .... zone; zero
zool. .... zoology, zoological

ABBREVIATIONS OF MONTHS AND DAYS

Jan.	. . . . January	July	. . . . July
Feb.	. . . . February	Aug.	. . . . August
Mar.	. . . . March	Sept.	. . . . September
Apr.	. . . . April	Oct.	. . . . October
May	. . . . May	Nov.	. . . . November
June	. . . . June	Dec.	. . . . December

Sun. *or* S.	. . . . Sunday
Mon. *or* M.	. . . . Monday
Tues. *or* Tu.	. . . . Tuesday
Wed. *or* W.	. . . . Wednesday
Thurs. *or* Th.	. . . . . . Thursday
Fri. *or* F.	. . . . Friday
Sat.	. . . . Saturday

ABBREVIATIONS OF ACADEMIC DEGREES

A

A.B. .... Bachelor of Arts
A.M. .... Master of Arts
Ar.M. .... Master of Architecture

B

B.A. .... Bachelor of Arts

B.Ag. *or* B.Agr. .... Bachelor of Agriculture
B.Ar. *or* B. Arch. .... Bachelor of Architecture
B.B.A. .... Bachelor of Business Administration
B.C. .... Bachelor of Chemistry
B.C.E. .... Bachelor of Chemical Engi-

neering; Bachelor of Civil Engineering

B.C.L. .... Bachelor of Civil Law

B.D. .... Bachelor of Divinity

B.D.S. .... Bachelor of Dental Surgery

B.E. .... Bachelor of Education; Bachelor of Engineering

B.E.E. .... Bachelor of Electrical Engineering

B.F. .... Bachelor of Finance; Bachelor of Forestry

B.Lit(t). .... Bachelor of Literature, *or* Letters

B.L.S. .... Bachelor of Library Science

B.M. .... Bachelor of Medicine

B.Mus. .... Bachelor of Music

B.Pd., B.Pe. .... Bachelor of Pedagogy

B.P.E. .... Bachelor of Physical Education

B.S. .... Bachelor of Science

B.Sc. .... Bachelor of Science

B.S.Ed. .... Bachelor of Science in Education

B.T. *or* B.Th. .... Bachelor of Theology

C

C.B. .... Bachelor of Surgery

Ch.D. .... Doctor of Chemistry

Ch.E. .... Chemical Engineer

C.S.B. .... Bachelor of Christian Science

D

D.C. .... Doctor of Chiropractic

D.C.L. .... Doctor of Canon Law; Doctor of Civil Law

D.D. .... Doctor of Divinity

D.D.S. .... Doctor of Dental Surgery

D.Lit(t). .... Doctor of Literature, *or* Letters

D. es L. .... Doctor of Letters (French)

D. es S. .... Doctor of Science (French)

D.L.S. .... Doctor of Library Science

D.M.D. .... Doctor of Dental Medicine

D.Mus. .... Doctor of Music

D.O. .... Doctor of Osteopathy

D.S., D.Sc. .... Doctor of Science

D.Th. *or* D. Theol. .... Doctor of Theology

D.V.M. ... Doctor of Veterinary Medicine

E

Ed.B. .... Bachelor of Education

Ed.D. .... Doctor of Education

Ed.M. .... Master of Education

E.E. .... Electrical Engineer

Eng.D. .... Doctor of Engineering

J

J.C.D. .... Doctor of Canon Law; Civil Law

J.D. .... Doctor of Laws

Jur.D. .... Doctor of Law

L

L.B. .... Bachelor of Letters

L.H.D. .... Doctor of Humanities

Lit(t).B. .... Bachelor of Literature, *or* of Letters

Lit(t).D. .... Doctor of Literature, *or* of Letters

LL.B. .... Bachelor of Laws

LL.D. .... Doctor of Laws

M

M.A. .... Master of Arts

M.Agr. .... Master of Agriculture

M.B. .... Bachelor of Medicine

M.B.A. .... Master in, *or* of, Business Administration

M.C.L. .... Master of Civil Law

M.D. .... Doctor of Medicine
M.D.S. .... Master of Dental Surgery
M.Ed. .... Master of Education
M.Pd. .... Master of Pedagogy
M.P.E. .... Master of Physical Education
M.S. *or* M.Sc. .... Master of Science
Mus.B. .... Bachelor of Music
Mus.D. .... Doctor of Music

P

Pd.B. .... Bachelor of Pedagogy
Pd.D. .... Doctor of Pedagogy
Pd.M. .... Master of Pedagogy
Phar.B. .... Bachelor of Pharmacy
Phar.D., Pharm.D. .... Doctor of Pharmacy
Pharm.M. .... Master of Pharmacy
Ph.B. .... Bachelor of Philosophy

Ph.D. .... Doctor of Philosophy
Pod.D. .... Doctor of Podiatry

S

S.B. .... Bachelor of Science
Sc.D., S.D. .... Doctor of Science
Sc.M. .... Master of Science
S.J.D. .... Doctor of Juridical Science
S.M. .... Master of Science
S.T.B. .... Bachelor of Sacred Theology
S.T.D. .... Doctor of Sacred Theology

T

Th.D. .... Doctor of Theology

V

V.M.D. .... Doctor of Veterinary Medicine

ABBREVIATIONS OF ORGANIZATIONS

A

ABA .... American Bankers Association; American Bar Association
AEC .... Atomic Energy Commission
AFL-CIO .... American Federation of Labor and Congress of Industrial Organizations
AIB .... American Institute of Banking
AMA.... American Medical Association
AP .... Associated Press
ARC .... American (National) Red Cross
ASA .... American Standards Association; American Statistical Association
ASTA .... American Society of Travel Agents, Inc.

B

Bd. of Rev. .... Board of Review
BTA .... Board of Tax Appeals

C

CAB .... Civil Aeronautics Board
CIA .... Central Intelligence Agency
CID .... Criminal Investigation Department
CSC .... Civil Service Commission

F

FAA .... Federal Aviation Agency
FBI .... Federal Bureau of Investigation
FCA .... Farm Credit Administration

FCC .... Federal Communications Commission

FDA .... Food and Drug Administration

FDIC .... Federal Deposit Insurance Corporation

FHA .... Federal Housing Administration

FMCS .... Federal Mediation and Conciliation Service

FPC .... Federal Power Commission

FRB .... Federal Reserve Board (or Bank)

FRS .... Federal Reserve System

FSA .... Federal Security Agency

FTC .... Federal Trade Commission

G

GHQ .... General Headquarters (Army)

H

HHFA .... Housing and Home Finance Agency

I

ICC .... Interstate Commerce Commission

IFTU .... International Federation of Trade Unions

ILO .... International Labor Organization

ILP .... Independent Labour Party (Brit.)

INP .... International News Photos

INS .... International News Service

IRO .... International Refugee Organization

IRS .... Internal Revenue Service

IWW .... Industrial Workers of the World

K

KC .... Knights of Columbus

KKK .... Ku Klux Klan

N

NAACP .... National Association for the Advancement of Colored People

NALS .... National Association of Legal Secretaries

NAM .... National Association of Manufacturers

NAS .... National Academy of Sciences

NASA .... National Aeronautical Space Agency

NATO .... North Atlantic Treaty Organization

NEA .... National Education Association; National Editorial Association

NLRB .... National Labor Relations Board

NMB .... National Mediation Board

NSA .... The National Secretaries Association (International)

R

ROTC .... Reserve Officers' Training Corps

S

SBA .... Small Business Administration

SEATO .... Southeast Asia Treaty Organization

SEC .... Securities and Exchange Commission

S.S.A. .... Social Security Administration

SSS .... Selective Service System

T

TC .... Tax Court of the United States

U

UN .... United Nations

UNESCO .... United Nations Educational, Social, and Cultural Organization

UNICEF .... United Nations Children's Fund

UNRRA .... United Nations Relief and Rehabilitation Administration

UPI .... United Press International

V

VA .... Veterans Administration

VFW .... Veterans of Foreign Wars

How to Handle Records and Correspondence for the Manager's Personal Matters

Part 4

CHAPTER 19

How to Keep Records of Personal Funds

The personal business records that the manager might expect his or her secretary to handle generally fall into three broad classes:

1. Records of what he or she owns, including insurance (see chapter 21), stocks, bonds, and other investments.

2. Records that must be kept for income and other tax purposes (see chapter 20). These include the records of income that must be reported and of expenses and losses that may be deducted (see chapter 22). Many secretaries are concerned only with income tax records.

3. Records of living expenses that are not deductible under the income tax law (this chapter).

The checkbook is the prime base of all of these records.

The manager may have one or several checking accounts in the same bank or in various banks. He must have a separate checkbook for each checking account. If he has more than one checking account in the same bank, each account will be distinguished either by special designation printed on the check or possibly by account number only, which is printed along the bottom margin of the check. For example, one account may be designated simply by the depositor's name—*Jonathan B. Daniels,* while another account may be designated *Jonathan B. Daniels, Special.*

The manager may also have savings accounts. Savings account *passbooks* are the depositor's records of savings account transactions. The passbook must accompany all withdrawals and deposits. The savings bank enters all deposits, withdrawals, and any interest earned on the account in the passbook at intervals, usually monthly.

The checkbook as a book of record. The bank supplies depositors with forms for making withdrawals. Checks bound in book form with three checks to the page may be convenient for the manager's use. The checks, which are usually numbered serially, may have the manager's name and address imprinted on them for a small charge. *Most important* is the account number encoded on the checks in magnetic printed numerals, which computers can "read." The Federal Reserve System requires that the account number be encoded on checks that clear through it. The day has passed when a bank depositor—with a small or large account—can fill in the name and address of his bank and his account number on a so-called *blank check* and cash it easily.

The *stubs* in the checkbook are your check register. Be sure to fill out the stubs accurately and with complete information for each transaction. Information to identify the payment and its nature clearly is essential. Any additional records you may keep are based on the information on these stubs. The manager (or his personal accountant) relies heavily on these stubs for income tax purposes.

1. Fill out the stub with the check number (if not already printed on the stub) and amount of the check, the date, the name of the payee, and the purpose for which the check is drawn before you write the check itself.

2. Be sure the explanation on the stub is specific enough to enable you or an accountant to post the payment to the proper records. If you spoil a check and have to write another one, *void* the stub for the record and rewrite the required information in the stub that corresponds to the new check you are writing.

3. When a deposit is made, enter the amount on the stub and add it to the last balance brought forward to show the amount in the bank account at that point. Subtract the amount of the check drawn to find the balance that is carried forward to the next stub.

   Checkbooks bound with three checks to the page do not provide for a balance after each check is drawn, but usually for a balance after the last check on the page is drawn. (See the recapitulation in Figure 37.)

4. After all the checks in a checkbook have been used, paste a label on the outside cover giving the name of the bank, title of the account, and dates on which the first and last checks were drawn. Number the books. This procedure facilitates finding a stub and numbers of the first and last check drawn.

How to reorder checkbooks. It takes about two or three weeks to get a new checkbook printed. Therefore, estimate the number of checks that you write in three weeks and order a new book in ample time to avoid running out of checks. The printer usually inserts a form for reordering near the end of the bound book. Complete this form and send it to your bank when you reorder, but do not depend upon the form as a guide as to *when* to reorder. The number of the first check in the new book will follow the number of the last check in the previous book, in numerical sequence.

How to write checks.   Always write checks on the typewriter or in ink in a clear, legible hand. Observe the following procedure:

Stubs. Fill out the stub before writing the check.

Number. Be sure that the number on the check corresponds to that on the stub. If the numbers are not printed on the checks, number consecutively all checks and stubs when you begin to use a new checkbook.

Date. Date the check the exact day on which it is drawn, or on the previous day if it is drawn on Sunday or a holiday. The bank will honor checks that are dated on Sunday or a holiday, however.

Payee. State clearly and accurately the name of the party to whom the check is payable. Do not prefix the name of the payee by a title, such as "Dr.," "Judge," "Rev.," or "Mr.," but you may use abbreviations of scholastic degrees after the name, thus: "Robert R.

	DEPOSITS		RECORD OF CHECKS AS DRAWN	AMOUNT OF CHECK	
BALANCE FORWARD	1	456 50	No. 1795 *February 10 19—*		
DATE			*Maintenance Corp.* ORDER OF	25	00
			House Expenses ACCOUNT		
			Oil burner repairs		
Feb. 15	1	000	No. 1796 *February 15 19—*		
			Adams & Nelson ORDER OF	255	38
18		250	*Clothes* ACCOUNT		
			($5.58 City Sales Tax)		
			No. 1797 *February 20 19—*		
			Greenwood Country Club ORDER OF	100	
			Recreation ACCOUNT		
TOTAL DEPOSITS	2	706 50			
LESS CHECKS DRAWN		380 38			
BALANCE FORWARD	2	326 12	TOTAL CHECKS DRAWN	380	38

FIGURE 37   STUBS FROM CHECKS BOUND THREE TO A PAGE

Wilson, M.D." If the payee is "Mrs. John E. Browne," include "Mrs." before the name, but if the payee is "Mrs. Ella Browne," do not include "Mrs."

If the check is payable to the officer of a club or society in his official capacity, follow his name with his office—"John E. Browne, Treas."

Amount. State exactly in figures and words the amount of the check. Write the figures close to the dollar sign that is on the check.

When writing the check by hand, write the cents or two zeros above the line in smaller figures, insert a virgule (a diagonal line), and then write 100. You cannot do this on the typewriter because your cents would look as if they were part of the dollar amount. When using the typewriter, separate the cents from the dollars with a decimal point, thus, $1,254.53 or $1,254.00. Do not separate the cents from the dollars with a space, for spaces make fraudulent alteration of the check easier.

In writing out the amount, express cents as fractions of 100. If there are no cents, use the word "no" as the numerator of the fraction. The following are approved forms for writing out amounts in checks:

One Thousand Two Hundred Fifty-Four and 53/100 . . . . Dollars
One Thousand Two Hundred Fifty-Four and no/100 . . . . Dollars

If it is necessary to write a check for less than a dollar, enclose the figures in parentheses, and precede the amount written out in words with the word "Only." Thus:

Pay to ————————————— John E. Browne ----------------------- $ (53¢)
Only Fifty-Three Cents --- Dollars

Blank spaces. Fill in all blank spaces before or after the name of the payee and of the amount of the withdrawal with hyphens if the check is written on the typewriter. Draw a straight line in the spaces if the check is written in ink.

Signature. The payer's signature should agree exactly with that shown on the signature card at the bank.

If you sign checks for the manager. If the manager wants you to sign checks for him, either in his absence or at all times, he will give you a power of attorney. This is made out on a form supplied by the bank and should be approved by your employer's attorney-at-law. A power of attorney creates fewer legal complications than carrying the account in your own name as secretary or as agent for your employer. Of course, a power of attorney does not imply that you are an attorney-at-law, or a lawyer.

If the name of the account is printed on the check, sign:

-------------------------------------, Att'y *or* --
Attorney

If the name of the account is not printed on the check, type it and sign, thus:

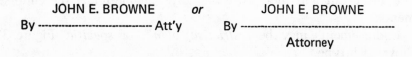

JOHN E. BROWNE   *or*   JOHN E. BROWNE

By ------------------------------- Att'y   By ---

Attorney

How to make deposits to the manager's bank account.   All banks supply depositors with deposit slips, usually with the depositor's name and account number imprinted on them. All you have to do to complete the deposit slip is to fill in the date and list the items that you are depositing. Enter all cash as one item, as called for by the deposit slip form, but list each check separately. (See page 440 for saving time in making deposits.)

How to deposit checks. Always examine a check carefully before depositing it to see that it is properly drawn. If the check is postdated, or if there is a discrepancy between the figures and the written amount, the bank will not accept the check. When the manager receives an improperly drawn check, do not deposit it but take the matter up with the person who drew (or made) the check.

If a check bears a notation or endorsement to the effect that it represents payment in full, do not deposit it without the manager's approval unless the check is actually for the full amount of the account referred to.

Endorse the checks (see below) and list them individually, by the name of the drawer, on the deposit slip. Some deposit slips call for an identification of each check by its A.B.A. transit number or by the place where it is payable. The small printed number that appears on the face of the check, for example $\frac{1\text{-}8}{2109}$ is the transit number assigned to a bank by the American Bankers Association. Banks do not insist that the depositor identify the checks, but they do insist that he itemize them.

How to endorse checks.   Always endorse checks on the back, across the left end as you turn over the check by tumbling top to bottom. Place the endorsement as near to the edge of the check as possible, unless the check is a punched card (i.e., perforated with holes for a computer to read). Do not write the endorsement through these markings. Frequently the check has a line across the back with instructions to "endorse below."

The endorsement should correspond *exactly* with the name of the payee. If the name of the payee is not correct, endorse the check as it is made out and then write the correct name under the endorsements.

Endorsements may be *restrictive, blank,* or *specific.* Figure 38 shows each type.

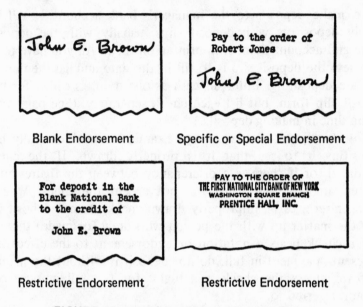

| Blank Endorsement | Specific or Special Endorsement |

| Restrictive Endorsement | Restrictive Endorsement |

FIGURE 38   ENDORSEMENTS OF CHECKS

Restrictive endorsement for deposit of checks. A restrictive endorsement restricts or limits the endorsee's use of the funds represented by the check. When the check is endorsed to a bank for the credit of the payee, it does not require a manual endorsement. A rubber stamp or typewritten endorsement is acceptable.

The usual phrasing for a restrictive endorsement is "Pay to the order of .... Bank for deposit only. John E. Brown." If the name of the payee is incorrect, type the name as it appears on the face of the check, and then stamp or type the endorsement for deposit.

Always use a restrictive endorsement on a check that is to be deposited by mail.

Blank endorsement. To endorse a check in blank, the payee simply signs his name on the back of the check, thereby making it negotiable without further endorsement. Anyone may then cash the check. Do not endorse a check in blank on the typewriter. The endorsement should be written in ink by the payee of the check or by someone authorized to endorse checks for him. Never endorse a check in blank until you are ready to cash or deposit it.

Specific endorsement. A specific or special endorsement specifies the person to whom the check is transferred. Thus, John E. Brown, the payee of a check, endorses it "Pay to the order of Robert Jones. John E. Brown." The check is then payable only to Robert Jones. A specific endorsement must be signed by the payee or someone authorized to endorse checks for him, but the other part of the endorsement may be written on the typewriter.

How to reconcile bank statement and checkbook. Upon receipt of the bank's statement, reconcile the balance shown by the bank with the balance shown by your checkbook as of the date of the bank statement. Here are the steps necessary to reconcile the bank statement with your checkbook balance:

1. The bank statement shows all withdrawals against, and deposits to the credit of, an account. When a statement is sent to you, the canceled checks are arranged in the order in which the items appear on the statement. Compare the amount entered on the statement with the amount on the check. If there is a discrepancy, call the bank immediately.
2. Arrange the canceled checks in numerical order.
3. Beginning with the first check, compare the amount of each canceled check with the corresponding stub in the checkbook. If the amounts are in agreement, put a check mark in front of the amount on the check stub. (If they are not in agreement, you have made an error and will have to adjust your balance accordingly.) Also compare the name of the payee on the check with the name on the stub.
4. Make a list of the outstanding checks—those that have not been paid, as indicated by the stubs that do not have check marks on them. Show the numbers and the amounts of the check on this list.
5. Record and subtract any bank service charges and/or bank debit memos. (Debit memos are notification of bank charges such as the charge for printed checks or correction of errors.) Bank service charges are generally of relatively small amount and can usually be accepted as accurately computed. However, if the amount of the service charge seems unusual, call the bank and ask to confirm its accuracy.
6. Check the deposits shown on the bank statement against those shown on your stubs. Make a list of deposits not shown on the bank statement. Deposits mailed the date the bank statement was closed and thereafter will not be credited on the current bank statement. If deposits that the bank should have received are not entered on the statement, get in touch with the bank immediately.

7. Some bank statements have a form of reconciliation printed on them. If they do not, make the reconciliation on a separate sheet or on the back of the stubs of checks written the last of the month, as follows:

Bank Statement Reconciliation

June 30, 19___

Balance per bank statement		$1,385.45
Add: Deposit mailed June 30, not shown on bank statement		865.80
Subtotal		$2,251.25
Deduct: Checks outstanding		
#734	$200.00	
#742	16.50	216.50
Reconciled balance per bank		$2,034.75

This last amount should be the same as the balance shown by your checkbook after you subtracted service charges and debit memos (see Step 5). Most banks offer a "no-service-charge checking account" if a minimum balance is maintained in the account. If the manager is still paying service charges, you should determine whether a no-service-charge account can be established for him.

If your checkbook balance and the bank balance are not reconciled after you have taken the foregoing steps, you have made an error in your stubs (or, although rare, the bank has made an error). Check carefully the addition and subtraction on each stub and, also, the balance carried forward from stub to stub. This will reveal any error you have made and you can then adjust the final stub to show the correct balance.

After the reconciliation has been made, O.K. and initial it. Put the reconciliation, the bank statement, and the canceled checks on the executive's desk, unless previously instructed to do otherwise.

TIPS TO BOOST YOUR EFFICIENCY IN TAKING CARE OF THE MANAGER'S BANK ACCOUNTS

A time-saving tip for making deposits. Save your time, or the time of a messenger, by making deposits by mail.

Banks usually supply their depositors with special deposit slips for mail deposits and also with special, postage-prepaid envelopes for mailing them. Prepare the deposit just as you prepare a deposit to be made in person. Observe the following precautions:

1. Never endorse a check in blank if it is to be deposited by mail. Endorse it to the bank for deposit to the account. If you do not have a rubber stamp, type the endorsement, for example: "For deposit with Carson City Bank for account of John E. Brown" (see also Figure 38).
2. If the executive's account number is not imprinted on the deposit slip form, insert it.
3. The bank will return to you a receipt for the deposit, with an envelope for mailing the next deposit.

RECORDS OF PERSONAL AND FAMILY EXPENSES

Expenses of which the manager may want records.   An executive may like to know what it has cost him over a definite period for a particular class of expenses, whether they are deductible for income tax purposes or not. The most common expenses on which he may want information are:

1. House expenses, if he owns the home he lives in. This includes expenditures for repairs, replacements, decoration, outside painting, grounds, and the like. See items 16 and 17 below for deductible expenses.
2. Wages paid to servants. He must keep these records for social security tax purposes and for filing an information return required by the government. Also, in some states an employer must pay unemployment and disability insurance taxes on the wages of domestic employees.
3. Life insurance and other premiums. The costs can be determined from the insurance records. (See chapter 21.)
4. Education of children.
5. Clothes.
6. Recreation, including expenses incurred at country and other social clubs.
7. Money spent in support of a dependent.
8. Travel, other than in connection with business. (A record of business travel expenditures must be kept for income tax purposes.)
9. Automobile expenses, other than in connection with business. (A record of business automobile expenses must be kept for income tax purposes.)
10. Membership dues, other than those that are deductible. For the latter, see page 490.
11. Hobbies expenditures.

12. Gifts. Gifts involving the payment of a gift tax are covered on page 494.
13. Taxes that are not deductible. The most important of these is the federal income tax.

In addition, the manager keeps records of the following personal expenditures for income tax purposes (see chapter 22):

14. Contributions.
15. Medical expenses.
16. Taxes.
17. Interest paid.
18. Expenses incurred in connection with income-producing property.
19. Expenses incurred in connection with his work, whether reimbursed or not.

System for recording expenses. The system described here for recording expenses does not call for a knowledge of bookkeeping; it is a simple system that anyone can set up and maintain.

	House Expenses, 19--			
Date 19--	Check Number or Description		Amount	Total
Feb. 10	*Maintenance Corp - Repair of oil burner.*		25 -	

FIGURE 39   RECORD OF ONE CLASS OF LIVING EXPENSES

Get a loose-leaf journal from a stationer, ruled as shown in Figure 39. You can use a loose-leaf ledger instead of a journal to conserve space. Disregard the debit and credit aspects of the ledger. When the left side of the sheet is filled, continue the entries on the right side. Set up a sheet for each class of living expense for which you are to keep records. Thus, if you are to keep a record for each of the first 13 items in the preceding list, you will start with 13 sheets. For the income tax items, use the records described in chapter 22 on the pages dealing with contributions, medical expenses, taxes, interest paid, expenses incurred in connection with income-producing property, and expenses incurred in connection with work.

At the end of each month, or more often if convenient, transfer or "post" the information on your check stubs to the living expense sheets and to the income tax records. Enter the date, the check number and/or description, and the amount. The description will make it unnecessary to go to the check stub to identify the item. Put a symbol, such as (En), on your check stub to show that you have posted it. If you post in a bound book, show the page number to which the item has been posted instead of using the symbol (En).

You can enter the total for the month on each sheet in the total column, or not, to suit your needs. When a page is full, carry forward the total to the back of the sheet or to the next page, as necessary. At the end of the year, show the totals for the year and rule a double line in red ink below the yearly total. Start new sheets at the beginning of each year, or continue the same sheets, indicating the new year under the double line.

The above system is by no means the only one that can be used. Nor is it essential that the records for living expenses be separated from the income tax records. However, the separation is recommended, for it enables you to keep together all the records pertaining to the income tax return.

How to Maintain Files and Records of Investments

If you are to keep records of the manager's investments in securities, you must be prepared to do the following:

1. Keep the files relating to security transactions.

2. Maintain a current list of investments owned.

3. Maintain the records of each security transaction, including records required for income tax purposes.

4. Supply the manager with information he may require about his securities or the corporations that issue the securities.

Importance of ownership in maintenance of securities records.
Frequently an executive looks after the investments of his or her spouse, his or her children, and other dependents. Thus, your job may consist of taking care of the investment records of several people.

You must bear in mind that each owner is separate and apart from every other owner. Investments jointly owned are separate and apart from the investments wholly owned by either one of the joint owners. Thus, if John and Mary Williams jointly own 100 shares of General Motors' stock, you keep the record of those 100 shares separate from the record of 50 shares of General Motors' stock that John Williams owns by himself. It would be as wrong to confuse the joint holding with the individual holding as it would to mix your own personal accounts with the manager's. What you do for one account, you do for all, keeping each person's records and accounts separate and distinct.

Filing system for security transactions. The following three file folders are all you need for a filing system relating to security transactions:

1. The security transactions file.
2. The broker's statements file.
3. The file for printed material about securities.

These three folders may be combined if the manager does not have many transactions in the market. Remember, keep these three folders for each account that you handle—the manager's account, his or her spouse's, their joint account, and the like.

How to keep the security transactions file. Keep a file entitled *Security Transactions 19___* for each broker if the manager uses more than one. When the manager handles transactions for other members of his family in their names, make a separate folder for each owner of securities as well as for each broker.

This file will hold all of the purchase slips, sales slips, receipts, delivery slips, correspondence, and other papers concerning each transaction of the year. It will include papers on transactions handled through brokers or directly with the corporations issuing the stocks.

Fasten together all papers relating to a particular transaction. Maintain the file in chronological order. Start a new file each year.

Broker's statement file. Keep a file entitled *(Name of broker) Monthly Statement, 19___.* Of course, if there are accounts with more than one broker, each will have its own folder. The only thing that will be kept in this file will be the monthly statements for the account. If more than one account is maintained with a broker—for example, one in the name of the manager and another in the name of his or her spouse—make a separate folder for each account. At the beginning of a new year, start new folders, keeping each year's accumulation separately.

Check the accuracy of the transactions on the broker's monthly statements against the purchase and sales slips in the security transactions file. Show the broker's statement to the manager after you have checked it, and then file in the broker's statement file.

Folder for printed material about securities. Keep a folder for annual reports, notices of meetings, prospectuses, and other printed matter relating to investments in securities. The material does not have permanent value and you can clear the folder out from time to time—unless the manager for some reason wants the material retained.

How to prepare and maintain a list of investments owned. The manager will want to know from time to time just what securities he or she owns. For this purpose, keep a running list of currently owned securities on a form similar to Figure 40.

Arrange the list in alphabetical order by security name. List each block of stocks, bonds, or certificates acquired at a different date or at a different price separately, dittoing the name of the same security. Leave space between each letter of the alphabet to enter additional securities bought during the month.

Make at least three copies of this list. Give the manager one, keep one for your own current use, and put one in the file. Some day the manager will leave his copy at home and will ask you for it. The extra file copy will then be useful. You will not want to give him yours because you need it for making current changes. The manager uses his copy to study his holdings. As a result of his studies, he will perhaps buy new securities or sell certain others.

When you get a purchase slip from the broker, enter the security bought on the list in its proper alphabetical order. Remember, you left space for this possibility. When you get a sales slip from the

Current List of Investments Owned									
Purchase Information					Sales Information				
Date Purchased	No. of Shares	Security Name	Cost per Share	Total Cost	Date Sold	Gross Sales Price	Sales Commissions	Net Proceeds	Long-term Gain or Loss (Held More Than One Year)	Short-term Gain or Loss (Held One Year or Less)

FIGURE 40   CURRENT LIST OF INVESTMENTS OWNED

broker, show the date sold on the list, preferably in red, and draw a *single* red line through that item to show that it is no longer owned. Make these entries at the same time that you enter the transaction on the security record (see next section). Place a symbol on the purchase slip to show that you have entered the item on the investment list.

Try to keep the manager's copy up to date, when you can get hold of it. If the list becomes too messy to be read or if you have not been able to get your hands on your employer's copy to bring it up to date, prepare a new list.

At the beginning of each year, start a new list of investments owned. This constitutes an inventory of the portfolio of securities. If it is so desired by the manager, this first-of-the-year list might include a column for market value as of December 31 to show the "paper" gain or loss.

HOW TO KEEP RECORDS OF SECURITIES TRANSACTIONS

The record of each security owned.   Keep a record of each security owned by the manager and by anyone else whose securities he or she handles. You may keep this record on cards or on loose-leaf sheets in a binder, depending upon which system best meets your needs and preferences and those of the manager.

How to keep a card record of a security transaction.   A card record of a security transaction is illustrated in Figure 41. Like all card records, it has the following disadvantages: (1) a card may be

LDM	JAN	FEB	MAR	APR	MAY	JUN	JUL	AUG	SEPT	OCT	NOV	

100 Shares FREDERICK COMPANY

Bt. Oct. 21, 19__, through Leonard James Co. at 33 1/4 ---- $3,325.00
plus Commission ---- 60.30
$3,385.30

Sold Oct. 17, 19__, through Leonard James Co. at 24 ------- $2,400.00
Dividends: Mar., June, Sept, Dec.

Date	Amt.	Date	Amt.	Date	Amt.	Date	Amt.	Date	Amt.

**FIGURE 41   SECURITY RECORD CARD SHOWING ENTRY OF
PURCHASE AND SALE OF STOCK**

misplaced, lost, or removed; (2) cards become dog-eared with handling. However, some secretaries have used a card system for years
and have experienced neither of these disadvantages. They prefer the
card method because (1) individual cards are easy to handle; (2) the
form can be designed to meet specific needs since it is ruled and run
off in the office on any duplicating machine; (3) if the records are
kept for more than one person, different-colored cards can be used
for each owner.

Operation of the card record system described. A record card
system is described here because it has features desirable for the
small investor, which are not found in the loose-leaf systems.

We describe here how an ordinary purchase, sale, receipt of
dividends, and interest are entered on the record card. Space does
not permit us to show the entries that would be made on receipt of a
stock dividend, stock rights, or new stock received in a split-up or
other exchange. However, you will have no trouble in keeping the
records of such items if you understand the record of the ordinary
purchase and sale and keep in mind that the record card should
furnish the information necessary to compute the gain or loss on any
security transaction.

Description of security record cards. The top line of months indicates the dividend-payment or interest-payment dates. The middle blank section carries the bulk of the record about the acquisition and disposition of the security. The bottom section is for recording dividends on stock or interest on bonds and certificates of deposit. In the case of a bond record, the lower part of the card would also show the amortization of bond premium that was deducted for income tax purposes.

How to enter a purchase on the record card. The card record calls for a separate card for each purchase of the same security. When a security that has been purchased is received, make up a security record card for it as follows:

1. In the upper left-hand corner insert the name of the owner of the security. You can use initials or other abbreviations because of point 6 below.
2. Immediately below the first ruled line, insert the number of shares or face amount of bonds or certificates and the title of the security. If it is stock, show whether it is common or preferred, unless the company has only one class of stock. If preferred, show whether it is redeemable or convertible. If a certificate of deposit or bond, give the percent of interest and the maturity date of the issue. Show whether it is redeemable or convertible. Indicate whether it is coupon or registered.
3. On the next line show when it was bought (the *date* of the trade as given on the broker's purchase slip), through whom bought (the broker), and the price per share or bond/certificate. Multiply the price per share or bond/certificate by the number to get the cost, and enter that cost. Immediately below this figure show the commission paid, because it becomes part of the cost for tax purposes. Add the commission to the cost to get the total cost. In figuring the cost, disregard only accrued interest purchased, since interest purchased, if any, will be reimbursed at the next regular interest payment date.
4. Leave a space for entry of any sale.
5. Write in the months when regular dividends are due or interest is to be received. This information shows where the tabs are to be set at the top of the card.
6. On the back of the card write the name of the owner exactly as it appears on the face of the security and enter the number of shares or amount of bonds it represents, together with the identifying number of the security.
7. Place the metal tab on the next dividend-payment date.

How to enter a sale on the record card. When a security is sold, pull out the card containing the record of its purchase or other acquisition and take the following steps.

If entire holdings shown on the card are sold:

1. Enter in red, immediately under the purchase entry, the following: Sold

(date) through *(broker's name)*; at *(price per share)*, and the total selling price. *Subtract* the commission paid because it affects the profit for tax purposes.

2. On the back of the card cross out the identifying number of the shares delivered for sale.
3. On the back of the card compute the profit or loss on the transaction. All basis figures necessary for the computation are on the face of the card; all sales figures are on the broker's sales slip.

If part of the holdings shown on the card are sold:

1. Enter in red, immediately under the purchase entry, the following: Sold *(number of)* shares, *(date)*, through *(broker's name)* at *(price per share)*, total sales price, less *commission.*
2. Cross out the number of shares owned and substitute the remaining quantity.
3. Cross out the old total cost figure and substitute the cost of the remaining shares. This is a simple mathematical computation. If the original total cost was $4,100 for 100 shares and 75 are sold, the cost of the remaining shares will be one-fourth of $4,100 or $1,025.

Entering dividends and interest on the record card. By entering the dividends and interest received on the record card of the particular security, your employer can see at a glance how the record of dividends on that security looks. A record of all the dividends and interest received during the year is kept separately for income tax purposes. The illustration of the record card (Figure 41) indicates how the dividend record is made on the cards.

In the case of a bond purchased at a premium, if amortization is deducted for income tax purposes (see page 488) that amount should be noted with the interest because the figure enters into the computation of the gain or loss when a sale is made. A separate column called "amortization," in the section containing the interest record, can be used for this purpose.

The file of security record cards. Arrange the file of investment record cards of securities owned by your employer alphabetically by the title of the security. Do the same for securities owned by your employer's spouse, or in other names.

If you prefer, you can arrange the cards by type of security and alphabetically within each class. Thus, all common stock, all preferred stock, and all bonds will be together. The first plan has the advantage of keeping all securities owned in a particular company in one place. The second plan makes it easier to see at a glance the various types of securities owned.

Have a tab card in the file called "Securities Sold 19____." When an entire holding of a security shown on a card is sold, remove the card from the active file and put it behind this tab. If only a portion of the securities shown on the card is sold, keep it in the "owned" section, but put a slip among the sales cards calling attention to the sale noted on the card in the owned file. At the end of the year remove all of the "sold" cards from the file and put them away for safekeeping, identified by year through the tab card. These cards are extremely valuable; they may be called for in later years by auditors, revenue agents, or lawyers to settle the estate in the event of your employer's death.

Cards for other completed transactions, such as securities redeemed or converted, are also filed among the "Securities Sold" cards.

Loose-leaf record sheets for security transactions.   Several forms of loose-leaf investment record sheets are illustrated below.

Figure 42 is used by the personal secretary to the former chairman of a large insurance company. When a security is sold, the item is merely crossed out and the sale entered in red. The illustration shows how stock dividends and splits in reverse are handled.

Figure 43 is a copyrighted form that can be purchased from local stationers.

Figure 44 is another form obtainable at local stationers, identified as Wilson Jones Form 636-40. One secretary who uses this form has added the words "No. of Shares" in the outer column and has substituted "Commission" for the "Maturity" column, to meet her needs.

| XYZ Corporation | | Location | Safe Deposit Box |
| Common Stock | | | First National |

No. Shs. Acquired	Date Acquired	Certificate Number-Date	Cost or Other Basis	Unit Cost	Average Unit Cost	Commission & Charges	Purchased from
100	3/15/40	23645 3/21/40	$1,515.82	15	15.1582	$ 15.82	J.Doe & Co. Company
10	3/15/40	29117 5/16/43	-0-	stk. div.			
110			1,515.82		13.78		
100	8/21/45	35823 8/24/45	2,018.32	20	20.1832	18.32	J.Doe & Co.
210			3,534.14		16.8292		
105	(3/15/60& (8/21/55	98504 1/15/60	-0-	rec'd in revaluation of stock 1 shr. for each 2 held			Company
315			3,534.14		11.2194		

FIGURE 42   INVESTMENT RECORD SHEET

NAME OF STOCK									COMMON PREFERRED		

NAME OF STOCK   **COMMON / PREFERRED**

EXCHANGE LISTED ON	WHERE KEPT	DIVIDEND RATE & WHEN PAYABLE	PAR VALUE $
AUTHORIZED ISSUE	OUTSTANDING	YIELD %	RATING	STATE OF INCORPORATION

CALLABLE

CONVERSION FEATURES

INCOME TAX STATUS   **TRANSFER AGENT**

REMARKS   **DATE OF ANNUAL MEETING**

DATE	NUMBER OF SHARES	CERTIFICATE NUMBER	PRICE PER SHARE	TAX	BROKER FEE	TOTAL	NAME OF BROKER	√4	√5	√10
BOUGHT						COST				
SOLD		NET RECEIVED				PROFIT OR LOSS				
BOUGHT						COST				
SOLD		NET RECEIVED				PROFIT OR LOSS				
BOUGHT						COST				
SOLD		NET RECEIVED				PROFIT OR LOSS				
BOUGHT						COST				
SOLD		NET RECEIVED				PROFIT OR LOSS				
BOUGHT						COST				
SOLD		NET RECEIVED				PROFIT OR LOSS				
BOUGHT						COST				
SOLD		NET RECEIVED				PROFIT OR LOSS				

DIVIDEND RECORD									MARKET QUOTATIONS		
RATE	DATE DUE	AMOUNT RECEIVED	4	5	RATE	DATE DUE	AMOUNT RECEIVED	4	5	DATE	QUOTED	GAIN OR LOSS + OR −
					TOTAL BROUGHT FORWARD							

| TOTAL CARRIED FORWARD | | | | | TOTAL CARRIED FORWARD | | | | | | | |

✿ = AVERAGE COST

FIGURE 43   INVESTMENT RECORD SHEET

STOCK AND BOND REGISTER

NAME

DESCRIPTION

DATE OF ISSUE | DATE OF MATURITY | INTEREST OR DIVIDEND | % PAYABLE | SEMI-ANNUALLY

DENOMINATION

MADE IN U S A

DATE 19___	OF WHOM PURCHASED	DATE 19___	SOLD TO	CERTIFICATE OR BOND NOS.	MATURITY	PAR VALUE	PRICE PAID	TOTAL COST	SOLD FOR	INTEREST OR DIVIDENDS EARNED	LOSS OR GAIN

FIGURE 44 INVESTMENT RECORD SHEET (STOCK AND BOND REGISTER)

Forms shown in Figures 42, 43, and 44 permit the use of one sheet for several purchases and sales of the same security. The card record calls for a separate card for each purchase of the same security. For this reason a loose-leaf record system may be more suitable than the card record system where there are numerous transactions in the same security.

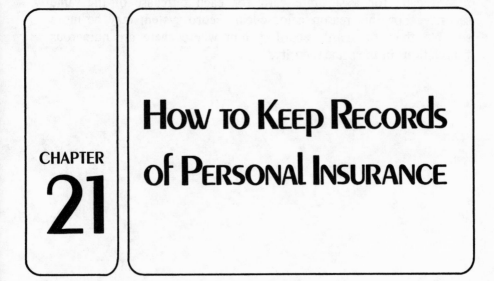

CHAPTER 21

How to Keep Records of Personal Insurance

The secretary has definite responsibilities in looking after the manager's personal insurance separate and apart from those assumed by his or her insurance agent or broker. The agent or broker advises his client about his insurance needs, places the insurance for him, attends to renewals, sends bills for premiums, has policies canceled on order of the insured and sends him return premiums on such policies, and reports claims under the policies to the insurance company. The secretary's duties complement these services. The purpose of this chapter is to explain those duties and to show how they should be performed.

Secretary's duties in regard to insurance. Personal insurance carried by an employer falls into two broad classes: (1) life insurance and (2) general insurance. The secretary's duties in regard to all insurance policies are:

1. To check policies as received.
2. To maintain records adequate for the following purposes:
    (a) Payment of premiums
    (b) Follow-up of expirations
    (c) Survey of the insurance program
3. To have policies canceled when necessary
4. To see that claims are reported, and settlements made
5. To suggest insurance action to be taken by the employer

Examination of policies. When any policy is received, the secretary should check it to see that all of the information that has been typed into the policy form is correct. In this connection, be certain that a policy on property is in the name of the person who owns it. If the property is owned jointly, the policy must be in the name of the joint owners. The insurance company will not pay a claim for more than the value of the insured's interest in the property, regardless of the amount of the policy or the value of the property.

When examining a life insurance policy, determine whether it protects the insured when traveling by air on scheduled or nonscheduled flights. If it does not, suggest separate coverage for air travel.

LIFE INSURANCE

Payment of life insurance premiums. The secretary must be most careful to watch the due dates for premiums on life insurance policies. Although there is a 28- to 31-day grace period after the due date during which payment may be made without lapse of the policy, the due date shown on the policy should be the secretary's guide for payment. Checks should be drawn in ample time to have them signed and sent to the insurance company or agent before the due date. If payment is not received by the insurance company by the end of the grace period, the policy will lapse unless it has a premium loan clause. If the insured is not in good health, it may be impossible to reinstate the policy. Some employers actually consider the secretary's attention to life insurance premium dates her or his main responsibility.

Retain the life insurance premium receipts in a file.

Under some life insurance policies, called "participating policies," the insured becomes entitled to a share of the divisible surplus of the company in the form of a dividend. The insured may choose to have his dividend (1) paid to him in cash, (2) applied as part payment of the premium due, (3) applied to the purchase of additional insurance, or (4) left with the company to draw interest. Dividends that are to be applied as part payment of premiums due are usually indicated on the premium notice. In that case pay the amount due less the dividend. For treatment of such dividends for income tax purposes, see page 474.

When the insured chooses to have his dividend applied to the purchase of additional insurance, the company sends a notice of the increase in amount. Attach the notice to the life insurance policy. Thus, the current value of the policy can be readily found.

Many policies now have a monthly automatic withdrawal plan; that is, the insurance company sends a notice to the bank and the bank charges the insured account for the amount of the premium that is due. The total monthly payments cost no more than the annual premium. The deductions will show as debits on the manager's bank statement. Remember, in these instances, to make the same deduction in the manager's checkbook.

If the manager's life insurance policy has a cash surrender value, he can borrow against it (in an amount equal to the cash surrender value). The interest rates for this are more favorable than bank rates. Terms and payments are arranged with the insurance company, and the secretary's responsibility is to keep a record of payment due dates and dates of remittances made. One method of record is the tickler card as shown in Figure 45. Instead of premium payments, you would be maintaining a reminder for loan payments.

Life insurance records.   The secretary should keep two classes of life insurance records: (1) a reminder of premium dates and (2) a description of the policies.

1. *Reminder of premium dates.* Keep a tickler card file for the payment of life insurance premiums. The procedure in maintaining a tickler file is described on page 33. Figure 45 is a reproduction of a 3″ by 5″ tickler card for the payment of life insurance premiums.

```
Premium due quarterly - 18th of Jan., Apr., July, Oct.
                        (30 days grace)

Amt. quarterly premium: $150
Make check to:          Nelson & Wolf Insurance Agency
Send to same            345 Seventh Avenue
                        Memphis, Tenn.

Policy #3498765 - Blank Life Ins. Co.

Insured: Anna Jane Smith
```

FIGURE 45   TICKLER CARD FOR PAYMENT OF LIFE INSURANCE PREMIUM

The card should show (1) due dates of the premiums; (2) amount of premium; (3) to whom the premium is payable (checks are made to the company, agent, or broker who bills you); (4) where to mail the check; (5) policy number; (6) name of company issuing the policy, and (7) name of insured. If dividends are to be applied as part payment of the premium, make a note to that effect on the tickler card. If you handle more than one bank account, the tickler card should also show the name of the bank account on which the payment check should be drawn. Some secretaries note on the tickler card the dates the premiums are paid.

A reminder system of premium dates must be kept.

2. *Sheet record describing policies.* For your employer's information, maintain a record describing the life insurance policies carried by him or her and by each member of his or her family if you are responsible for those policies. A desirable form for this purpose is a sheet record, which shows at a glance the entire life insurance program. Make a separate sheet for the policies carried by each person for whose insurance you are responsible. The sheet record should have columnar captions similar to those shown in Figure 46. When each policy is received, enter the information called for in the appropriate column. The advantage of the sheet record is that the insured can see the entire picture of his or her life insurance program without studying separate sheets or cards.

You may keep your insurance record in another form if you prefer. Alternate methods are suggested in the following paragraph.

Alternate life insurance records.   Here are two alternate methods of keeping life insurance records. Either may be kept in lieu of, or in

POLICY RECORD										
COMPANY	NUMBER	AMOUNT	TYPE	DATE OF ISSUE	AGE AT ISSUE	GROSS YEARLY PREMIUM	DISABILITY		DOUBLE INDEMNITY	BENEFICIARY
							PREMIUM WAVER	MONTHLY INCOME		

FIGURE 46   SHEET RECORD OF LIFE INSURANCE POLICIES

addition to, the sheet record shown in Figure 46, but neither is a substitute for the reminder record.

1. A visible card record is explained on page 463 for use in connection with insurance other than life. Cel-U-Dex (North Windsor, New York) produces a record card for life insurance policies, also, to be used in the visible record binder manufactured by them.

2. The form shown in Figure 47 provides for a detailed description of the policy and for a record of dividends and their application. The record also has a column that shows the cash or loan value of the policy. This is an excellent form to use when complete details of a policy and its status are desired. One sheet is adequate for entries for many years.

Life insurance premium distribution record. People who carry a heavy life insurance program are interested in knowing how the premiums are distributed throughout the year. Figure 48 is a form that may be used for that purpose. Enter the day of the month on which the premium is due in the "Day of Mo. Due" column, and the amount of the premium opposite the policy number in the column

FIGURE 47   DETAILED RECORD OF LIFE INSURANCE POLICY

Policy Number	Day of Mo. Due	DISTRIBUTION OF LIFE INSURANCE PREMIUM PAYMENTS												
		Jan.	Feb.	Mar.	Apr.	May	June	July	Aug.	Sept.	Oct.	Nov.	Dec.	Total
397456	6			$100						$100				$200
497653	15						$150							$150
309634	30										$75			$75
				$100			$150			$100	$75			$425

FIGURE 48   LIFE INSURANCE PREMIUM DISTRIBUTION RECORD

for the appropriate month. Show the totals for each month and for the year.

If desired, premiums for other types of insurance may be shown on the life insurance record.

This record may be used in either of two ways: (1) to show the distribution of premiums for the forthcoming year, or (2) to enter payments as they are made, thus providing a running record of all premiums paid in a given year. This record is kept in addition to, and not as a substitute for, the reminder of premium dates and description of the policies.

GENERAL INSURANCE

Payment of general insurance premiums.   Payment of premiums on policies other than life insurance must also be attended to promptly, although the urgency may not be as great as in the case of life insurance premiums. All premiums on general insurance are due on the date of the issuance of the policy or on the anniversary of the issuance, although the broker usually has a short period following the due date of the policy to account for the premiums to the insurance company. The broker will usually remind the insured of past-due premiums.

Follow-up of expiration.   The insurance broker usually attends to the renewal of expiring policies well in advance of the expiration date. However, it is your duty to see that the renewals are received. Your tickler system serves to remind you of expirations. If a renewal policy or certificate is not received, get in touch with the broker.

General insurance records.   The records that the secretary should keep for insurance other than life are determined by the extent of the insurance program. A *reminder system* must be kept, but as to other records there may be a choice. Suggested records are described below.

1. *Reminder of expirations.* Whenever a policy or certificate is received, whether as a first contract or as a renewal of an expiring contract, make up a 3" by 5" tickler card to act as your reminder of the expiration date. What you write on the card will vary with the type of policy. The following, however, are the minimum essentials to be noted: (1) type of coverage and expiration date; (2) identifica-

tion by company and policy number; (3) agent's name; (4) insured;
(5) property covered; (6) amount of premium. Figure 49 illustrates a
tickler card for an automobile policy.

```
Blank Casualty Co. Policy #MF 248392
Automobile Combination Policy

Plymouth, 19__           Expiration date: Sept. 16, 19__

Insured: Richard Dale

A.B. Cole, Agent
200 Main Street
Memphis, Tenn.

Annual Premium:     P.I.    $120.00
                    P.D.      90.50
                    F&T       40.00
                            $250.50
```

FIGURE 49   TICKLER CARD FOR EXPIRATION OF AUTOMOBILE POLICY

You do not need a tickler card for the premium due date because
a bill ordinarily accompanies the new policy. The bill is your
reminder that a premium payment is due.

2. *Visible card record.* A visible card system is a convenient
method of keeping a record for insurance survey purposes. Cel-U-Dex
Corporation, North Windsor, New York, manufactures an insurance
binder containing space for visible records of 12 policies. That
company also supplies the record cards that fit into the pockets.

When a policy is received, a card is made up for it. At the bottom
of the card is the identification of the kind of policy, the amount,
and the expiration month. A celluloid marker is placed over the
expiration month. Thus, you can see at a glance what policies expire
each month. Describe the property covered and type of coverage in
the blank space at the top of the record card.

If you wish, you may give each policy an entry number, which
should be placed in the "Item No." column. Or, you may use the
item number simply to indicate that there is more than one policy of
a kind. Thus, there may be three fire insurance policies on three
separate record cards, numbered 1, 2, 3; three automobile combination policies, numbered 1, 2, 3, and so on. If you use the latter
method, it is advisable to code the types of policies and put a symbol
before the number. For example, fire insurance policies might be
numbered F-1, F-2, and so on. When a policy is canceled, the item

number may remain blank or all of the cards may be renumbered in proper consecutive order.

Alternate property insurance records.   1. Instead of the visible card record, you may keep a *sheet record* of property insurance on a form similar to the one shown in Figure 50. This form is not suitable for liability insurance. The disadvantage of the sheet record for property insurance is that expired policies are on the same sheet as policies in force. If there are many policies, an analysis of the record is required to separate the policies in force from those that have expired. You may lessen this disadvantage by having a separate sheet record for each property. In that case, omit the columnar heading "Property and where located" and describe the insured property in the upper left-hand corner of the sheet record.

						PROPERTY INSURANCE RECORD			
Kind	Policy Number	Company	Agent or Broker	Ins. Begins	Ins. Expires	Property and Where Located	Amount of Policy	Amount of Premium	Premium Paid
Fire	K-349875	Capital Fire	William & Norris	3/14/--	3/14/--	Cottage, Atlantic Beach	$10,000	$80	3/20

FIGURE 50   SHEET RECORD OF PROPERTY INSURANCE

2. The form shown in Figure 51 provides for a *detailed description* of policies other than life insurance policies. A separate sheet is kept for each kind of insurance on each piece of property. The entry showing value of the property is particularly useful for reference when market values fluctuate and the insured wants to check on whether he is fully insured or overinsured.

General insurance premium distribution record.   A form similar to the one shown in Figure 47 for distribution of life insurance premiums may be used to show a distribution of premiums for general insurance. The premium distribution for all general and life insurance may be kept on the same sheet.

Reporting claims.   Claims under insurance policies should be reported immediately to the agent or broker. He will make specific inquiries about the details that the insured must supply. The agent or

FIGURE 51   DETAILED DESCRIPTION OF POLICIES OTHER THAN LIFE INSURANCE

broker, in turn, will report the claim to the insurance company, and the insurance company will usually make an investigation. The company will furnish a blank proof of claim to the agent or broker, who sends it to the insured. When the proof of claim is completed, it is customary to return it to the agent or broker. Losses are usually adjusted with the company's adjuster. Sometimes, however, losses are paid without adjustment after the proof of loss is filed. The agent or broker usually receives the company's settlement check and delivers it to the insured.

For records of losses for income tax purposes, see page 487.

When a loss is paid under a fire insurance policy, the face amount of the policy is reduced by that amount. After the damage to the property is repaired, care must be taken to see that the proper amount of insurance is again carried on the property.

Cancellation of policies and follow-up   When the protection offered by an insurance policy is no longer needed, return the policy for cancellation and a return premium obtained for the unexpired period. You will act on instruction from the manager, but you should bring the need for cancellation to his attention. You will notify the agent or broker and return the policy as he directs.

Make a note that a return premium is expected, if that is the case, and follow up if it is not received.

Suggesting insurance action.   The secretary must be alert to situations that call for insurance action, just as the insurance agent or broker would be if he were present to observe what is taking place. It is the secretary's duty to remind the manager of changes that might be needed in existing policies and to suggest that it might be advisable to ask the insurance agent or broker about insurance to meet particular situations. Thus, when the employer moves his or her residence, buys a new car, sells an old car, puts a car away for the season, invests in a building, plans a trip, buys his or her spouse additional valuables—these and many other situations call for insurance action. Information on available coverages can be obtained from the insurance agent or broker. Some of the general insurance coverages available to an individual are listed below.

Accident	Blanket policy
All risk	Boiler explosion
Automobile	Burglary
Aviation	Disability income

Extended coverage endorsement   Liability
Fire   Moving
Health   Property floaters
Homeowners   Rent and rental value
Hospital and medical   Travel

The above list does not include business insurance, because responsibility for such insurance usually rests with someone other than the secretary. The list shows only some of the available coverages. Today nearly every type of potential loss can be covered by insurance.

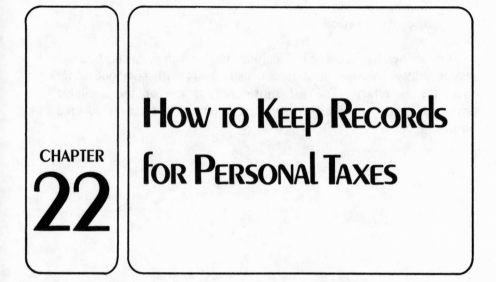

CHAPTER 22

How to Keep Records for Personal Taxes

The purpose of this chapter is to show the secretary how to keep track of the manager's activities, earnings, losses, expenses, and other payments that in any way affect any of his personal income taxes. It does not go into an explanation of business taxes, because the tax problems of a business, whether conducted as an individual proprietorship, partnership, or corporation, are usually taken care of by the firm's accountants.

A secretary can acquire from this explanation (1) suggestions for keeping running records of items that affect taxes; (2) basic income and other tax information necessary for her to recognize items that affect personal taxes. Since tax laws change from time to time, the secretary should keep informed of new regulations, which may necessitate the keeping of additional records.

Duties in connection with federal income tax.   The secretary assists the manager in federal income tax matters by doing the following:

1. Keeping the income tax files
2. Keeping records of all taxable income received during the year
3. Keeping records of all deductions to which the manager may be entitled
4. Following up to see that returns are filed and payments made

The following explanation shows how to perform each of these functions.

Tax records for the manager with a family.   If the manager is married, the secretary must be careful to identify every item involving a tax question with the manager's wife or husband, for it is not always possible to know in advance whether the manager will file a joint return with his or her spouse or a separate return. The secretary will usually know whether the husband or the wife is concerned, for tax purposes, with a particular activity, receipt of income, expenditure, or loss; but if the secretary does not, she or he should inquire *at the time* the event takes place. The secretary must make full notes and records at the time a thing happens; otherwise, when the time comes to make out the tax report, she and the manager will be wracking their brains to recall the facts.

A basic rule, then, is to keep separate records for each individual in the family if the transactions of more than one person pass through your hands.

The income tax files.   The income tax files consist of all previous years' records relating to income taxes and a current income tax folder. It is best to keep the previous year's records in large red expansion portfolios labeled "Federal Income Tax, 19___ (*name of taxpayer*)." These records are kept perpetually and are never destroyed, unless your employer decides to discard them *after all possible statutes of limitation have run out.*

At the beginning of the year, set up a folder labeled "Federal Income Tax, 19___ (*name of taxpayer*)." This is a general folder for income tax material that does not get into the separate folders or records that will be described in the following pages.

Records of income and deductions.   Keep a running record of all items that affect the manager's taxable income and of all items that affect the deductions he or she may be allowed. Two types of running records are described: (1) a simple daily record of taxable income and deductions; and (2) a classified record book.

Since we will describe special records for expenses of business trips, contributions, investment expenses, and medical expenses, none of these items appears in the forms illustrated below. The special records for these items are explained in connection with the basic income tax information that pertains to them, beginning on page 471.

Simple daily tax record.   Some secretaries will find the simple daily record shown in Figure 52 sufficient for keeping track of taxable income and deductible expenses. Each day, the entries that affect the income tax are made in this record book, which is a simple journal that can be purchased in any stationery store. At the end of the year, the items are analyzed to get them into their proper classifications for income tax purposes.

Date		Description	Received		Paid	
Mo.	Day					
Mar.	15	Semimonthly salary	$1,800	00		
	24	Dividend on 10 shares ABC Common stock	58	00		
	31	Semimonthly salary	1,800	00		
Apr.	1	School tax paid on residence			440	00

Daily Record of Income 19--

FIGURE 52   DAILY RECORD OF TAXABLE INCOME AND DEDUCTIONS

If the manager has only one source of income—his regular salary—it is possible to omit these entries of income and depend upon the earnings statements received with the salary checks for the information. At the end of the year, his company will give him a statement showing his total earnings and the income tax withheld. In your record, enter the amount of the salary, not the "take-home" pay.

Classified record book. For a person with various and irregular sources of income and numerous items of various kinds of deductible expenditures, a record book, bound or loose-leaf, for all income and deductions that enter into the computation of federal income tax is advisable. Get an ordinary journal, or a columnar journal, just large enough to take care of the year's records. Start a new book each year so that you can file away the year's records with the income tax papers for that year. Divide the book or sheets into the following parts:

1. Income
2. Deductions (to include all deductions except contributions, expenses of business trips, investment and medical expenses)
3. Contributions (described on page 481). If there are only a few contributions each year, a separate record need not be kept. The donations would be entered with other deductions, as described on page 480.
4. Expenses of business trips (described on page 480)
5. Investment expenses (described on page 489)
6. Medical expenses (described on page 484)

Record of income in classified record book. The income record in the classifed record book should show, for each item of income, the date received, from whom and for what paid, and the amount. Circle dividend items for convenience in calculating the tax. Figure 53 illustrates a basic form of record.

Income 19-

Date		From whom received and for what	Amount Received	
Mar.	3	Dividend on 10 shares of ABC common stock	58	00
	15	Salary	1,800	00

FIGURE 53 RECORD OF INCOME IN CLASSIFIED RECORD BOOK

If the manager has various sources of income and many recurring items, use a columnar page with a column for each type of recurring income and a miscellaneous column for the nonrecurring items. It is advisable to include a total column, as illustrated in the columnar record shown in Figure 54. The addition of this total column will show at any time what the total income is. Also, this total can be used as a check against the accuracy of the addition of the other columns which, when added together, should equal the figure in the total column. You must use your ingenuity in adapting this form to your needs. For example, you might need a column for interest, instead of trust income.

Record of deductions in classified record book. In the deduction section of the record book, use enough columns to take care of all recurring items that are deductible for income tax purposes and a miscellaneous column for unusual items. The record should show the

Income 19--							
Date		From whom received and for what	Total	Salary & Commiss.	Dividends & Interest	Trust Income	Misc.
Feb.	3	Semimonthly salary ABC Co.	250 00	250 00			
	5	Neville Trust	125 00			125 00	
	15	ABC Co. Reimbursement travel expense	80 00				80 00
	15	Cash dividend on 10 shares X Co. common stock			15 00		

FIGURE 54 COLUMNAR RECORD OF INCOME IN CLASSIFIED RECORD BOOK

Deductions 19--							
Date		Item	Total	Losses	Taxes	Interest	Misc.
Jan.	3	R C Scholl, Receiver of taxes—residence	445 00		445 00		
	10	Hempstead Bank interest on loan	125 00			125 00	

FIGURE 55 RECORD OF INCOME TAX DEDUCTIONS IN CLASSIFIED RECORD BOOK

date paid, to whom and for what, and the amount. Figure 55 illustrates a practical form that you might use.

Following up income tax matters.   Follow-up of income tax matters includes:

1. Maintaining a tax calendar
2. Getting the necessary forms
3. Reminding the manager of tax dates
4. Having available, when needed, a copy of the previous federal income tax return filed and all the records that will be used in preparing the return
5. Attending to the filing of the report and paying the tax
6. Filing all the federal income tax papers for the particular year in an envelope labeled "Federal Income Tax, 19___"
7. Filing information returns

Maintaining a tax calendar.   The tax calendar may be part of the regular calendar maintained for all purposes, as described on page 33. In bringing this calendar up to date each year, the tax items should be checked against a tax service (see page 508).

Getting the necessary forms.   The following income tax forms may be needed:

1. The current year's income tax form, and applicable subsidiary schedules.
2. The form for declaring the estimated tax.
3. The form for taking credit for taxes paid to foreign countries or other states.
4. The form for reporting social security taxes.

Obtain the necessary forms from the local post office during tax-reporting time each year or from the District Director of Internal Revenue. His address can be secured at the local post office. Get at least three copies of each form, one for filing with the tax official, one to be retained by your employer, and one to be used as a worksheet.

Reminding the employer of income tax date.   The manager is not likely to forget the important federal income tax dates, but it is nevertheless wise to remind him as the final dates for filing returns and paying taxes approach. Also, if you are taking care of his personal checking account, inform him at the same time of his bank balance.

BASIC INFORMATION CONCERNING
FEDERAL INCOME TAX

HOW TO KEEP TRACK OF TAXABLE INCOME

Wages, salaries, and other compensation. Keeping track of wages, salaries, and other compensation received by the manager involves having available at the end of the year, or before the income tax report must be filed, a record of the total amount received by him as wages, salaries, and other compensation. The amounts must be those *before deduction* for such items as federal income tax withheld, federal insurance (social security) contributions, and hospital and other insurance. This means that gross earnings, not merely the amount of the manager's salary check, must be recorded. There is ordinarily no need for making a record of the deductions from his salary, except the deduction for hospitalization, insofar as the income tax is concerned. Save the earnings statements that accompany his salary check. At the end of the year, he will receive from his company the statement showing his total earnings and how much federal income tax was withheld.

Also, if the manager has an ordinary life policy under which the beneficiaries are his or her spouse or family (not a group life policy) on which *his or her* employer pays the premiums, those premiums are regarded as part of the manager's compensation. You must also include among his or her earnings any amounts received as reimbursement or allowance for trips made in connection with employment. The expenses of these trips, however, are deducted from the manager's total compensation.

How to keep a record of dividends and interest for tax purposes. Keep a record of all dividends and interest received. Keep separate records for dividends and for interest because of the favorable tax treatment given dividends. The form shown in Figure 56 may be used. The "total" column at the right shows how much was received from each investment during the year. The totals at the bottom show how much was received each month. The grand total is entered at the end of the year in the appropriate space at the bottom of the outer column. To identify quickly any dividends from foreign corporations on which a tax has been withheld, enter the dividend in red or circle the amount; the manager may be entitled to a credit for such taxes. The dividend notices contain the information on the amount of tax that has been withheld and whether it is one for

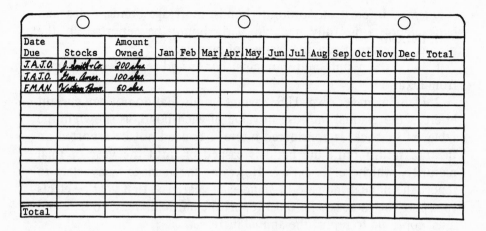

Date Due	Stocks	Amount Owned	Jan	Feb	Mar	Apr	May	Jun	Jul	Aug	Sep	Oct	Nov	Dec	Total
J.A.J.O.	J. Smith & Co.	200 shs.													
J.A.J.O.	Gen. Amer.	100 shs.													
F.M.A.N.	Western Bros.	50 shs.													
Total															

FIGURE 56   DIVIDENDS RECEIVED

which a tax credit can be taken. Be sure to retain these dividend notices.

The record for interest should be similar to that for dividends. Circle in red any nontaxable interest.

Special information about dividends and interest for tax purposes.

Dividends. The taxpayer is permitted to deduct $100 from dividends received. On a joint return, $200 is excludable if husband and wife each had dividends of $100 or more.

Dividends paid *in stock* of a corporation are not usually taxable. The corporation declaring a stock dividend notifies the stockholders whether the dividend is taxable or not. If the manager receives a *taxable* stock dividend, he must report as income the fair market value of the stock received.

Sometimes a corporation will give its security holders the option of taking a dividend in cash or in stock. In that case the dividend is always taxable, even if the security holder elects to accept stock that would otherwise be exempt.

Dividends paid in stock of a company other than the one paying the dividend are income to the extent of the market value of the stock.

Dividends received from a mutual life insurance company that are merely an adjustment of the premiums paid are not included in taxable income. However, amounts received in excess of the aggregate premiums or other consideration paid for the policy are taxable. The same rule applies to dividends on paid-up policies, whether they are received or left with the company. Interest on such dividends is taxable.

Interest. Interest on corporate bonds, mortgage bonds, notes, and bank deposits is fully taxable and should be reported in the manager's return. Some interest is not taxable.

1. Interest on state and municipal bonds and securities is exempt from taxation.

2. If the manager owns U.S. Savings Bonds that do not pay current interest, the gradual increase in value of each bond, as shown in the table on its back, is considered interest. It need not be reported on the tax return until the bond is cashed or until the year of final maturity, whichever is earlier. However, the manager may elect to report the annual increase in value each year. The first year he elects to report the increase, he must report the entire increase to date and must continue to report the annual increase.

If the manager has bought bonds selling "flat" with defaulted interest coupons attached, later collection of a defaulted coupon is not regarded as a collection of interest. To the purchaser, it is a return of capital, and the amount so collected reduces the cost basis of his investment.

How to keep records of rents received.   Reporting rents received for income tax purposes calls for records showing depreciation, expenditures for repairs, and other expenses. For that reason it is almost essential that the secretary keep a real estate record similar to that shown in Figure 57.

The following is a checklist of the more common items that could be considered as deductible in computing the net rent. All except depreciation and repairs should appear in the expense column of the form shown in Figure 57.

Building maintenance expenses
Carpentry expenses
Casualty loss
Commission for obtaining lease (amortized, which means applying the commission over the life of the lease and taking as a deduction each year's portion of the commission)
Damage claim payments
Decorating expenses
Depreciation, building and equipment
Fire loss

Interest on mortgage
Liability insurance
Painting
Plumbing repairs
Property insurance
Real estate taxes
Repairs
Salaries and wages
Social security taxes
Storm damage loss
Theft
Travel expenses
Unemployment insurance taxes

REAL ESTATE

LOCATION

DESCRIPTION

| PURCHASED FROM | DATE PURCHASED | PURCHASE PRICE | AGENT EMPLOYED | ASSESSED VALUE |
| RECORDED IN | COUNTY OF | STATE OF | DEED BOOK NO. | PAGE NO. | WHERE DEED KEPT |

MORTGAGE DATA

REMARKS

| SOLD TO | DATE SOLD | SALE PRICE | AMOUNT CASH RECEIVED | HOW BALANCE PAYABLE |
| AGENT EMPLOYED | | AGENT'S FEE | | PROFIT OR LOSS |

MORTGAGE DATA

REMARKS

DATE	DESCRIPTION		EXPENSE	DEPRECIATION AND REPAIRS	✓ 10	FIXED IMPROVEMENTS	NET INVESTMENT	RETURNS RECEIVED ✓ ✓ 4 8
	MAKE AS FIRST ENTRY UNDER "NET INVESTMENT," THE ORIGINAL PURCHASE PRICE							
	TOTALS BROUGHT FORWARD							
	TOTALS CARRIED FORWARD							

FIGURE 57   REAL ESTATE RECORD

How to keep a record of royalties. If the manager receives author's royalties, royalties for musical compositions, works of art, and the like, renting fees from patents, or license fees for the use, manufacture, or sale of his patented article, the amounts so received are taxable income.

Certain deductions may be made. For example, the cost of developing a patent may be written off ratably over the life of the patent, and the amount attributable to the particular year deducted.

Keep the record of the amounts received; the deductions, in most cases, are figured when the return is filed. The receipt of royalties can be entered in the columnar record of income shown in Figure 54.

In most cases the royalties are fully taxable. In some instances, depending upon the arrangement your employer made, the "royalties" may in effect be the proceeds of a sale of his interest in the product and, hence, may be subject to capital gain treatment.

Profit and loss from the conduct of a business. The federal income tax return has a section in which a person engaged in a business or profession as an individual owner enters his net profit or loss from that source. Such income should not be confused with income from salary, discussed on page 474.

The secretary to a person who is engaged in business for himself will usually not be responsible for determining the income or loss of that business. The secretary to a professional person—a doctor, lawyer, dentist—may have to keep the records of the employer's income and deductions arising out of his professional activities. For professional expenses, see page 490.

Only in rare instances will the secretary to an executive of a corporation find that her employer has income from another business or from professional activities. Any amounts received from such sources may be entered in the columnar record of income shown in Figure 54.

Gain or loss from the sale of property. Any profit arising from the sale or exchange of such items as stocks, bonds, land, or residence property constitutes taxable income. Where the taxpayer buys or builds a new home within a year before or after he sells his old home, gain on the sale will be recognized only to the extent that the selling price exceeds the cost of the new home. Special rules as to costs also apply in the event of construction of a new home started within 12 months after the sale of the old.

Losses from the sale or exchange of such items as stocks, bonds, land, or residence property, if incurred in a transaction entered into *for profit* (and, consequently, *not* losses arising from the sale of a taxpayer's own private residence), may be deducted.

Special rules govern the gain or loss from sale or exchange of the so-called "capital assets." These are explained beginning on page 447 in connection with keeping records of security transactions.

Income from estates, or trusts, and other sources.   The manager may have income from any of the sources mentioned below, which you must record for income tax purposes.

Income from estate or trust. Gifts or bequests are not included in income. However, a share of an estate or a trust's distributable income (whether received or not) is taxable and must be included in the income tax return.

Income from other sources. Income received by the manager from such sources as the following is taxable:

Bad debt recoveries, state and city tax refunds, and the recovery of certain other items, but only to the extent that such items were deducted on a prior year's federal tax return.

Accident and health insurance benefits received as reimbursement for medical expenses for which a deduction was taken in a prior year.

With a few minor exceptions, rewards and prizes received from someone other than an employer (awards and prizes received from an employer are considered, along with salaries and commissions, as compensation for services).

Record of miscellaneous income.   When any amount of income is received from any of the sources described in the preceding paragraphs, a record must be made of it. This can be handled through the record of income. A detailed memorandum of such items as recovery of a bad debt or insurance benefits, covering all the pertinent facts, should be placed in the income tax folder for the year.

Annuities.   If the manager is receiving a company pension or an insurance annuity that he bought or to which he contributed, he is entitled to recover the amount he paid for it tax-free. A certain percentage, called the *exclusion ratio,* is excluded from taxable income each year. The exclusion ratio is determined by dividing the amount your employer invested by the amount he expects to receive. For example, if he paid $12,000 for an annuity and expects to receive $16,000, 75% ($12,000 ÷ $16,000) of each payment is tax-free. If the annuity is to be paid for life instead of for a definite number of years, the expected return is based upon tables furnished by the government.

If the manager receives pensions or annuities *paid for in whole by his employer,* they are fully taxable as income when received. If he paid part of the cost, and the payments he will receive within three years aggregate the total amount he invested, the entire annuity is tax-free until he recovers the amount of his investment. Thereafter, the entire amount received each year is taxable.

As secretary to a person who is receiving an annuity, your obligation is to keep a record of the amounts received as an annuity. These can be shown in the record of income described on page 471. The accountant (or whoever prepares the executive's income tax return) can work out the division of the total into the taxable and nontaxable portions when he prepares the return.

HOW TO KEEP RECORDS OF
FEDERAL INCOME TAX DEDUCTIONS

Importance of deductions.   Current tax laws make it essential that you know what deductible items are and how to record them. It may be that when the manager files his return he will take the "optional standard deduction" allowed under the federal income tax law, or he may elect to itemize. Detailed records are required in either case, since he may deduct travel expenses even when he uses the standard deduction. Have in mind that it is very probable the manager will actually have to prove that these expenses were actually incurred. In some instances he will have to show receipts or lose an entire deduction. Your job is not only to maintain the records but to retain original papers, such as receipted bills and memoranda, that permit easy verification of the deductions.

Expenses of business trips.   Expenses for travel, meals, and lodging incurred while the manager is away from home *overnight* on company business are deductible. These expenses must be listed in a separate schedule and attached to the return. Expenses for travel, but *not* meals, incurred in connection with company business not requiring overnight travel are also deductible. Such expenses, however, are deducted separately from overnight travel expenses. Separate records of overnight and nonovernight expenses must be kept. Expenses in going to and from work are *not* deductible. Also record any expenses the manager incurs in the course of his employment for which the company reimburses him or gives him an allowance. The sum of these expenses is subtracted from his total wages, salary, or compensation (which should include amounts received as reimbursement or allowance). Any form that shows the date, description of the expenditure, and the amount will suffice for keeping a record of business trip expenses. If the manager travels frequently, use the form illustrated in Figure 58.

Here is a checklist for business trip expense deductions:

Airplane fare	Railroad fares
Automobile expenses	Steamship fares
Baggage transfer costs	Taxi fares
Bus fares	Telephone and telegraph expenses
Excess baggage charges	Temporary lodging
Meals	Tips
Porter charges	

Caution: It is frequently difficult to persuade the manager to keep an accurate record of travel expenses. Internal Revenue Service rules relating to deductibility of travel expenses are becoming more strict. The need to substantiate such expenditures is critical. Documentary evidence may be required. Supply him with several of the forms shown in Figure 58 for each trip; remind him to bring back receipts for expenditures, and immediately record any expenses you know about. For example, if you arrange to get his plane ticket, note immediately the amount spent. If the manager does not use the forms, be sure to get the record orally from him immediately on his return. It is easy to forget what was spent after a few days.

Contributions. Contributions to most charitable, religious, scientific, or educational corporations or funds, museums, colleges, and the like, or veterans' organizations are deductible for the year in which they are paid. If payment is made by check, the courts say that payment is made when the check is delivered and not when it is cashed.

The charitable deduction is limited, but if a complete record is kept of *all* contributions, the accountant can figure the correct deduction for contributions at the time that the income tax return is prepared.

EXPENSE AND REIMBURSEMENT RECORD

Name of Company:_____ Period covered: from _____ to_____

Name:_____ Occupation:_____

Item	When and How Long Away	Where and How Far	What I Did	Whom I Saw	Why	How Much I Charged or Spent	Amounts Reimbursed Plus Charges
Travel Away from Home						Fare____ Gas____ Oil____ Meals____ Room____ Extra____	
Local Transportation (not including to and from work)							
Entertainment							
Other Business Expenses							
Comments							
					Totals:		

FIGURE 58   EXPENSE AND REIMBURSEMENT RECORD

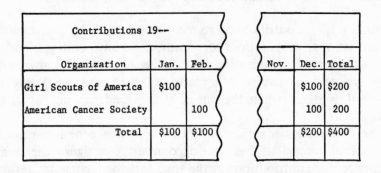

Contributions 19--				Nov.	Dec.	Total
Organization	Jan.	Feb.				
Girl Scouts of America	$100				$100	$200
American Cancer Society		100			100	200
Total	$100	$100			$200	$400

FIGURE 59   RECORD OF CONTRIBUTIONS

The record of contributions. A form for maintaining a running record of contributions is given in Figure 59. This record will enable the secretary to give the manager the answer to such questions as, "What have I given the Red Cross so far this year?" It will also furnish data required to compute the contribution deduction.

To keep this record, rule a sheet with 13 columns. Head it as shown in Figure 59. Enter the name of the organization receiving the contribution in the "Organization" column and the amount of the contribution in the appropriate monthly column. The exact date need not be shown since the check stub can be referred to for that information if needed. Enter successive contributions to the same organization on the same line as the first contribution to it, but in the appropriate column. Thus, each organization will appear only once on the list and all contributions to it will be together. The total of the figures across the column will show how much was contributed during the year to each of the organizations.

At the end of the year, enter the total for each month at the bottom of the monthly columns and the total to each organization in the outer "total" column. The grand total of the totals of the monthly columns should equal the grand total of the outer column.

Figure 60 is suitable for keeping a running record of donations if the manager customarily makes his donation to each organization in a lump sum.

```
CONTRIBUTIONS                          19--


Jan.  9     Girl Scouts of America                       $100
     15     Bucknell University, Lewisburg, PA             150
     18     NJ Association for the Blind                   200
     20     Cerebral Palsy Association                     100

Feb. 10     North Jersey Speech and Hearing Center         100
     14     Ridgewood Valley Hospital, Ridgewood, NJ       100
     18     American Cancer Society                        100
```

FIGURE 60   RUNNING RECORD OF DONATIONS FOR CURRENT YEAR

Alternately, enter each organization alphabetically and the total of the year's contribution to it in a column headed with the particular year. If kept from year to year, this record will enable the secretary to give the manager a quick answer to such questions as, "What did I give to the American Cancer Society last year and the year before?" "How much have I given the Girl Scouts in the past five years?"

Medical expenses for income tax purposes.   *Deductible medical expenses.* The manager may deduct medical expenses to the extent that they exceed three percent of his adjusted gross income. He may deduct medical expenses incurred for himself, his spouse, or any dependent who receives over half of his support from the taxpayer. Although he cannot claim a child who earned over a specified amount as an exemption in arriving at the maximum yearly deduction (unless the child is a student or under 19), medical expenses for such a child can be included in computing the amount spent in medical bills.

The cost of medicines and drugs is deductible to the extent that it exceeds one percent of the manager's adjusted gross income *and* to the extent that it, along with other medical expenses, exceeds the previously mentioned three percent limitation.

Only expenses actually paid during the year enter into the computation. It does not matter when they were incurred.

"Medical expense" is broadly defined; it includes any payment for diagnosis, cure, treatment, transportation to and from medical care, mitigation or prevention of disease, or for the purpose of affecting any bodily function or structure; also premiums paid for accident or health insurance. (One-half of premiums paid for medical insurance or $150, whichever is less, is deductible without regard to the three percent limitation. The balance of medical insurance premiums paid is deductible, along with other medical expenses, to the extent that it exceeds the three percent limitation.)

Examples of deductible medical expenses:

ambulance hire
artificial limbs
artificial teeth
fees of authorized Christian Science
    practitioners
chiropodist's fees
licensed chiropractor's fees
dental fees
drugs and medicine prescribed by
    doctor *to the extent that they
    exceed one percent of gross in-
    come*
eyeglasses
hospital fees
hospitalization insurance

laboratory fees
membership fees in associations fur-
    nishing medical services, hospi-
    talization, and clinical care
cost of operations and related treat-
    ments
osteopath's fees
physicians' and surgeons' fees
practical or registered nurses' fees
surgical fees
therapy treatments
transportation expenses to and
    from medical care
x-rays

Payments to a person who acts as both nurse and domestic give rise to a medical deduction only to the extent of the payment allocable to nursing duties.

The deduction must be reduced by reimbursements (from health or hospitalization insurance, workmen's compensation, or through a damage claim) that are received in the same year the expense is paid. If received in a later year, the reimbursements may be taxable income.

How to record medical expenses. Perhaps the manager's total medical expenses for the year will not be sufficient for a tax deduction. Nevertheless, you must keep a record of every penny spent during the entire year.

Become thoroughly familiar with the preceding list of expenses that qualify as "medical" expenses. Only then will you be able to keep an accurate record of the expenditures that enter into the computation of the medical expense deduction.

Keep the medical expense record separate from all other expense records, using a form similar to that shown in Figure 61. Keep the receipted bills in support of these expenses and file them with the papers pertaining to the particular year's income tax return.

		Medical Expenses 19 —			
Date	Whose Illness	Nature of Expense	Name + address of Payee	Amount	
1/10	Son, James	Eyeglasses	Charles Johnson, Optometrist 21 Main St.	$35	—
2/3	Wife	X-ray	Dr. Robert Smith Lakeville, N.Y.	40	—
2/7 2/8	Daughter, Florence "	Hospital bill,	Memorial, N.Y.	120	—
3/1	Family	Hospitalization insurance	Quarterly deduction from salary	40	68
3/8	Daughter, Florence	Trip to Florida on Dr. Smith's recommendation	Various	500	00

FIGURE 61   RECORD OF MEDICAL EXPENSES

Notice that expenses for medicine and drugs do not appear on the record of medical expenses. Keep the expenditures for medicine and drugs separate from the other medical expenses. You may keep this record by clipping your drug bills and receipts for cash payments together until the accountant is ready to make out the income tax return. (Some drugstores give their charge customers statements that show the running total of expenditures for medicine and drugs.)

Taxes—deductible and nondeductible. The following *nonbusiness* taxes are deductible:

State personal income taxes

Personal property taxes (including those for autos)

Real estate taxes (except assessments levied for paving, sewers, or other improvements that increase the value of the property)

City or state sales taxes (unless levied on the seller and not collected as a separate item from the purchaser)

State gasoline taxes

Taxes incurred in the *production of income,* such as renting real estate, are deductible as a business expense (to arrive at adjusted gross income).

In no case are the following taxes deductible:

Federal income tax or estate, inheritance, legacy, succession or gift taxes.

Federal social security and unemployment taxes paid by employers on wages of domestic servants.

Federal social security taxes paid by employees are not deductible by them.

Federal excise taxes on safe deposit box rental, railroad tickets, theater tickets, club dues, telephone and telegraph messages unless paid as an expense in carrying on a business or investment activities.

How to keep records of taxes paid. If the secretary keeps a record of real property owned by the manager, as described in Figure 57, the real estate taxes paid will appear on this record. The record of city or state sales taxes are usually available only if you handle the manager's household accounts.

Whether or not you perform these functions, you must devise a way of keeping track of *all* deductible taxes. The following methods have been used successfully.

1. Keep a *tax folder* for the year and place in it all receipts and memos for taxes paid that year. At the end of the year, whoever prepares the tax return will analyze the receipts and memos of payments and prepare a summary of deductible items by kinds of taxes.

2. Keep a record of deductions as illustrated by Figure 55, with a special column for taxes paid. At the end of the year, make the analysis and summary of the deductible tax items from the entries in the tax column. In addition, maintain a tax folder for keeping the receipts and memos.

Casualty and theft losses.   Net losses from fire, storm, hurricane, flood, shipwreck, or any other casualty or theft, to property the manager rents to others or to his business or professional property are deductible.

If such losses are incurred in connection with property used for personal purposes, such as personal belongings, home and furniture, and the like, the net loss may be entered as a separate deduction.

The actual loss is computed by determining the value of the property just before the loss and its value immediately afterwards. The difference must be reduced by any insurance or other recovery. A statement explaining the nature of the loss and how the loss was computed should be attached to the return. No amount can be deducted that exceeds the original cost less depreciation allowable.

How to record casualty and theft losses. Make a record of the casualty or theft loss at the time it occurs, and place it in the folder relating to the year's income tax. The memo should contain all of the details needed for preparing the statement that will be attached to the return. If you keep a record of deductions as shown in Figure 55, enter this item in the "losses" column.

Interest paid on personal debts.   Interest on debts, such as a bank or finance company loan or a mortgage on a home, is deductible. But note that interest on money borrowed to buy tax-exempt securities is not deductible. This deduction does not include the financing fees, taxes, and insurance that are sometimes paid on a mortgage or installment contract. Enter the interest paid in the record of deductions (Figure 52 or 55).

Bad debts.   A deduction is allowed for debts that become worthless within the year for which the return is made. A *nonbusiness* bad debt is treated as a short-term capital loss. Each bad debt deduction should be explained on an accompanying statement showing (1) of what the debt consisted, (2) when it became due, (3) what efforts were made to collect the debt, (4) how it was determined to be worthless.

No bad debt deduction should be taken unless the debtor was legally liable to the taxpayer. Advances to relatives made out of moral considerations with no thought of repayment are gifts, not loans, and no deduction is allowed for nonpayment.

You should prepare a memorandum covering the four points mentioned above when you learn that the manager has suffered a bad debt loss. Place the memorandum in the year's tax folder and enter the loss in the record of deductions (Figure 52 or 55).

Amortization of bond premium. The deduction for amortization of bond premium may arise if the manager purchases taxable bonds at a premium; that is, at a price above the face value of the bonds. He has the right to elect to deduct that portion of the premium that is amortized during the taxable year. In the case of convertible bonds purchased at a premium, a special computation must be made to eliminate from the premium the part attributable to the conversion feature.

> *Example:* On January 1, 1976, the manager purchased five $1,000, wholly taxable bonds for $5,100, maturing on January 1, 1996. The interest would be included in his gross income. If he elects to amortize the premium, he will be allowed a deduction of $5 ($100 premium ÷ 20 years) for each year during which he owns the bonds.

If the election to take the amortization deduction is made with respect to any bond issue, it applies to all similar bonds owned when the election is made and all such bonds later acquired and is binding for all future years, unless permission to revoke the election is given by the Commissioner of Internal Revenue.

Alimony. If the manager is paying alimony that his or her spouse must include in her or his return, the manager can deduct it on his or her return. You can include the record of payments in the record of deductions. Sums specially designated as support for minor children are not deductible.

Ordinary and necessary expenses. Since this chapter is limited to personal taxes, the deductions that arise in connection with carrying on a trade or busines (business expenses) are not treated. However, since the explanation is intended for secretaries to people who may have investments that are held for the production of income and for secretaries to professional people, the deductions that are classed as investment expenses and professional expenses are covered here.

Investment expenses. Any ordinary and necessary expenses paid during the year are deductible if they are incurred for the production or collection of income, or for the management, conservation, or maintenance of property held for the production of income (investment expenses). Thus, if the manager invests money in stocks and bonds, certain expenses incurred, such as investment counsel fees, are deductible. Or, if he owns real property that he rents, any expenses incurred in producing the income, for example, traveling expenses incurred in looking after the property, are deductible. Some of the most common of these deductible expenses are:

Attorneys' fees, such as would be paid in suing for the collection of rents

Auditors' and accountants' expenses

Automobile expenses (When car is used for both pleasure and investment purposes, expenses may be prorated and the portion attributable to investment use may be deducted.)

Clerical help, such as salary of a bookkeeper

Custodians' fees paid to banks or others

Depreciation on office equipment used in connection with property held for income

Insurance and bonding expenses

Investment counsel fees or commissions

Maintenance costs of idle property where effort has been made to sell or rent

Rental of safe deposit box used in connection with investment activities

Traveling expenses of trips away from home overnight made for purpose of looking after investments (includes fare, meals, and lodging (but not laundry), tips to porters, cost of hiring a public stenographer, and baggage charges incurred while away from home overnight.)

How to keep a record of investment expenses. Record the following data in any record of investment expenses: date, description of the item, and amount. If there are recurring expenses, such as counsel fees, salary to clerical help, telephone, postage, and the like, it is advisable to set up the record in columnar form so that the recurring items can be entered in the proper columns.

Traveling expenses should not be confused with the expenses of business trips for which a person is reimbursed by his employer. In the investment expense record there may be one column for traveling expenses, to be supported by separate itemization of the individual fares, meals, lodging, trips, and so on.

You must also get information from the manager about personal business trips just as you do in keeping the record of expenses of a business trip for which the manager is reimbursed.

Items that are to be apportioned, such as automobiles used for pleasure and investment activities, may be entered in full as they occur. At the end of the year or when the income tax return is prepared, they can be apportioned.

Professional expenses. Office rent, salaries to employees, social security tax paid on employees' salaries, subscriptions to technical journals and current magazines used in the reception room, cost of supplies, fees paid to other professional persons for professional assistance, dues to a professional society, and similar expenses, are deductible as ordinary business expense. However, no deduction may be taken for the cost of books, instruments, and equipment having a useful life of more than one year (capital items on which depreciation may be taken); membership in a purely social club; bar examination fees and other costs of securing admittance to the bar; and similar fees paid by physicians, dentists, accountants, and others for securing the right to practice.

A professional person who uses his residence both as office and home (physician and dentist in particular) must carefully draw the line between professional and personal expenses. The professional may deduct the rental value of rooms occupied by him as an office (if he actually pays rent) and the cost of electricity and heat furnished in these rooms. If he does not pay rent but owns the property, he may deduct a pro rata part of the annual depreciation. He also may deduct wages of domestic servants in proportion to the time devoted to taking care of his office. When an office is maintained apart from the home, the entire rent may be deducted, as well as the cost of electricity, heat, telephone, and the like.

Expenses that may not be deducted include social security tax paid on his own income as a self-employed person; capital expenditures; personal items, such as living and recreation expenses; cost of taking special courses of training; and expenses for improving personal appearance.

Because of the large number of professional expenses, some method must be devised for recording the expenditures and deductions as they occur. Usually this is part of a system of keeping a professional person's accounts that is set up by an accountant and maintained by the secretary. The records are therefore not discussed further here.

Other taxes that may require attention. Besides the federal income tax, you may have to know about the following taxes if you are to help the manager with all of his or her personal tax matters:

1. State income taxes
2. State and local property taxes
3. Real estate taxes
4. Social security taxes
5. State unemployment insurance taxes
6. State disability insurance taxes
7. Gift taxes

State income taxes. You will be concerned with state income taxes payable by the manager if (1) he lives in a state that has a personal income tax, or (2) is employed in a state that taxes him as a nonresident.

In almost all instances the records maintained for, and used in, filing the federal income tax will be adequate for taking care of the state income tax. One *caution* must be noted: There may be deductions permissible in a particular state that are not allowed under the federal income tax law. For example, under the New York State income tax law premiums paid for life insurance are deductible.

Specifically, the secretary should do the following in regard to state income taxes:

1. Include on your calendar the dates when reports must be filed and taxes paid.
2. Obtain the required forms from the state tax commission or other taxation authority. Get at least three copies of the form, one for filing with the tax official, one to be retained by your employer, and one to be used as a worksheet.
3. Keep any necessary records of deductions beyond those required for federal income tax purposes.
4. Prepare reminders of reports to be filed and taxes paid.
5. Have available, when needed, a copy of the latest federal income tax return filed and the return for the previous year; also, a copy of the previous year's state income tax return. These are invariably needed in preparing the current year's return.

6. File reports and pay taxes.

7. File all the state income tax papers for the particular year in an envelope folder labeled "State Income Tax, 19___."

State and local personal property taxes.   If the manager happens to live in a jurisdiction that taxes the ownership of household goods, automobiles, stocks and bonds, and other personal property, he may be subject to a personal property tax. Also, if he happens to have such kinds of property permanently located in a state that imposes personal property taxes, he may be subject to a personal property tax.

Usually a return is required to be filed in which the properties taxable must be listed and their values indicated. The manager should know what percentage of value is used in the particular jurisdiction in assessing the tax so that he may be guided in filling in the values in his return. For example, it may be unwise to fill in a valuation of 100 percent if the prevailing assessment is at 50 percent of value, unless the full value is required. The tax assessor makes his assessment and usually renders a bill for the taxes. In some cases, however, it is necessary to call at the assessor's office to find out the amount of the tax.

Specifically, you should do the following in regard to personal property taxes:

1. Include on your calendar the dates when reports must be filed and taxes paid.
2. Obtain the necessary forms from the tax jurisdiction.
3. Get information as to the prevailing percentage of assessment for employer's use in filing the report. This may be obtained from the tax jurisdiction authority.
4. Prepare reminders of reports to be filed and taxes paid.
5. Have available, when needed, a copy of the previous report to be used in preparing the current report.
6. File the reports and pay the taxes.
7. File the copy of the return and the tax receipts for the particular year where they will be available when the federal income tax return is prepared.

Real estate taxes.   Owning property involves payment of taxes. Usually there are several taxes, such as a county tax, a village tax, and a school district tax. Tax bills are received from the taxation authority. They show clearly what they are for, the assessed value of the property, when the tax must be paid, to whom it must be paid, the penalties that will be imposed if the tax is not paid when due, and the discount that will be allowed if the bill is paid in full by a certain date. Usually payment can be made in halves. If only one half is paid, there is no discount; no bill is rendered for the second half. Failure to receive a tax bill is no excuse for delay in payment or for nonpayment. You must therefore note tax payment dates on your calendar.

Social security taxes paid on behalf of domestic employees.   The secretary may also be concerned with the social security tax that the manager is required to pay on the wages of employees in his home. If a person working for the manager receives at least $50 in cash wages in a three-month period, the manager must send in a tax report at the end of the quarter. Even if the employee only works an hour or two a day or only one day a week and earns $50 during the quarter, the tax report is required. The form of report used for domestic employees is also furnished by the government, but it is different from that used in business organizations. It is a special envelope addressed to the Internal Revenue Service, with spaces for the employee's name, social security account number, wages paid, and taxes due. Enclose in the envelope a check or money order for the amount withheld from the employee's salary and the amount of tax the manager is required to pay.

Keeping the record of wages paid to domestic employees. If the secretary actually takes care of the payroll of the manager's house employees, she will have no difficulty maintaining the record of wages paid. But if the wages are paid by the manager's spouse, the secretary may have difficulty getting information about employees dismissed and hired and wages paid. She must then devise some routine by which she is informed of changes in the household staff as they occur and of the wages paid to the help.

The following procedure is suggested:

1. Keep a book in which the necessary information is recorded.
2. Regularly, the first Monday of each month, place a memorandum on the employer's desk asking whether there have been any changes in the domestic staff or get the information by telephone from the manager's home. If there have been changes, get the name, address, telephone number, *and social security number* of the new employee and information as to which employee left.

3. Deduct the required percentage from each wage payment until the servant has earned the maximum taxable amount during the calendar year. In figuring the withholding, the cash wages are rounded to the nearest dollar. For example, if a daily wage is $21.50, consider it as $22.

State unemployment and disability insurance taxes. These taxes usually concern only the secretary to a professional person. In such instances the secretary prepares the insurance returns and pays the taxes from her payroll records. In all other cases the responsibility for these taxes usually rests with the person who handles the firm's payroll.

In some states the manager may be required to pay state unemployment and disability insurance for his domestic employees.

Be on the lookout for good employment records (merit rating) and the notices of credit. When they are received from the taxation authority, be sure that the credit is taken into account in paying the tax.

In addition to keeping a record of amounts paid for unemployment and disability insurance, you should do the following:

1. Include on your calendar the dates when reports must be filed and taxes paid.
2. Prepare the necessary unemployment insurance reports for the manager's signature.
3. Make remittances of tax payments.
4. Keep all papers relating to the unemployment and disability insurance reports together in a file. It is not necessary to start a new file for each calendar year.

Gift tax. It is quite common for a person of means to make substantial gifts to members of his or her family. Because of the nature of the gift tax law, these gifts may be made quite regularly.

The manager will undoubtedly have an accountant or other tax expert handle the rather complicated tax aspects of these gifts.

What the secretary does about the gift tax. 1. Keep all copies of the gift tax returns made in successive years together in a folder and bound with a fastener. This practice is important because of the manner in which the gift tax is computed.

2. Keep a record of gifts made that will enable you to supply the information necessary to complete the gift tax form. One method is to prepare a sheet record showing the date of the gift, to whom it is made, and the money or property given as a gift. If securities are

given, list the names of the securities and the fair market value of each at the date of the gift.

HOW TO BOOST YOUR EFFICIENCY
AS A KEEPER OF TAX RECORDS

To be really helpful to the manager concerning his income tax return, you must consult the up-to-minute tax information published regularly by experts in the field. *The Prentice-Hall Personal Income Tax Guide Book,* published annually as a specialty by Prentice-Hall, Inc., Englewood Cliffs, New Jersey 07632, is an inexpensive paperback booklet that can be your "right hand" in the tax field. This booklet sets forth in easy-to-follow steps the usually complicated process of making out accurately a federal income tax return. Prentice-Hall sells this booklet in bulk to companies that give it as a courtesy to their employees or customers, but you can buy a single copy from the Special Publication Division of Prentice-Hall. The booklet answers clearly and simply the tax problems that confront most individuals in the preparation of their income tax returns. For unusually complicated tax problems and for tax problems of corporations, partnerships, and sole proprietors of businesses, consult the *Sources of Information* described in chapter 23.

The Secretary's Handy Information Guide

**PART
5**

CHAPTER

23

Selected Sources of Information for the Manager

Every good secretary knows that today's successful executive reaches the top by working harder than others and by continuing education in ever-growing general areas of national and international matters, as well as in the area of his or her own special field. Every good secretary also knows that keeping up with the manager, continuing to serve the manager and the company in the best tradition of the secretarial profession, requires pursuit of her or his own continuing education.

A manager often asks the secretary to look up information for him, or asks questions that the secretary is not expected to answer without getting the information. She has two recourses: her own ingenuity and knowledge of where the facts are compiled, and where they are available.

Your ingenuity as a guide to information. A good secretary needs a little ingenuity. The knowledge of where to look up information is a basic requirement, and one of the more obvious sources of all kinds of information is the library—your company library, the public library, state libraries, and the libraries of other companies and organizations, particularly research organizations. If you visit any of these facilities, do not be afraid that you will not know where to begin—simply explain your problem to the librarian and you will doubtless receive all of the help that you need.

Many executives want the answer to a question "right now" and you do not have time to go to the library. The thing to do is to use your ingenuity and think of places to telephone. (The yellow pages of your telephone directory will serve you well on these occasions.) If the manager asks a question about animals, where could you get the answer? Try the zoo. Does he want to know the foreign exchange rate on a particular currency? Call a commercial bank that has a foreign department. The technical term used to describe a certain item? Call the manufacturer of, or dealer in, that item if one is available in your locality.

Always use the latest available edition of a book! If your fact-finding leads you to a particular reference book with a pattern of regularity, order a copy for your office or company library. (You can get the name and address of the publisher from the title page of the book.) If you have to go to a library, an idea of the scope of the books in its reference department is necessary. Following are some of the reference books that you are likely to encounter in your fact-finding for the manager. These sources are divided below into basic library sources and information of a specialized nature. If the information you seek is not in the material described here, a librarian can usually suggest the reference book that will help you.

BASIC LIBRARY SOURCES

Encyclopedias.

Encyclopaedia Britannica articles, in the main, are scholarly, detailed, and well illustrated. They are particularly good for historical and background material, and for general information on the arts, sciences, technology, and political and economic developments of foreign countries and cities. Yearbooks are published to describe the developments of the year and provide a chronology of important events.

Encyclopedia Americana contains accounts of scientific and technological developments that are in general more complete and up to date than those in the other encyclopedias. The descriptions of American cities are particularly good; they give an historical account of their founding, statistics of commerce and manufacturing, and some indication of the cultural and educational advantages available. Each account is followed by a carefully collected bibliography. The yearbooks contain descriptions of events of the year and keep statistical material current.

There are less ambitious encyclopedias, such as the one-volume *Columbia Encyclopedia.* The cost is also much less than the larger works, *Britannica, Americana,* and *Collier's Encyclopedia.*

Reference books of facts.

Either the *World Almanac and Book of Facts,* published by Newspaper Enterprise Association, or the *Information Please Almanac Atlas and Yearbook,* published by Simon and Schuster, can be very useful as a one-volume source of general facts of all kinds. These books are crammed with statistics on government (state, national, and international), history, geography, science, religion, sports, famous people, and so on. You can find out such facts as the center of population in the United States, when Hawaii was admitted into the Union, or what a patent is and how you can apply for one.

Almanacs are published annually, so in order to have the latest information you will have to purchase a new edition each year. Almanacs are soft-covered and inexpensive. No secretary should be without one in her office library.

Statistical Yearbook (Annuaire Statistique) is published by the United Nations. This is an annual publication that includes separate tables of all pertinent statistics for all nations of the world.

Statistical Abstract of the United States, published annually by the U.S. Government Printing Office, is a major source of socioeconomic statistics for the United States, with many tables broken down by state.

Atlases.

Encyclopaedia Britannica World Atlas, published by Encyclopaedia Britannica, Inc., contains politico-social maps, economic, soil and climatic maps, and a gazetteer index.

Rand McNally Commercial Atlas and Marketing Guide, published annually by Rand McNally & Co., includes highly detailed maps and indexes of United States and foreign places; up-to-date, comprehensive marketing information on state, county and city levels; retail sales maps to assist in territory evaluation, setting quotas, potentials, and so forth. Monthly business trend map and correspondence services are included. It is designed primarily for the businessperson.

Rand McNally Road Atlas, published annually by Rand McNally & Co., is a popular large-size paperback guide for managers who travel by car. It includes large, full-color road maps, toll road and expressway information, and special maps of major cities.

Dictionaries, word books, and sources of quotations.

Dictionaries give you the spelling, pronunciation, and definition of a word, and, in some cases, synonyms and antonyms. They break words into syllables and show you where to hyphenate. You will also find the correct spelling of the plural forms of many nouns and the spelling of unusual variant forms of verbs.

Dictionaries give you the accepted way of pronouncing words, with the words phonetically spelled out in parentheses. A phonetic key is at the front of the dictionary and (in some dictionaries) at the bottom of each page.

The same word can have different meanings. If such is the case, the different definitions are grouped accordingly under separate headings as to the part of speech. Specialized meanings (such as those related to law, architecture, chemistry) are labeled as such. You will find some words labeled "slang," but most dictionaries are very conservative in their outlook.

For most purposes, a desk, or abridged, dictionary is adequate. Paperback "pocket" dictionaries are available, but are not advisable for office use. Even if you have an unabridged dictionary in your office, you should have an abridged desk version on your desk for quick reference.

Dictionary of synonyms and antonyms. When using a dictionary, you start with a word and find its meaning. With a dictionary of synonyms and antonyms, such as *Roget's Thesaurus,* you start with a meaning and find a word to fit it. A thesaurus entry gives the synonyms of a word, and all related words, phrases, expressions, and opposites, carefully graded according to their fine shades of meaning. Another good synonyms reference, with well-annotated entries, is *Funk and Wagnalls Modern Guide to Synonyms.*

Bartlett's Familiar Quotations is probably the best-known book for sources of quotations. It is a collection of passages, verses and proverbs traced to their source in English and modern literature. It is published by Little, Brown and Company of Boston and is frequently revised. Another good quotations reference is *Dictionary of Quotations,* edited by Bergen Evans and published by Delacorte. It includes unfamiliar as well as familiar quotations.

INFORMATION OF A SPECIALIZED NATURE

Firm names and addresses.   The need for firm names and addresses arises constantly. For that reason a great number of directories have been published for different fields of business. Thus, for example, there are directories of manufacturers, showing who manufactures what; of banks, hotels, exporters and importers, newspapers, warehouses, shipping firms, and many others too numerous to mention. Some sources through which the appropriate directory can be found are given here, as well as some specific references to publications with which you ought to be familiar.

Industrial Marketing, Market Data and Directory Issue contains a list of directories and trade catalogs published in the preceding year. (Note that *Industrial Marketing* is a periodical.)

A well-known directory for locating names and addresses of manufacturers is *Thomas Register of American Manufacturers.* This shows who manufactures what. More than 70,000 products are listed, with names of the manufacturers under each product, arranged by state and city. The compilation of trade names and trademarks is excellent for locating the manufacturers of widely advertised products.

Other helpful sources are the classified telephone directories, and the rating books of general mercantile and special agencies. Chief among the latter is *Dun & Bradstreet Reference Book,* which is available only to subscribers, supplies credit and capital ratings of large and small businesses, their addresses, and type of business. The financial services described on page 507 are also useful in locating names and addresses of firms.

Information about individuals.   The manager may want you to find out facts about someone's life. If that person is fairly well known, the sources of information are plentiful. For example, there might be a full-length biography written about the person. There might be a reference to the individual in an encyclopedia, or you might find a complete synopsis of the person's life in an obituary column of the *New York Times;* get the date the obituary appeared in the paper from the *New York Times Index.*

Who's Who. The biographical dictionaries of the Who's Who type give data about living individuals, such as date of birth, marital status and children, education, positions held, club affiliations, and directorships. They are published in numerous fields; some cover the United States, some cover foreign countries. You can tell the subject matter by the title, for example, *Who's Who in Labor.* Always be aware that the biographical information is gathered from questionnaires filled out by the persons themselves and might not be entirely objective.

See *Webster's Biographical Dictionary* for biographical material of historical figures.

Two other good sources of biographical information about people currently in the news are the periodical *Current Biography,* published by H. W. Wilson, and *Taylor's Encyclopedia of Government Officials—Federal and State,* published by Political Research, Inc. The latter is continually updated through loose-leaf supplements. Both contain photographs.

Professional information.   Often, an excellent source of professional information is the association that serves the manager's profession. For example, if your company manufactures home appliances, the Association of Home Appliance Manufacturers could be most helpful to you and your manager, particularly if he is a member of that organization.

Three directories listing all major associations in the United States are *Gale's Encyclopedia of Associations,* the largest volume, published in hardcover by Gale Research Company; the *National Trade*

& *Professional Associations of the United States,* published in paperback by Columbia Books, Inc. Publishers; and *Who's Who in Association Management,* published in paperback by the American Society of Association Executives for its members.

The U.S. Government Printing Office in Washington, DC produces most of the federal literature, usually available in paperback or pamphlet form at modest prices. An inquiry on almost any topic will bring you a list and order form of available publications.

The Department of Commerce continually prepares statistical data on all industries. In addition to the large census volumes found at the library, quarterly reports are available by subscription, such as the *Current Industrial Reports,* prepared by industry classification (e.g., metalworking machinery).

GUIDES TO REFERENCE WORKS ON SPECIFIC SUBJECTS

The manager may ask you to get the facts for him on a subject of current interest or on a subject that was current some years ago. The indexes to periodical literature furnish references to articles that have been published in books, magazines, pamphlets, and newspapers on all subjects. These indexes usually give references under subjects, titles of articles and publications, and authors. Any large library has them, and small libraries have some of them.

One of the best guides to sources of information for a secretary who does a great deal of research is *How and Where to Look It Up: A Guide to Standard Sources of Information,* by Robert W. Murphey, published by McGraw-Hill. This volume describes many more reference works than can be given in this chapter of *Complete Secretary's Handbook.* (The basic sources listed in this chapter will serve for most of the research projects or questions you are likely to meet.) Another good work of the same type is *How to Use the Business Library, with Sources of Business Information,* by Herbert W. Johnson, published by South-Western.

Guides to periodicals and newspapers.   Newspapers and magazines are often excellent sources of information, especially for a business-person who needs current facts or wants to quote a public figure in a speech or report. Fortunately, there are indexes that can direct you to particular articles.

N. W. Ayer and Son's Directory of Newspapers and Periodicals, a bibliography, has a complete compilation of published newspapers and periodicals. The basic arrangement is by the state of publication, with cities and towns listed alphabetically under these headings. Included in this compilation are the frequency of publication, special features, circulation, size of page and column width, subscription price, policies and character, and names of editor and publisher.

Readers' Guide to Periodical Literature, published by H. W. Wilson Company, covers over 100 periodicals of general nature. Each article in these periodicals is referred to by author and subject; titles are given only for works of fiction.

The *Business Periodicals Index,* published by H. W. Wilson Company, is an index, by subject matter, to various business periodicals. The fields that are covered include accounting, advertising, banking and finance, general business, insurance, labor and management, marketing and purchasing, public administration, taxation, specific businesses, and specific industries and trades. *Business Periodicals Index* is published monthly (except July), with a bound cumulation each year.

Applied Science & Technology Index, published by H. W. Wilson Company, is an index, by subject matter, to various scientific and technological periodicals. Some of the fields that are covered in the *Index* are aeronautics, automation, chemistry, construction, electricity and electrical communication, engineering, geology and metallurgy, industrial and mechanical arts, machinery, physics, and transportation. The *Applied Science & Technology Index* is published monthly (except August) with a bound annual cumulation.

The *New York Times Index,* published by the New York Times Company, is an index to the contents of that newspaper. The index comes out frequently, with a final cumulative index for each year. Reference is given to the date of the paper, page number, and column number. You will find the *Times Index* particularly helpful when you have occasion to look up an obituary, the full text of a speech or document, or book and theater reviews.

Periodicals: Price List 36, published by the U.S. Government Printing Office, provides the titles of all periodicals published by the United States government. It also describes the contents and names the publishing agency, subscription price, and catalog number. The

Monthly Catalog of U.S. Government Publications, prepared by the Superintendent of Documents, lists mostly pamphlets and leaflets prepared by various agencies (subject, author, and title indexes).

The *Book Review Digest,* published by H. W. Wilson Company, is an index to book reviews appearing in magazines and newspapers. Quotations are printed from many of those reviews that are cited.

The *Wall Street Journal Index,* published by Dow, Jones & Company, is divided into two sections, the first devoted entirely to corporate news, the second to general news.

SOURCES OF FEDERAL GOVERNMENT INFORMATION

The *Official Register of the U.S. Government* is a publication that appears annually, listing, by agency, all persons holding administrative or supervisory positions in the legislative, executive, and judicial branches of the federal government and the District of Columbia. It gives each person's name, title, legal residence, and (in most cases) salary. The book is indexed by agency and by name.

The *Official Congressional Directory* lists the names and addresses of officials associated with the federal government, including members of the press. The directory, published by the U.S. Government Printing Office, also contains biographical data on each member of Congress and maps of Congressional Districts. The directory is issued normally at least once during each session of Congress.

The *Congressional Record* is a daily record of the proceedings of Congress, including a complete history of all legislation. Texts of bills are not included. Indexes give names and subjects of bills and a history of them under their respective numbers. The final index to a volume, covering one session, thus provides references to the complete history of all legislation introduced during that session.

SOURCES OF FINANCIAL INFORMATION

The secretary may have occasion to look for the following three types of information about the securities owned by the manager:

1. Current information, such as quotations of security prices, dividend action, securities called for redemption, new issues, announcements on stock

rights, financial and business news affecting the securities market, trends of security prices, stock and bond yields, and the like.

2. Compiled information about companies and their securities, such as the history of the company; its business and products; the address of the general office; the name and address of the transfer agent, registrar, and dividend-paying agent; statistical records of dividends, price range, income statements and balance sheets; complete descriptions of each class of stock outstanding and of bond issues.

3. Tax information, such as taxation of capital gains and losses, taxation of stock dividends, stock rights, exchanges of stock, dividends received in stock of another company, and the like.

There are many sources of information for each of the above-mentioned groups. The most important are noted below. Most of the sources mentioned can usually be found in any large public library.

Newspapers.

New York Times. New York: The New York Times Company, Daily.

The Journal of Commerce and Commercial. New York: Twin Coast Newspapers, Inc., Daily.

Wall Street Journal. New York: Dow, Jones & Company, Daily. Other large city dailies.

Periodicals.

Barron's National Business and Financial Weekly. Boston: Dow, Jones and Co.

Business Week. New York: McGraw-Hill, Weekly.

Commercial and Financial Chronicle. New York: National News Service, Weekly.

Dun's Review. New York: Dun and Bradstreet, Monthly.

Financial World. New York: Butler Publishing Corp., Weekly.

Fortune. New York: Time, Inc., Monthly.

Nation's Business. Washington, DC: Chamber of Commerce of the United States, Monthly.

Survey of Current Business. Washington, DC: U.S. Department of Commerce, Monthly.

Security services. The three leading security services are Bernard, Moody, and Standard and Poor's. They attempt to give as complete a picture on all phases of investment as possible. The heart of each service is the data assembled on individual companies. These publications are kept current through loose-leaf services with periodic cumulations. Some of the publications of these three companies are mentioned below.

Value Line. A loose-leaf service of Arnold Bernard and Co. that provides detailed investment information on both companies and industries.

Moody's manuals giving securities information are now published in six areas: *Municipal and Government; Bank and Finance; Industrial; OTC Industrial; Public Utility;* and *Transportation.*

Standard Corporation Records. Complete factual information on major American and Canadian corporations and their securities. Six loose-leaf volumes, revised monthly, supply the bulk of the data on balance sheets, earnings, and market prices.

Standard and Poor's Trade and Securities Service. Three sections include: Weekly Outlook for Securities Markets, Monthly Earnings and Ratings Stock Guide, and a statistical section.

Standard and Poor's Bond Guide. Pocket-size booklet with information all on one line for each security.

Other useful publications are: *Moody's Handbook of Common Stocks,* published quarterly, which gives a one-page summary of financial background, recent developments, and prospects for the future for numerous stocks; *Value Line Investment Survey,* published weekly by Arnold Bernhard and Co., which analyzes selected stocks and the most favorable industries for investment; *Standard and Poor's Industry Surveys,* published quarterly, which gives in-depth analyses of industries.

SOURCES OF TAX INFORMATION

Federal income tax.   Numerous books, pamphlets, and digests, as well as several complete and abridged loose-leaf tax services, are published on federal taxes.

For accurate, up-to-date information, a tax service would serve the manager best—for example:

Prentice-Hall Federal Tax Guide. Prentice-Hall, Inc., Englewood Cliffs, NJ: Annual with frequent supplements.

For tax treatment of exchanges of securities in reorganizations of particular companies and distributions of stock dividends and rights for individual security issues, a ready reference table is furnished in the following service:

Capital Adjustments. Prentice-Hall, Inc., Englewood Cliffs, N.J.: 2 bound and 2 loose-leaf volumes with current supplements.

Other taxes.   The two principal publishers of loose-leaf tax services, Prentice-Hall, Inc., and Commerce Clearing House, cover all taxes imposed by federal, state, and local governments. Write to the publisher asking the name of the service that covers your specific requirements; then consult the service. If the service is not available in your company or in a nearby large library, write to the particular taxation authority for the information desired.

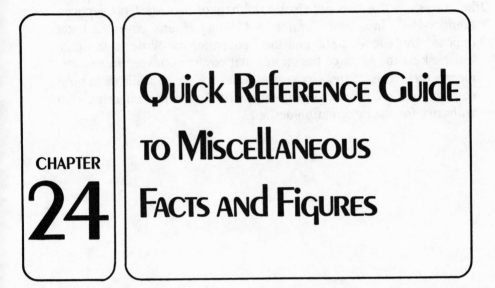

Quick Reference Guide to Miscellaneous Facts and Figures

CHAPTER 24

This chapter contains various types of miscellaneous information that is most often needed by the secretary and is set out in the following categories for your quick reference:

´	Accent, acute	-	Hyphen
`	Accent, grave	—	Em dash
' or '	Apostrophe	-	En dash
*	Asterisk	...	Leaders
{ }	Braces	¶	Paragraph
{ }		‖	Parallels
[ ]	Brackets	( )	Parentheses
∧ or ⌒ or ~	Caret	.	Period
, (ç)	Cedilla	?	Question mark
∧	Circumflex		(Interrogation point)
:	Colon	" "	Quotation marks
,	Comma	§	Section
†	Dagger	;	Semicolon
¨ (ö)	Dieresis	~	Tilde
‡	Double dagger	‗	Underscore
*** or .. or ——	Ellipsis	/	Virgule
!	Exclamation point		

I	1	XI	11	XXX	30	CCC	300
II	2	XII	12	XL	40	CD	400
III	3	XIII	13	L	50	D	500
IV	4	XIV	14	LX	60	DC	600
V	5	XV	15	LXX	70	DCC	700
VI	6	XVI	16	LXXX		DCCC	800
VII	7	XVII	17	or XXC	80	CM	900
VIII	8	XVIII	18	XC	90	M	1,000
IX	9	XIX	19	C	100	MM or mm	2,000
X	10	XX	20	CC	200		

General rules for Roman numerals.

(1) Repeating a letter repeats its value: XX = 20; CCC = 300.

(2) A letter placed after one of greater value adds thereto: VIII = 8; DC = 600.

(3) A letter placed before one of greater value subtracts therefrom: IX = 9; CM = 900.

(4) A dash line over a numeral multiplies the value by 1,000. Thus, $\overline{X} = 10,000$; $\overline{L} = 50,000$; $\overline{C} = 100,000$; $\overline{D} = 500,000$; $\overline{M} = 1,000,000$; $\overline{CLIX} = 159,000$; $\overline{DLIX} = 559,000$.

STANDARD
PROOFREADING MARKS

∧	Make correction indicated in margin.	////	Hair space letters.
Stet	Retain crossed-out word or letter; let it stand.	*wf.*	Wrong font; change to proper font.
Stet (dotted)	Retain words under which dots appear; write "Stet" in margin.	*Qu?*	Is this right?
		lc.	Set in lower case (small letters).
X	Appears battered; examine.	*s.c.*	Set in small capitals.
═══	Straighten lines.	*Caps*	Set in capitals.
√√√	Unevenly spaced; correct spacing.	*c&sc*	Set in caps and small caps.
‖	Line up; i.e., make lines even with other matter.	*rom.*	Change to roman.
run in	Make no break in the reading; no paragraph.	*ital.*	Change to italic.
		═══	Under letter or word means caps.
No ¶	No paragraph; sometimes written "run in."	═══	Under letter or word means small caps.
Out-see copy	Here is an omission; see copy.	──	Under letter or word means italic.
¶	Make a paragraph here.	∼∼∼	Under letter or word means boldface.
tr.	Transpose words or letters as indicated.	∧	Insert comma.
∂	Take out matter indicated; delete.	⅋	Insert semicolon.
∂	Take out character indicated and close up.	⁏	Insert colon.
		⊙	Insert period.
∅	Line drawn through a cap means lower case.	/?/	Insert interrogation mark.
⊘	Upside down; reverse.	/!/	Insert exclamation mark.
⊃	Close up; no space.	⁼/	Insert hyphen.
#	Insert a space here.	V	Insert apostrophe.
⊥	Push down this space.	ⱽⱽ	Insert quotation marks.
⌐	Indent line one em.	ℓ	Insert superior letter or figure.
⊏	Move this to the left.	⋀	Insert inferior letter or figure.
⊐	Move this to the right.	[/]	Insert brackets.
⌐⌐	Raise to proper position.	(/)	Insert parentheses.
⌐⌐	Lower to proper position.	⊸∕ₘ	One-em dash.
		⊸⊸ₘ	Two-em parallel dash.
		⊛	Spell out.

HOW TO CORRECT PROOF

It does not appear that the earliest printers had any method of correcting errors before the form was on the press. The learned learned correctors of the first two centuries of printing were not proofreaders in our sense; they were rather what we should term office editors. Their labors were chiefly to see that the proof corresponded to the copy, but that the printed page was correct in its Latinity, that the words were there, and that the sense was right. They cared but little about orthography, bad letters, or purely printers' errors, and when the text seemed to them wrong they consulted fresh authorities or altered it on their own responsibility. Good proofs, in the modern sense, were impossible until professional readers were employed, men who had first a printer's education, and then spent many years in the correction of proof. The orthography of English, which for the past century has undergone little change, was very fluctuating until after the publication of Johnson's Dictionary, and capitals, which have been used with considerable regularity for the past 80 years, were previously used on the miss or hit plan. The approach to regularity, so far as we have, may be attributed to the growth of a class of professional proofreaders, and it is to them that we owe the correctness of modern printing. More errors have been found in the Bible than in any other one work. For many generations it was frequently the case that Bibles were brought out stealthily, from fear of governmental interference. They were frequently printed from imperfect texts, and were often modified to meet the views of those who published them. The story is related that a certain woman in Germany, who was the wife of a printer, and had become disgusted with the continual assertion of the superiority of man over woman which she had heard, hurried into the composing room while her husband was at supper and altered a sentence in the Bible, which he was printing, so that it read Narr instead of Herr, thus making the verse read "And he shall be thy fool" instead of "And he shall be thy lord." The word not was omitted by Barker, the King's printer in England in 1632, in printing the seventh commandment. He was fined £3,000 on this account.

CHECKLIST OF
BUSINESS INSURANCE COVERAGE

Accident
Accounts receivable
Acid and chemical damage
Aircraft: hull & liability
Air passengers
Airport liability
Air insurance
Alteration bond
Arrest bond
Art glass
Arts: all risk
Assumed liability
Auctioneer's bond
Automobile: car & liability
Auto trailers

Baggage
Bail bond
Bailee's customer's
Bank burglary & robbery
Banker's blanket bond
Banker's forgery & alteration bond
Blanket bonds, fidelity, forgery,
    alterations
Boiler policy
Bonds, all purposes
Breeder's policy
Bridge policy
Builder's risk
Burglary
Business interruption

Camera: all risk
Cargo
Car rental
Casualty: all types
Chain stores, multiple locations
Checks
Civil commotion
Cloudburst
Collision
Common carrier's legal liability

Compensation
Completion bond
Consequential damage
Consignee
Contruction bond
Contents of buildings
Contractors:

    bonds
    compensation
    equipment floater
    liability
    protective policy

Conversion
Crash: aviation
Credit insurance
Crime: comprehensive
Crop insurance
Curios
Cyclone

Dentist's liability
Depositor's forgery bond
Destruction: money, securities,
    records
Dies
Drawings

Earthquake
Electric motors & equipment
Elevator liability
Embezzlement
Employer liability
Engines: all types
Equipment floater
Excess commercia! bond
Exhibitions
Explosion
Extraordinary alterations

Farm equipment & liability

Fidelity bonds
Fiduciary bonds
Fine arts floater
Fire
Fleet coverage
Flood
Flywheel
Forgery bonds
Fraud bonds
Freezing
Freight policy
Fur floater
Furrier's customer's floater

Garage-keeper's liability
Garage liability
Glass
Goods-in-process
Guarantee bonds

Hail
Hangar-keeper's liability

Inland marine floater policies
Inland transit policy
Insurrection

Landlord's liability
Larceny
Laundry policy
Leakage
Leasehold insurance
Legal liability
Liability: all types
Lightning
Livestock

Machinery
Malicious mischief
Manufacturer's liability
Manuscripts
Marine insurance
Mercantile burglary
Merchant's protective bond

Messenger robbery
Money & securities
Motor truck carrier's form
Musical instruments floater

Negligence liability

Occupancy insurance
Office burglary & robbery
Officer's & director's liability
Owner's liability

Parcel post insurance
Patterns
Paymaster robbery
Performance bond
Personal effects floater
Personal liability
Personal property floater
Physician's liability policy
Plate glass insurance
Power interruption
Products liability
Professional liability
Property: all types
Property damage liability

Rain
Records destruction insurance
Rental insurance
Repair & replace insurance
Riot
Rising water
Robbery

Safe: burglary
Safe deposit boxes
Safe depository liability
Service station liability
Smoke damage
Sports liability
Sprinkler leakage
Steam boiler insurance
Stored goods

Strikers, damage from	Unoccupied buildings
Surety bonds	Use & occupancy
Surgeon's liability policy	
	Vandalism
Team's liability	
Tenant's liability	Warehouseman's liability
Theft insurance	War risk
Third-party liability	Water damage
Title insurance	Windstorm
Tornado	Workmen's compensation
Tourist's baggage floater	
Transportation floater	

TABLES OF WEIGHTS, MEASURES, AND VALUES

Long Measure

12	inches	1 foot
3	feet	1 yard
5½	yards, or 16½ feet . .	1 rod
320	rods, or 5,280 feet	1 mile
1,760	yards	1 mile
40	rods	1 furlong
8	furlongs	1 statute mile
3	miles	1 league

Square Measure

144	square inches	1 square foot
9	square feet	1 square yard
30¼	square yards	1 square rod
272¼	square feet	1 square rod
40	square rods	1 rood
4	roods	1 acre
160	square rods	1 acre
640	acres	1 square mile
43,560	square feet	1 acre
4,840	square yards	1 acre

Solid or Cubic Measure (Volume)

1,728	cubic inches	1 cubic foot

27	cubic feet	1 cubic yard
128	cubic feet	1 cord of wood
24¾	cubic feet	1 perch of stone
2,150.42	cubic inches	1 standard bushel
231	cubic inches	1 standard gallon
40	cubic feet	1 ton (shipping)

Dry Measure

2	pints	1 quart
8	quarts	1 peck
4	pecks	1 bushel
2,150.42	cubic inches	1 bushel
1.2445	cubic feet	1 bushel

Liquid Measure (Capacity)

4	gills	1 pint
2	pints	1 quart
4	quarts	1 gallon
31½	gallons	1 barrel
2	barrels	1 hogshead
1	gallon	231 cubic inches
7.4805	gallons	1 cubic foot
16	fluid ounces	1 pint
1	fluid ounce	1.805 cubic inches
1	fluid ounce	29.59 cubic centimeters

Mariners' Measure

6	feet	1 fathom
100	fathoms	1 cable's length as applied to distances or intervals between ships
120	fathoms	1 cable's length as applied to marine wire cable
7½	cable lengths	1 mile
5,280	feet	1 statute mile
6,080	feet	1 nautical mile
1.152 2/3	statute miles	1 nautical or geographical mile
3	geographical miles	1 league
60	geographical miles, or	
69.16	statute miles	1 degree of longitude on the equator, or 1 degree of meridian
360	degrees	1 circumference

Note: A knot is not a measure of distance but a measure of speed. Current usage makes a knot equivalent to a marine mile per hour (properly it is 1/120 of a marine mile). Hence, when the speed of vessels at sea is being measured, a knot is equal to a nautical mile, or 6,080 feet, or 2,026.66 yards, *per hour.*

United States and British Weights and Measures Compared

1	British Imperial bushel . . .	1.03205 United States (Winchester) bushels
1	United States bushel. . . .	.96895 British Imperial bushel
1	British quart	1.03205 United States dry quarts
1	United States dry quart . .	.96895 British quart
1	British quart (or gallon) . .	1.20094 United States liquid quarts (or gallons)
1	United States liquid quart (or gallon)	.83268 British quart (or gallon)

Avoirdupois Measure (Weight)

(Used for weighing all ordinary substances
except precious metals, jewels, and drugs)

27-11/32	grains	1 dram
16	drams	1 ounce
16	ounces	1 pound
25	pounds	1 quarter
4	quarters	1 hundredweight
100	pounds	1 hundredweight
20	hundredweight . . .	1 ton
2,000	pounds	1 short ton
2,240	pounds	1 long ton

Troy Measure (Weight)

(Used for weighing gold, silver,
and jewels)

24	grains	1 pennyweight
20	pennyweights . . .	1 ounce
12	ounces	1 pound

Comparison of Avoirdupois and Troy Measures

1	pound troy	5,760 grains
1	pound avoirdupois .	7,000 grains

1	ounce troy	480 grains
1	ounce avoirdupois .	437½ grains
1	karat, or carat . .	3.2 troy grains
24	karats	pure gold

Apothecaries' Measure (Weight)

20	grains 1	scruple
3	scruples 1	dram
8	drams 1	ounce
12	ounces 1	pound

Apothecaries' Fluid Measure (Capacity)

60	minims 1	fluid dram
8	fluid drams 1	fluid ounce
16	fluid ounces 1	pint
8	pints 1	gallon

Surveyors' Long Measure

7.92	inches 1	link
25	links 1	rod
4	rods, or 100 links . . 1	chain
80	chains 1	mile

Surveyors' Square Measure

625	square links 1	square rod
16	square rods 1	square chain
10	square chains 1	acre
640	acres 1	square mile
36	square miles 1	township

Circular or Angular Measure

60	seconds (60") . . 1	minute (1')
60	minutes (60') 1	degree (1´)
30	degrees 1	sign
90	degrees 1	right angle or quadrant
360	degrees 1	circumference

Note: One degree at the equator is approximately 60 nautical miles.

Counting

12	units or things	. . .	1	dozen
12	dozen, or 144 units	.	1	gross
12	gross		1	great gross
20	units		1	score

Paper Measure

24	sheets	. . . . . .	1	quire
20	quires	. . . . . .	1	ream
2	reams	. . . . . .	1	bundle
5	bundles	. . . . . .	1	bale

Note: Although a ream contains 480 sheets, 500 sheets are usually sold as a ream.

United States Money

10	mills	. . . .	1	cent
10	cents	. . . .	1	dime
10	dimes	. . . . . .	1	dollar
10	dollars	. . . . . .	1	eagle

COMPARISON OF CENTIGRADE AND FAHRENHEIT TEMPERATURES

Degrees Centigrade		Degrees Fahrenheit
0	Freezing Point	32
10		50
20		68
30		86
40		104
50		122
60		140
70		158
80		176
90		194
100	Boiling Point	212

Note: To convert from °F to °C, subtract 32 from °F and divide by 1.8.
To convert from °C to °F, multiply °C by 1.8 and add 32.

METRIC SYSTEM

LENGTH

unit	abbreviation	number of meters	approximate U.S. equivalent
myriameter	mym	10,000	6.2 miles
kilometer	km	1,000	0.62 miles
hectometer	hm	100	109.36 yards
dekameter	dam	10	32.81 feet
meter	m	1	39.37 inches
decimeter	dm	0.1	3.94 inches
centimeter	cm	0.01	0.39 inch
millimeter	mm	0.001	0.04 inch

AREA

unit	abbreviation	number of square meters	approximate U.S. equivalent
square kilometer	sq km or km^2	1,000,000	0.3861 square mile
hectare	ha	10,000	2.47 acres
are	a	100	119.60 square yards
centare	ca	1	10.76 square feet
square centimeter	sq cm or cm^2	0.0001	0.155 square inch

VOLUME

unit	abbreviation	number of cubic meters	approximate U.S. equivalent
dekastere	das	10	13.10 cubic yards
stere	s	1	1.31 cubic yards
decistere	ds	0.10	3.53 cubic feet
cubic centimeter	cu cm or cm^3 also cc	0.000001	0.061 cubic inch

CAPACITY

unit	abbreviation	number of liters	approximate U.S. equivalent cubic	dry	liquid
kiloliter	kl	1,000	1.31 cubic yards		
hectoliter	hl	100	3.53 cubic feet	2.84 bushels	
dekaliter	dal	10	0.35 cubic foot	1.14 pecks	2.64 gallons
liter	l	1	61.02 cubic inches	0.908 quart	1.057 quarts
deciliter	dl	0.10	6.1 cubic inches	0.18 pint	0.21 pint
centiliter	cl	0.01	0.6 cubic inch		0.338 fluid ounce
milliliter	ml	0.001	0.06 cubic inch		0.27 fluid dram

MASS AND WEIGHT

unit	abbreviation	number of grams	approximate U.S. equivalent
metric ton	MT or t	1,000,000	1.1 tons
quintal	q	100,000	220.46 pounds
kilogram	kg	1,000	2.2046 pounds
hectogram	hg	100	3.527 ounces
dekagram	dag	10	0.353 ounce
gram	g or gm	1	0.035 ounce
decigram	dg	0.10	1.543 grains
centigram	cg	0.01	0.154 grain
milligram	mg	0.001	0.015 grain

By permission. From Webster's New Collegiate Dictionary, © 1975 by G. & C. Merriam Co., Publishers of the Merriam-Webster Dictionaries, Springfield, Massachusetts.

METRIC SYSTEM OF WEIGHTS AND MEASURES

Prefixes	Meaning		Units
milli-	= one-thousandth	.001	
centi-	= one-hundredth	.01	
deci-	= one-tenth	.1	"meter" for length
. . .	Unit = one	1.	"gram" for weight or mass
deka-	= ten	10	"liter" for capacity
hecto-	= one hundred	100	
kilo-	= one thousand	1000	

DIAGRAM OF TOWNSHIP
DIVIDED INTO SECTIONS

LAND MEASUREMENTS

- A rod is 16½ feet.
- A chain is 66 feet or 4 rods.
- A mile is 320 rods, 80 chains or 5,280 feet.
- A square rod is 272¼ square feet.
- An acre contains 43,560 square feet.
- An acre contains 160 square rods.
- An acre is about 208¾ feet square.
- An acre is 8 rods wide by 20 rods long, or any two numbers (of rods) whose product is 160.
- 25 by 125 feet equals .0717 of an acre.
- A section is 640 acres.

MATHEMATICAL TABLES

Mathematical Signs and Symbols

Symbol	Meaning
+	Plus, the sign of addition.
−	Minus, the sign of subtraction
x	The sign of multiplication.
÷	The sign of division.
.	Is to } The signs of proportion.
::	As } portion. Thus
:	Is to } 3 : 6 :: 4 : 8.
∵	Because.
∴	Therefore.
=	Equals, the sign of equality.
>	Greater than.
<	Less than.
√	Square root.
$\sqrt[3]{}$	Cube root, $\sqrt[4]{}$ fourth root, $\sqrt[5]{}$ fifth root, etc.
( ) [ ] { }	Indicate that the figures enclosed are to be taken together. Thus 10 x (7 + 4); 8 − [9 ÷ 3]; $3\left\{\dfrac{7+3}{4-2}\right\}$
° ′ ″	Degrees, minutes, seconds. Thus 25° 15′ 10″ represents 25 degrees, 15 minutes, 10 seconds.
′ ″	Feet, inches. Thus 9′ 10″ = 9 feet 10 inches.
∞	Infinity.
⊥	Perpendicular to.
‖	Parallel to.
#	Number; numbered.
°	Degree.
O	Circle.
∠	Angle.
L	Right-angle.
□	Square.
▭	Rectangle.
▱	Parallelogram.
△	Triangle.
0	The cipher, zero.
%	Percent.
℈ Scruple)	
ℨ Drachm } Apothecaries' weight.	
℥ Ounce)	

Shortcuts in Multiplication

To multiply by

1-1/4	add	0	and	divide by	8
1-2/3	"	0	"	"	6
2-1/2	"	0	"	"	4
3-1/3	"	0	"	"	3
5	"	0	"	"	2
6-1/4	"	00	"	"	16
6-2/3	"	00	"	"	15
8-1/3	"	00	"	"	12
12-1/2	"	00	"	"	8
14-2/7	"	00	"	"	7
16-2/3	"	00	"	"	6
25	"	00	"	"	4
31-1/4	"	000	"	"	32
33-1/3	"	00	"	"	3
50	"	00	"	"	2
66-2/3	"	000	"	"	15
83-1/3	"	000	"	"	12
125	"	000	"	"	8
166-2/3	"	000	"	"	6
250	"	000	"	"	4
333-1/3	"	000	"	"	3

For example, to multiply 5 times 2: add 0 to 2 (20) and divide by 2 (20 ÷ 2 = 10). Thus, 5 x 2 = 10.

Shortcuts in Division

To divide by

	multiply by	8	and	divide by	10
1-1/4	"	6	"	"	10
1-2/3	"	4	"	"	10
2-1/2	"	3	"	"	10
3-1/3	"	8	"	"	30
3-3/4	"	16	"	"	100
6-1/4	"	4	"	"	30
7-1/2	"	12	"	"	100
8-1/3	"	11	"	"	100
9-1/11	"	9	"	"	100
11-1/9					

To divide by

12-1/2	multiply by	8	and divide by		100
14-2/7	"	7	"	"	100
16-2/3	"	6	"	"	100
25	"	4	"	"	100
31-1/4	"	16	"	"	500
33-1/3	"	3	"	"	100
75	"	4	"	"	300
125	"	8	"	"	1,000
175	"	4	"	"	700
275	"	4	"	"	1,100
375	"	8	"	"	3,000
625	"	8	•	"	5,000
875	"	8	•	"	7,000

For example, to divide 5 by 6¼, multiply 5 times 16 (80) and divide by 100 (80 ÷ 100 = .80). Thus, 5 ÷ 6¼ = .80.

RATE OF SAVINGS UNDER VARIOUS DISCOUNT TERMS

½%	10 days net	30 days	=	9%	per annum
1%	" "	" " "	=	18%	"	"
1½%	" "	" " "	=	27%	"	"
2%	" "	" " "	=	36%	"	"
2%	" "	" 60 "	=	14%	"	"
2% 30	"	" " "	=	24%	"	"
2%	" "	" 4 mos.	=	8%	"	"
2% 40	"	" 60 days	=	36%	"	"
2% 70	"	" 90 "	=	36%	"	"
3% 10	"	" 30 "	=	54%	"	"
3%	" "	" 4 mos.	=	10%	"	"
3% 30	"	" 60 days	=	36%	"	"
4% 10	"	" " "	=	29%	"	"
4%	" "	" 4 mos.	=	13%	"	"
5%	" "	" 30 days	=	90%	"	"
5%	" "	" 60 "	=	36%	"	"
5%	" "	" 4 mos.	=	16%	"	"
6%	" "	" 60 days	=	43%	"	"
6%	" "	" 4 mos.	=	20%	"	"
7%	" "	" " "	=	23%	"	"
8%	" "	" " "	=	26%	"	"
9%	" "	" 60 days	=	65%	"	"
10%	" "	" 90 days	=	45%	"	"

Exact Number of Days Between Dates

From Any Day Of	To the Same Day of the Next											
	Jan.	Feb.	Mar.	Apr.	May	June	July	Aug.	Sept.	Oct.	Nov.	Dec.
January	365	31	59	90	120	151	181	212	243	273	304	334
February . . .	334	365	28	59	89	120	150	181	212	242	273	303
March	306	337	365	31	61	92	122	153	184	214	245	275
April	275	306	334	365	30	61	91	122	153	183	214	244
May	245	276	304	335	365	31	61	92	123	153	184	214
June	214	245	273	304	334	365	30	61	92	122	153	183
July	184	215	243	274	304	335	365	31	62	92	123	153
August	153	184	212	243	273	304	334	365	31	61	92	122
September . .	122	153	181	212	242	273	303	334	365	30	61	91
October	92	123	151	182	212	243	273	304	335	365	31	61
November . . .	61	92	120	151	181	212	242	273	304	334	365	30
December . . .	31	62	90	121	151	182	212	243	274	304	335	365

Exact Interest Table

Interest on $100 at Various Rates for Various Periods

	5%	6%	7%	8%	9%	10%	11%	12%
1	.01389	.01667	.01944	.02222	.02500	.02778	.03056	.03333
2	.02778	.03333	.03888	.04444	.05000	.05556	.06111	.06666
3	.04167	.05000	.05833	.06666	.07500	.08333	.09167	.10000
4	.05556	.06667	.07778	.08888	.10000	.11111	.12222	.13333
5	.06945	.08333	.09722	.11111	.12500	.13889	.15278	.16667
6	.08333	.10000	.11666	.13333	.15000	.16666	.18334	.20000
7	.09722	.11667	.13611	.15555	.17500	.19445	.21389	.23333
8	.11111	.13334	.15555	.17778	.20000	.22222	.24445	.26666
9	.12501	.15000	.17500	.20000	.22500	.25000	.27500	.30000
10	.13889	.16667	.19444	.22222	.25000	.27778	.30556	.33333
20	.27778	.33334	.38888	.44444	.50000	.55556	.61112	.66666
30	.41667	.50001	.58332	.66666	.75000	.83334	.91668	.99999
40	.55556	.66668	.77776	.88888	1.00000	1.11112	1.22224	1.33332
50	.69445	.83335	.97220	1.11110	1.25000	1.38890	1.52780	1.66665
60	.83333	1.00002	1.16664	1.33332	1.50000	1.66668	1.83336	1.99998
70	.97223	1.16669	1.36108	1.55554	1.75000	1.94446	2.13892	2.33331
80	1.11112	1.33336	1.55552	1.77776	2.00000	2.22224	2.44448	2.66664
90	1.25010	1.50003	1.74996	1.99998	2.25000	2.50002	2.75004	2.99997
100	1.38890	1.66670	1.94440	2.22220	2.50000	2.77780	3.05560	3.33330

Time in Which Money Doubles Itself at Interest

Rate percent	Simple Interest		Compound Interest		
2	50 years		35 years	1 day	
2½	40 "		28 "	26 days	
3	33 "	4 months	23 "	164 "	
3½	28 "	208 days	20 "	54 "	
4	25 "		17 "	246 "	
4½	22 "	81 days	15 "	273 "	
5	20 "		14 "	75 "	
6	16 "	8 months	11 "	327 "	
7	14 "	104 days	10	89 "	
8	12 "	6 months	9 "	2 "	
9	11 "	40 days	8	16 "	
10	10 "		7	100 "	

COMMEMORATIVE
WEDDING ANNIVERSARY LIST

First	*Paper*	Thirteenth	*Lace*
Second	*Cotton*	Fourteenth	*Ivory*
Third	*Leather*	Fifteenth	*Crystal*
Fourth	*Linen*	Twentieth	*China*
Fifth	*Wood*	Twenty-fifth	*Silver*
Sixth	*Iron*	Thirtieth	*Pearls*
Seventh	*Wool or copper*	Thirty-fifth	*Coral or jade*
Eighth	*Bronze*	Fortieth	*Rubies*
Ninth	*Pottery*	Forty-fifth	*Sapphires*
Tenth	*Tin*	Fiftieth	*Gold*
Eleventh	*Steel*	Fifty-fifth	*Emeralds*
Twelfth	*Silk*	Sixtieth	*Diamonds*

Merchants' associations revise the list from time to time

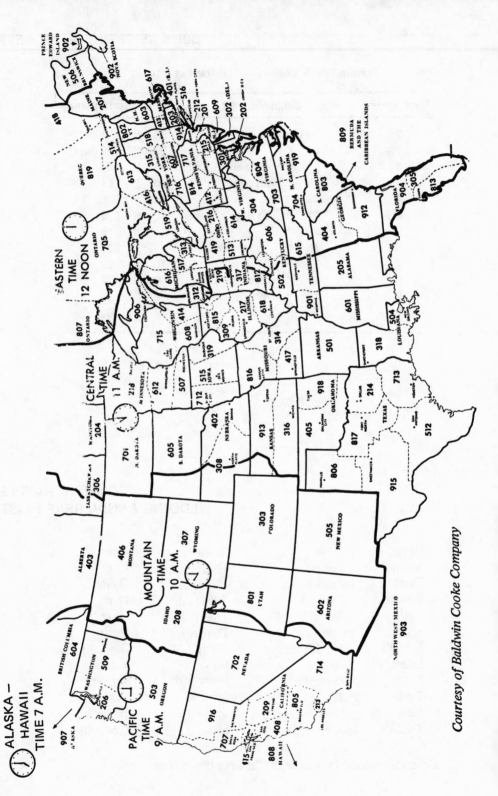

Courtesy of Baldwin Cooke Company

528

1976–1981

1976

1977

1978

1979

1980

1981

1982–1987

1982

JANUARY
S	M	T	W	T	F	S
					1	2
3	4	5	6	7	8	9
10	11	12	13	14	15	16
17	18	19	20	21	22	23
24	25	26	27	28	29	30
31						

FEBRUARY
S	M	T	W	T	F	S
	1	2	3	4	5	6
7	8	9	10	11	12	13
14	15	16	17	18	19	20
21	22	23	24	25	26	27
28						

MARCH
S	M	T	W	T	F	S
	1	2	3	4	5	6
7	8	9	10	11	12	13
14	15	16	17	18	19	20
21	22	23	24	25	26	27
28	29	30	31			

APRIL
S	M	T	W	T	F	S
				1	2	3
4	5	6	7	8	9	10
11	12	13	14	15	16	17
18	19	20	21	22	23	24
25	26	27	28	29	30	

MAY
S	M	T	W	T	F	S
						1
2	3	4	5	6	7	8
9	10	11	12	13	14	15
16	17	18	19	20	21	22
23	24	25	26	27	28	29
30	31					

JUNE
S	M	T	W	T	F	S
		1	2	3	4	5
6	7	8	9	10	11	12
13	14	15	16	17	18	19
20	21	22	23	24	25	26
27	28	29	30			

JULY
S	M	T	W	T	F	S
				1	2	3
4	5	6	7	8	9	10
11	12	13	14	15	16	17
18	19	20	21	22	23	24
25	26	27	28	29	30	31

AUGUST
S	M	T	W	T	F	S
1	2	3	4	5	6	7
8	9	10	11	12	13	14
15	16	17	18	19	20	21
22	23	24	25	26	27	28
29	30	31				

SEPTEMBER
S	M	T	W	T	F	S
			1	2	3	4
5	6	7	8	9	10	11
12	13	14	15	16	17	18
19	20	21	22	23	24	25
26	27	28	29	30		

OCTOBER
S	M	T	W	T	F	S
					1	2
3	4	5	6	7	8	9
10	11	12	13	14	15	16
17	18	19	20	21	22	23
24	25	26	27	28	29	30
31						

NOVEMBER
S	M	T	W	T	F	S
	1	2	3	4	5	6
7	8	9	10	11	12	13
14	15	16	17	18	19	20
21	22	23	24	25	26	27
28	29	30				

DECEMBER
S	M	T	W	T	F	S
			1	2	3	4
5	6	7	8	9	10	11
12	13	14	15	16	17	18
19	20	21	22	23	24	25
26	27	28	29	30	31	

1983

1984

1985

1986

1987

GEM BIRTHSTONES
FOR THE VARIOUS MONTHS

January	*Garnet*	July	*Ruby*
February	*Amethyst*	August	*Sardonyx*
March	*Bloodstone*	September	*Sapphire*
April	*Diamond*	October	*Opal*
May	*Emerald*	November	*Topaz*
June	*Pearl*	December	*Turquoise*

DESK REFERENCES
FOR THE SECRETARY

General Reference Books[1]

Complete Book of Business Etiquette, by J. Vermes, Parker Publishing Company, Inc., West Nyack, NY.

Fowler's Modern English Usage, Oxford University Press, New York and Oxford.

A Manual of Style, The University of Chicago Press, Chicago.

The New Roget's Thesaurus, G. P. Putnam's Sons, New York.

The Prentice-Hall Complete Secretarial Letter Book, by Mary E. De Vries, Prentice-Hall, Inc., Englewood Cliffs, N.J.

Private Secretary's Encyclopedic Dictionary, 2nd Ed., by the Prentice-Hall Editorial Staff, revised by Mary A. De Vries, Prentice-Hall, Inc., Englewood Cliffs, N.J.

Sisson's Word and Expression Locator, by A. F. Sisson, Parker Publishing Company, Inc., West Nyack, NY.

Webster's New Collegiate Dictionary, G. & C. Merriam Company, Springfield, MA.

Zip Code Directory, U.S. Government Printing Office, Washington, DC.

Specialized Secretarial Books[2]

Data Processing Secretary's Complete Handbook, by E. Laird.

Legal Secretary's Complete Handbook, by B. Miller.

Legal Secretary's Encyclopedic Dictionary, P-H Editorial Staff, Rev. by B. K. Thomae.

Medical Secretary's Guide, by E. Kabbe.

The Real Estate Office Secretary's Handbook, by L. Doris.

School Secretary's Handbook, by J. Smith.

Sletwold's Manual of Documents and Forms for the Legal Secretary, by E. Sletwold.

---

[1]These are a few of the books that a secretary will find especially useful in her daily work. In each instance the latest edition is recommended. For a more complete list of secretarial books available from Prentice-Hall, write to Prentice-Hall, Inc., Englewood Cliffs, NJ 07632.

[2]Available from Prentice-Hall, Inc.. Englewood Cliffs, NJ 07632.

Index